DISPARATE REGIONAL DEVELOPMENT IN BRAZIL

For my parents, Ivônio and Verinha

Disparate Regional Development in Brazil

A Monetary Production Approach

ADRIANA AMADO
Department of Economics
University of Brasilia, UnB

Routledge
Taylor & Francis Group
LONDON AND NEW YORK

First published 1997 by Ashgate Publishing

Reissued 2018 by Routledge
2 Park Square, Milton Park, Abingdon, Oxon OX14 4RN
711 Third Avenue, New York, NY 10017, USA

Routledge is an imprint of the Taylor & Francis Group, an informa business

A Library of Congress record exists under LC control number: 97073376

ISBN 13: 978-1-138-31154-1 (hbk)
ISBN 13: 978-0-429-45880-4 (ebk)

Contents

Acknowledgements

I am intellectually indebted to my Ph.D.supervisor Professor Victoria Chick who gave substantial contributions to this book, commenting on each part, pointing out the inconsistencies and suggesting improvements and who also, very kindly, submitted to boring and endless readings of various drafts of each chapter.

Maria de Lourdes Rollemberg Mollo contributed significantly to the conclusion of this book, reading parts of it and making relevant comments on some ideas that I exposed in some seminars at the University of Brasília. She also supported me with her kind friendship in moments of down-turn that the whole process of writing the book imposed on me.

My father, Amado, and my mother, Dely, gave me the confidence and support necessary to keep going in all the phases of my Ph.D. course. I must especially thank my mother for her help with the contacts necessary to the data collection and for her patience in getting papers and specific references on Brazil. My sister and best friend, Verinha, with her joy and love contributed significantly to my emotional equilibrium over all those years giving me all the support that I needed and encouraging me to keep going. I also thank my mother and sister for their weekly letters, which were a magnificent way to continue taking part in our family life.

My husband and love, Ivônio, contributed in almost all possible ways to this book: he accepted my absence and opened hand of three important years of our joint life supporting me to keep going with my projects, helped me with the necessary contacts in the agencies that I have been visiting in the data collection process, helped me with software advice and searched and collected some bibliographic references in Brazil while I was in London and especially wrote me daily long letters that made me feel closer to him.

Moacir and Nona with their friendship were extremely important to my adaptation in London. They contributed in all the ways they could to make my life less hard and to reduce my loneliness.

All my friends and especially the ones to whom I have had more contact in those four years: Celina, Jorge, Marília, Alfredo, Rita, Liginha, Dênio, Jorge, Pop, Cláudia, Beatriz, Hulda, Silke, Cristovam, Gladys, Júlia, Paula, Maria Luiza, Joaquim, André Eduardo, Helô, Tarcísio, Thompson, Rogério Studart, Naércio, Adriana, Susana, Rogério Andrade, Cristiane, Viju and Carlos Eduardo contributed in a way or another to this book.

The staff of SUDENE, BNB, IBGE, National Congress, Fundação Joaquim Nabuco, FUNDAP among others were essential to the collection of data and most kindly accepted to open their personal files, to reaggregate some data, to produce new data etc.. I also thank Tânia Bacelar de Araújo and Leonardo Guimarães Neto for the comments on the general idea of the book and the help they gave me on the contacts in some institutions.

The editing job done by Shirin Patel is thankfully aknowledged.

The financial support of CAPES was essential to the realization of this project and is thankfully acknowledged.

Introduction

Regional development theory has ever lacked an adequate approach to money and financial elements as a source for differentiated patterns of regional growth. This is comprehensible within orthodox theory, since for those theorists, money is a neutral element which is just supposed to enter their models to establish the price level once equilibrium has been settled by real variables. Therefore, the role of money is restricted to the short run and is the result of misformed expectations or of some rigidities which characterise this period.

Money is also considered neutral in its effects, or its effects are not analysed at all, in most heterodox regional analyses. Some models do not have a well specified monetary framework. Other models follow the orthodox characterisation of finance as representing saving and, thus, present a monetary theory which is in essence orthodox. Finally, some models assume absolute endogeneity of the money supply and so see money as merely an accommodating variable. These models find causes for different patterns of regional development only among real elements. Therefore, even among the heterodoxy we have a "real" bias in the analysis of regional development.

The non-neutrality of money is one of the central elements in the Post Keynesian analysis of Monetary Production Economies. These economies are characterised by the central role played by entrepreneurs in the decisions of investment and production. These decisions are based on a profit seeking logic, but as their results are manifested in the future, entrepreneurs have to base their decision making process on expectations. Entrepreneurs know that their decisions are not only irreversible but can also be disappointed: time is irreversible, and there are no mechanisms for pre-conciliation of wants. These elements give way to the prospect of uncertainty. Uncertainty is so essentially different from risk: risk is quantifiable; uncertainty is unquantifiable. The uncertainty surrounding economic events creates the need for social mechanisms which allow agents to act by reducing their individual level of uncertainty. Contracts reduce uncertainty and money is the social element which allows the existence of monetary contracts. Money and monetary contracts reduce uncertainty, but do not eliminate it. On the contrary, it is the existence of money that breaks with the perfect world of Say's Law. Agents base their decisions on conventions and animal spirits that are the two elements that can conduct the decision making process. The liquidity preference of agents is also explained by their need to reduce uncertainty (the precautionary motive) and gain from unpredicted opportunities and even to exploit them (the speculative motive) besides the traditional transaction motive. Therefore, the greater the instability, the higher the liquidity preference of agents in monetary production economies. The interest rate is the price which makes agents depart from the safe haven of liquid assets. Therefore, it is a monetary variable. As the investment level is determined by equalising the marginal efficiency of capital with the monetary rate of interest, interest is a fundamental element connecting the monetary and real spheres of the economy. Since monetary factors determine the rate of interest and investment is a key factor in growth, money is non-neutral in monetary production economies. The financial system, as the creator of liquidity, has a fundamental role to play in the "real" story.

Contrary to classical, neoclassical and new classical theory, in the Post Keynesian perspective, finance and saving are two different elements. There are no saving constraints to investment decisions. Credit is the element which releases investment from saving. The creation of credit allows investment to take place and so income is generated and then savings equalise investment. Therefore, credit creation has an important role to play in the real growth of monetary production economies. The monetary logic behind these models is that credit creates deposits and not the other way round, as is still assumed by orthodox models.

As all the elements which lead to the non-neutrality of money are present in regional economies and they are not homogenous across regions, they are supposed to interfere in the various patterns of growth of the regional economies. Dow's pioneer work on the non-neutrality of money at the regional level adopts some elements of dependency theory and, based on the Post Keynesian monetary approach, constructs a theory which explains the financial behaviour of agents in different regional economic structures. She observes the different elements which lead to the non-neutrality of money at the aggregate level and examines what happens when two economies have different economic structures and do not have barriers to financial or trade flows. For the structural differences between regions, she adopts the characterisation of dependency theory, but she does not assume the causal relations established by this theory since she is mainly concerned with the monetary dynamic of the regional economies. However, her theory is not only interested in financial variables: she develops a joint analysis of the financial and real determinants of disparate patterns of growth and in doing so establishes feedback mechanisms which tend to reinforce the uneven regional development of a country. The exploration of some of the real elements described by dependency theory and the analysis developed by these theorists can bring some important clarification to the regional monetary dynamic as the Brazilian case illustrates.

The theoretical framework adopted in the book establishes that central economies present a more stable pattern of development: its dynamic is internally generated, the productive structure is concentrated in the industrial sector and institutions are more solid and developed. On the other hand, peripheral regions typically have a productive structure based on primary sectors, a more unstable pattern of development which is mainly export led, higher import coefficients, less developed institutions and less developed financial markets. The differentiated level of instability of these two sets of regions leads to a stronger liquidity preference in the periphery than in the centre. However, as the periphery has a less developed financial market and financial system, agents prefer to express their liquidity preference in assets of the centre; thus they create leakages of financial resources from the periphery toward the centre. This source of leakage added to the leakages caused by the higher import coefficients in the periphery result in a reduced possibility of money creation by the banks in the periphery and endows banks of the centre with a relative advantage compared to the ones of the periphery. This tends to stimulate banking concentration in favour of banks of the centre.

The bases for the diffusion of information also are weaker in the periphery. This makes banks which have their head offices in the centre more wary of extending credit to these regions, since the remoteness of the bases of information and the strong conventional character on which they base their decisions do not favour credit creation in these regions. When banks of the centre extend credit toward the periphery, they will favour firms which have their head offices in the centre, since the remoteness of the information base is reduced in such cases. However, this tends to create an additional problem of retention of liquidity in the region, since these extra-regional firms tend to present a higher import propensity than the local firms, which reduces the possibility of credit creation within the region. Banks in the periphery also tend to keep larger reserves in relation to their deposits since the higher level of instability of these economies makes them more wary of being in an illiquid position. Therefore, there is a series of mechanisms which interact to create financial limits to growth in peripheral economies. The only way of breaking these vicious circles is interference by an exogenous element. This element, suggests Dow, is the State.

The Brazilian experience is extremely rich in elements for the analysis of this model because Brazil is marked by a tremendous imbalance in its regional development and because it gives us the opportunity to observe the results of a certain kind of State intervention in the pattern of regional development. However, clearly, the Brazilian regional problem does not have a financial origin: regional imbalances arose when financial variables did not have a very precise role to play, and many of the regional economic structures were determined during this period. Nevertheless, the financial sphere does have a role to play in the whole economic story, and this role has never been properly studied. Therefore, the main aim of this book is to analyse the Brazilian regional question from a new perspective which seeks to investigate the interrelations between monetary and real phenomena in such a way as to establish the bases for the dynamic of a monetary production economy marked by regional imbalances.

In dealing with the Brazilian case, we will set out three different periods. In the first, primary export model, we analyse the process which led to the settlement of the regional problem in that country. During this period finance was provided from abroad and was a fundamental element in the extraction of surplus from the periphery by the international centre. However, the financial element did not have a substantial role to play in the determination of the regional question. Great part of the country was excluded from the monetary sphere of production, which was mainly restricted to the dynamic region linked to the international markets, this reduced the effects that financial elements could have on those sub-peripheral regions. In the second period, the country embarked upon an import substitution process without strong explicit policies for the periphery. In the period after the 60s, the State adopted powerful strategies of intervention in the economic structure of the region. These policies, however, did not realise their full potentials because they created new forms of leakages in the financial flows of the peripheral regions. Thus part of the benefit of those policies were captured by the central regions. The seven Chapters of the book are divided in four Parts.

Part I reviews the theoretical background for regional development analysis which deals with the idea of vicious circles. Chapter 1 reviews the theories that work with the notion of vicious circles: Dependency Theory, Myrdal's models and Kaldorian models. We point out the role that is attributed to the financial elements in each model and their relation to real elements. Chapter 2 is divided into two sections. The first one reviews the elements that lead to the non-neutrality of money in the Post Keynesian analysis of the monetary production economies and the second section observes how these elements, when acting on regional economies that are structurally different but have no barriers to monetary and commercial flows, can generate non-neutrality in regional terms.

Part II reviews the earlier economic history of Brazil observing the bases on which the regional problem was settled in that country. Chapter 3 analyses the economic history of Brazil from its European settlement until it reached the import substitution process. The role of the financial variables during this period was explained well by Dependency Theory models and was related to the extraction of surplus from the world peripheral economies. The sub-peripheral economies (economies peripheral to the national centre, which is peripheral to the world centre) remained apart from the monetary system, which was just linked to international trade of some staples. It is in this period that the main structural characteristics of the regions were settled. For instance, it is almost impossible to understand the weakness of the labour markets of the Northeast and the concentration of the economic structure of this region without understanding the sugar cane activity and its main characteristics. Similarly, the main characteristics of coffee production and of the economy of São Paulo at this time shaped the path that this region followed in later periods. Therefore, the study of the historic formation of the Brazilian economy is relevant in the analysis of recent periods developed in later chapters.

Part III analyses the regional economies under the import substitution process. In this period the State did not have a well defined policy for the regions. Its actions were based mainly on ad hoc action. Chapter 4 points out the main structural characteristics of the regional economies and observes the dynamic of the Brazilian economy as a whole in order to analyse the impacts that this dynamic had on the regional economies. As we are interested in analysing a monetary production economy, it is important to analyse the real and financial sides of the story in order to integrate these two elements into a whole coherent picture. With this aim, we will pay special attention to the sectorial composition of each regional economy, to the dynamic elements in the process of growth, to the way by which these economies are internally integrated and that they integrate with other regions and abroad, to the structure of the labour markets and so on. These elements are important to understand the integration and the dynamic of the financial system of each different regional system. Chapter 5 assumes the analysis made in Chapter 4 and develops the elements which explain the financial patterns followed by the regional economies. To do so, we analyse the data on the banking system from the perspective of the regional economic dynamic observed in Chapter 4.

Part IV analyses the regional economies after the adoption of explicit State policies for the regions. Chapter 6 examines some of the main regional economic policies implemented after the 60s, notes the impacts of these policies in the real economy and gives a general description of the regional economies during the period. It examines the new economic integration of the regions and the impact that this new order has on the structural elements of the regional economies, such as the labour markets, the absorption of labour etc. Chapter 7 observes the financial behaviour of the regional economies under the new regional policies and aims to examine jointly the real and financial impacts of these policies in terms of what was predicted by the theoretical model.

The conception of region

Regional economic theory should be concerned mainly with the socio-economic concept of region and not with the geographic/political delimitation of regions. Instead of geography being the benchmark in the determination of regions, socio-economic relations should define the boundaries of the system which, having a geographical counterpart, could be defined as a region. As Perroux observes: "The spaces that directly interest us are the economic spaces. They are defined by economic relations established among economic elements" (Perroux, 1967, p. 149).

Put another way, the socio-economic concept of region is more an ideal construct than concrete, in the sense of a geographical definition (Lipietz, 1988). It refers more to the spatial dimension of the ways in which different modes of production are articulated than to a concrete geographical demarcation. And inside the same mode of production, it refers to different ways in which the socio-economic relations are particularized in the system, thus forming a subsystem with concrete characteristics. Therefore, given these peculiarities of the socio-economic relations of a subsystem within a spatial dimension, we can think in regions and their relations and in doing so analyse the interrelations of the socio-economic subsystems and how they are articulated.

However, the available data are defined for geographic and political regions. In this book, when possible, we will attempt to reduce the type of distortion that this can cause. That is why in our analysis we will try, when possible, to separate socio-economic subsystems which present some characteristics that do not allow joint analysis. This is the case of the State of São Paulo, which in our analysis, appears separate from the rest of the Southeast, given its particularities in the process of capital accumulation and in its relations to other regions, and the states of Pernambuco and Bahia in the Northeast. Notwithstanding, some raw generalisations persist as a consequence of the lack of more precise data.

The data

The regional aggregation of Brazil underwent significant changes through the analysed period. These changes are associated with the creation and changes of status of some territories to the status of states, the creation of new states, and the aggregation of these political units into regions. However, for our work, the important aspect is the regional aggregation of the country. A major change of the aggregation occurred in 1970. Until then, the national territory was aggregated in the following regions: North: Territory of Rondônia, Territory of Acre[1], Amazonas, Territory of Rio Branco[2], Pará, Territory of Amapá; Northeast: Maranhão, Piauí, Ceará, Rio Grande do Norte, Paraíba, Pernambuco, Alagoas, Territory of Fernando de Noronha; East: Sergipe, Bahia, Minas Gerais, Espírito Santo, Rio de Janeiro, Guanabara; South: São Paulo, Paraná, Santa Catarina, Rio Grande do Sul; Centre-West: Mato Grosso, Goiás, Distrito Federal. After 1970 the aggregation was changed to: North: Territory of Rondônia[3](RO), Acre (AC), Amazonas (AM), Territory of Roraima[4] (RR), Pará (PA), Territory of Amapá[5] (AP), Tocantins[6] (TO); Northeast: Maranhão (MA), Piauí (PI), Ceará (CE), Rio Grande do Norte (RN), Paraíba (PB), Pernambuco (PE), Alagoas (AL), Sergipe (SE), Bahia (BA), Territory of Fernando de Noronha[7] (FN); Southeast: Minas Gerais (MG), Espírito Santo (ES), Rio de Janeiro (RJ), Guanabara[8] (GB), São Paulo (SP); South: Paraná (PR), Santa Catarina (SC), Rio Grande do Sul (RG); Centre-West: Mato Grosso (MT), Mato Grosso do Sul[9](MS), Goiás (GO), Distrito Federal (DF).

This caused some problems with homogeneity of data and comparisons between them. In order to facilitate comparisons between the two periods analysed in Parts III and IV, we decided to develop the analysis on the real side of the economy based on the present regional aggregation. This was so also because part of the data was available only in this new aggregation and to make possible a certain homogeneity. On the other hand, the chapter on the financial system was developed on the basis of the pre-70s aggregation. This does not damage the analysis, as the reader is reminded of the basis of the aggregation and to note the differences which it presents in relation to the aggregation of Chapter 5. As some parts of this chapter needed data from the real side of the economy, eg. GDP, population etc., these data were reaggregated in order to be consistent with the old aggregation.

For these data, we used the IBGE regional aggregation. In Part IV, part of the data refers to the "legal" concept of region, that is, the definition of the regions in which the Development Agencies for the Regions (SUDENE and SUDAM) operate. For this purpose, there is a wider concept of Northeast and the Amazônia Legal. The Northeast comprises the North region as defined by IBGE plus the North of the State of Minas Gerais. And the Amazônia Legal comprises the North of the states of Goiás, Mato Grosso and the west of Maranhão. When we analyse the government incentives to these regions, the area that receives these incentives is wider than the area defined in the rest of the book, which follows the aggregation of IBGE.

Table 1

Regional Aggregation According to SUDENE and SUDAM

	SUDENE	SUDAM
North		North and north of the state of Goiás, Mato Grosso and the West of Maranhão
Northeast	Northeast and North of Minas Gerais (Vale do Jequitinhonha)	

The main sources for the chapters that deal with the real side of the economy are: Anuário Estatístico (IBGE), PNAD (National Survey by Household Sample), Census and the Regional Accounts produced first by Fundação Getúlio Vargas and later on by IBGE. The duration of the analysed period creates some difficulties in dealing with the data. The first problem refers to the change in the regional aggregation in this period. We had to reaggregate part of the data to make it compatible with the aggregation used in each chapter. The second problem concerned changes in the composition of the variables analysed. As a consequence of these changes, we had to adapt our analysis to different levels in different periods.

Apart from the change in the regional aggregation of IBGE, we also have different aggregations, depending on the source we are using. For instance, the data on employment from PNAD is expressed at a level of aggregation completely different from the level of regional aggregation of IBGE.

Another problem is the continuity of the series. The largest part of the series was discontinued. For instance, the demographic census collected data every ten years but was discontinued in 1990. At the same time, the economic census collected data every five years, but was also discontinued in 1990, and according to informal sources, it will not be resumed.

The same problem applies to methodological questions. The regional accounts were the responsibility of IBRE of FGV (Brazilian Institute of Statistics of Getúlio Vargas Foundation). The last available data from this institution are from 1977. In 1980, these data became the responsibility of IBGE (Brazilian Institute of Geography and Statistics Foundation) and were calculated every five years. However, the series ends in 1985 and, according to informal sources, will not be continued any more. They now pass the methodology to the states so that each can calculate its own stadual account. SUDENE (Superintendency for the Development of the Northeast) has its own department of regional accounts; however, it operates within the broad concept of legal Northeast and so includes part of Minas Gerais which is in Southeast in IBGE data. At the same time, SUDENE produces data just for the Northeast, which does not allow comparison of trends with other regions.

In terms of data on commerce, we also have problems. The source of data available until 1969 was a research developed by CEDEPLAR/UFMG (Regional Developing and Planning Centre of The Federal University of Minas Gerais) and the data for the years 1975, 1980, 1985 were published in the Revista de Finanças Públicas (Review of Public Finance). However, the last available set of data is for the year 1987. And there is no sign of giving continuity to this series.

Another important source for the analysis of data on the structural changes which took place in the Northeast after the 1960s is the two direct researches developed by SUDENE/BNB (Superintendency for the Development of the Northeast/Bank of the Northeast of Brazil) in the incentivated industry. However, the first research was lost. It was not published and the bank destroyed the computer files in which the data were stored. There are some remains of the research which members of staff kept in their personal files, but they are not enough to give an idea of the whole research. For this reason, we had to use part of the data made available in a Ph.D. thesis of the University of São Paulo and which was later published as a book (Magalhães, 1983). In 1988, SUDENE/BNB produced another research on the incentivated industry of the Northeast and, this time, it was published and we had access to it. Nevertheless, the questionnaires of these two researches were not compatible and, because of this, we had to make tables for the two sets of data and the comparison between them is only partially possible.

If the data on the real side of the economy present problems, these problems are much more intense in the financial side of the regional question.

There are few works which have tried to analyse the regional financial system in Brazil. These studies were based mainly on the analysis of the distribution of the bank network and on data on the ratio of deposits to credit. Their analyses was mainly concerned with the aggregate of the banking system and did not give special attention to the different sets of institutions which operate in each market. The lack of development in this area compared to the analysis of the real side of the economy could be due to two factors: a) the lack of theoretical models in this area which could satisfactorily explain the reality of the regional financial system and b) the lack of regional financial data in Brazil. Probably both elements have had a role to play.

The analysis developed in this book, in contrast to other analyses developed for Brazil, has adopted a wider perspective on the regional financial system. We thought that the simple analysis of the deposits to credit ratio was not enough to explain the financial dynamic of the regions, so we analysed other variables in order to attain more precise results. We also thought that to isolate the financial system from the real sphere would not help in understanding the financial dynamic of the regions. Therefore, this book presents elements of the real side of the economy, which allows us to integrate these two spheres.

Until 1975 we basically used the Movimento Bancário do Brasil and the special inquiries of the economic census as our main sources. However, although raw data were available we had to undertake a huge work of reaggregation, since the regional aggregation of the country changed, and the Movimento Bancário do Brasil continued to present data with the old aggregation. We attempted to make the data in Part IV compatible with the new regional aggregation of Brazil.

Another point to emphasise is the aggregation of different institutions which Movimento Bancário do Brasil presented. Until 1968, this publication allowed a less rich analysis of the different institutions, since it presented more aggregate data. After 1968, data for private banks were produced separated. The publishing of Movimento Bancário do Brasil has ended in 1975; thus, libraries have disconnected series of this publication. Therefore, it was extremely difficult to get a complete series based on this publication. Unfortunately there is not a great demand for it in libraries, the volumes get lost very easily and there is no interest in rearranging the series.

However, as this publication has not been available since 1975, the only source available for financial data aggregated in regional terms is the Anuário Estatístico of IBGE. However, this publication is not consistent in the institutions and accounts of the balance sheets of the banks covered. In some years, it just publishes data on Banco do Brasil, in other years, it presents just the general total and so on. Nonetheless, we have had to use this source for the period 1980-1985. This explains the different institutional aggregation of this period. The Banco Central do Brasil published in June 1985 an appendix (separata) to its monthly bulletin (Boletim Mensal) containing data on banking at the regional level. However, the data was aggregated over all banks except Banco do Brasil, which was not compatible with our aggregation. But as this was the only source for all the commercial banks in 1980, we used it and pointed out the reason for presenting a different aggregation for this year.

The data for 1990 was obtained from the Central Bank of Brazil. As they do not have regional data they had to aggregate the data of branches and head offices in order to obtain the aggregation which we use in this thesis. They could only give us data beginning in 1988, because in this year they changed their account plan and disposed of all the old data, now lost.

The data on the participation of specific banks[10] in particular markets were also given by the Central Bank, which again had to prepare a special software package to produce these data since they were not available at the stadual level.

The information on the regionally differentiated legislation on reserves was also obtained from the staff of the Central Bank.

The FEBRABAN (Federation of the Brazilian Banks), although having part of the data we intended to use, denied us access to them on the grounds that the organising of the data would divert staff from their normal duties. Therefore, we could not have access to these data.

Finally, the data on differentials in interest rates across regions were not available. What we could do was to use some proxy to attempt to approach the question in the Brazilian case. We tried to work with the data available in the especial inquiries of the economic census. These inquiries, however, were not done in all the years of the census and IBGE told us that there was no other source. Furthermore, they were not homogenous to allow us to construct series from these inquiries, since some variables were presented sometimes as flows and in other years as stocks.

As there were no sources to estimate the regional interest rate differentials we used the interest rates that BNDES allows banks to charge when relending its funds. These data were collected in the instructions that BNDES gave to the banks, as reported by BNB.

Therefore, given the difficulties in getting regional financial data in Brazil, it is not difficult to understand the reasons for the limited amount of research in this area. We hope that this book contributes to the understanding of the dynamics of the banking system across regions in Brazil and alerts organisations to the need for more data on this sector.

Notes

1 Acre changed its status from Territory to state by a law of 15/06/1962.

2 The Territory of Rio Branco had its name changed to Territory of Roraima by a law of 13/12/1962.

3 This Territory was transformed into a state by a Law of 22/12/81.

4 This Territory was transformed into a state with the Constitution of 1988.

5 This Territory was transformed into a state with the constitution of 1988.

6 This state was created with the constitution of 1988.

7 This Territory was incorporated into the state of Pernambuco with the Constitution of 1988.

8 The states of Rio de Janeiro and Guanabara were merged with a Law of 01/07/1974.

9 This state was created in with a Law of 11/10/1977.

10 The list of these banks was based on the share of the banks in the Brazilian deposit market. These data were available in Balanço Anual, a special issue of the Gazeta Mercantil.

Part I
Heterodox theories of regional development

1 Uneven patterns of regional development: some heterodox interpretations

Introduction

Our main purpose in this chapter is to analyse different heterodox theoretical models that predict non-convergent regional growth. The first model explains the historical experience of insertion of peripheral countries in the world capitalist system, how this process generated an uneven pattern of development at the world level and how this process tends to be reproduced internally in terms of the economic regions of a country. In this model, financial conditions are sometimes considered as a restriction to the process of growth. However, there is a tendency to identify finance and saving as the same thing, treating, in this way, finance as a real constraint and not as a monetary constraint to the real variables in the process of growth. This treatment, we argue, may have been appropriate to an early stage of banking development (Chick, 1986) but is not appropriate to the analysis of a modern economy. The second type of model follows the idea of cumulative causation theory, where growth by itself tends to be self-reinforcing. Therefore, regions that attain a positive differential in growth tend to reproduce it over time. Kaldorian models use these ideas and, working with a demand-led model, stress that differentials in growth among regions can be explained by differences in the structure of the external sector of those economies. In these models, finance does not have any role to play. Those models, instead of presenting a heterodox approach do not assign any relevant role to monetary and financial constraints that the process of development of peripheral economies present. They are basically concerned with real forces that interact to generate cumulative processes that tend to stress the inequalities between regions.

Dependency Theory

The conception of a dependent pattern of development of the third world appeared in the years following the Second World War. The foundation of ECLA (Economic Commission for Latin America) added an extra impulse to a new way of thinking about the questions and challenges that the underdevelopment of the third world posed for economic growth theory. However, the Theory of Dependence cannot be reduced and, in some sense, is not mainly related to ECLA's ideas, especially as expressed by Prebisch, Furtado, Sunkel, Paz and Rodriguez. The formation of a new conception of peripheral development prepared the field for new ways of interpreting the relationship between centre and periphery. The great majority of the theories was related to what can be called the "neo-marxist approach"; these ideas are expressed principally in the works of Baran, Frank, dos Santos, Marini, Caputo and Cardoso.

The main concern of these theories is not to explain regional inequalities, but to stress that polarization between centre and periphery at the world level tends to be reproduced internally in underdeveloped countries. Thus, it is useful, for our purposes, to analyse the main contributions of these theories, both at the international and at the national level, in order to understand the process that generates central and peripheral economic structures that are parts of the same general process of capitalist development.

The above mentioned authors share some common points of analysis. The first one is that the idea of a unique pattern of development which all countries must follow[1], must be questioned. The phenomenon of underdevelopment is not considered a quantitative matter; it is not relative to the position of a country at a different stage of economic development within a general pattern of development which is common to all social and historical formations. Development and underdevelopment are different roles that distinct countries or regions play in the same process[2]. Underdevelopment is explained by these theories through the analysis of the structural characteristics of underdeveloped countries and through the investigation of the way in which these economies have been inserted in the world capitalist system. These authors observe that these economies have been playing a peripheral role in the world process of development, having their dynamic determined from abroad, this dynamic being mainly determined by a certain kind of response to the needs of the central economies.

On the other hand, those theories explain in different ways the main facts that characterise the phenomenon of underdevelopment; they have different points of view about the structural limitations of underdeveloped economies and different conceptions of the interdependence of external and internal determinants of the pattern of development. Therefore, it is necessary to differentiate between those authors who, in one way or another, are related to this School. We will, therefore, follow Palma's (1981) criterion of classification and will analyse, on the one hand, the theories of ECLA, on the other, the ideas of Baran, Frank, and dos Santos and finally Cardoso's analysis of underdevelopment.

ECLA and the idea of centre and periphery

The main purpose behind the founding of ECLA was to bring together different theorists to analyse and interpret underdevelopment in Latin America. This group not only had the objective of creating a "new theory" that could explain the main structural characteristics and their role in the process of underdevelopment in Latin American countries, but also had the aim of formulating positive proposals that would make it possible to overcome the peripheral underdevelopment of those countries. Prebish, Furtado, Sunkel and Rodriguez, among others, were mainly concerned with explaining the dichotomy in the international economy through a theory that denied the main postulates of the classical and mainstream theories of international trade[3].

They regard underdevelopment as being characterised by structures that interact to perpetuate this situation if "natural" forces are allowed to take their course. In this sense, they were mainly concerned with analysing how those structures were created, how they interacted and perpetuated themselves and how those "natural" patterns could be changed. Among the elements that are typical of underdevelopment, they observe: low per capita income, concentration of income, instability of the process of growth, under and unemployment, regional imbalances and foreign dependence. But according to this school of thought, these phenomena cannot be understood without analysing the process that creates them. Moreover, these features are the other side of the process of development of the central economies and play an important and functional role in the determining the international division of labour which allows the centre to be in a developed position[4]. Therefore, the uneven regional pattern of development is conditioned by and itself conditions the underdeveloped character of the country, and in order to understand underdevelopment at a regional level, it is necessary to understand it on the national level and on the international level.

ECLA's analysis pointed out, basically, two different phases in the underdevelopment of Latin America. The first one extends from the Iberian colonization to the beginning of the 20th century, more precisely, to the 1930s. This period is characterised by the absolute orientation of these economies towards their external markets. In ECLA's terminology this phase is referred as "Desarollo Hacia Afuera" (Development Towards Outside). In this phase, the periphery is typified mainly by the concentration in production of primary products; normally, each country specialised in only one product and derived all the dynamic elements of its economy from the external market of this commodity. Therefore, the dynamic element is situated outside its economy, that is, within the market demands of the markets of the Centre. The internal demand for consumption goods, on the other hand, is mainly supplied by the Central countries who export their industrialized products to the periphery. There is a complete and well defined international division of labour in which the periphery produces raw materials and primary products in general, while the centre produces a very large variety of industrial products for self consumption and export to the periphery. The second phase is referred to as "Desarollo Hacia Adentro" (Development Towards Inside), is marked by the maintenance of the dependent development; however, in this period, the dynamic element of the economy is transferred to the internal market of these economies[5].

However, this situation cannot be changed simply by introducing a capitalist enterprise into the archaic, traditional structure as this would not necessarily modify it in a significant way; because profits, which are considered by Furtado the main source of saving that serves as the basis for investment[6], are not necessarily attuned to the region in which they are generated. The main relationship between the dynamic and the archaic sectors of the economy is determined by wages, which are generated in the dynamic sector and that can, potentially, be a source of change in the traditional sector (Furtado, 1964, p. 132). In some specific cases, the amount of wages gives a sufficiently monetary character to the periphery and this allows a certain diversification of the structure of consumption within substantial segments of those economies which are linked to the external markets. However, as this increased demand is supplied by imports of industrialized products that originate in the centre, the international/interregional division of labour is again reproduced and reinforced.

Industrial production tends to have externalities associated with it that by themselves cause an increase in productivity of labour in this sector[7]. This is a sufficient element to increase the difference between the average incomes in economies specialized in industrial production and those ones based on primary production. But the main factor observed by ECLA as the source of disparity of the average incomes between peripheral and central economies is the inherent long run tendency towards the deterioration of the terms of exchange against the peripheral economies. If the differential in the increase of productivity between the centre and the periphery is considered constant, the mere deterioration of the terms of exchange will lead to an increasing gap between the average income of those regions/nations and if a productivity gain in the peripheral region is assumed, the fruits of these gains will be transferred to the central economies through the mechanisms of trade (Prebisch, 1949 and Rodriguez, 1981).

The main elements that explain the deterioration of the terms of exchange, according to ECLA's view, are: a) the fact that the demand for industrial goods is more diversified and is more income elastic than the demand for primary goods; b) the structural surplus of labour that characterizes the peripheral economies[8]. This is the main factor that contributes to the deterioration of the terms of exchange, as the surplus of labour exerts a downward pressure on wage levels in the export sector resulting in the reduced prices of those products; c) the oligopolistic/monopolist structure of the markets of the central economies that exerts a certain control over the prices of raw material produced in the peripheral countries and, on the other hand, exerts a greater control over their own prices of industrial products; and finally d) the better organization of the labour force in the centre into unions that allows this segment to retain the gains of productivity achieved in each sector (Prebisch, 1949, p. 59 and Rodriguez, 1981, p. 42).

Cardoso, therefore, points out that:

> It is not difficult to see why these apparently simple statements cause so much ado. They negate the importance of international trade per se, as the foundation for economic equality among nations, and incorporate the explanation both of institutional and structural factors that were situated beyond the sphere of the market and of the free fluctuation of prices: labor union struggles, the organizational capacity of workers and employers in the center, the effect of monopoly." (Cardoso, 1982, p. 143)

ECLA has based a great part of its theoretical work on the assumption that the industrialization of Latin American economies would by itself bring the structural changes necessary to overcome the underdevelopment of this region (Prebisch, 1949). But the evolution of industrialization in Latin America has shown that it has represented only a change in the situation of dependence and the main obstacles to development still persist[9].

The industrialization of Latin America was unable to produce the source of structural reforms that were necessary to overcome the main causes that put limits to the previous way of development which was led by the external market. The new needs for foreign finance, that this new pattern of development brought, were not satisfied by increases in the earnings from exports, mainly because the elements that contributed towards the depreciation of the terms of exchange still persisted.

The structural surplus in the labour force was maintained and in some occasions was intensified when the technology imported from the central economies was adopted and was not well adapted to the available resources of the peripheral economies (Furtado, 1964, p. 139).

Another important bottleneck that this process enforced was related to the limits of the internal supply of agricultural products. The typical ownership structure of land in Latin American consists of a combination of large and very small properties. This makes the supply of products from the agricultural sector extremely inelastic and strengthens the structural surplus of labour supply since it contributes to the expulsion of labour from this sector in a higher proportion than if there were a different structure of ownership[10].

The new dependent pattern of development continued to depend on the external sector, mainly to increase export demand and resulting increases in incomes and consequently in savings. The new dependence creates a new bottleneck of the point of view of the transformation of internally generated savings into capital: since the real capital necessary to production has a large import coefficient and accumulation, thus, generates persistent disequilibria in the Balance of Payments (Prebisch, 1949, p. 51). Therefore, the need for external finance seems imperative to continue the process of import substitution, although, if the internal structures do not change, the service of external finance can in the long run aggravate the external imbalance (Sunkel, 1973, p. 20).

The dichotomy centre/periphery is reproduced internally. Inside peripheral countries there is a centre which is developed and modern and attuned to the international market and which produces and commercializes export products, while there is also a backward, archaic sector that is related to a traditional production system normally linked to subsistence activities[11].

Therefore, the dualistic world model of development that generates central and peripheral economies tends to be reproduced internally. One of the manifestations of this excludent reality is the unequal regional development that reproduces the conditions observed in the world economy. The basic difference between the two models is the foreign exchange constraint, which, of course, does not operate regionally. However, the need for external finance to the peripheral regions still persists, as also the self-reinforcing character of this need.

Baran, Frank and dos Santos: world capitalist development as the source of underdevelopment

Baran began the tradition of "neo-marxist" analysis of underdevelopment with his book *The Political Economy of Growth* in 1957. These ideas have had a considerable influence on the work of Frank and dos Santos[12].

According to Baran, the accumulation of wealth in the metropolis, which was the base of the industrial revolution, originated to a great extent in the appropriation of wealth from the colonies. The appropriated wealth had a cumulative effect on the metropolis' economy which reinforced the process of intensive industrial growth of this region/country (Baran, 1957, p. 139). Therefore, in order to continue this process of surplus extraction and the concentration of it in the world metropolis, it was necessary to have mechanisms to forbid the creation of self-generating processes of growth in the satellite economies, and to condition those economies to play a functional role in the process of growth of the metropolis. Then, it was the dynamic of growth of the centre itself which generated the source of unequal development at the world level (Baran, 1957, p. 141).

The contact between the central capitalist economies and the peripheral economies at the beginning of colonization destroyed and transformed the peripheral economies' traditional and archaic structures[13] and introduced capitalist elements in those economies. However, while the insertion of capitalist elements, on the one hand, created the possibility of development, on the other hand it also put limits to it, depending on the specific ways in which those elements were introduced and the specific roles that they played in expropriating the previously accumulated surplus. And so, the capitalistic elements introduced in those economies were more related to the growth needs of the centre than of the development of the periphery (Baran, 1957, p. 144).

One of the main characteristics of backward areas is the predominance of the agricultural sector within the whole productive system. The extreme volatility of the prices of the products of these markets and the dependence of those prices on the state of the demand of central regions make investment in these sectors extremely uncertain. The low level of investment is also explained when these elements are taken together with the higher rate of interest that prevails in the peripheral economies and the tendency to avoid long term credit as demonstrated by lenders in those regions, because of the risk involved (Baran, 1957, p. 166).

The market for industrial goods that appears in these economies, instead of constituting a market for the incipient industrial nucleus generated inside these countries can be observed as an appendix of the internal market of the central economies. Investment in the internal markets of the peripheral economies is also obstructed by a lack of policies to protect these markets and so allow development of an incipient industry. Absence of investment prejudices against further investment, resulting in a self-perpetuating situation.

Baran observes the possibility of industrialization of the peripheral economies. However, he argues that this industrialization is led normally by multinational or foreign firms which tend to present productive processes that are intensive in capital. This creates two types of difficulties for peripheral economies: a) they suffer a strong leakage, since the capital goods used in the productive process are normally imported and b) they intensify their structural problem of unemployment, since their technological profile is not adapted to the distribution of the productive factors of peripheral economies. Furthermore, since the markets of these peripheral economies are normally very restricted[14], they only subscribe to one firm or a few firms in each sector, resulting in a strong tendency in these economies towards oligopolistic market structures (Baran, 1957, p. 177).

Therefore, it can be seen that underdevelopment is conserved in these backward economies as a consequence of the interplay of external and internal forces that have convergent interests in maintaining this state. Thus, Baran analyses the class arrangements and alliances between the external and internal spheres that perpetuate the underdevelopment of these regions. Baran stresses, therefore, the fact that underdevelopment is not a consequence of lack of surplus, but a problem of : a) transference of that surplus and b) bad use of the economic surplus, which is spent in luxury and unproductive consumption by the dominant class of satellite countries (Baran, 1957, p. 227).

The ideas developed by Baran formed the basis of Gunder Frank's analysis. According to Frank, the phenomena of development and underdevelopment are the necessary outcome of the development of capitalism.

The main element characteristic of Frank's theory is the negation of the idea of dualistic models that attribute underdevelopment to the continued existence and of some "archaic" or "feudal" structures in underdeveloped regions or countries[15]. According to him, the problem of development in Latin America has no relation with such a formation, because this type of structure is specific to the development of Western Europe and has never existed in these peripheral countries. Underdevelopment is a consequence of the natural development of capitalism and of the free play of its logic and contradictions (Frank, 1967, p.3). The historic process by which peripheral economies are incorporated in the world capitalist system has been conducted according to capitalist logic; therefore the main structures of these peripheral economies have been adapted to and transformed into capitalist ones[16] (Frank, 1966, p. 17).

Frank pointed out that the phenomenon of development/underdevelopment can be characterized, basically, by three essential contradictions: a) the expropriation/appropriation of the economic surplus; b) the metropolis/satellite polarization and c) the continuity in change (Frank, 1967).

The expropriation/appropriation contradiction refers to the role of economic surplus in the process of economic development. According to Frank, the strong level of monopoly both at the internal and at the external level which characterized the insertion of Latin America into the world capitalist system has made easy the expropriation of surplus from those countries/regions. The expropriation of this surplus and its appropriation by the central countries/regions tends to make underdevelopment a generalized phenomenon and development a restricted one (Frank, 1967).

The contradiction of metropolis/satellite polarization is, perhaps, the most important contradiction in Frank's analysis of capitalism (Frank, 1967, p. 8). This contradiction affirms that polarization and exclusion are fundamental features of world capitalist development. Therefore, development/underdevelopment, centre/periphery are opposite sides of a unique process and each can only be analysed in relation to the other. "Underdevelopment was and still is generated by the very same historical process which also generated economic development: the development of capitalism itself" (Frank, 1966, p. 23).

The polarization of metropolis/satellite economies is not concerned only with the expropriation and appropriation of surplus. It has to do with the reproduction, at the internal level of the satellite economies, of the contradictions that are inherent in capitalism at the world level. Therefore, satellite economies tend to reproduce internally the political, social and economic structures of domination that make possible this polarization. This process creates a national metropolis and satellites and the tendency towards development in the former and towards underdevelopment in the latter is reproduced. This in turn, creates internal regions which could be considered "sub-satellites", and which have their development conditioned by the development of their own metropolis, that in its turn plays the role of satellite in relation to the world metropolis, and has its development conditioned by it.

This contradiction shows that the more tied the satellites are to the metropolis, the greater is the structural underdevelopment of their economies because the contradictions that express the relation underdevelopment/development are accentuated. Conversely, satellite economies that have less contact with the metropolis have less of a tendency towards the "development of underdevelopment".

Finally, there is the contradiction of continuity in change. Frank is concerned with the maintenance and continuity of the main and fundamental structures of the capitalist system that allow the polarization of development and underdevelopment in the world capitalist system. These structures are maintained throughout time, despite some changes in their forms.

According to Frank, the main way of extracting the surplus used by the internal and external metropolis is through commercial and financial monopolies. He emphasizes the role that credit plays in these economies, and moreover the role that financial concentration plays. In terms of external indebtedness of the peripheral economies, he points out that this corresponds to a special way of appropriation of surplus. On the other hand, at the national level, credit is not evenly distributed and tends to exacerbate the monopolistic character of these economies since it is directed towards sectors that have a higher technological advantage and that have, normally, a stronger monopolistic feature. These firms, usually, also have easier access to international sources of finance. Thus they have two advantages in relation to the competitive sectors of the economy. These firms, usually, are multinational or national (operating nationwide) enterprises that have a strong oligopolistic character. Therefore, the financial sector tends to increase the internal disparities between national and international enterprises, between the internal metropolis and the satellites and between sectors with different degrees of technological development and market power (Frank, 1967, pp. 199-200).

Frank observes that the main source of the new character of dependence in the third world economies is the increasing control of the central economies over the industries of these countries. This control takes place in two ways: a) through direct investment in these countries and b) by the control of the technology used in the productive processes of the satellite economies. According to Frank, these two processes reinforce his thesis of continuity in change, for they emphasize the maintenance of the old structures of dependence in a new economic environment.

Dos Santos developed his ideas in great part using Frank's framework, although he criticized Frank's thesis that the process that generates underdevelopment is fundamentally a process of surplus extraction from the satellites to the centres. According to dos Santos, this process, instead of being a satellization process is a case of formation of a specific kind of internal structure in the satellite countries that is conditioned by the external relations of dependence.

> Underdevelopment, far from constituting a state of backwardness prior to capitalism, is rather a consequence and a particular form of capitalist development known as dependent capitalism. The process under consideration, rather than being one of satellization as Frank believes, is a case of foundation of a certain type of internal structure conditioned by international relationships of dependence. (dos Santos, 1973, p. 76)

Dos Santos, therefore, is concerned with analysing the peculiarities of the different ways of determining the internal structures in each historical period of the dependence relations of peripheral countries. This is the opposite position to that of Frank, who was interested in analysing and emphasising the similarities of those different periods (Palma, 1981, p. 402).

Dos Santos is interested in the specific historical ways in which the relations of dependence evolve. The first historical way that he observes is colonial dependence, the second refers to financial/industrial dependence and the third refers to the expansion of multinational corporations (dos Santos, 1970, p. 232). The analysis of these three "stages" does not mean that some of them cannot live together during particular periods, but it accentuates which one is more relevant in some specific historical periods. The pattern of these situations is determined externally, however, the internal forces produce the resultant concrete way throughout those dependent economies evolve through time.

The external relations of dependence tend to be transferred into the economy and reproduce its main characteristic in such a way that the extraction of surplus from the backward regions and from the traditional sector is the main base on which to develop the dependent capitalism of the national centre (dos Santos, 1970, pp. 234-235). Therefore, according to this point of view, the internal structure of dependence and underdevelopment can only be understood in a wider sense if it incorporates the external dependence and the way in which the internal structure combines with the external ones in order to form a dependent structure of capitalist development.

Cardoso and the analysis of the relation between the new forms of dependence and growth

Cardoso develops his theory on a theoretical framework that is similar to that of dos Santos[17]. However, Cardoso is more concerned with the concrete and specific forms that dependency has assumed through Latin American history and especially with the role that internal structures play in this process[18].

Dependency is analysed, as in other theories mentioned above, as a consequence of the development of the world capitalist system. The dynamic of the whole system is located in the centre and peripheral development could be considered a reflex development, whose dynamic is a dependent one. But for the broad analysis of this process it is necessary to consider dependency and dependent development not only as a purely economic process, but as an economic, social and political process where all these spheres are essential to the comprehension of the concrete form that dependence assumes and the way in which it evolves through time. The analysis of the specific form of dependence emphasises the insufficiency of the mainly economic parameters established by other theories to characterize underdevelopment[19].

In his book with Faletto (1979) and in his article of 1972, Cardoso notes how the relations of dependency have evolved in Latin America, and moreover, the relevance and specific ways of articulation of the internal structures of class and power that allowed and reinforced the changes. Therefore, he points out that it is necessary to analyse the relations of underdeveloped economies with international markets, but it is also fundamental to understand how the formation of a certain internal social structure creates the necessary conditions for the external relations of dependence[20].

Therefore, dependency is only possible with an internal base that makes possible its evolution and maintenance. The whole organization of the internal society tends to create the conditions to perpetuate a specific situation of dependence.

Cardoso shows that the previous method of characterizing underdevelopment is inadequate in dealing with the "new" relations of dependence that are observed in the world economy into which Latin American countries are inserted. He observes that after the 1950s and mainly after the 1960s the economic structure of underdeveloped countries was increasingly characterized by the diversification of their industry and their production. This could be observed as the overcoming of underdevelopment or the dependent situation[21], but as he notes, these changes are only a new way of expressing those relations of dependence (Cardoso, 1979, p. 19).

Analysing the new pattern of development in Latin America, Cardoso points out that, contrary to what was thought, dependency, monopoly and capitalist development are not necessarily mutually exclusive[22]. After the 50s, Latin American countries were mainly characterized by an intense process of industrialization that was mainly based on oligopolistic/monopolistic structures. However, instead of this process representing a barrier to growth, it intensified it. But, far from constituting a way of overcoming dependent relations inside and outside the country, this process has constituted a new base for the new relations of dependence in these economies.

The source of inequality and dependence is no longer a productive structure concentrated on raw materials or agricultural products. The new dependence and conditions for extraction of surplus are based on a new international division of labour and on a new internal social and political base. Cardoso analyses the peculiarities of these new relations of dependency at the international level and the way they interact with the internal economic and social structures, when the State began to play a fundamental role in allowing the implementation of new alliances of class that are the basis of this new situation of dependency (Cardoso, 1978).

In this new phase, international capital migrates from the primary sectors in the peripheral economies, where it produces raw materials to sell in the international market, to industrial production, whose main goal is the internal market of the periphery. Therefore, the main decisions and the dynamic of the process of development continued to be based outside the peripheral economies and this tended to perpetuate their dependent character.

The key role of third world internal markets creates the necessity to promote a certain type of internal prosperity: the type of demand attuned to its products tends to transform internal structures in order to create markets that integrate into the world economy. Thus, the new structure of these economies allows new forms of association between international and national capital and in a certain sense, international capital allows national capital some degree of participation in the process of production. On the other hand, this process tends to deepen the unequal relations that characterize dependent development because now we have both external and internal dependence, since there is an internal sector that is associated with the international capital that tends to reproduce internally all the elements related to the general pattern of dependent development above analysed. These inequalities can be observed at the social, political and regional level (Cardoso, 1972, p. 90)[23].

In this new world, economic dependence manifests itself basically in two ways: a) production decisions are located outside these peripheral economies (given the control of the market by the multinational corporations); b) the peripheral countries depend on the import of technology and on the import of some means of production. In this new stage of the world capitalism, the main sources of extraction of surplus appears in the form of payment abroad of interest, royalties, dividends and remittance of profits (Cardoso, 1973, p. 57).

Therefore, this conception of dependence emphasizes that a dependent pattern of growth does not necessarily lead to stagnation, although it does not allow the internalization of the dynamic of growth[24]. This process tends to accentuate the internal differentiated relations, that is, it takes one sector of the economy (the modern sector that is related to the international capital) to a level of development similar to those sectors in all the central economies. On the other hand, it stresses inequalities of income, of political power and of regional development. This process is extremely functional in allowing and creating the necessary conditions for the promotion of the modern sector of the economy to the level of central economies.

Cumulative causation theory and dome Keynesian models of uneven regional patterns of development

Myrdal and the cumulative causation theory

Myrdal (1972) develops his theory of regional and international disparities based on the idea of cumulative causation[25]. This principle is strongly opposed to the prediction of mainstream theory that regional and international inequalities will decrease through mechanisms of trade and migration of factors and products.

According to Myrdal the main problem with conventional theory is the inadequacy of the theory to deal with inequality, and further, to deal with persistent and sometimes growing inequalities (Myrdal, 1972, p. 9). He notes that the main cause for this inability is a consequence of the assumptions of this theory, especially the role of the notion of a stable equilibrium in this theory. According to him, mainstream theory assumes that for each movement or action of the economic system there are some forces that move at the same time in the opposite direction in such a way that equilibrium is restored. What Myrdal points out is that these forces can act in the same direction as the first one, thus accentuating the disequilibrium instead of achieving equilibrium, reinforcing the direction of the primary disturbance and generating a cumulative process[26]. These cumulative processes can only be stopped by exogenous forces acting in the opposite direction to the primary movement (Myrdal, 1972, p. 13).

Normally, the effects of a cumulative advantage in one region are not restricted to that particular region; they interact with other regions since factors and products can move from one place to another. Again, contrary to the mainstream approach, Myrdal observes:

> By themselves, migration, capital movements and trade are rather the media through which the cumulative process evolves - upwards in the lucky regions and downwards in the unlucky ones. In general, if they have positive results for the former, their effects on the latter are negative. (Myrdal, 1972, p. 27)

Banks play an important role in this process, for they allow the transfer of savings from the poorer and stagnant regions to the richer and dynamic regions. Thus, they accentuate the cumulative process and contribute towards amplifying the gap between regions (Myrdal, 1972, p. 28).

These negative effects on a depressed region that result from a positive change in the dynamic region are the so-called "backwash effects" and act to increase the regional disparities instead of narrowing the gap between different regional developmental levels. Myrdal, however, observes that some elements act in a "centrifugal" way and tend to extend the effects of the economic expansion from its centre to other regions; these are called "spread effects". These effects operate under the same principle as cumulative causation. The observance of such an effect, however, does not mean that there is an inherent tendency towards stable equilibrium (Myrdal, 1972, p. 32). Although analysed in general terms, the cumulative causation and mainly "backwash" and "spread" effects assume different features in economies that are at different levels of economic development. Myrdal observes that developed economies tend to have a lower level of regional disparities than underdeveloped ones, and moreover, in the richer countries, these disparities tend to decrease through time, while in the poorer economies, these disparities tend to increase (Myrdal, 1972, p. 34).

Therefore, economic development in an environment of free market forces tends to increase the internal disparities between countries and tends to increase the internal differentiation between regions within the poorest countries. These processes can be stopped or at least their impacts reduced by the exogenous action of the State that can, through coherent policies, generate upward cumulative causation processes and reverse the tendencies dictated by the market. However, instead of the theoretical possibility of reversing the "natural" tendencies of the market toward growing inequalities through the discretionary intervention of the State, these actions, as Myrdal observes, are themselves governed by the cumulative causation process that has its origins in the interests of the powerful classes and regions. In this way, the State's intervention is limited by the play of power within the country.

Kaldor and a Keynesian version of cumulative causation theory

Following Myrdal's ideas of cumulative causation processes, Kaldor (1970) developed a model to explain the sources of uneven patterns of development among regions. Dixon and Thirlwall (1975) formalized this model and reached some specific conclusions that differ in some sense from Kaldor. In the same agenda of research, Thirlwall (1980) developed a model using basically the same previous framework and recovered Harrod's trade multiplier in order to explain the mechanisms through which different regions reach different levels of development.

Kaldor (1970) attempted to elaborate a model that gave an alternative argument to neoclassical regional locational theory. Instead of explaining the location of certain industries through exogenous elements, like natural endowment and transport costs[27], he searched for endogenous elements that were capable of explaining different patterns of development and different rates of growth.

Following the Keynesian tradition, these models assume that the long run rate of growth of the product is determined by the growth of autonomous demand of the economy, since induced investment and consumption are strictly related to the autonomous demand. Kaldor argues that in the regional context the main source of autonomous demand is the demand that is originated outside the region, that is, the demand for exports. Thus, the regional rate of growth is mainly determined by the rate of growth of exports, to which the rate of growth of investment and consumption adjust. The foreign trade multiplier is the mechanism responsible for the adjustment of imports to the new level of exports.

These models establish that there are two main sources of change in the demand for exports: the first one is exogenous and refers to the rate of growth of world demand for products of the region; the second is endogenous and refers to the movements at the competitive level of the products of the region. The competitiveness of these products is basically a function of changes in the efficiency wages in the region[28].

As efficiency wages represent the relation between monetary wages and labour productivity, and as money wages are assumed to be relatively invariable across regions, for institutional reasons, the main point to be analysed, and, consequently, the main source of disparities among the regions' growth rates, will be found in the behaviour of labour productivity. The cumulative causation process of growth rests on the Verdoorn Effect, which assumes productivity as a positive function of the growth of output. Therefore, higher rates of increase in productivity are associated with higher rates of growth. Thus, given an initial advantage in the competitiveness of one region which generates a positive differential in the rate of growth of this region, this advantage will be perpetuated, by the action of the Verdoorn Effect on regional productivity and, consequently, on the efficiency wage and on the competitiveness of the products of the region.

The Verdoorn Effect is, however, a source of regional inequalities only when the Verdoorn coefficient varies across regions or when other parameters that influence the rate of growth of the economy vary. The values attained to each of those parameters are related to the economic structure of each region.

Dixon and Thirlwall (1975), on establishing a specific function for demand for exports, observe that the long-term rate of growth of the region is a positive function of the rate of change of the following variables: the income elasticity of demand for exports; the cross elasticity of demand for exports; the autonomous changes on productivity; the Verdoorn coefficient; the competitive prices abroad; and world income. Regional growth varies negatively with the rate of change in nominal wages and with the rate of change in the mark-up, precisely because these two elements represent a loss in competitiveness of the products of the region. The elasticity of demand for exports will depend basically on the structure of the products that each region produces. The rate of autonomous growth and the Verdoorn Coefficient will depend upon the extent that accumulation is induced by growth and incorporates technical progress and, thus, will depend on the industrial composition of each region. These features will determine the extent to which each region keeps and reinforces the benefits originating from an increasing demand.

Thirlwall (1980), on considering the work of the trade multiplier and the determinants of the rate of growth compatible with the balance of payments equilibrium, reaches the conclusion that the regional rate of growth is fundamentally determined by the rate of growth of exports divided by the income elasticity of demand for imports[29]. Assuming the Verdoorn Effect, again, we have some sort of cumulative causation process, with a self-reinforcing effect of growth that tends to amplify or maintain the differences in regional rates of growth.

The divergence or convergence of different regional rates of growth, according to Dixon and Thirlwall (1975), is basically an empirical matter and depends on the values of the parameters necessary to determine the equilibrium rate of growth. As we observed before, Kaldor (1970) notes the possibility of divergence in the regional equilibrium rate of growth that is made possible by the Verdoorn Effect. On the other hand, Dixon and Thirlwall (1975) affirm that divergence is an "unrealistic assumption"[30] and what is closer to reality is the maintenance of a constant difference in regional rates of growth that is determined by differences in equilibrium rates.

Those models, in accordance with Myrdal's explanation of differences in the regional rates of growth, show that the free play of the market tends to increase differences between regional rates of growth or at least maintain these differences constant. Thus, there is the necessity for exogenous actions in this "natural" process in order to restore its "natural" trend. These actions, according to these authors, may have their origin in State economic policies that can interfere in the rate of growth of depressed regions and through the Verdoorn Effect can expand this first impulse in the region.

There are two main lines of economic policy proposals. On the one hand, Kaldor proposed the devaluation of the rate of exchange in the case of regions with different currencies (different nations) or a policy of wage subsidies which through their effect on the efficiency wage can expand the demand for exports and increase the competitiveness of the region[31].

On the other hand, Dixon and Thirlwall affirm that:

> Wage subsidies at the regional level are equivalent at the most to an autonomous shock which, as we regard earlier, could only affect the growth rate permanently if the structural parameters of the growth model were thereby affected favourably. (Dixon and Thirlwall, 1975, p. 211)

Dixon and Thirlwall defend the idea that the government policy must act on export promotion and import substitution through mechanisms that attune taxes and subsidies at the regional level to sectors that must be stimulated, eg. those with high income and price elasticities of demand, or a high Verdoorn Coefficient. These sectors must be encouraged to locate in depressed regions through capital incentives and labour subsidies.

The unique constraint imposed on the regional rate of growth in these models is the level of autonomous demand, and in the specific case, the level of external demand. Therefore, the explanation of uneven patterns of regional development is based only on real variables. The financial conditions of the economy do not have any role to play in the cumulative causation process and in the determination of the regional level of output and employment. This fact is the result of the Kaldorian conception of finance, money and the absolute endogeneity of money supply[32]. According to Kaldor, the state of liquidity of the economy should be considered rather than money in a narrow sense. All those assets that are used for clearing contracts could be considered as forming the money supply (Kaldor, 1978, p. 10). Those assets have the common feature of not yielding interest. Otherwise, Kaldor considers the range of financial assets that yield interest but can be almost instantaneously converted into money as forming a broad concept of money supply (Kaldor, 1985, p. 71), or the state of liquidity of the economy (Kaldor, 1985, p. 71).

The introduction of interest-bearing assets in the concept of money supply opens the door to the introduction of an ample range of financial assets within this concept and this fact accentuates the problem of controlling the money supply. According to Kaldor what is really relevant to the decisions of spending is the state of liquidity of the economy and this variable is totally out of control of the monetary authority[33].

In a credit economy, with the Central Bank playing its role of lender of last resort, the supply of money is endogenous and is determined by the demand of the public; it is totally out of control of the monetary authority. Even the monetary base is endogenous, since it is responsive to changes in the demand for money (Kaldor, 1978, p. 16).

Therefore, in a credit economy, since the supply of money is absolutely demand determined, the unique instrument of monetary policy is the control of the interest rate in order to preserve the reserves of the Central Bank. At this level of interest rate thus determined, the elasticity of credit supply is infinite, the money supply will be absolutely demand determined and the financial system is absolutely passive in relation to the extension of credit. In some specific moments the monetary authority can use its power to fix the rate of interest as a means of making credit extension easier or restricting it, but even in those instances, the supply of money continues to be demand-determined. Such a policy can have indirect effects on the supply of money, since it affects the decision to invest and, consequently, the level of income and, finally, the demand for money to which the supply of money will adjust (Kaldor, 1985, p. 25). But in this context, the Central Bank's power to fix the rate of interest is still limited by the necessity of maintaining the solvency of the financial institutions.

In Kaldor's theory, as the supply of money and credit is endogenous and adapts almost automatically to the demand determined by the real side of the economy, finance cannot represent any constraint to growth. The interest rate is a policy variable; liquidity preference has no effective role to play (Kaldor, 1985, p. xviii).

This analysis can be extended to the regional level. It is assumed that the interest rate is fixed by the Central Bank and that at this level the credit supply is infinitely elastic to all regions; thus the financial market is neutral in relation to the uneven pattern of development. Therefore, the unique source of inequality between regions is found in the real side of the economy.

Notes

1 For this type of argument see Rostow (1971).

2 For this topic see Dos Santos (1973, p. 59).

3 They noted that the mainstream theory of international trade and the regional locational theory were based on very unrealistic assumptions. The main hypothesis criticized by them was the one that referred to the even distribution of the "fruits of the technological progress" among regions and countries. For a good analysis of this point see Prebisch (1949, p. 47).

4 See Sunkel (1973) and Rodriguez (1981).

5 See Paz (1975 second part) and Furtado (1971).

6 Furtado, and the majority of dependency theorists, considers savings or surplus as a previous condition to investment. This could be analysed as a result of a simplistic treatment given to the banking system and to its evolution through history.

7 This point was observed by Myrdal and was stressed by Kaldor in his article of 1970.

8 This excess tends to be amplified with the introduction of new techniques that are more intensive in capital.

9 For a more detailed analysis see Palma (1981); Bodenheimer (1971); O'Brien (1975) and Petras (1967).

10 See Prebisch (1970, pp. 203-204).

11 The observation of the dualistic position of the peripheral countries is one of the fundamental elements in the differentiation between the various streams of the Dependency Theory.

12 See Palma (1981) and Frank (1967, p.xvii).

13 Baran's analysis accepts the existence of these structures, although, the main explanation for the underdevelopment of the peripheral regions is not centred on this element, but more precisely in the relationship of these economies and the capitalist world system.

14 The reduced size of the peripheral markets is due to the concentration of income and the poor capacity to internalize the linkages that production generates. The latter is a consequence of the productive structure of these economies.

15 Frank points out: "I believe on the contrary that the entire 'dual society' thesis is false and that the policy recommendation to which it leads will, if acted upon, serve only to intensify and perpetuate the very conditions of underdevelopment they are supposedly designed to remedy" (Frank, 1966, p. 19).

16 There are some disagreements about the characterization of capitalism adopted by Frank. Palma observes that the unique way that Frank can

develop his theory is by supposing that peripheral economies are fully inserted in a capitalist system is taken as the main, or unique, characteristic of capitalism the production towards the market and oriented by the profit-seeking behaviour of the entrepreneurs (Palma, 1981, p. 402). Laclau highlights the point that the more relevant element to the characterisation of the capitalist mode of production: the use of a free labour force under a wage payment system is not considered by Frank in his description of the satellite capitalist structures (Laclau, 1973).

17 However Cardoso makes some fundamental critiques of this stream of dependence theory. For a good example of these critiques see Serra and Cardoso (1986).

18 See Cardoso (1973, p. 46).

19 For this argument see Cardoso (1979, p. 18).

20 Cardoso does not have a mechanistic way of analysing the determination of the internal structures by the external structures. He is much more concerned with the interplay of those structures in the generation of concrete forms that dependence assumes. Palma (1981) observes that this is the opposite position in relation to Frank's analysis.

21 This is true if underdevelopment is associated with the concentration of production on the primary sector.

22 This point is opposed to Frank's idea of the "development of underdevelopment" and also opposes the stagnationist models developed by Furtado and to the models developed by Marini (1969 and 1973).

23 de Mattos (1989) observes that territorial concentrating processes can only be reversed based on general deconcentrating policies. This is because he observes the process of reversal of concentration at the territorial level as a process of a decrease in the dependent position of the peripheral regions and a decline in the differences of living standards of the local population.

24 Moreover, it does not allow for the possibility of the overcoming of the main socio-economic problems of dependent countries (Cardoso, 1978, p. 9).

25 Hicks also observes some sort of cumulative process in his article of 1959, but he perceives other forces that act to reduce regional disparities, such that the model does not present any unique result concerning the deepening or reduction of regional disparities (Hicks, 1959, p. 162). Nurkse (1955) also develops a model of cumulative causation. However, as with Myrdal, Nurkse considers financial

constraints as saving constraints and in this way does not advance significantly the discussion of the vicious circle generated on the financial side of the economy.

26 These cumulative processes are not unidirectional: they can act in both directions, upward and downward.

27 According to Kaldor these elements are relevant to the explanation of the location of agricultural activity, but not to analysing the location of industry.

28 Prices in these models are formed through mark-up on the efficiency wages. That is why Kaldor proposed wage subsidies and not other kinds of subsidies.

29 Davidson (1990) Prices in these models are formed through mark-up on the efficiency wages. That is why Kaldor proposed wage subsidies and not other kinds of subsidies.refers to this result as Thirlwall's Law.

30 This is a consequence of the empirical observation of the values of each parameter that enters in the determination of the equilibrium growth rate.

31 In this way Morgan (1973) observes:

Measures to reduce the cost of capital and labour in the depressed regions enhance their competitive position vis-a-vis the rest of the world in the same way as a country's competitive position is improved by currency devaluation, but with two important differences. Devaluations normally turn the terms of trade against the deficit country and so reduces the real incomes of its inhabitants, whereas regional policies protect the real income of the inhabitants of depressed regions by a subsidy from more prosperous ones. Secondly, devaluation, if carried to the point at which a new equilibrium rate is established, provides a permanent cure, whereas the benefits of subsidies last only as long as the subsidies themselves (Morgan, 1973, p. 28).

32 See Dow (1990). For a Kaldorian model that considers the monetary aspect of the economic process see Palley (1991/92) and for the an alternative treatment of the "horizontalist" approach of the money supply see Moore (1979/80 and 1988).

33 For this point see Kaldor and Trevithick (1981), Palley (1991/92) and also Moore (1979/80, 1983 and 1988) that for different reasons reach the same conclusions of a horizontal curve of money supply.

2 Money, finance, financial system and uneven patterns of development

Introduction

The relevance that economic theory attributes to money has been changing through time, but as a generalization it can be said that it has been treated much more as a mere convenience and an element without importance rather than as an element that can really affect the short and long run trend of the economy. The orthodoxy has always treated money as a helpful means of exchange but what really matters in the process of exchange is the trade of one good for another: money is considered only an oil that makes exchange easier. The relevance that this school attributes to money is reduced to its short-term effect, which is a reflection of the frictions that are characteristic of this period and not of any intrinsic element that characterizes the economic process or monetary economies[1].

The treatment that Keynes gives to money in his later works, confers on money a fundamental role that is inherently linked to his conception of a monetary economy, which is one where "money plays a part of its own and affects motives and decisions and is, in short, one of the operative factors in the situation, so that the course of events cannot be predicted, either in the long period or in the short, without a knowledge of the behaviour of money between the first state and the last" (Keynes, 1973a, pp. 408-9). Therefore, money is conceived as being non-neutral both in the long and in the short period. The conception of the economy that the orthodoxy has in mind when thinking about money is what Keynes named a barter or real-exchange economy. This can be observed in: "The distinction which is normally made between a barter economy and a monetary economy depends upon the employment of money as a convenient means of affecting exchanges, as an instrument of great convenience, but transitory and neutral in its effect". Furthermore, "an economy, which uses money but uses it merely as a neutral link between transactions in real things and real assets and does not allow it to enter into motives or decisions, might be called - for want of a better name - *a real-exchange economy"* (Keynes, 1973a, p. 408)[2].

The conception of money, monetary economies and the role that money plays in these economies is inherently linked to the analysis of the historical development of money. Therefore, the mainstream could have an appropriate analysis for economies that are in the earlier stages of banking development but this analysis loses sense completely when we are dealing with economies that have overcome stage 1 of banking development[3]. Thus, although Keynes affirms in the *General Theory* that in this book "money enters into the economic scheme in an essential and peculiar manner, technical monetary detail falls into the background" (Keynes, 1936, p. xxii). These "monetary details" are fundamental to the full comprehension of the different roles of money in different stages of banking development. In the *Treatise on Money*, Keynes was especially concerned with the roles and ways in which the financial system creates money and with the consequent roles of money in the economy (Keynes, 1971), while in the *General Theory* those elements are a side issue. Here we shall analyse the specific roles that money, comprehended as State money and private money, can play in the real side of the economy.

There are three basic conceptual elements in the monetary theory of Keynes and of the Post Keynesian School: time, uncertainty and money. These three elements when put together generate the non-neutrality of money. In the first section of this chapter we present the case for non-neutrality of money and credit. We argue that this non-neutrality is fundamental. In the second part of the chapter, we will observe the specific roles that money and the financial system play in the determination and intensification of disparities between regions that are in different stages of development.

As has been observed in Chapter 1 the models concerned with explaining uneven patterns of development are mainly based on real elements that characterize those economies, though Dependency Theory does introduce some financial constraints to the explanation of different patterns of development. However, Dependency Theory does not develop all the potential roles that finance and money can play in emphasising inequalities between centre and periphery[4].

In order to fill this gap and to show that finance and money have a crucial role to play in regional development, Dow presents some models that are concerned exactly with the functions of the financial system in the promotion of uneven patterns of development [5].

Time, uncertainty and money in a monetary production economy

Keynes, in the preface to the *General Theory*, affirms: "A monetary economy, we shall find, is essentially one in which changing views about the future are capable of influencing the quantity of employment and not merely its direction" (Keynes, 1936, p. xxii). This quotation emphasises the importance of time and expectations-formation in a monetary production economy. However, the conception of time to which Keynes and Post Keynesians refer is fundamentally different from the notion of time on which the orthodoxy bases its analysis[6]. The notion of time relevant to Keynes's theory is historical time, which is characterised by complete irreversibility. This makes agents to undertake their economic decisions, which have their effects in future, based on expectations which they know cannot be revised and are subject to disappointment (Amadeo & Dutt, 1987, p. 574).

Since we propose to analyse regional growth in a monetary economy of production perspective in which the formation of expectations and the interplay of forces within the economic system are fundamental, the relevant notion of time will be historical time.

In the perspective of Keynes and the Post Keynesians, there is a fundamental difference between the concepts of uncertainty and risk. The first can be identified by its non-quantifiable character and the second by its possibility of measurement in quantitative terms (Knight, 1933, pp. 19-20). However, all the spheres of the economy are not under the same degree of uncertainty. The nearer, in time, the result of the outcome of a decision, the smaller the degree of uncertainty in the decision making process. At the same time, the larger the commitment of the agent, both in terms of volume of resources and time, the stronger the uncertainty and more volatile the bases on which he undertakes the decision (Keynes, 1937, p. 213). Pointing out the differences between risk and uncertainty Keynes states: "By 'uncertain' knowledge, let me explain, I do not mean merely to distinguish what is known for certain from what is only probable. The game of roulette is not subject, in this sense to uncertainty; nor is the prospect of a Victory bond being drawn, or, again, the expectation of life is only slightly uncertain. Even the weather is only moderately uncertain. The sense in which I am using the term is that in which the prospect of an European war is uncertain, or the price of copper and the rate of interest twenty years hence, or the obsolescence of a new invention, or the position of private wealth-owners in the social system in 1970. About these matters there is no scientific basis on which to form any calculable probability whatever. We simply do not know" (Keynes, 1937, pp. 213-4).

The Uncertainty that characterizes economic activity is a result of the non-ergodicity of economic events, that is, events in the economy are not time independent (Davidson, 1988, pp. 331-2). The non-ergodicity of such events results from their non-seriable and non-divisible character[7], that is, the probability distribution is not the same as one reached by a series of trials executed at the same moment or by a series of trials each one taking place in each moment isolated in time from the others.

Another fundamental point is that in classical probability the probabilistic weight in each outcome of the total set of outcomes of an event must add up to one. That is, the set of outcomes must be complete in order to allow the application of traditional probability theory. This, however, does not occur in the real world. As Keynes puts it: "The calculus of probability, tho mention of it was kept in the background, was supposed to be capable of reducing uncertainty to the same calculable status of certainty" (Keynes, 1937, p. 213).

There are basically two points here that make the economy an improper object for traditional statistical method (Davidson, 1982-83, p. 192). The first one refers to the presence of historical time and its consequent irreversibility. The second one refers to the creative character of the economic process as a whole. These two elements make the economic events "crucial experiments": as they are non-divisible and non-seriable, replication of the experiment is impossible, since the conditions in which the experiment takes place are destroyed by the realization of it (Shackle, 1979, p. 135). Furthermore, the incompleteness of the set of outcomes (that is, the probabilities of the set of possible outcomes do not add up to one) leads agents to fill this gap using their creativity, which makes economic events "crucial" and thus not proper subjects for the traditional probability method.

Few references have been made to the different degrees of uncertainty across regions. If there are substantial differences in the degree of uncertainty among regions, the behaviour of agents in relation to money will also be differentiated. The analysis of this element will be one of the bases for the model developed in the second section of this chapter.

Agents who have to make decisions in a monetary production economy where uncertainty is present, and who know that the results of those decisions will only present themselves in a distant future, must develop some mechanisms that reduce uncertainty, at least at the individual level. Since the results of their decisions cannot be predicted through the use of the calculus of probability, they must develop other mechanisms in order to form their expectations and enter into commitments that have uncertain results. Keynes presents two main bases on which these expectations are formed: one is conventional behaviour and the other is the "animal spirits" characteristic of human actions.

Expectations that are formed on these conventional principles tend to reduce uncertainty at the individual level and at the social level, but as soon as there are changes in the degree of confidence in these expectations and there is a social distrust in them, they are subject to violent changes. This fact tends to create an extremely volatile environment to the decision-making process, which enforces still more the conventional character of these processes (Keynes, 1937, pp. 214-5, and Keynes, 1936, p. 154). On the other hand, "animal spirits" are also extremely volatile and cannot be predicted (see Keynes, 1936, Chapter 12).

These mechanisms on which agents base their expectations are also non-neutral in terms of the regional dynamic. Conventions tend to accentuate situations that are settled and in this sense tend to enforce a given regional structure. This element will be important when we analyse the formation of expectations of agents in regions that are subject to different economic structures and different degrees of uncertainty.

In such a world, there is the necessity for the social creation of other mechanisms or institutional arrangements that allow the decision-making process within some protective boundaries (Davidson and Kregel, 1980, p. 142). Among these mechanisms are contracts, and money, which is the fundamental basis of those contracts.

In an environment surrounded by uncertainty, the flexibility of action becomes a fundamental value. The commitment of resources in long term projects leads agents to lose some opportunities of unforeseen gains or to suffer unexpected losses. Liquidity becomes relevant in this context. The measure of the liquidity of a good or an asset is considered in three dimensions: the time for the transformation into another goods, the power of maintaining its value in the process of transformation and the probability to realising its full value. The majority of assets and goods presents a trade-off between the fist two dimensions, which makes them present a reduced liquidity. But one asset presents "full liquidity": the "probability of one of realising its full value immediately" (Chick, 1983, p. 304). This is money. The liquidity preference of agents refers to this position within the scale of liquidity.

Therefore, as money is the perfectly liquid asset and as liquidity means flexibility, it represents absolute flexibility to agents who own it. The retention of money represents, thus, the potential retention of all other goods.

The liquidity of assets is related to institutional arrangements especially the degree of organisation and breadth of the spot markets, which allows the reduction of transaction costs (see Davidson, 1980, p. 280). The more organised and broader the spot market for an asset, the more liquid is this asset, for same the same level of transaction costs.

The institutional arrangements that give liquidity to assets vary across regions. Hence, the liquidity of assets that each region supplies is also supposed to vary. Cash[8] is the unique absolute liquid asset across regions. Therefore, regions in which institutional arrangements are less developed have less liquid assets and the distance in the scale of liquidity between cash and other assets becomes greater. Cash, therefore, is more strongly demanded for liquidity purposes. If we add this to the previous tendency of having different levels of uncertainty across regions, we will notice that regions which have higher liquidity preference as a consequence of their higher levels of uncertainty, also present less liquid assets. Therefore, there are two elements, which, put together, indicate a higher demand for money and especially a higher demand for cash in certain regions. This will be extensively discussed later on in section 2.

Uncertainty plays a fundamental role in the demand for money as a store of wealth, in relation to the speculative and precautionary motives. In a world where risk is the key element, these two motives could be eliminated. However, in a world where uncertainty is the relevant element these two motives for demanding money play the key role. Uncertainty may vary across regions and liquidity of assets may also differ because the institutional arrangements are not homogeneous across regions. Now we can point out that these elements end up by generating different levels of demand for money in different regional economies; since the level of uncertainty in peripheral economies is higher, the demand for money for speculative and precautionary motives will be also higher. Moreover, as the institutional arrangements that give liquidity to assets are not homogeneous across regions, the demand for money in regions that have less developed financial markets will be higher due to the transaction and speculative motives. These two tendencies together will result in a higher liquidity preference in the periphery.

> Partly on reasonable and partly on instinctive grounds, our desire to hold money as a store of wealth is a barometer of the degree of our distrust of our own calculations and conventions concerning the future. Even tho this feeling about money is itself conventional or instinctive, it operates, so to speak, at a deeper level of our motivation. It takes charge at the moments when the higher, more precarious conventions have weakened. The possession of actual money lulls our disquietude; and the premium which require to make us part with money is the measure of the degree of our disquietude. (Keynes, 1937, p. 216)

The interest rate is not related in any way to savings; rather it is defined as the necessary incentive to make agents give up liquid assets: "The interest rate is not the 'price' which brings into equilibrium the demand for resources to invest with the readiness to abstain from present consumption. It is the 'price' which equilibrates the desire to hold wealth in the form of cash with the available quantity of cash" (Keynes, 1973b, p. 167). Hence, the interest rate is a monetary phenomenon and depends, basically, on the liquidity preference of agents and on the conditions of the money supply.

Now we shall analyse the ways by which money acts on the real side of the economy. In Keynes's theory, interest has nothing to do with the equilibrium between investment and saving. Here saving has not a defined relationship with the interest rate, but with income. Investment is not constrained by saving, but actually the causality is the other way round: investment creates the necessary savings through the multiplier (Keynes, 1973c, p. 281).

Investment decisions are based on the marginal efficiency of capital, which corresponds to the rate that equalizes the present value of the flow of expected yields of a capital asset to its flow supply price, that is, the minimum price necessary, given the market conditions, to induce the production of one extra unit of this capital asset (Keynes, 1936, p. 135). This definition emphasises the uncertain character of the investment decision. In an uncertain world, the prospective yields of a capital asset cannot be calculated on the basis of a probability distribution, nor on any other absolutely reliable method. Thus, long run expectations are formed on the grounds of purely subjective perceptions. Keynes postulates a downward schedule of the marginal efficiency of capital. Hence, as the level of investment is determined by the equalisation of the marginal efficiency of capital and the money rate of interest, this last factor puts a ceiling on the rate of accumulation. Therefore, money, credit and the money rate of interest have a fundamental role to play in the process of accumulation of monetary production economies.

The elements that make money non-neutral at the general level make it also non-neutral at the regional level, since we have economies that present distinct economic structures and those structures induce agents to present behaviours in relation to financial and monetary elements that are differentiated across regions.

The investment finance constraint

Keynes defines finance as the liquidity that entrepreneurs need to retain between the moment in which they decide to invest, that is the moment when investment is only a planned expenditure, and the moment when the expenditure really occurs. As was mentioned when we analysed the finance motive, this extra demand for liquidity represents an extra pressure on the liquidity position of the economy as a whole. This means that an increase in investment intentions may increase the interest rate if there are no offsetting movements in the liquidity preference of the society as a whole or in the liquidity supply. The supply of liquidity can be altered by a change in the liquidity preference of the banks (increase in credit) or by the action of the monetary authority.

This means that the simple fact of the investment decision taking place, before any expenditure has been made, represents an increase in demand for liquidity and if all other conditions are maintained, this represents a limit to investment, since the interest rate, that is the ceiling to the marginal efficiency of capital, has increased.

The investment decision and investment itself are independent of any decision of saving, since saving has nothing to do with the release of extra finance and saving cannot finance anything ex ante (see Keynes, 1973c). The fundamental variables in this process are investment and the financial conditions of the economy that release the necessary liquidity for investment to take place. These elements allow Keynes to affirm: "The entrepreneur when he decides to invest has to be satisfied on two points: firstly, that he can obtain sufficient short-term finance during the period of producing the investment; secondly, that he can eventually fund his short-term obligations by a long-term issue on satisfactory conditions." (Keynes, 1973c, p. 217).

Only when the first of these conditions is satisfied can investment take place. Therefore, the true constraint on investment comes from the monetary side of the economy. Saving is a consequence of the process of investment and not a pre-condition of it. The generation of saving that allows the equalisation of investment to saving, ex post, is a consequence of the implementation of the investment decision and of the play of the multiplier. Therefore, saving only plays its role ex post (Keynes, 1973c).

Since it is finance that "rules the roost" in the investment decision, it is fundamental to comprehend what determines its supply[9]. Keynes observes that if investment proceeds at a steady rate finance will come as the outcome of a revolving fund[10]. The release of finance by an investment that has just been implemented will finance another investment that is in the phase of planned expenditure. This is a consequence of the fact that finance is not a real resource but is represented by book entries on the balance sheets of the banks (see Keynes, 1973b, p. 209 and 1973c, pp. 219-20)

The problem arises when there is a change in the pattern of investment; as was mentioned before, this is what characterises the finance motive (see Chick, 1983). When there is an elevation in the planned level of investment, the demand for liquidity expands and if there is not a simultaneous enlargement in the supply of finance, there will be an increase in the level of the rate of interest that will discourage investment. It is exactly in this sense that the actions of banks become fundamental to the pattern of accumulation of the economy, since they are the main finance suppliers acting through the extension of loans and the concomitant creation of liquidity.

> The banks hold the key position in the transition from a lower to a higher scale of activity. If they refuse to relax, the growing congestion of the short-term loan market or of the new issue market, as the case may be, will inhibit the improvement, no matter how thrifty the public purpose to be out of their incomes. On the other hand, there will always be exactly enough ex post saving to take up the ex post investment and so release the finance which the latter had been previously employing. The investment market can become congested through shortage of cash. It can never become congested through shortage of saving.

> This is the most fundamental of my conclusions in this field. (Keynes, 1973c, p. 222)

In this sense, banks have a fundamental role to play in the determination of the pattern of accumulation of the economy. But, contradicting some authors, not every banking system accommodates all the needs of the real sector of the economy. Banks have their own liquidity preference that follows the same principles that determine the liquidity preference of the society as a whole, but as they play a fundamental role in the determination of the supply of liquidity, their preferences have a much more powerful role. Banks tend to present a higher liquidity preference exactly at moments when there is an intensification of uncertainty in the economy and when the expectations as a whole are pessimistic. This fact tends to accentuate the depressed character of the economy, since banks deny expanding the supply of money and thus intensify the conditions to increase the level of the interest rate as the liquidity preference of the society as a whole is also increased.

Minsky observes:

> During periods of tranquil expansion, profit-seeking financial institutions invent and reinvent "new" forms of money, substitutes for money in portfolios, and financing techniques for various types of activity: financial innovation is a characteristic of our economy in good times .(Minsky, 1986, p. 178)

And:

> Although financial innovations are common, their acceptance depends upon an attenuation, however trivial, in the subjective evaluation of the liquidity premium embodied in holding money. A period of successful functioning of the economy leads to a decrease in the value of liquidity and to an acceptance of more aggressive financing practices. Banks, non-bank financial institutions, and money-market organizations can experiment with new liabilities and increase their asset-equity ratio without their liabilities loosing any significant credence. In these circumstances the readily available supply of finance from aggressive financial institutions raises capital-asset prices and induces short-term (i.e., speculative) finance of capital-asset positions and investment. (Minsky, 1986, p. 249)

Therefore, in a monetary economy where there are idle resources, the constraints on output come from the monetary side. It is the combination of the characteristics of a monetary or entrepreneur economy of production with the peculiarities of money that creates the limits to the extension of output and accumulation.

We can observe now if such an important element (money and liquidity) in the aggregate level can be neutral in the determination of income in economies that are intrinsically linked to each other and that do not present boundaries to monetary and production factor movements. This is precisely our objective in the next section of the present chapter.

The role of finance in the determination of uneven patterns of regional development

With the objective of analysing different regional patterns of development, Dow adapts Keynesian monetary theory to the regional level. She takes some elements of Dependency Theory and creates a cumulative causation theory that emphasises the vicious circles that the financial system can originate in countries with strong differences in development levels between regions. In her model, real and financial elements are interlinked and generate a dynamic process that tends, if allowed free play, to intensify the unequal pattern of regional development.

In Dow (1982), she analyses the money multipliers when disaggregated to the regional level and defines the influence of the monetary and financial spheres on employment and income. In Dow (1987), she explains the role of the financial system when it is operating under different degrees of information and uncertainty, and when the degree of confidence with which agents hold their expectations varies according to regions. In this model, finance represents a more severe constraint on investment in regions with a high level of uncertainty and, therefore, finance is an effective source of inequalities. In both articles she uses a model that presents two distinct regional poles. In so doing she follows the characterisation adopted by dependency theorists to typify central and peripheral regions.

The characterisation of centre and periphery

Dow points out that central regions are characterised by a more stable pattern of development, more developed financial markets, a lower propensity to import and a self-generated pattern of growth. On the other hand, peripheral economies are characterised by low levels of income, an unstable pattern of development which is mainly export led, concentration of production in the primary sector[11], less developed financial markets and, consequently, a more volatile base for diffusion of information. Dow points out: "Centre, an archetypal central region, is characterized by prosperity which is expected to continue, active markets, and financial sophistication. Periphery, an archetypal peripheral region, has a stagnating economy, thin markets and a lesser degree of financial sophistication. The additional transactions and information costs associated with remoteness help to preserve a continuing differential in financial sophistication between the two regions. The liquidity of any given asset is thus less in periphery than in centre" (Dow, 1982, pp. 25-6). As was mentioned before, this characterisation originates mainly in the analysis of Dependency Theory, but instead of observing these characteristics as intensifying the real process of underdevelopment, Dow associates these general real and institutional features with the resulting behaviour of agents in relation to money and financial assets and establishes some mechanisms that explain the roles of finance in the determination of the pattern of development of different regions.

J. Friedman (1972) also develops a theory of regional growth using a polarized system, where the dynamic element is innovation. The core regions are considered the locus of the "innovative change" and the periphery is defined according to the dependent relation that it develops in terms of the capacity to absorb changes from the central region (Friedman, 1972, p. 85). He characterises development as "a discontinuous, cumulative process that occurs as a series of elementary innovations which become organized into innovative clusters and finally into large-scale systems of innovation. The innovations may be technical or institutional and, if the latter, may be usefully subsumed under the customary categories of social, economic, political and cultural" (Friedman, 1972, p. 86). The introduction of the idea of institutional innovation in the characterisation of the centre/periphery model is fundamental when we analyse the appropriation of the gains that the evolution of the banking system can bring to the regions where these innovations take place. It is exactly these innovations that are responsible for the change to the stages of the development of the banking system and are, normally, led by the central region.

The stages of banking development and the regions

Following the research line of Chick (1986), Chick and Dow (1988) and Dow (1990), Dow develops a model that explains the role of the financial sector in regional development from a Post-Keynesian point of view, but now considering the different stages of the history of banking development, and analysing the specificities of each stage.

This section will be organised according to the stages of banking development, although the empirical part of the book will not follow the same organisation.

The analysis of the evolution of the banking system demonstrates that the system gradually gets rid of the boundaries to its action: first it got rid of the deposits as a full constraint to the extension of loans; then it got rid of the fractional reserve basis to the extension of loans; then it pushed to the creation of a lender of last resort which made it even more free to extend loans without any constraint, and so it evolves through successive stages. This is the perfect representation of a system that overcomes the frictions and the "legal" and real impediments to the full play of market forces, since this was a process led by market mechanisms. At the same time this evolution makes money become gradually less neutral and gives relevance to banks in the economy as a whole, which is the opposite result that orthodox theory expects. Orthodoxy observes the short-run non-neutrality of money as a result of the frictions that are imposed over market mechanisms. Thus, they suggest that those boundaries should be removed. However, their model for dealing with banks in later stages of banking development is a model that treats finance as saving and so conforms to the first stage of banking development, thus being useless to the understanding of a modern monetary production economy.

The evolution of the banking system also has important effects on the regional economies. As the banking system evolves it gradually emphasises more the uneven pattern of regional development and, therefore, it moves away from the results predicted by orthodox theory. Therefore, there is an important theoretical point in analysing the banking system regionally and nationally throughout its history.

However, as all general characterisations, the stages of banking development suggested by Chick (1986) and Chick and Dow (1988) present problems when we are dealing with specific regional economies. For instance, the mere legal possibility of inter-bank lending does not mean that banks actually use this facility to extend loans. Therefore, we can have a banking system that apparently is in stage 3 of banking development, but just a small part of it is really in this stage. Another typical example is the existence of a lender of last resort that should imply in the banking system being in stage 4 of banking development, but this mechanism could have restrictions in terms of banks that actually have access to it. That is, banks that have momentaneous shortage of reserves can eventually make use of this mechanism, however, banks that structurally face shortage of reserves may not have access to this scheme. As will be observed later, the centre's banks normally are in the first situation, while peripheral banks are in the second. So, we can have an economy whose centre apparently is in stage 4 of banking development, but which has great part of its banking system operating in stage 2. This is the reason for not establishing those rigid boundaries when working with the specific case of Brazil.

First stage of banking development and the regions The first stage of banking development is characterised by the constraints that deposits represent to reserves and loans: the liabilities of the banks are not yet used widely as means of payment and deposits correspond to saving. Thus banks are merely intermediaries between savers and investors. Therefore, at this stage, saving precedes and constrains investment. In terms of the regions, it can be said that financial flows correspond to saving flows. Savings go from regions in which they are in excess, or in which there is a positive difference between saving and investment to regions in which there is an excess of investment in relation to the level of local saving. Consequently, financial flows tend to equalize saving and investment within the region and between regions.

Second stage of banking development and the regions In the second stage of banking development, the liabilities of the banks begin to be treated as money, since it is used as a means of exchange in addition to its use as store of value. Thus, deposits generated by banks tend to stay in the banking system and banks can now extend credit as a multiple of their reserves. Saving is not a constraint to investment any more and now the constraints to the extension of credit by the banks are represented by the availability of reserves. The basis for a financial explanation for uneven regional development is established at this stage of banking development; the later stages tend to amplify the general tendencies that are implicit or latent at this stage.

Regional money multipliers and the endogenous regional money supply Adapting Tsiang's model (1978) to the regional level, Dow (1982) analyses the diffusion of reserves and the behaviour of regional money multipliers in order to observe the roles that the financial sphere can play in determining employment and income at the regional level[12]. The regional money multipliers, just as the national money multipliers, are larger the lower the liquidity preference of the agents. This can be observed by the analysis of the reserve/deposit ratios of the banks and cash/deposit preferences presented by the public and the relations of these two elements in the money multiplier. At the regional level, the money multiplier suffers from the influence of leakages caused by the propensities to import and invest outside the region. The larger the leakages, the smaller the multiplier. The level of reserves is mainly determined by the inflow of new reserves of the Central Bank or by the flows of trade between regions and capital flows.

The fact that the possibility of leakages of finance from one region to the other exists invalidates, at the regional level, the idea of a "revolving fund" of finance, developed by Keynes. This is the case both when investment does not evolve through time and when there is growth in the economy. In both cases, leakages of finance from one region to the other cause a drain on the "revolving fund". This is exactly one of the peculiarities of monetary analysis in regional terms.

This analysis, therefore, points out the endogeneity of the monetary base at the regional level, since it can be altered by financial flows between distinct regions. This element, when put together with regional differences in the money multiplier originating in different portfolio choices, creates the conditions for finance to play its role in different patterns of regional development.

Peripheral economies are typically characterised by strong instability. Thus, liquidity preference tends to be more intense at the periphery than at the centre[13]. The greater liquidity of the portfolios at the periphery reduces the money multiplier and makes finance comparatively scarce. The lower level of income observed in these economies also tends to make the cash/deposit ratio larger, and the money multiplier lower in peripheral regions. There is a negative relation between the level of income and the demand for cash, since, lower income agents normally use a larger proportion of cash, in relation to their total income, for their day to day expenditures. In extreme situations, agents that do not achieve a determined level of income have no access to current accounts and other financial instruments. These factors tend to make the money multiplier lower in peripheral regions than in central ones.

Not only does the multiplier tend to be lower in the periphery but also the multiplicand (reserves) tends to be lower despite the higher reserve/deposits ratio. The tendency for peripheral agents to satisfy their liquidity preference with centre assets creates a flow of funds (cash drain) from the periphery to the centre that causes a decrease in the reserves of the former. Morgan (1973), analysing the British economy, observes that the higher attraction that central assets exert on portfolio choices on the periphery agents is one more element that allows disequilibria in the capital account of those regions:

> Although there is a capital market in South Wales (and in most of the other problem regions), a high proportion of the stock exchange securities held locally are those either of the central government or of companies based outside the region. Again, therefore, there will be a net capital export, unless there is a sufficient indirect reflux through the activities of the borrowing institutions. (Morgan, 1973, p. 21)

On the same lines, McKillop and Hutchinson (1991) observe that the employment and output of banks in a specific region are functions of the demand for their services. In this way, as part of the demand, relative to speculative activities, is directed towards banks outside the region, this tends to cause a process of banking concentration in favour of the central regions. Since credit creation is limited by the availability of reserves, this fact generates a decrease in the potentiality of credit expansion in the periphery. The comparative "underdevelopment" of the financial system of the periphery and the instability of the real side of this economy leads agents to present a higher liquidity preference as a consequence of the precautionary motive. That is, their demand for money to face unexpected expenditure is higher in relation to their income. One might expect that the underdevelopment of the peripheral financial markets implies a smaller liquidity preference in relation to the speculative motive. To the contrary, their speculative demand for money manifests itself in the financial markets of the centre and is higher in the periphery than in the centre. Therefore, both precautionary and speculative motives accentuate the higher liquidity preference at the periphery.

The institutional differences between the two types of region also act to accentuate the leakages of finance from the periphery to the centre. On the one hand, the higher activity of the markets of the centre makes assets traded there more liquid than the peripheral ones. On the other hand, securities of firms of the centre have conventionally a much more solid institutional background, which makes agents prefer them in relation to the ones of the periphery. This ends up reducing the money multipliers in the periphery because these leakages represent drain of finance from the periphery to the centre.

Thus, given these characteristics of peripheral and central economies, we expect to find that the former present a smaller monetary multiplier and multiplicand than the latter. In the long run, this tendency is maintained but the expansions of high powered money and its effects on the regional availability of finance independ on the place where the injection of high powered money occurs (Dow, 1982).

Another element that contributes to the smaller peripheral money multiplier is the higher liquidity preference of the banks, which tend to keep a higher reserve/deposit ratio. This is a consequence of the strong instability and consequent uncertainty that characterises these economies.

The extension of loans by banks of the centre to peripheral regions is also limited by the remoteness of the place where the investment will take place from the point of view of the decision centre and the resulting imprecision of knowledge. Therefore, there will be an inherent tendency by banks of the centre to restrict loans to peripheral regions by centre's banks. The process of decision-making by the banks will have, therefore, a strong conventional basis which in the majority of the cases tends to put limits to peripheral investment and thus to reinforce the tendency towards depression in those regions (Dow, 1987).

Another element that tends to reinforce the constraint on credit extension to peripheral areas is the persistent tendency of their assets to depreciate in value, given the region's stagnant character. This fact tends to put extra limits on the availability of credit since the value of the regions' collateral base for an extension of new credit is devalued. Thus, Dow observes, "financial integration does not necessarily entail an absence of credit constraint; credit constraints may persist, but for reasons other than simply the reserve base of the local banking system. Attention will thus be focused on the factors constraining both the supply, and the demand for credit" (Dow, 1992, p. 620).

Nevertheless, if changes in the multiplier parameters are considered, the location of the injection of new money begins to be analytically relevant.

However, not only must the regional place of the injection be analysed, but also the sectors where this injection takes place within the region must be examined in order to observe the changes in expectations and thus changes in portfolio choices in the multiplier parameters and in the outflow of capital. If these changes are considered, the location of the expansion of the monetary base is not neutral at all (Dow, 1982).

The main concern of Dow is to analyse the money multiplier in the short run, since it is in this period that the location of the injection of the new high powered money really matters[14]. Straszheim (1971) also observes that the different impacts of monetary policy in regional terms are restricted to the short run and may vary with the sector on which the differentiated policy is acting. These short run effects are important since they interact with the real side of the economy, putting a ceiling on the decision to invest, and consequently determining the level of income and employment. In order to observe the interrelations between the money multiplier and the income multiplier, Dow (1982) elaborates a model that interlinks the money multiplier with the accelerator-multiplier model and puts finance as a constraint on investment.

Considering this new model and its feedback effects, the results of a monetary expansion are different depending on whether it occurs in the central or in the peripheral regions. The location of the injection determines a faster pattern of growth in income which in turn generates changes in expectations that reinforce the original tendency (Dow, 1982).

Dow's analysis is developed assuming a segmented banking system[15], but, as she pointed out, the same kind of reasoning can be developed for a nationwide branch banking system (Dow, 1982, 1987). Nationwide bank systems can exacerbate the shortage of finance in peripheral regions, by making capital outflows easier; here, the supply of finance is no longer limited mainly by the regional availability of reserves but depends on the decision of the banks that operate in both regions whether to extend credit to peripheral regions or not.

The characterisation of the peripheral and central financial markets accentuate an inherent tendency toward banking concentration. As Chick and Dow point out:

> If there is a high import content to investment expenditure, the income multiplier in the periphery will be low, as will savings growth, and the redeposit ratio in periphery financial institutions will also be low, as money returns to the centre to pay for the imports. In addition, the stage of development and the level of income being lower, the use of cash rather than deposits is likely to be more widespread. Difficulty in rationing reserves is exacerbated by the great fluctuations in deposits in periphery

> banks, caused by volatility of both investment in and export proceeds from the periphery. Periphery banks will therefore at best need higher than average reserves (usually, centre assets) and at worst are vulnerable to bankruptcy. Thus the competitive advantage lies with centre banks: there will be pressure towards banking concentration and branch banking by the centre in the periphery. (Chick and Dow, 1988, p. 238)

Therefore, the inherent tendency towards banking concentration that this model stresses through the comparative advantage that the banks of the central region present is widespread and intensified with a nationwide bank system. Considering banks that act at the local level and banks that act at national level, we can observe that there is a kind of coincidence of stages of banking development in time, since local banks are strictly limited by their reserves that are generated locally while nationwide banks develop mechanisms of inter-branch and inter-banking lending that allow them to be free of the constraint of locally generated reserves. In a certain sense, this corresponds to regional banks being in the second stage of banking development and nationwide banks being in the third stage. This is one more point that tends to increase the comparative advantage of the banks of the centre that operate at the nationwide level.

> Thus a national banking system may exacerbate net capital outflows from a region. Such behaviour is efficient to the extent that the assessment of relative returns is correct and also because it increases the national money multiplier (and thereby the bank's profit base). But the judgement as to relative returns may be self-fulfilling if the supply of credit is sufficiently low to discourage investment. (Dow, 1982, p. 42)

Centre's and periphery's nationwide banks There is a significant difference between the behaviour of peripheral nationwide[16] and central nationwide banks. To analyse this difference we can make use of the model of bank behaviour developed by Tobin (1982), which establishes a positive relation between loans and the retention ratio, defined as the redeposit ratio, and a negative relation between a bank's defensive position, defined as the level of reserves that the bank keeps, and the deposit retention ratios (Tobin, 1982, p. 521). At first, we could be led to think that this made banks of the centre (which have a higher retention ratio, given their higher participation in central and peripheral markets) more able to extend credit to the periphery than the peripheral nationwide banks, which share their local markets with banks from the centre and have a lower participation in the central markets. However, this is not a necessary outcome. If we disaggregate the retention ratio of banks, we will see that different classes of banks can be expected to have different retention ratios according to the region in which they are acting and the activity inside the region that they are financing. Peripheral nationwide banks tend to present higher retention ratios when operating in their local markets and a marginal participation in central markets. Central nationwide banks, on the other hand, tend to present higher participation both in peripheral markets and in central ones. In this way, their retention ratios tend to be higher in both markets than periphery's nationwide banks. Consequently, when a bank of the centre that operates nationwide lends to the periphery[17], if the activity represents a great leakage through its higher integration with the central region, this bank will get back its deposit in the centre's markets and, if the activity is regionally integrated, this bank will also have higher redeposits in the peripheral region.

On the other hand, peripheral nationwide banks tend to give loan preference to activities that have strong regional linkages and smaller leakages within the periphery, since their retention ratio is high at the local level but inexpressive in the central markets. In this way, any leakage of finance from the region will have an important impact on the retention ratio of the bank. In this sense, peripheral banks will discriminate against activities that present higher leakages from the periphery and, therefore, they will have a more positive impact on the periphery's regional money multiplier than centre's nationwide banks extending credit to the periphery.

At first, we may think that, given these conditions, central nationwide banks have a much more positive role to play in peripheral regions since, as they present higher retention ratio levels than peripheral nationwide banks, they extend more loans and keep lower defensive positions. However, if we consider the problems of the remoteness of the basis of information of activities developed in the periphery in relation to those banks, this whole picture changes. Moreover, if we observe that for the central nationwide banks the leakages of finance do not constitute a problem, but for the region they do, the whole picture also changes. When these two elements are considered together, the action of central nationwide banks will be much more to reduce the money multiplier in the region, since they stimulate activities with higher leakages than the peripheral nationwide banks, and, in this sense, they reduce the possibility of retention of finance in the region.

Third stage of banking development and the regions In stage 3 banks develop mechanisms of inter-bank lending; therefore reserves no longer represent a constraint to each bank individually, but only at the aggregate level. What is true for banks in general is true for banks operating in a defined area, that is, the regional reserve constraint is fundamentally reduced at this stage of banking development. The main ideas developed for the second stage of banking development are emphasised in this stage.

In regional terms the deficits of the regions do not limit at the same extent the credit creation since reserves are not an absolute constraint to the extension of credit. However, the results of the regional balance of payments continue to be an important variable in determining the availability of loans, although, now, the elements that determine a deficit in the regional balance of payments are fundamental in the formation of expectations and, consequently, in the decisions by the banks of the centre to extend loans to the regional branch or to the periphery banks. If a deficit is observed as being temporary, probably there will not be any severe constraint on the extension of new loans. However, if the deficit is considered structural, there will be a tendency to constrain the extension of new loans to this region, since the extension of loans will end up in a leakage of reserves from the banking system towards another region. A regional shortage of reserves can now be compensated by interbranch and interbank lending, but this is fundamentally determined by the centre banks' expectations on the state of peripheral economies.

Observing the stronger confidence in assets from the centre and the stronger confidence with which expectations are held at the centre, Dow (1987) elaborates a model that is based on Hill and Moore (1982), but which inverts the direction of causality of their model[18], establishing a Keynesian chain of causality. In this model, Dow, assuming a banking system segmented and composed of local banks and nationwide banks, shows that there is a national rate of interest and that local banks extend credit to particular regions, charging different rates of interest[19] according to the degree of trust that they have in the regional assets. She observes that not only is the segmentation of the financial market manifested through differences in the rate of interest but it is even manifested through the quantitative availability of credit. That is, the interest differential does not fully compensate for the higher perceived risk of lending to the periphery. The differences in the rates of interest and the quantitative constraint to the expansion of credit both put a ceiling on investment and income. Hence, "it was suggested that the increase in liquidity preference of financial institutions in declining regions might be manifested in rationing credit as well as increasing its price" (Dow, 1988, p. 215)[20].

Therefore, instead of following the monetarist chain of causality where income generates deposits and deposits generate credit, Dow observes that the conditions of demand for and supply of credit determine the level of income[21], as Moore observes: in the real world loans make deposits" (Moore, 1982, p. 11)[22]. Hence, the specificities of regional financial markets really have a role to play in determining regional inequalities. In these models, the great difference between a regional banking system and a nationwide branch banking system is pointed out by Dow:

> Branch banking rather than unit banking was shown to render the credit supply curve horizontal, as in a standard Keynesian model. But its position and length are still variable regionally,

> generating results similar to those for a unit banking system. The main difference would be in reducing the credit availability constraint on prosperous regions, but strengthening it in depressed regions. (Dow, 1987, p. 23)

At this stage of banking development, as nationwide branch banks have more facility to allocate reserves between branches than local banks, the tendency to banking concentration becomes stronger, since the former gains an extra competitive advantage over the local banks. When the tendency towards banking concentration is combined with information problems that concentrating decision-making at the centre's head offices brings with it, a new tendency appears, that is the tendency towards industrial concentration. This process is a result of the remoteness of the peripheral regions and of the subsequent strong conventional character that the loan decisions assume. These elements favour the extension of credit to nationwide corporations operating in peripheral regions with head offices at the centre than to local enterprises, because the information base of the projects of those corporations is less uncertain to head offices of banks of the centre (Dow, 1987 and 1990).

Therefore, the regional financial constraint has origins in the two sides of the balance sheets of the banks. On the one hand, there are problems related to the redeposit ratio in the periphery. This makes banks constrain their levels of extended credit, since there is a continuous leakage of reserves from the peripheral banking system to the central banking system. On the other hand, there is the problem with the more uncertain environment of the periphery that makes banks more cautious about extending credit to those regions. If the bank is a bank from the centre, there is an extra element that tends to reduce the willingness to extend credit towards the periphery that refers to the more remote information base for the formation of expectations. Therefore, the two sides of the banks' balance sheets feed each other to further constrain the available finance at the periphery.

Fourth stage of banking development and the regions In stage 4 the monetary authority or the Central Bank assumes the function of lender of last resort: banks can borrow reserves from it at moments of reserve shortage at a given interest rate. This stage makes banks comparatively free from the constraint of reserves that was characteristic of the previous stages, and, consequently, an expansionist bias is created. Credit creation now depends mainly on the decision of banks to extend loans. At this stage, the extension of credit to the periphery no longer needs to be at the expense of the expansion in the centre.

The regional pattern of the financial system is accentuated at this stage. Now the exogenous limits to credit creation have disappeared, but credit is still endogenously limited by the willingness of banks that are mainly determined by their expectations about the economic conditions of the region. As Dow points out:

> The availability of borrowed reserves from a central monetary authority does not mean that the supply of credit for any borrower or group of borrowers is unlimited. Indeed the supply of credit is likely to conform to the same type of regional pattern as outlined for earlier stages of the banking system. But that pattern is now likely to be even more marked, with credit creation in both Peripheral and Central regions more constrained during boom conditions. (Dow, 1990, p. 22)

Instead of being unconstrained by reserves, banks use the behaviour of deposits as an indicator for further credit extension; therefore, reductions in the level of new deposits or rate of redeposit must indicate a deficit in the balance of payments of the region that may express a stagnating tendency, this is a signal to reduce credit creation. As Dow observes:

> Branch banking and the availability of a lender of last resort facility remove the absolute reserve constraints on regional credit creation. Lending in any region can then be expanded on the strength of reserves borrowed from the Central Bank (rather than other regions). But the factors which determine the net deposit creation resulting from credit creation for any region (which would earlier have determined the regional reserves constraint) will still be important as determinants of further credit creation. Credit creation will still be unconstrained if a tendency to deficit is temporary, but not if it is an indicator of economic stagnation. The regional pattern of liquidity preference will become a progressively more important factor in regional credit creation, influencing perceptions of return from the uses of credit, as the financial sector becomes more sophisticated. (Dow, 1990, p. 21)

Goodhart (1989, Chapter XVI) also observes that banks tend to analyse their regional level of reserves as a way of determining the continuity of extension of loans toward a particular region. Although reserves no longer constitute a narrow limit to the extension of credit, they maintain their indicative role.

At this stage, the tendency of banks to concentrate in the central region and the consequent increase in industrial concentration still persists and is reinforced.

Fifth stage of banking development and the regions The most recent stage of banking development is characterized by active deposit-seeking behaviour by the banks' liability management. Banks compete for funds by offering higher rates of interest on deposits when deposits and reserves are needed to support new loans. This reinforces the tendency towards increase in the rates of interest charged on loans and, therefore, brings a tendency towards depression in economic activity. The effect of higher interest rates may, however, be counterbalanced by increased credit availability.

At this stage, the financial costs of running firms may increase. This means that only firms with stronger market power, that is firms that can transfer their higher financial costs to prices, continue to have access to credit[23]. This is one more element leading to concentration of production as a consequence of the structure of the financial system. This reinforces, in terms of the financial system, the argument of ECLA that the differences in the market structures of the central and peripheral regions can perpetuate uneven growth, for the centre is characterised by an oligopolistic market structure that not only allows it to capture the fruits of technical progress, as described by ECLA, but also to have access to credit that is extended at higher rates of interest, since their market power allows it to transfer this higher financial cost to the final buyers. Conversely, the peripheral economies, which present more competitive markets, suffer two types of negative impacts: a) they have to pay higher prices for the input from the central economies, as a consequence of the transference of the higher financial costs and b) they have to pay higher interest that cannot be transferred to prices.

Therefore, the evolution of the banking system tends to intensify the tendencies that were latent at stage 2 of banking development, that is, an inherent tendency towards a disparate development of credit creation that generates an unequal pattern of real development of central and peripheral economies. This tendency is intensified by another element that contributes to the smaller peripheral money multiplier, which is the higher liquidity preference of peripheral banks that tends to result in a higher reserve/deposit ratio. This is a consequence of the strong instability and consequent uncertainty that characterises these economies. This tendency intensifies the process of banking concentration, since banks that operate at a nationwide level present competitive advantages over local banks in their capacity to extend loans and increase deposits. These facts are self-reinforcing and are mainly generated by the logic of the free play of market forces, which tends to intensify the uneven pattern of development generated by real and financial causes:

> There may be a trade-off between efficiency and equity in segmented financial markets, though we tend to believe that in financial matters, a move toward unification, which improves micro-efficiency, may be macro-inefficient: it may impede the

> relative development of peripheral economies and encourage concentration which may benefit the centre at the expense of the periphery, but may not even serve the long-term interests of the centre. Our analysis suggests that a policy of financial segmentation - if it is not already too late to consider - would need to be taken in conjunction with policies to encourage periphery entrepreneurship and to discourage the wide fluctuations of the periphery's product prices which result in generally pessimistic valuations of periphery assets and projects. (Chick and Dow, 1988, p. 24)

Consequently, if market forces are let free, there would be a strong tendency towards financial concentration at the centre[24]. This would bring an inherent tendency to industrial concentration, in which nationwide enterprises would have comparative advantages in relation to peripheral enterprises, since the decision to extend loans is strongly based on conventional procedures and will tend further to constrain the possibilities of growth at the periphery.

The concentration of new loans in nationwide/multinational companies tends to emphasise again the volatility of financial flows in the periphery, as those enterprises present more mechanisms to transfer finance from one region to the other when there are changes in the state of expectations. On the other hand, these enterprises tend to present a larger import coefficient, which again reinforces the smaller income multiplier effects that they produce and accentuates even more the tendency of reduced availability of finance in the regional level, even considering that banks are not constrained by reserves. Therefore, financial and industrial concentration mutually reinforce each other to increase regional disparities.

Policy implications of the model

In order to break these cumulative processes, the intervention of some exogenous element is necessary. Dow (1990) points out that the state is the unique force that can act according to a logic that is not necessarily related to the logic of private markets. In this sense, government policies can act basically in two different ways: a) through instruments of monetary policy and b) by acting on the structure of the financial system (Dow, 1990).

As was mentioned before, monetary policy is not neutral at the regional level. The region in which high powered money is introduced matters both in the short and in the long run if the accelerator/multiplier mechanism is considered together with the effects of the expansion in the reserve levels. However, if changes in the parameters of the money multipliers are considered endogenous, depending on the sectors in which the new high powered money enters, there will be changes in those parameters and consequently in the possibility of extension of finance. Thus, in terms of public policies, it is more convenient to extend high powered money towards depressed regions than towards dynamic regions, for, on one side, there will be a tendency towards the reduction of disparities and the effects at the national level of liquidity will be smaller than if the supply of money were extended by the dynamic region (Dow, 1982).

The second source of interference of the government relates to the direct intervention in the organisation of the financial market. The regionalisation of the banking system makes the outflow of finance more difficult and creates a regional basis for the extension of credit. Thus, credit extension to enterprises, especially the small ones, that operate only at the regional level is made easier, as a consequence of a more solid information base that regional banks have in relation to remote areas. This policy reverses not only the tendency towards banking concentration, but also inverts the tendency towards industrial concentration. Following these principles, Dow proposes the direct intervention of government in restructuring the financial system. According to Dow, the intervention of the State in the structure of the financial market must be to establish:

> i) provincial government-owned banks,
> ii) more active provincial promotion of private sector non-bank financial intermediaries,
> iii) provincial government-sponsored regional financial centres. (Dow, 1990, p. 150)

However, mere intervention in the structure of the financial system and regional differentiation of the monetary policy are not enough to reduce regional disparities. Dow points out the necessity of developing a fiscal policy that reduces fluctuations of the level of activity in peripheral regions in order to change expectations and, consequently, portfolio behaviour of agents in those regions. These two sets of policies would avoid the outflow of finance and alleviate the constraint on investment that outflows represent to those regions.

The reversal of these cumulative causation processes that develop through the interaction of real and financial spheres and that are mutually reinforced is not a simple task. As was pointed out, it is necessary to create monetary and financial policies that are mutually coherent, but it is also necessary to develop an industrial policy that allows the integration of different sectors and that reduces the outflow of finance through the import content of the new activities that the fiscal policy attracts. This element is fundamental in order to fix the benefits of the differentiated monetary and fiscal policy in the target region. Otherwise, the extended credit or finance will have a reduced effect, only circulating in its first round in the peripheral region, and afterwards returning to the central regions and there playing its full role as liquidity. Therefore, finance, in regional terms, cannot be considered a revolving fund even if we analyse the steady state, because of leakages. The idea of a revolving fund is developed by Keynes considering a closed economy. If we consider an open economy this idea becomes problematic, but if we consider an absolute open economy, as regional economies are, this idea loses its meaning, since the financial leakages that financial and commercial flows allow make it impossible to think in terms of a revolving fund of finance.

Therefore, it is important to recover the concept of "linkage" as defined by Hirschman (1958) and integrate this notion into Dow's model, highlighting that the extension of new credit - especially that provided by government-owned banks - is supposed to occur in the direction of sectors that potentially present higher intra-regional linkages[25]. And adapting the ideas of Perroux (1967) it is necessary to establish "propulsive" industries[26] that can induce the creation of new industry and in this way spread the positive effects of government policy inside the periphery.

However, the mere analysis of the potential generation of linkages of one specific sector is not enough for the actual creation of those linkages. Other elements must be taken into account for the effective attachment of the results of special policies to the target region. For instance, the origin of the capital of the newly created firm matters in terms of the generation of linkages with the local economy. As will be observed in the Brazilian case, the origin (intra or extra-regional) of the capital of the newly installed firms at the periphery is important in terms of the generation of linkages at the regional level. This is because firms that act nationwide establish their targets at the national level. The whole strategy of the firm is determined at the national sphere and, therefore, the degree of linkages that these firms can present in regional terms is reduced, since it is expected that these industries have stronger relations with the region in which they have their head offices than with the region where they have just one plant. Conversely, we can observe that locally owned firms have more "linkages" with the local economy, since local entrepreneurs establish their plans in a much more locally constrained way and, in this sense, they tend to prioritise local links for informational and strategic reasons. Hence, one criterion to decide which sectors will or will not receive credit in peripheral regions should be the possibility of generating internal linkages and dynamizing the economy. Some empirical studies have been produced which analyse the relation between intra-regional/extra-regional ownership of firms and the capacity to generate linkages within the region. For example: Lever (1974), analysing the Scottish case, observes that the intra-regional origin of the firm is an important element in determining the capacity to generate local linkages. Hoare (1978), studying Northern Ireland, reaches the same sort of conclusion. However, Marshall (1979), analysing Northern England, reaches the conclusion that just the ownership variable is not enough to explain different degrees of material linkages (physical inputs and outputs). Nevertheless, he notices that the firm ownership variable is significant in generating demand for local services. Firms whose ownership is extra-regional do not demand local services; they tend to have and keep close relations to their original regions. Thus, local firms should be priorised in the decision to extend loans.

In this sense, we can imagine certain kinds of financial linkages since some firms or sectors, by their own characteristics, are capable of creating more real and financial linkages as a consequence of the more reliable information base on which they took decisions than others. This more reliable information base will permit these sectors or firms to take their decision in a way that does not allow leakages of finance that will be observed if the decision making were undertaken by another firm or sector. For example: a peripheral firm tends to have a more reliable information base on the peripheral economy in which it operates than a central one making decisions on the periphery; so it is more likely to invest in this economy than a firm that originated from the central region. At the same time, a firm that has its head office outside the region tends to present higher leakages of resources, as it is predisposed to be more integrated with the economy in which it has its head office. At the same time, the firm that has its head office at the periphery tends to speculate more with assets of the region than the firm that has its head office outside the region, since the information available on these markets is much less remote for this firm than for a central firm, although both tend to prefer to speculate with assets of the central region. In this sense, we can say that the origin of the capital of the firm matters both in terms of real and financial linkages of one specific sector. Therefore, the results reached by Marshall (1979) are relevant since they show that the linkages in the service sector of extra-regional firms are not kept by the local economy. On the contrary, he observes that these linkages are generated within the original region of the firm and so represent a leakage for the host economy.

Hence, the degree of linkages, real and financial, that one particular sector can present in one determined region[27] is fundamental in order to achieve the full power that a specific credit/monetary policy can generate. Therefore, the capacity of keeping the created liquidity in the region is one important element to be considered by the banks, especially the public banks, when extending credit to specific projects. Thus, if there is not a complete integration between governmental policies for the regions it may occur that monetary and fiscal policies that seem to be acting in the right direction can present outcomes that reinforce the cumulative effects that the free market forces generate.

The model developed by Dow introduces some fundamental points that are necessary to highlight. The first one is that money is non-neutral, in general terms and in regional terms. As Keynes and the Post Keynesians emphasised, the non-neutrality of money is a central characteristic of a monetary economy. In contrast to what neoclassical or new classical theorists postulate, the non-neutrality of money is not the result of frictions that disturb the perfect and smooth functioning of the markets, nor is it the result of unexpected surprises in terms of the model that describes the generation of rational expectations. Rather, it is the consequence of the mechanisms that agents develop to protect themselves in a world of radical uncertainty. The non-neutrality of money in regional terms is not the consequence of the barriers to capital flows. On the contrary, the less barriers that exist, the more non-neutral are money and the financial system. The regional non-neutrality of money is the result of the private logic of markets operating in economies that are structurally differentiated but which do not present any sort of barriers to the flow of goods and capital. The structural discrepancy of these economies generate different levels of uncertainty and so agents defend themselves by maintaining more liquid portfolios in regions where the level of uncertainty is more accentuated. There is, thus, a perverse logic that allows the generation and perpetuation of vicious circles or cumulative processes that reinforce an uneven situation of development at the centre and peripheral underdevelopment.

Notes

1 For the position of the orthodoxy on the neutrality of money see Ricardo (1970 and 1973), Friedman (1956, 1977), Hahn (1982 and 1984) and Lucas (1973).

2 For a good differentiation of monetary economies of production and a real exchange economy see Carvalho (1988) and Keynes (1979, pp. 77-89).

3 See the characterization of Chick (1986). This characterization will be explained in the second part of this chapter.

4 The great majority of models that deals with monetary and financial problems at the regional level is based on the orthodox framework and observes money as having only a role to play in the short run, its neutrality being restored in the long run, Dreese (1973-74) and Beare (1976). On the other hand, there are other models that follow the same theoretical framework and tend to observe the non-neutral role of money as a consequence of some rigidities and imperfections of the markets. Fishkind and Roberts (1979) construct a model where monetary policy has different impacts on different regions as a consequence of information costs that make the elasticity of the LM curve vary across regions. This is clearly a consequence of frictions in the capital market. On the other hand, Fishkind (1977) observes that different impacts of the monetary policy on the regions can be a consequence of differences in the structure of the productive sector of each region that determines different interest elasticities of the IS curve.

5 See Dow (1982, 1987, 1990) and Chick and Dow (1988).

6 For a good analysis of the differences in the notion of time see Dow (1985). Carvalho (1983-84, p. 266), also presents interesting notes on the fundamental differences between time and space. Shackle (1965, pp. 3-4), develops interesting observations on the relevance of the difference between mechanical time and historical time.

7 See Davidson (1982-83, p. 187).

8 We are considering cash and not money as the homogeneously liquid asset because deposits can have less liquidity in regions where the banking system is less developed.

9 For further discussion on the limits that finance puts to investment see Davidson (1986); Kregel (1986) and Studart (1995).

10 The idea of a "revolving fund" must be modified when we are thinking in terms of regional economies, as will be observed later on, for the leakages that can occur in regional economies do not allow the full play of a "revolving fund".

11 This general characterization presents elements of what ECLA considers the phase of "Desarrollo Hacia Afuera" (Development Towards Outside). Dependency theorists have shown that the relations of dependence evolve over time, and some features of dependent economies disappear without the main relations of dependence disappearing. This fact must be considered on amplifying the analysis of Dow.

12 In order to develop the regional money multipliers, Dow works with a segmented bank system. Therefore, the banks' credit expansion is limited by the regional level of reserves to expand credit.

13 It can be argued that if central and peripheral assets are available to individuals at both the centre and the periphery, there would not exist any reason for agents at the periphery to present a higher liquidity preference, since the range of assets with which both groups can operate is the same. However, if we observe closely the process of expectations formation, we will notice that there are reasons for agents presenting higher liquidity preferences at the periphery. Agents in those regions form their expectations remote from the assets of the centre. This gives the stability of prices of those assets a more remote character in the process of expectations formation at the periphery. On the other hand, agents at the periphery are much closer (in terms of expectations formation) to the instability that surrounds these markets and the local assets and this has a great weight in the whole process of formation of expectations. Therefore, these two elements lead to a higher liquidity preference at the periphery than at the centre. Nevertheless, the more remote base of information about reevaluation

of centre assets for peripheral agents does not offset the preference of peripheral agents for assets of central regions. The more active centre markets and the consequent higher liquidity of centre assets create the conditions for the manifestation of the liquidity preference of agents from the periphery in the demand for centre assets at the expense of the peripheral ones.

14 This analysis was based on some simulations using the model developed. For further details see Dow (1982).

15 Scott (1955) observes that in a segmented banking system there is a lag between the adjustment of portfolio due to a change in the monetary policy between central and peripheral banks, the first adjusting sooner. He also notices that the removal of barriers which make the system segmented leads to a faster adjustment to changes in the monetary policy in the system as a whole. However, he does not observe the side effects that those freer movements of capital can have on the peripheral banking system. Thurston (1976) reaches the same sort of conclusions in terms of lags of adjustment of the reserves in the peripheral and central banks.

16 Although being allowed to operate nationwide, peripheral nationwide are more constrained than central nationwide banks as a consequence of their smaller size.

17 The discrimination of the banks at the centre will be in terms of assessing the information and in terms of the degree of trust that they have in the information that they get. As the activities of the peripheral regions have a more "remote" base of information for the banks of the centre, they will discriminate against those regions, as will be observed later on.

18 Hill and Moore (1982) assume the direction of causality to be from income to deposits and then to credit. Moreover, they are basically concerned with market frictions, such as imperfect information in the explanation of differentials of interest rate and ceilings on credit extension. Moore, Karaska and Hill (1985) maintain the direction of causality of the previous model, so they assume that income generates deposits and deposits allow the extension of credit on a fractional reserve base, therefore, credit is a more or less passive element in the whole process (Moore, Karaska and Hill, p. 32, 1985).

19 The regional rate of interest is determined by a mark-up process and the mark-up margin varies with the expectations of the value of regional assets and with the level of uncertainty that is observed in the economy. These elements are an important contribution to the traditional mark-up models of determining the interest rate (see for example Rousseas, 1985).

20 Hutchinson and McKillop (1990) and McKillop and Hutchinson (1990) develop a model for Northern Ireland that assumes the neutrality of the financial system in a nationwide integrated financial system. After this, they observe the non-neutral effects that segmentation due to different costs of obtaining information and institutional segmentation can present.

21 In this process both sides are influenced by the degree of confidence in expectations of the future values of local assets.

22 However, this position of Moore must be analysed carefully since banks do not respond passively to demand of loans. For this point see also Rousseas (1985, p. 135).

23 See Minsky (1986, pp. 159, 161, 163, 170).

24 Gentle and Marshall (1992) observe the increased concentration of the banking system in the South East of Britain as a by-product of the process of financial liberalisation undergone by this country in the late 1970s and 1980s. Gentle (1993) points out some positive elements in this process, as large firms are supposed to play a crucial role according to his theoretical framework: "the evidence of this book suggests that it is large firms that are the agents of capitalist development". Furthermore: "it is large firms which have facilitated the convergence of markets and in so doing have adopted a variety of organisational designs" (Gentle, 1993, p. 290).

25 Hirschman (1981, chapter 4) observes that in particular sectors of the economy, the linkages can be negligible and even negative; therefore, policies that stimulate these sectors will have smaller effects in terms of reversing the general environment of underdevelopment of the economy as a whole.

26 Hansen, reviewing the ideas of Perroux, establishes the following characteristics of the propulsive industry:

> Despite some differences of emphasis, three basic characteristics of a propulsive industry (or firm) emerge from the relevant literature. First, it must be relatively large in order to assume that it will generate sufficient direct and potentially indirect effects to have a significant impact on the economy; second, it must be a relatively fast growing sector; and third, the quantity and intensity of its interrelations with other sectors should be important so that a large number of induced effects will in fact be transmitted (Hansen, 1967, p. 717).

27 Here we are referring to one particular sector in one specific region. This is so because the same sector can present absolutely different levels of linkages in different regions depending on the structure of property, on the consumer market, etc.

Part II
Some notes on the regional economic history of Brazil

3 Some notes on the regional economic history of Brazil

Introduction

To understand the uneven pattern of regional development in Brazil one needs to comprehend how the country came to be formed and the role that each region has played in its formation. It is, therefore, necessary to analyse the elements responsible for the growth and dynamics of this economy in each particular historical period and how the changes in the dynamic variables influenced the regional patterns of development. It is in the earlier phases of Brazilian economic history that some of the bases of the economic structure of the regions were shaped, and this explains a part of the current trend of regional development in Brazil. In those earlier stages, real factors were the main determinants of the regional patterns. Though financial elements interplayed with real factors, they did so on a smaller scale, especially at the regional level, than in periods when the domestic banking system was more developed. Financial considerations of this period are very similar to the analysis developed by Dependency Theory as explored in Chapter 1: international financial capital supported the real development dictated by the needs of the developed world.

There are fundamentally two periods that divide the regional economic history of Brazil. The first period is the colonial era and it also comprises the subsequent phase when, despite being politically independent from Portugal, Brazil continued to follow a traditional, primary-export model. In this period, all the dynamics of the economy were derived from the external market. The second period is characterised by the shift from the external market for a limited number of products to the internal market as the main source of dynamics in the process of growth of this economy. This period can also be divided into two phases. The first refers to the extensive import substitution process, that is, the goods which were originally imported but were substituted by domestic production bring about a simple productive process mainly in the consumer goods sector and are linked to the traditional sectors of the economy. The second phase refers to the heavy industrialisation when import substitution reaches the capital goods producer sector and the durable consumer goods sector (Mello, 1982, p. 93). The transition from the first to the second phase was the coffee economy of the second half of XIX century and the first two decades of the XX century. In this period, some anachronistic relations of production that did not allow development of the internal market were changed and joined other favourable structural and conjunctural elements that allowed the transition from the agrarian export model to the import substitution model. During this period are laid the bases for the process of import substitution and here we can find some of the fundamental elements that will contribute to the enormous concentration of production in the Centre-South of Brazil.

Now we will analyse the first period and the transition to the second and examine what are the principal elements that characterise them, which are the dynamic elements and which factors contributed to the concentration of wealth, production and dynamics in specific regions. Where possible[1], we will make reference to the role of the financial system.

This part of the book provides a wide vision of the regional economic history of Brazil. It is through the comprehension of the dynamic variables shaping the regional economies and the nation as a whole, the labour relations that were developed in each context and the economic activities that were developed in each region that the reader will be able to appreciate the content of the following chapters, their structure and the context in which they have been developed.

Colonization, sugar and cattle-raising activities

The discovery and occupation of Brazil took place in the context of the discovery of many new lands world wide. But in contrast to the discovery of gold and silver in the Spanish territories, Brazil, apparently, did not have such immediately valuable products. On the other hand, Portugal traded in spices that were obtained in the Orient and were sold in European markets for excellent prices. As Portugal itself had problems with its scarce population, there was no reason for a part of its population to migrate in order to colonise a land that did not represent any promise of wealth. Furthermore, the differences in and the hostility of the climate and natural environment[2] were extra reason to discourage the colonization of the country.

The first product that attracted the attention of Portugal was brazil wood (Pau-Brasil), widely used to dye textiles in Europe. This product had a collector character that did not allow the spread of its economic effects to other sectors of the economy. It was mainly carried out by Portuguese and French using local indians who worked as slaves. It did not contribute to the concentration of economic activity in specific parts of the territory since brazil wood was spread over the entire coastal strip of Brazil. The profitability of this activity, however, was restricted to the first half of the XVI century since after this period, devastation of the forests resulted in a reduced supply. With the decline in profitability of brazil wood, sugar cane cultivation substituted it as the main economic activity of the country.

Sugar cane was introduced in Brazil by the Portuguese, who had some experience with cultivating it in some African islands. Sugar by this time was an extremely expensive product and was commercialized in Europe with an enormous margin of profits. The decline in the extraction of brazil wood coincided with the introduction of the cultivation of sugar cane. This was an activity that contributed to the Portuguese objectives of population settlement in its new territory, and it was a very profitable product on the international market.

Sugar cane adapted well to the new land. Soon it was evident that the best lands and climate for this activity were located in the Northeast. The technical needs of sugar's cultivation made the adoption of large land holdings (latifundia) a feature in the agrarian structure of regions that were linked to this activity[3]. Indians were not used widely as labour force in sugar cane cultivation: imported African slave labour was used instead. The combination of latifundia and slavery was a constant in the colonial history of the Northeast of Brazil, especially in the sugar-producing areas. The use of slave labour constrained the formation of an internal market, since slaves are not consumers, in the broad sense of the word, and the free labour force that worked in the "engenho" (sugar mills)[4] was very small.

The settlement of these areas was extremely expensive to individual entrepreneurs who were rewarded with large extensions of lands; the capital was financed by the Portuguese crown, by Dutch banks and traders, and to some extent by Jewish bankers (Prado, 1976, p. 32). After the beginning of the sugar production it became a self-financing activity. As Furtado calculates it could finance up to double its productive capacity within two years of production. However, leakages of surplus during commercialisation of this activity resulted in making it dependent on external sources of finance, mainly Dutch (Prado, 1976, p. 32; Furtado, 1971, p. 10). The Dutch not only financed commercialisation of this product in Europe, but they also financed the production, installation, constant capital and the purchase of African slaves, the main labour force. Therefore, commercialisation and finance of sugar cane crops and the production of sugar were carried out by the central economies (Portugal and Netherlands). These two phases were the central elements in the transformation and extraction of surplus from the periphery, and as they were controlled by foreigners, the surplus leaked from these economies to the central ones. This restricted any possibility of self-financing of the sugar cane crops and sugar production and left the financial and commercial spheres of those activities clearly as sources for the extraction of surplus from the colony or periphery. Therefore, in this case we have the two spheres, commercial and financial, playing the roles depicted by Dependency Theory as the sources of extraction of surplus from the periphery to the centre in colonial societies and in this way they intensify the uneven pattern of development at world level.

The main regions where this activity was concentrated were Pernambuco and Bahia. There were other concentrations in São Paulo (São Vicente) and Rio de Janeiro but they were far less important and, after some time, they were abandoned and the regions "specialised" in other activities.

At the beginning of the XVII century, a new product began to gain importance in international markets: tobacco. In Brazil it was produced mainly in Bahia, and later its culture was extended to Sergipe and Alagoas (Prado, 1976, p. 40). Therefore, the main dynamic cultures that were linked to external markets were located in the Northeast of Brazil[5]. This product, however, was far from having the same importance as the activities associated with the production of sugar, it counted as merely a peripheral activity.

The great profitability of sugar made it an extremely specialized activity. The opportunity cost of producing other kinds of products was enormous; it was more profitable to import necessary goods from abroad. The exceptions to this general rule were the production of cattle and wood to provide the energy that the production of sugar demands. And, in this sense, a new peripheral activity developed and gave a new shape to the regional distribution of the economic structure of the country[6].

The increasing demand of the "engenhos" for cattle expanded the economic frontiers of the colony, since, given the higher opportunity costs of rearing cattle in lands that could be used for sugar cane plantations, cattle-raising was carried out increasingly in the interior, far from the "engenhos". From the interior in the Northeast of Brazil cattle-raising spread all over the territory reaching the far South of the country.

The cattle-raising developed some peculiarities that were very important in the later analysis of the economic history of Brazil. As the supply of land was extremely elastic, this activity tended to be extensive and to occupy enormous portions of land in the interior of Brazil. It also acquired a nomadic character, especially in the Northeast, where droughts were a constant phenomenon, making it necessary to migrate in search of water (Furtado, 1971, p. 57).

Another common feature of this activity was the small fixed capital required. Basically, the investment consisted of cattle, the other factor, land, was extremely abundant and did not have economic value, especially the land of the "sertão" in the interior of Brazil. As the value of cattle was very low, there was no economic rationale in using African slaves, who were extremely expensive, in this activity. Thus, the labour force used in this activity was mainly indians captured in the interior of the country and free workers (Prado, 1976, p. 44).

It can be seen that the settlement of the interior of the country was complementary to the main activity, the production of sugar for external markets. By this time, the economy of the country was divided basically into two big groups. The first one consisted of the dynamic activity linked to the external market with a high profitability; the second one was a complementary activity whose demand was derived from the first activity and had a low profitability and a strong subsistence character. The peripheral activity, though, tended to spread all over the territory and by the beginning of the XVIII century, was an important activity in both the Northeast and South of the country.

Cattle-raising had more than a complementary role to play in the economy. Leather derived from it was largely used in Brazil in almost all activities and had some importance in exports of some regions. The South had a stronger position in production of exportable leather than other regions, since the quality of the leather produced there was superior to the one from the Northeast and the centre of the country.

Instead of the relative dynamism of the region linked to the external market (Northeast), there were other regions that suffered almost absolute misery, their main activity being linked to subsistence sectors and to the capture of indian slaves who were used as the main labour force in the region or were sold in other regions. This was basically the case of the "capitanias", captaincy system, that nowadays constitutes the state of São Paulo (Simonsen, 1937, Vol. I, p. 351).

Therefore, we had a dynamic pole in the country that was basically attuned to international market interests, which, however, was not well linked with other sectors in the economy. Moreover, as the more profitable sectors of the dynamic activity were the monopoly of foreigners, little surplus remained in the country, which limited the possibilities of stimulating other internal sectors of the economy. The main sources of surplus extraction were the financial and commercial spheres. This is perfectly in accordance with what is observed by Dependency Theory in colonial economies and which also observes that some of these characteristics are maintained even after political colonisation of peripheral countries is overcome. That is, these theories note, as was seen in Chapter 1, that the situation of dependence and the conditions of extraction of surplus are essentially maintained, even if they change their forms.

With the unification of the Portuguese and Spanish crowns between 1580-1640, the Dutch-Portuguese partnership in the sugar activity was broken. As the Dutch controlled all the commercial and financial spheres of this activity, and Portugal only controlled the production part of it, this activity reached a crisis, because the success of this activity depended too much on the commercial sphere and on the control that was exercised over the international market for this product (Furtado, 1971, pp. 45-6). The crisis became more apparent when Brazil was invaded by the Dutch, who took over the production of sugar, occupying the capitanias of Pernambuco, Itamaracá, Paraíba, Sergipe and Rio Grande do Norte. This allowed them to control 50 per cent of the entire sugar production in Brazil (Simonsen, 1937, pp. 171, 178).

The expulsion of the Dutch from Brazil in 1654 did not put an end to the problem. On the contrary, before the invasion of Brazil, the Dutch only controlled the commercial and financial spheres of the sugar activity. After the invasion, they controlled the technology of production also. And after being expelled from Brazil, they began sugar production in the Caribbean islands. Therefore, they competed in better conditions than Brazil in this activity, since they had control of the international markets of this product and Brazil did not.

This was the beginning of a long period of decline in sugar production. As the main dynamic activity declined, the population was absorbed into peripheral activities that increasingly gained a subsistence character. As the monetary value of production decreased, as a consequence of the degeneration of the dynamic activity linked to the external market, there was a constraint on the capacity of the economy to import. This resulted in the advent of a handicraft sector that supplied some basic goods that were previously imported (Furtado, 1971, pp. 62-3).

Gold mining and the central region

The discovery of gold in the central region of Brazil at the end of the XVII century restored the external determination of the dynamic location of economic activity. The Northeast, which was under a severe crisis, lost its position to the Centre-South which in this phase was the dynamic region. The principal region responsible for the production of gold was what is now the state of Minas Gerais, but Goiás and Mato Grosso had some importance in this activity also, especially after 1720 (Simonsen, 1937, Vol. II, p. 41).

Gold mining was carried out mainly by African slave labour, although slaves had never been the majority population in these regions (Furtado, 1971, p. 78).

The initial investment necessary to create a mine was not very great, especially compared to the investment necessary for sugar production. This allowed a better income distribution in this region and created a much more diversified demand than the one observed in the Northeast of Brazil. This, when put together with the fact that the use of free workers was greater in this region than in sugar production and the fact that the imports of this region were smaller than in the part of Northeast that was linked to the production of sugar, brought about a bigger consumer market in this region. Another peculiarity of the mining region is its urban character, in contrast to the agricultural regions. These characteristics also allowed the development of a middle class formed mainly of traders who were concerned with the supply of goods to urban centres, civil servants who were related to the collecting of tax and to the supervision of mines, some workers who were linked to the handicraft sector and so on (Hollanda, 1964, II-III, p. 371). All these factors created the conditions for a self-reinforcing process of growth based on a more diversified structure of supply, but, as Furtado observes, this aim was not reached. The main explanation that this author gives for this failure is the total lack of technical knowledge of the local population, which did not allow the development of a local industry or developed handicraft sector (Furtado, 1971, p. 79)[7].

The new economic cycle that the discovery of gold set up in Brazil brought some fundamental changes in the organisation of the economy of the country as a whole. First of all, there was intense migration from the stagnant Northeast to the dynamic centre of the country. This migration was constituted not only of free labour; one of the fundamental sources of slaves necessary to the mines was the Northeast, since the general crisis in this economy made some slaves redundant there.

Another fundamental point is the dynamism that the production of gold brought to the economy of the South. As was previously mentioned, this economy was mainly linked to the production of cattle[8]. When the dynamic centre of the economy of Brazil was transferred to the Centre-South, as the South was nearer this region and the South produced better quality livestock than the Northeast, the prices of the livestock of the South increased and became higher than the prices of Northeastern livestock, reversing the traditional relation. This gave dynamism to the economy of the South.

However, not only did cattle-raising in the South gain from the increased demand from the mines region, the Northeast, too, had its demand increased and the cattle-raising activity spread all over the São Francisco river region in the direction of the mines.

By this time, the political capital of the country was transferred from Salvador to Rio de Janeiro (1763). São Paulo and Rio de Janeiro began to be important centres of commercialisation and export of gold. On the other hand, the commercial activity of Rio de Janeiro was greatly increased by the demand from the mining (Hollanda, 1964, II-II, p. 317).

The maximum point of the production of gold in Brazil was reached in 1760. Its decline was swift and, by the end of the XVIII century, it was no longer an important activity, as the gold reserves of the country were almost exhausted and a new phase of stagnation began in this region. Economic activity was transferred from mining to the agricultural sector and to activities related to cattle-raising. When the coffee boom began, this region turned to production of coffee but still maintained a certain diversification of its productive structure, mainly linked to agriculture, cattle-raising activities and the industrialisation of some dairy products[9].

The basic characteristics of the extraction of surplus from sugar production were maintained for gold mining. This made that the decline in this activity very rapidly reverted this region to the relative poverty that was characteristic of regions that were not attuned to external markets. As these regions did not keep the surplus that was generated by them and had a very limited success in creating new economic sectors related to the dynamic activity, once the natural resource was exhausted or the conditions of the external markets changed, they reverted to their initial conditions of internal periphery. However, some of the characteristics with which the period of the dynamic activity had shaped the region persisted even when the main activity lost its dynamism. This is very important for comprehending the later regional analysis of the Brazilian economy.

During periods of decline in the main economic activity of the country (this can be observed with sugar cane and gold) plenty of peripheral products gained importance within the total exports of Brazil until a new product gained dominance and put the other products into a peripheral position.

At the end of the XVIII century, there were political disruptions in the Caribbean islands which reduced the production of sugar in this region. This permitted an increase in the international prices of sugar, which allowed a relative recovery to the importance of this activity in the exports of Brazil, and, consequently, the Northeast, which was the main supplier of sugar, partially recovered its position at the national level.

Another product that gained relative importance in the exports of Brazil since the second half of the XVIII century was cotton. The cultivation of cotton presented substantial differences with relation to the cultivation of sugar cane. It had lower fixed costs than sugar cane. It also allowed co-production of some crops which were used for the subsistence of the workers. These permitted the production of this crop by small land owners or by persons that were not land owners and had not developed any previous accumulation (Castro, 1980, Vol. 2, p. 19). Initially, it was used only by the internal market and to produce clothes for slaves. With the industrial revolution in England, and with new technologies that allowed extensive use of this raw material by the textile industry, the international market of this product grew enormously. The production of cotton was mainly centred in the Northeast, especially in the states of Maranhão, Bahia and Pernambuco, and later was spread all over the country[10]. However, international prices of this raw material declined greatly after the beginning of the XIX century and this contributed towards the decline of its cultivation in Brazil (Prado, 1976, pp. 81-2).

Therefore, by the end of the XVIII century, Brazilian exports were much diversified, but this diversification and the prosperity observed at the time had very volatile bases, as was observed by Furtado (Furtado, 1971, p. 92). The foundations on which the prosperity of some regions lay was determined from abroad, and because the dynamic activities had short linkages with other sectors of the economy, the effects of this prosperity were limited to one sector of the economy of these regions. Once the conditions of the external markets changed, there was a complete stagnation in those regions. However, some peculiarities of the previous dynamic economic activity were maintained. This was clearly the case in sugar production, which shaped the social and economical structures of the Northeast until today leaving a bequest of latifundia and weak labour relations in the region. The same phenomenon can be observed within the economy of the mining region, where a larger consumer market was developed as mining allowed a better income distribution than the sugar cane cultivation did and this allowed the diversification of the economic structure of the region, although, this diversification was also limited by other factors previously discussed.

Therefore, the prosperity of the regions that were attuned to external markets was much more a consequence of the needs of the central economies than a consequence of internal determinants. Furthermore, just a small part of the benefits of external markets remained within the region and the country since the more profitable parts of the productive process and the parts that really allowed the extraction of surplus was carried abroad by foreigner entrepreneurs and this did not allow the benefits of the prosperous times to be maintained or continued when there was a change in the conditions of the external markets or in the natural resources of the region. This typifies the model developed by Dependency Theory to explain the dynamics of the colonial societies. And moreover, this depicts well the role that Dependency Theory attributes to the financial system in colonial economies. On the one hand, it allowed the development of activities linked to the interests of the central economies and, in this sense, acted in their own interest. On the other hand, by controlling key phases of the productive process (commercial and financial spheres) they extracted the surplus generated by these activities and did not allow their self-perpetuation, thus keeping the control of these activities and maintaining the relation of dependency of the periphery on the centre.

The North, which has not been mentioned until now, was colonised much more for political reasons than for economic purposes. Portugal decided to colonise this region in order to avoid penetration by Spanish and French in the first half of the XVI century. The first and most profitable activity of this region was the capture of indians to be sold in Pernambuco to the "engenhos". As this activity declined with the spread of African slave labour in Pernambuco, this region turned to extractive activities. These activities were mostly carried out by missionaries who used indian labour. The main products were spices, cocoa and other products that were native in the Amazon jungle.

These were basically the regional characteristics of Brazil at the beginning of the XIX century, when it became independent.

Some considerations on the monetary and financial relations of the period

There are few references to the financial and monetary organisation of Brazil from the XVI century to XIX century, and some of the references contradict each other. However, some general features of this period can be observed.

The monetary standard of the colony and its regulation was strictly linked to the interest of Portugal[11]. Therefore, until independence we cannot talk of a Brazilian monetary standard, instead of the fact that, in some periods, some regions or state of the colony presented a relative degree of freedom in relation to the monetary policy imposed from Portugal.

The first feature present throughout the economic history of the colony is the scarcity of coinage and legal tender money. This persisted even during the time that gold mining was the main economic activity of Brazil, and can be viewed as a consequence of the export of surplus which has characterised the whole colonial period and of the strict monetary policies that Portugal imposed on the colony. The lack of legal tender money was especially accentuated in peripheral regions, since these regions did not have any links with the monetary source of the economy, which was the external sector. This fits in absolutely with the logic of the colonization as depicted by Dependency Theory. The sectors related to external markets were the only ones where monetary relations were supposed to develop, since external trade was the main factor in monetary relations. However, even these sectors were under monetary pressure, since the extraction of surplus via commercial and financial mechanisms did not allow a substantial part of the surplus to remain inside the country. Regions which were peripheral to the peripheral national economy had further problems with the availability of money, since they had no contact with external markets and, so, had greatly reduced possibilities for developing monetary relations.

The scarcity of legal tender money means that a variety of other "monetary" standards were adopted at the time, especially at the regional level. For instance, the use of sugar as a means of payment in the purchase of goods was very common in all the regions (Levy, 1979, p. 27). The use of legal tender money was basically restricted to commercial areas, which traded in products that were linked to the external market. Thus, activities that were developed within the country in order to maintain its market had a weak monetary character. A great part of the domestic trade was based on barter (Schwartz, 1987). Therefore, it is not only in periods when we have a developed financial system that we have monetary restrictions to development. As this period demonstrates, the peripheral regions suffered an absolute constraint of money and "finance" since only the sectors linked to external markets had access to these two elements and this put limits to the capacity of accumulation in regions that do not have their activities linked to this sector. Since this shortage of money was so extreme, it jeopardised the local and day-to-day capacity to trade of those economies and ended up by creating social alternatives to legal tender money that assumed diverse forms in each region. However, these alternatives were bound by the partiality of the alternatives created.

Labour relations were also largely non-monetary. Since the main part of the labour force was slaves, the monetary character of this relation was only present at the initial purchase of the slave and, after that, in the purchase of goods that allowed the physical reproduction of the slave labour force. These transactions cannot be considered as a potential source of development of an internal market[12]. The use of indian free workers did not develop monetary relations either, since this relation was based mainly on a barter form of payment.

Therefore, the monetary relations of this economy tended to develop only around the dynamic activities. Once they lost their dynamics, as a consequence of changes in external market conditions or the exhaustion of natural resources, as was the case with mines, the economy of these regions tended to turn to subsistence activities that did not have a strong monetary character.

The scarcity of gold coins was more important in some regions, especially in those that were not linked to the external market. Maranhão used several different goods as means of exchange, especially some goods made of cotton, because of the absolute scarcity of coins in the regions (Simonsen, 1937 vol I, p. 114). The "capitania" of São Paulo had also its own coin by the end of the XVII century (Simonsen, 1937, vol I, p. 114 and Levy, 1979, p. 54). Other goods that were produced in São Paulo were also used as means of exchange and a standard of value as a consequence of the scarcity of legal tender money (Simonsen, 1937, vol I, pp. 336-7). São Paulo was relatively independent of the restrictive nature of the monetary policy of Portugal. By the end of the XVII century, it decreed its own measures of monetary policy, going against the interests of Portugal. When Portugal tried to impose its own monetary policy on the region, there were a few rebellions. Portuguese monetary policy was only conformed to once again with the discovery of mines and a consequent increase in gold available to the regions[13].

The first activity to present more complex financial processes, because of the proportion of initial capital required to install and develop it, was sugar production. As analysed before, the finance of this activity came mainly from an association of private and public Portuguese and Dutch capital. Dutch capital had played a special role in this activity, since the Netherlands had a developed financial system and had financed not only the initial investment but also the sugar trade. The control of the financial and commercial spheres of sugar production was fundamental to the extraction of surplus. Therefore, it was expected that these two phases would not be carried out by Brazilian entrepreneurs, since colonial logic expects these activities to be undertaken by the metropolis as a way of extracting surplus from the colony, as was seen in Chapter 1. In the case of Brazil the colonial metropolis (Portugal) was not able to develop these two spheres properly because it did not have a well developed financial system that could cope with financing an activity of the scale of sugar production and it did not have control of the sugar market. Therefore, a great part of the benefits of this activity was transferred to the Netherlands and the surplus extracted from the colony was used mainly in accumulating capital in that country, which was also a world metropolis.

As Levy (1979) points out, scarcity of money led to a widespread use of credit[14] in the colony. These credit relations were, however, developed without the intervention of specialised institutions and were based on barter. Typically goods were advanced before the production of a crop. These credit relations instead of primitive were responsible for some exchange relations in the economy. But, apart from the experience of sugar production, there was no development of credit to finance external market operations of Brazil, not at least until the beginning of the XIX century (Simonsen, 1937, vol II, pp. 266-7).

The Jesuits had a part to play in creating some "institutions" of credit, since some of the money that was available in the colony was deposited with them and they began to extend credit based on these deposits. But their role was not so widespread as to alter fundamentally financial relations in the colony (Levy, 1979, p. 56).

Another important incentive to the development of financial relations in the colony was the foundation in the Northeast of the Company West Indias by the Dutch during of their invasion of Northeast. They brought more sophisticated financial techniques to this country, which were in contrast to its primitive and very simple local financial and credit relations. But because they charged excessively high interest rates and extended credit so easily, some land owners of Brazil became over indebted. These debts made the colonists cooperate in the expulsion of the Dutch from Brazilian lands[15].

The decline in the sugar activity which coincided with the expulsion of Dutch from the Brazilian territory, meant that the relations of credit that were previously observed in the colony were reestablished.

The increasing importance of gold mining did not result in new financial techniques in the region. Despite the fact that a great part of financial transactions in the regions were undertaken through credit relations, these relations were very archaic and were not developed by specialised institutions (Levy, 1979, p. 93). Interest rates charged on this credit were extremely high, and after the beginning of the decline of sugar production, they increased, which contributed further to the deterioration of the economic situation of the region (Levy, 1979, p. 107).

By the end of the XVIII century, the external trade of Brazil began to be financed by English companies, bringing about change in the sphere of influence in Brazil from the Netherlands to England. However, the dynamics and mechanisms of surplus extraction from the country persisted. The financial and commercial spheres continued to be dominated from abroad and leakages in the flow of income persisted, which continued to constrain a self-generating process of growth in the country.

This shows that, during this phase, when there was no national banking system, international finance intensified regional inequalities. The international financial system financed international trade and part of the production of staples during specific periods. However, as these economies were "enclaves" within the country, the money or "liquidity" created by the main activity did not leak to other sectors and so the absolute monetary constraints on peripheral regions were not overcome.

By this time, the first bank was created in Brazil. On the initiative of some traders, in order to confront the constant scarcity of currency, the bank began to issue some notes on the warranty of public deposits in the bank (Simonsen, 1937, Vol II, p. 267). But the first really important initiative in organising something that could really be called a financial system came after the installation of the Portuguese Court in Brazil in 1808[16]. The Banco do Brasil began to operate in 1809. It accepted deposits, discounted commercial and personal notes (Letras de Câmbio) and had the power to issue its own notes that must be payable on the spot. The notes of the bank gained legal tender status and circulated as money. The bank was a private bank[17], but received incentives from the government to operate. The head office of the bank was in Rio de Janeiro, where the Portuguese Court was installed, and later it established two branches, one in Bahia and other in São Paulo[18].

Besides Banco do Brasil there were other banks who issued their own notes. The allowance to these banks to issue notes varied according to the necessities of money of the economy. The Banco Comercial do Rio de Janeiro (1838), Banco Comercial da Bahia (1845), Banco do Maranhão (1846), Banco Comercial de Pernambuco (1851), Banco do Brasil Mauá (1851), and others issued their own notes which were sometimes in serious competition with the notes issued by the government (Hollanda, 1964, II-III, p. 44).

In 1853, the Banco do Brasil[19] obtained a monopoly on issuing bank notes. But in 1857, the commercial banks were again allowed to issue notes; this was due to a shortage of means of payment in some regions of the country, especially the North. In 1866, the Banco do Brasil regained its monopoly. Granting banks the power to issue notes or restricting them were forms used to regulate the availability of means of payment in the economy (Hollanda, 1964, II-III, p. 79).

Although, at this time we had a national banking system, the financing of the activities related to external markets continued to be undertaken by the external financial sector. The national banking system had a more limited influence and was more closely associated with business and produce that were not important to external relations. The financial regional model developed in Chapter 2 demonstrates successfully what was going on in this period in terms of international and national financial systems. The national financial system was in tune with activities that were not strongly related to external markets, while the international financial system specialised in financing produce that was directed at international markets and did not concern itself with financing activities related to the internal market or peripheral activities that were also related to external markets.

The coffee activity and the transition to the import substitution model

The upturn in the Brazilian economy by the end of the XVIII century, as observed above, did not last very long. By the beginning of the XIX century, the economy declined again as a consequence of changes in the international markets of its main export products. When sugar began to be produced from beet, the market in Europe was diverted. Europe not only began to produce sugar but also created some exportable surplus (Prado, 1976, p. 158). Extra pressure on the external market of sugar from Brazil was brought about by the protection that the United States gave to sugar from Hawaii, Puerto Rico and Louisiana, and, in some sense, from Cuba (Denslow, 1977, p. 57). This caused a severe deterioration in the international prices of this product and resulted in stagnation in the Northeast. Cotton also saw its international conditions deteriorating, when production in the USA was reorganized and it became a strong competitor in the international market undercutting the cost of production and consequently the price of this product (Denslow, 1977, p. 57). Therefore, by this time the Northeast saw stagnation in two of its most important products. This crisis was deepened by the interruption of the slave trade from Africa (Prado, 1976, p. 159)[20].

However, the crisis that the economy of the Northeast faced at the beginning of the XIX century did not continue through the century. During some periods, there was recovery in the international prices of its main export products, sugar and cotton, and there was a certain diversification of its main products of export. This was the case with cocoa in Bahia, and tobacco. However, the main export products of the Northeast continued to be sugar and cotton.

Between 1820 and 1850, there was an increase in the world production of sugar and in the value of the exports of this product. International prices of this commodity faced a new crisis after the second half of the century, and this crisis prevailed until the end of the century and until the beginning of the XX century[21].

The modernisation of the sugar industry allowed a certain development of other sectors indirectly linked to this industry, stimulating an incipient internal market in the Northeast, especially in urban centres (Guimarães Neto, 1989, p. 37). The significant extension of the railways and the commercial use of steam ships allowed integration of regional markets and reduced the costs of the main crops. The extension of the use of these two forms of transport took place mainly after the second half of the XIX century (Guimarães Neto, 1989, pp. 37-40).

In this scenario of crisis, a new product began to gain importance in the external markets: coffee. It was introduced in Brazil in 1727 (Prado, 1976, p. 159), but until the beginning of the XIX century, it was used only for local consumption. It spread all over the territory of Brazil. With the increase in international prices of coffee, it began to assume a relative importance in the external trade of Brazil and its production was concentrated in the regions that were better suited to its production in terms of soil and climate.

The first region where coffee cultivation was introduced on a large scale was the Paraíba Valley, close to the port of Rio de Janeiro for export and, therefore, joined the natural conditions and the transport facilities that this location represented. By the middle of the XIX century, coffee was the main export product of Brazil, responsible for 40 per cent of total exports (Furtado, 1971, p. 113).

The area where it had been previously produced had not been used economically and had substantial available labour which had became redundant with the decline in mining. Therefore, coffee was developed using mainly under-employed resources, which allowed expansion of this activity even when external prices of the product were declining, as was the case during 1820-1850 (Furtado, 1971, pp. 113-4)[22].

The whole process of production, financing and commercialisation of coffee was carried out in Brazil. Rio de Janeiro, by this time, had become the commercial and financial centre that supported the expansion of this activity and its economy was dynamised by coffee production.

The main constraint on extending coffee cultivation was a certain inelasticity of the labour supply, which became greater with the interruption of the slave trade in 1850 (Silva, 1976, p. 41)[23]. The solution to this problem was found in the internal reallocation of the slave labour force. At first slaves were bought from the declining mining regions, but after the availability of slaves in these regions was reduced, coffee cultivation began to compete with sugar production for the labour force. This caused a huge flow of slaves from the Northeast to the Paraíba Valley resulting in an increased price for slaves in the Northeast, an extra factor in deepening the crisis in the sugar producing regions of the Northeast.

However, the productivity of the Paraíba Valley declined rapidly. The type of soil of that region was not well suited to coffee cultivation and coffee production shifted to the west region of São Paulo. This coincided with the increased pressure that the inelasticity of the labour supply represented to coffee production. By this time, it was evident that the need for labour which this crop had created would not be met by the internal availability of labour. By the beginning of the XIX century, some experiences of bringing immigrants from abroad to work in coffee crops began to take place, but this proved unsuccessful as they created a condition of almost total dependence of the immigrant on the owner of the lands[24]. The inelasticity of the supply of labour tended to become more and more serious, especially as the price of coffee increased in international markets. In 1860, a change in the form of payment to immigrants reduced the importance of "parceria," the system by which the immigrants did not have a fixed wage but shared the crops and the risks involved in producing them with the landowner. In 1870, the government of Brazil began to pay for the travel of the immigrants, which gave an extra impulse to the enlargement of the supply of labour in the region. So, in 1880, coffee activity was mainly based on the use of free labour force[25].

Some of the activities that were a condition to the later development of coffee production were financed by foreign capital which received some warranties for the payment of interest from the Brazilian government. Therefore, these complementary activities were undertaken financed by external capital, the government and the private national sector. The main source of external capital, during this period, was England[26]. The evolution of activities directly or indirectly linked to coffee production led to the creation of new sectors in the economy and to the diversification of investment. It is during this time that a network of transport was created, important export firms appeared and a financial system really developed. The financial system was mainly based on banks[27] which were linked to the financing of coffee production (Silva, 1976, p. 50)[28].

By this time, on the whole, there was no scarcity of means of payment that characterised the colonial era. Normally banks had the power to issue notes and when this power was suspended and the economy was seen to contract, they gained the right of issuing once again. There were, by this time, strong speculative movements in the economy that reflected the instability of trading conditions and the financial situation of the country (Prado, 1976, p. 201). Until the end of the XIX century, important intermediators in coffee cultivation were called "comissários"[29]. They financed new coffee plantations and the modernisation of these plantations. Usually they bought coffee produced in each year and traded it in the commercial centres. Later in the XIX century, the activities of these "comissários" were substituted by banks and by institutions that specialised in coffee trade (Silva, 1976, p. 59).

After 1880, the majority of plantations in the west of São Paulo employed free labour in its production (see Prado, 1976, p. 190). This was fundamental for the later development of an incipient internal market that allowed diversification of the productive structure. Wages in this region were higher than in the traditional sugar producing regions or in the Paraíba Valley[30]. This was a consequence of the favourable weather for this crop and of the constrained labour force in this activity, since the other main factor of production, land, was relatively elastic. This elasticity of the supply of land was an extra factor which allowed higher wages in this region. Land availability gave the workers the opportunity to produce for their own subsistence, which put an extra upward pressure on wages in the region. This fact was an additional incentive to the creation of a stronger internal market in this region (Furtado, 1971)[31].

The transference of the centre of coffee production from the Paraíba Valley to the west of São Paulo reduced the importance of Rio de Janeiro as the main export port of coffee and the port of Santos in 1894 assumed the function of the first coffee export port of Brazil (Simonsen, 1939, p. 16). However, this was only possible because, by this time, the network of railways developed greatly in the São Paulo region. The development of this network reduced between 30 per cent and 50 per cent of the cost of exporting coffee (Cano, 1977, p. 34), with a consequent increase in profit margins.

By the end of the XIX century, there were crises and depression in the international prices of coffee[32]. These crises were normally overcome by deliberate policies of devaluation of the rate of exchange in such a way as to maintain the monetary income of the sector that produced and exported coffee. These policies, although maintaining the internal purchasing power, and although very important in terms of the future development of an incipient industrial sector, had a strong concentrating character, since the entire population imported almost all the goods consumed in the country, and the exports were mainly concentrated in the coffee producing sector[33].

The formation of an internal market in the west of São Paulo and the policies of maintaining internal income in times of crisis led to the beginning of industrial growth[34]. These movements, however, were weak and involved sectors that had very simple technology. In 1850, the number of industries remained constant around fifty; in 1866, there was a strong movement towards the creation of new industries; and, in the 1880s and 1890s, this movement strengthened (Simonsen, 1939, pp. 22-4). The regional distribution of industry in Brazil can be observed by the analysis of the distribution of the textile industry in Table II.1[35].

Table II.1
Distribution of the Textile Industry of Brazil by State
1881

State	Number of Industries	Spindles	Looms
Bahia	0.27	0.21	0.170
São Paulo	0.20	0.05	0.168
Minas Gerais	0.18	0.00	0.039
Rio de Janeiro	0.13	0.62	0.425
Federal District	0.11	0.09	0.166
Other States	0.09	0.03	0.030

Source: Simonsen (1939, p. 23).

The origin of industrialisation in Brazil is a controversial subject. There are two opposing arguments in this debate. One assumes that external shocks, and the policies of maintaining the internal income, through the policies of coffee valuation and exchange rate devaluations[36], played a fundamental role in the movement towards industrialisation. Therefore, at times of crisis, there was a constraint on the capacity of the Brazilian economy to import, and as internal incomes were maintained, usually as a result of the devaluation of the rate of exchange, the demand, that was previously supplied by imports, was diverted to the internal market. This allowed expansion of internal industrial production, mainly using idle capacity (Furtado, 1971; Simonsen, 1939; Baer, 1965; Mello, 1982; Aureliano, 1981).

From the opposing point of view, there are those who believe that the supply side of the industrialisation process was more important than the demand side. Therefore, they assume that external shocks played a negative role in the movement towards industrialisation, since the devaluations of the exchange rate made import of capital goods and raw material more expensive which constrained the process of industrialisation. Furthermore, it is assumed that the policy of coffee valuation had played a negative role by providing an incentive to misallocate resources in favour of coffee cultivation (Leff, 1972a; Villela and Suzigan, 1975; Peláez and Suzigan, 1976 and Dean, 1969).

In an intermediate position, we have those who believe that the movement towards industrialisation can only be understood if demand and supply constraints are analysed together. That is, they note that the external constraints at times of decline in the international prices of coffee and the use of policies to maintain the internal income when the rate of exchange was devalued, are important factors in explaining the growth of industrial production. And this growth in industrial production, was only possible because there was idle capacity in the economy. On the other hand, they note that when the international demand for the export products of the country had recovered, the valuation of the exchange rate made possible because it made imports cheaper expansion of the productive capacity, using the accumulated profits from the period of expansion of production. Therefore, they note movements in the demand side and the supply side of the economy at different periods and note that both movements were fundamental to the industrialisation process (Versiani & Versiani, 1977; Fishlow, 1977).

In 1888, a monetary reform allowed some regional banks to issue inconvertible money. This was followed in 1889 by further policies of easy credit which led to a great expansion in the country's means of payment. The speculative and fictitious character of this period is noted by some authors (Prado, 1976; Versiani & Versiani, 1977), but there are some authors who see this period as being fundamental to the process of industrialisation. According to Fishlow, there was a time lag between the inflationary pressures of such a policy and the adjustments of the rate of exchange. This allowed re-valuation of the exchange rate, and consequently more capital goods were imported. When the time lag between the changes in these two variables disappeared, the productive capacity could respond to the demand which had been stimulated by the devaluation of the exchange rate and for the expansionary monetary policy (Fishlow, 1977, pp. 12-3). In 1891, the expansionist policy was interrupted and, in 1896, the issuing power of banks was suspended. The economy contracted and there were many bankruptcies.

The policies that allowed development of the industries at this time were related to the policy of coffee valuation, and the consequent maintenance of the internal level of income by the devaluation of the exchange rate, which really represented an obstacle to imports. Tariffs did not play a relevant role as a protectionist mechanism[37]. The main nature of the tariffs was fiscal[38]. That is, the main source of fiscal revenue was the tariffs on imports, and therefore, they were fixed based on the necessities of the government and not on protectionist principles[39] (Dean, 1969, p. 85; Fishlow, 1977, p. 8; Vilella & Suzigan, 1975, p. 58; Simonsen, 1939, p. 33; Baer, p. 13).

During the first three decades of the XX century, more aggressive policies to maintain the income of the coffee producing sector were undertaken. Besides the action on the rate of exchange, policies were developed to control the coffee supply in the international markets were developed. The first measure in this direction was undertaken with the "Convênio de Taubaté"[40] and, later, during the Great Depression, further measures were undertaken to maintain the internal revenue of the producer and exporter sector of coffee.

The country that experienced its first crisis of overproduction of coffee in 1898 and which faced a decrease in its imports by this time, began the new century with a restrictive monetary policy and with some fiscal difficulties. This was one of the elements which led to a change in the tariffs, which in

1905 began to be charged in gold. Instead of the fiscal nature of this measure, some authors observed that it was fundamental to the process of diversification which took place in the economy of the region of São Paulo, at that time[41].

However, the tendency towards overproduction of coffee still persisted and was intensified at the beginning of the century. This led to the creation of special mechanisms for the export of coffee in order to maintain the international prices of this product (Convênio de Taubaté, 1906)[42]. These measures were based on the action of the government as a buyer of the excess of coffee stocks which if reached the market, would push prices downward. These purchases were financed by external loans and the payment of their interest was funded by a tariff charged in gold on the export of coffee (Furtado, 1971, p. 179).

At this point the diversification of the economic structure within the coffee producing region in the west of São Paulo gained dynamism. This dynamism originated partly in the regime of "parceria" labour relations where the worker received a part of his earnings as a fixed wage[43], and partly in the policy of landowners to allow their workers to use part of their land to produce food for their consumption. This made possible a much more diversified agriculture than in other regions of the country[44] (Cano, 1977, p. 60). As the population in urban centres began to grow and as the measures that created obstacles to imports (devaluation of the exchange rate and some tariffs[45]) began to be put in place, this production began to gain an increasingly commercial character and began to diversify and gain importance in terms of generating income. At the same time, there was a segmentation in agriculture which took place as a subsidiary activity in the coffee plantations and in agriculture which had developed independently of the main crops (Cano, 1977, p. 61).

Another element which contributed to the diversification of the economic structure of São Paulo was another by-product of the crisis in the coffee activity: at moments when the crisis deepened the less productive farms sold their lands to smaller producers who produced mainly agricultural products for the internal markets (Prado, 1976, p. 251 and Cano, 1977, p. 62). Therefore, the movement toward industrialisation which took place in Brazil and especially in the Southeast (São Paulo, Guanabara, Rio de Janeiro and Federal District) was followed by a movement toward diversification and intensification of agriculture, mainly in the state of São Paulo.

The capital which allowed the movement toward industrialisation was mainly linked to the coffee sector. As the coffee crisis began to deepen, those who did not sell their lands felt it necessary to diversify their investment structure in order to avoid the deep crisis caused by the fall of the international prices of coffee. As the coffee crisis did not coincide with the crisis in the internal demand for internally produced industrial goods[46], diversification into producing these goods allowed the entrepreneurs a more secure position.

Importers also played an important role in the industrialisation process. Since they had the control of the market for industrial goods, they knew how this market functioned and they had direct access to international banks in order to finance their investments. When the exchange rate began to be devalued, as a consequence of the policies of coffee valuation, importers tended to diversify their investment and invest in the internal industrial sector (Dean, 1969).

The crisis in the international markets as a consequence of the First World War did not present the same intensity in the internal market of Brazil. On the contrary, this was a period of intense growth in internal industrial production and in profits in the industrial sector. The level of employment in the economy was maintained as a consequence of the policies of coffee valuation, and industrialisation was deepened. The same happened with the diversification of agriculture.

The First World War marks a change in the position of the banks in São Paulo. Until this period, the market of São Paulo was mainly dominated by foreign banks (Neuhaus, 1975, p. 26). As Cano notes of the Paulistas Banks: "Until 1918, they had installed 11 branches in the state; this number grew to 53 in 1924 and 88 in 1927, when they began to finance agriculture more intensively...as well as the better and bigger distribution of credit to agriculture, their role is supposed to have increased also in financing industry and commerce" (Cano, 1977, p. 74, our translation)[47].

It is in the 1920s that the process of industrial concentration which was taking place in São Paulo was really consolidated. This can be seen in Table II.2.

Table II. 2
Industrial Concentration in Brazil

States	Participation in the Value Produced (%)		
	1907	1919	1939
São Paulo	15.9	31.5	45.4
Guanabara	30.2	20.8	17.0
Rio de Janeiro	7.6	7.4	5.0
Minas Gerais	4.4	5.6	6.5
Rio Grande do Sul	13.5	11.1	9.8
Others	28.4	23.6	16.3
Brazil	100.0	100.0	100.0

Source: Cano (1977, p. 253).

The Great Depression of 1929 brought about an enormous decline in the exports of Brazil, and consequently in its imports. Exports in 1929 were at the level of US$ 416.6 millions and in 1932 they were reduced to US$ 108.1 million (Baer, 1965, pp. 21-2). This was, to a great extent, a consequence of the drastic fall in the international prices of coffee during this period. In 1929, the price of coffee was US$ 0.225/pound and in 1931 this became US$ 0.08/pound (Furtado, 1971, p. 187). As Furtado observes, this drastic fall can only be understood as a combination of two crises, one in the demand side and the other in the supply side. The first refers to the crisis which affected the international markets as a whole and the second refers to the overproduction in Brazilian markets which the valuation policy was not able to control (Furtado, 1971, p. 187).

The devaluation of the exchange rate reduced the loss in the coffee producing sector, but despite this, the incomes of the coffee producing sector decreased. Furthermore, this policy of devaluation proved to be of limited value in dealing with the continuous problem of overproduction of coffee, since it sustained the prices of coffee in terms of national money, and this made it possible to continue increasing production of this product, which in turn put extra pressure on its international price. It was now acknowledged that further measures needed to be taken to sustain the internal income and protect the coffee producing sector (Furtado, 1971, Chapter XXXI).

So, a more radical policy was instituted by which excess of stocks would be destroyed after government purchase. Again, in contrast with the previous policy which financed the formation of stocks through foreign loans, this new policy financed the purchase of the stocks and their destruction through the extension of internal public credit (Furtado, 1971, p. 196)[48].

This policy had two consequences for the Brazilian economy, and especially for the region which was most involved in coffee production. The first was a more intense devaluation of the exchange rate than would have been the case if this policy had been financed with foreign loans. The second consequence was to maintain the level of employment in the economy and consequently the level of internal income. According to Furtado: "The policy of protection of the coffee sector during the years of the great depression was actually an authentic program of boosting the national income. Brazil was actually engaged in an anticyclical policy of much broader scope than any even suggested in any of the industrialized countries" (Furtado, 1971, p. 192)[49].

These policies were fundamental to the transference of the dynamic centre of the Brazilian economy from its external sector to its internal market. Therefore, with this transfer the diversification and intensification of the process of industrialisation which began in the second half of the XIX century increased and in the 1930s gained a new dynamic centre: the movement of the internal market.

This process coincided with the intensification of industrialisation and diversification of the economy of the Southeast, especially that of São Paulo, and seems to have represented an essential element in its evolution.

Therefore, in this earlier phase of financial development, when we had few local banks and financial operations were mainly related to foreign banks, financial elements played a small role compared to the dimension that this role assumes in later phases of development (both of the financial system and of the real economy), in what concerns the regional question. But this does not mean that monetary matters did not have a part to play in the process of development. The analysis previously developed shows that the external financial system tended to have a concentrating role. That is, it financed activities linked to the external markets, and, as these activities did not present internal links, the benefits of production allowed and stimulated by this finance were restricted to the dynamic activities. In this way, the monetary constraint that bound the peripheral economies was not reduced with the financing of the dynamic activities.

This period of the economic history of Brazil is well represented by the models of Dependency Theory analysed in Chapter 1. The role of finance as an element that put extra constraints on regional development is, to a certain degree, bounded because the financial system was at an incipient stage of development. However, the role of financial elements was far from neutral: the external financial system was mainly responsible for the financing of the activities related to the external markets and, in this sense, it allowed the development of these activities and of the regions in which they were produced. Nevertheless, the financing of these activities represented one of the most important elements in the extraction of surplus from the periphery by the central countries and this inhibited the internalisation of the benefits of growth and any possibility of self-perpetuating growth process. In this way, the sort of role played by the international banking system was well represented by Dependency Theory models.

Some considerations on the economies of the North, Northeast and South

Some important changes were taking place in the peripheral regions while the Southeast and especially São Paulo were undergoing the above analysed structural changes. These transformations were by-products of the changes in the dynamic centre or were consequences of modifications in the conditions of the external markets. In this section we will attempt to observe what was going on in the peripheral economies at the end of the XIX and beginning of the XX centuries.

North

The first process to be analysed refers to the substantial increase in the international prices of rubber at the end of the XIX century and beginning of the XX century. This represented an enormous source of new wealth to the North region, which formerly concentrated on collector activities, especially cocoa. These activities were based on indian labour organised by the Jesuits until the XVII century. The main constraint to the development of rubber production was scarcity of labour. The Jesuits no longer played a role in organising the indian labour force, there was a total lack of free workers in the region, but as the prices of rubber continued to increase until the First World War, the lucrative nature of this activity caused an immense dislocation of the labour force from the Northeast, mainly to the Amazon. The beginning of immigration from the Northeast to the Amazon began in 1808-1809 when there was an intense drought in the Northeast (Santos, 1980, p. 98). This process tended to increase when the rubber activity gained importance in regional and national terms.

Compared to what was happening in coffee plantations, in the North, the participation of foreign immigrants was negligible; the source of an external labour force to work in the rubber activity was actually found in the reallocation of the internal labour force from the Northeast (Santos, 1980, p. 88).

The production of rubber maintained the collector character of the previous activities which had been carried out in the North and maintained a special regime of labour which was characteristic of this region since its settlement. This special regime was called "aviamento" and consisted of credit relations transmitted in a more or less extensive chain of debtors and creditors. This chain normally began with a big "Casa Aviadora", an institution which gave credit to a smaller "aviador" who were individuals who in turn extended this credit to other "aviador" and so on until this credit chain reached the direct producer. The special characteristic of this source of credit was that it was given in kind, that is, the credit consisted of tools, necessary instruments for the production of rubber, some goods necessary for the subsistence of the direct producer and so on. On the other hand, this credit was repaid with rubber, and not in monetary terms. Thus, there was no monetary influence in these credit relations, or such influences were very restricted. These relations meant that the "aviador" maintained control of both sides of the process, that is, he fixed the prices of the products that he was given as credit and at the time that this credit was repaid, he fixed the price of the product that he was receiving as payment, rubber. It is quite obvious that this system allowed an immense margin of exploitation of the labour force, and as we will show later, this is considered one of the causes which did not allow a self-generating process of growth in the North at the time of the rubber boom[50].

However, banks[51] did not participate in this process of labour/credit relations. The main activities of banks in the North, at this time, were external exchange operations. Only occasionally they extended credit to the "casas aviadoras", but they asked for an unrealistic basis of collateral, which kept them out of this system (Santos, 1980, p. 142).

Relations between the North and other regions of Brazil were very fluid, but, until 1900, the North maintained an equilibrated balance of trade with other regions; although at the beginning of the 1900s this situation changed and the North ran up deficits in its balance of trade with other regions which were paid with the conversion of its external exchange surplus. That is, in some sense, the external potential of import of the North was being transferred to other regions and the North itself was intensifying the demand for products of the Centre-South of the country.

But as rubber began to be produced in the East in an organised way, and lost its character of a collected product its international price began to fall and Brazil soon lost its importance in the external market of this product. The increase in the decline of the international price of rubber took place during 1911-1914. As the international prices of rubber began to decline, the region turned to other collector activities and the subsistence sector and lost its importance in the national economy.

The relative importance that rubber had assumed in the Brazilian economy during this period can be observed in Table II.3.

Table II.3
State of São Paulo and Amazônia
Exports of Coffee and Rubber and the Population Ratio

Years	Exports: 1000 Contos			Population
	Rubber AM	Coffee SP	AM/SP	AM/SP
1871-1880	107.9	221.8	48.6%	39.7%
1881-1890	185.5	490.7	37.8%	34.4%
1891-1900	1163.3	2860.0	40.7%	30.5%
1901-1910	2268.8	2899.2	78.3%	-
1911-1920	1406.8	4942.0	28.5%	31.3%

Source: Cano (1977, p. 89).

Analysing Table II.3 we can ask why the relevance of the export sector allowed development of an industrial sector in São Paulo while in the North this phenomenon did not take place. Cano observes that inspite of the relatively great importance of the rubber boom at the end of the XIX century and the beginning of the XX century in the North, the way that the rubber production was organised resulted in certain fundamental elements which did not contributed to a movement toward industrialisation and diversification of the productive structure. The first element was the relations of credit between the direct producers and traders, as mentioned before. These relations obstructed the introduction of payment of wages. The "aviamento" made each small producer a direct producer, and this contributed to shrinkage of the internal market of the region, as their revenues took the form of goods and the monetary income that the direct producer attained was extremely small. This system of labour organisation allowed leakages in terms of payment of interest to elements that were not economically linked to the region. And finally, the collector character of rubber extraction contributed to the non-utilization of the land in the agriculture production for local consumption. This did not allow diversification or the formation of commercial agriculture in the region and increased leakages through the import of the majority of goods consumed in the region. As we will see, this is the opposite process of what was happening in the Centre-South of the country during the same period[52].

Northeast

By the end of the XIX century, the Northeast faced a new crisis on the international market for its main products (sugar and cotton). Both products declined in quantities exported and in their total proceeds. But, at this time, the economy was not moving towards the subsistence sector. On the contrary, it diverted its market from the external market to the internal market. Therefore, the economy of the Southeast began to absorb gradually the production of the Northeast. This integration of the national market was only possible because there were certain conditions in the infrastructure which allowed the movement of goods at reduced cost compared to the previous period (Guimarães Neto, 1989, Chapter II)[53].

The change in the consumer markets of the Northeast can be seen in the case of sugar by an analysis of Table II.4.

Table II.4
Pernambuco: Sale of Sugar in the Internal Market
1856-1928
(Average Annual Quantities)

Years	Index
1856-60	49
1861-65	42
1866-70	42
1871-75	54
1876-80	70
1881-85	87
1886-89	87
1897-1901	100
1902-17	315
1918-20	-
1921-25	352
1926-28	464

Source: Guimarães Neto (1989, p. 59).

Leff (1972b) observes that the main determinant of the backward position of the economy of the Northeast since the second half of the XIX century, can be found precisely in the analysis of the behaviour of the external markets of the products of the Northeast and of the Southeast, especially of São Paulo. According to him, as the main dynamic element of the Brazilian economy was its external market, the regional allocation of the products which had favourable positions in those markets determined the location of the dynamic region of the country, and at the crucial period when industrialisation was taking place would determine the region where this process would be concentrated.

His analysis began by observing the different pattern that the exports of sugar and cotton (the main export products of the Northeast) had followed compared with the pattern of coffee. These differences in trends can be seen in Table II.5.

Table II.5
Share of Cotton, Sugar and Coffee
in Total Brazilian Export Receipts
(%)

Product	1821-23	1871-73	1912-14
Cotton	25.8	16.6	2.9
Sugar	23.1	12.3	0.3
Coffee	18.7	50.2	60.4

Source: Leff (1972b, p. 246).

The dominance that coffee assumed in the external trade of Brazil made the exchange rate of the country reflect the conditions of this product and not the conditions of the marginalized products such as cotton and sugar. The result was a fall in the domestic currency prices received by the producers of cotton and sugar as opposed to when the exchange rate was determined by the export conditions of these products. This led entrepreneurs to reduce their levels of production. It also prevented the introduction of new technologies which producers in other countries were utilising (Leff, 1972b, p. 257). Following this line of argument, Leff concludes: "Under these conditions, the Northeast might well have been better off as a separate political unit, with its own currency system. Its trade and development would then have been determined by the region's own comparative advantage" (Leff, 1972 b, pp. 258-9).

However, this argument has been criticised. The strongest counterargument was presented above, that is, the limitations to the exports of the Northeast were not only on the supply side, but due to new substitute products which were developed by the main former importers of the products of the Northeast (the classic example is of sugar beet) or of protectionist policies followed by the main consumers of the products of the Northeast (Denslow, 1977). Therefore, instead of facing problems on the supply side, the Northeast actually had constraints on the demand side in the international demand for its products.

South

During the first half of the XIX century and especially at the end of that century, there was an inflow of European immigrants to the South, where the climate and the land structure were more similar to Europe. The structure of ownership of the land, especially after the colonisation by European immigrants in the second half of the XIX century, was based on small estates and the structure of industries and firms followed the same model (Hollanda, 1964, II-III, p. 227). The structure of industry tended to be diversified among several sectors and the ownership tended to be more highly concentrated.

The South region was not so integrated with other regions because of a poor transport system, which was only improved at the beginning of the XX century. This was one of the causes that did not allow a more profound integration of the region with São Paulo during the coffee boom. But the main element which obstructed this integration was the relative diversification of the structure of both industrial and agricultural production. An extra element which obstructed this integration was the consumption habits of São Paulo, which were not compatible with the main products of the South. The most important product of the region was dry and salted meat. This product was not largely accepted in the market of São Paulo, mainly because of the consumer habits of the immigrants. On the other hand, this product was largely consumed in other regions of the country, especially in regions where there was an important influence from slavery, as was the case with Guanabara, Rio de Janeiro and the Northeast. Therefore, the economy of the South tended to have closer economic relations with those regions than with São Paulo (Cano, 1977, p. 111).

The three states which formed the South were settled at different times. Paraná was only properly settled in the 1930s and as it had a limited transport network, its integration was closer with São Paulo than with other states of the region. But this integration was mainly in terms of the use of the transport system, commercialization system and the financial system of São Paulo. The integration of the markets was not towards São Paulo, but towards other states. That is, the commercial surplus of the region was sold in the markets of Rio de Janeiro, Guanabara and the Northeast (Cano, 1977, p. 106)[54].

The value of the industrial production of the states of the South can be seen Table II.6.

Table II.6
Participation of the States of the South in the Industrial Sector of the South
(Value of Industrial Production)

	1907 (%)	1919 (%)
Paraná	4.5	3.4
Santa Catarina	1.9	2.0
Rio Grande do Sul	13.5	11.8

Source: Cano (1977, pp. 108, 112, 119).

Although Rio Grande do Sul showed a relatively high participation in the Brazilian industrial sector, the main industries present in the state and in the region were related to the primary sector, e.g. processing of mate, lard, dry and salted meat, wood etc.. Therefore, to characterise this sector as industrial is to overlook its actual character which is more linked to primary activities rather than industrial activities (Cano, 1977, section 2.2.3).

Notes

1 We can deal with this question with only relative consistency after the beginning of the XX century, due to lack of either data or discussion of the financial nature of the earlier period.

2 These differences ironically were fundamental to profitable colonization, as they allowed cultivation of exotic raw materials and natural products that could get high prices in Europe.

3 For an explanation on this question see Prado (1976, p. 33).

4 Engenho is the name given to the unit that produces sugar; normally it includes the plantation of sugar cane also.

5 Schwartz (1987) presents a good analysis of the peripheral cultures developed in Brazil in the colonial era.

6 See Schwartz (1987) for the analysis of cattle raising as a peripheral activity in the colonial period.

7 Castro observes that this process of diversification ended much more as a consequence of the limits that the metropolis put on the colony, than as a consequence of the lack of technical knowledge (Castro, 1980, Vol. 2, p. 28).

8 In spite of the fact that cattle-raising was important to the Northeast, part of its demand came from the South, especially because of the production in this region of dry salted meat which was mainly

consumed by slaves.

9 For an analysis of this period in the region of the mines see Hollanda (1964, II-II, p. 391).

10 Although the Northeast maintained its leading position in the production of this raw material.

11 Simonsen (1937 vol I, chapter III) presents a good description of the monetary system of the colony and its relations with Portugal. The Portuguese monetary system and its monetary standards are also very well described in this chapter.

12 For the almost total lack of diversification in the nutrition habits of slaves see Castro (1977).

13 For a more detailed analysis of these facts see Simonsen (1937, vol I, pp. 342-4).

14 These credit relations were based on real exchange practices.

15 A detailed analysis of the financial conditions of this period can be found in Levy (1979, pp. 58-83).

16 Until this time the legal tender money of Brazil was gold Peláez and Suzigan(1976, p. 34).

17 For the change of Banco do Brasil from a private to a public bank and vice versa and for the interrelations between this bank and the government see Neuhaus (1975).

18 See Simonse (1937, vol II, pp. 268-70).

19 For the analysis of the movement of monopoly/break of monopoly of the privilege of issuing notes of Banco do Brasil see Neuhaus (1975) and Peláez and Suzigan (1976).

20 England began its attempts to put an end to this trade by the beginning of the XVIII century. Actually, there was a Law of 1831 which forbade slave trade in Brazil. However, the Brazilian government did not enforce this law, and, in real terms, it had no effect on the traffic. Only in 1850 with the so-called Eusébio de Queiroz Law was this traffic really interrupted in actual terms. For an excellent discussion on the extinction of the Brazilian slave trade and of the involvement of England in the whole process see Bethell (1970).

21 There are interesting data on the evolution of prices and the production of sugar in Pernambuco (the biggest sugar producer of Brazil) in the XIX century in Guimarães Neto (1989, p.33).

22 For this point see also Mello (1982, p. 54).

23 See also Delfim Netto (1979, p. 8).

24 Hollanda (1964, II-III book II chapters III, IV, V, VI) presents an excellent description of European immigration in Brazil at this time.

25 For a detailed description of the immigration process see Prado (1976, chapter 19); Furtado (1971, pp. 126-8) and Silva (1976, p. 44).

26 Silva analyses these external loans and their contribution to the financing of new activities in Brazil (Silva, 1976, p.34).

27 The stock exchange was only created in 1917 and was not of great importance in the financial system as a whole.

28 Banks established links with the "comissários" that intermediated the loans to the coffee growers. This intermediation was valid both for national banks and foreign banks (Lima, 1976, p. 298).

29 Aureliano points out the role of intermediation that the "comissários" played in the coffee economy (Aureliano, 1981, p. 110). Following the same argument, Mello observes that there was a certain dependency between the reproduction of the commercial capital and the action of the "comissários" in this economy (Mello, 1982, p. 68).

30 However, Cano (1977), observes that this phenomenon did not last too long; immigration, both of foreigners and people from other regions, put extra pressure on the level of wages, depressing them.

31 This, however, was modified later. The immigration of people from other regions, specially from Northeast, made that São Paulo did not pay the highest wages in the country (Cano, 1977).

32 See Delfim Netto (1979), for the analysis of the three cycles that took place in the coffee economy before 1906.

33 The consequences of these devaluation policies can be observed in Furtado (1971, Chapters XXVIII and XXIX).

34 As we will see this position is not accepted by all the streams of the economic history of Brazil. There was an enormous controversy generated on the question of the origin of the process of industrialization of Brazil. The beginning of the industrialization process only took place after 1929 crisis; in the moment we only observe the intensification of the industrial growth. Mello observes that we only can talk about the process of import substitution and industrialization when the primary export model is overcome, that is, when the dynamic variable of the economy moves from the external market towards the endogenous variable investment (Mello, 1982, p. 92).

35 The analysis of the distribution of the textile industry in the territory gives an idea of the distribution of the industry , not related to the processing of primary products. Textile was one of the most important industrial elements in the Brazilian economy by this time. This fact can be seen analysing the composition of the industrial product of Brazil in the period 1880/1889. The industrial product presented the following composition: 60% Textile Industry, 15% Food, 10% Chemical Products, 4% Wood, 3.5% Clothes, 3% Iron (Prado, 1976, p. 259).

36 We are considering the rate of exchange as the rate of Brazilian

currency to dollar.

37 Versiani & Versiani (1977) maintain a different standpoint. They claim that tariffs played a fundamental role as a protectionist mechanism in the process of industrialisation.

38 There is an excellent discussion on the role that tariffs and protectionist instruments played in the early industrialisation of Brazil in Luz, 1961.

39 Some facilities were provided in obtaining exemption on the import of machinery and some raw material. This could be considered a source of stimulus to the national industry. A law which was reformulated in 1890 which prohibited the exemption of tariffs on goods that had similar produced in Brazil (Dean, 1969, p. 85).

40 "Convênio de Taubaté" was an agreement to maintain artificially the prices of coffee.

41 See Lima (1976, p. 324).

42 For further details on the "Convênio de Taubaté" see Delfim Netto (1979, pp. 48-52).

43 Cardoso (1960) stresses the role which a more developed capitalist production relation played in the industrial growth that took place in São Paulo and which in 1930 began a process of industrialisation.

44 For an analysis of the process of agriculture diversification that took place in São Paulo see Aureliano (1981, pp. 23-28) and Castro (1980, Vol. II, pp. 69-70).

45 Cano (1977, p. 62) observes the tariffs of 1905 as a protectionist mechanism that has expressively contributed to the diversification of the agriculture in São Paulo.

46 This was a consequence of the fact that the main instrument used to maintain the profits of the coffee sector was the exchange rate and at times of crisis inf the coffee sector it tended to divert the demand for imports to the internal demand of industrialised goods.

47 However, the financial system at this time was not very organised and developed. An institution that fulfilled the functions of a Central Bank was created only in 1932 (Caixa de Mobilização Bancária do Banco do Brasil). The role which banks played at this time was limited to the functions of short-term finance. Only in 1937 was an institution created(Carteira de Crédito Agrícola e Industrial do Banco do Brasil) which functioned as a Development Bank and extended long-term credit to industry (Villela & Suzigan, 1975, pp. 32, 60).

48 There are some divergences of opinion on whether the coffee valuation policy was funded by internal credit or not. For this debate see Silber (1977) and Villela and Suzigan (1975, p. 178).

49 This quotation was made from the translation of Furtado (1971) in Furtado (1963).

50 There is an excellent description and analysis of the system of "aviamento" in Santos (1980, chapter 6).

51 By this time, English banks played a major role in the Amazon (Santos, 1980).

52 This analysis is carried on by Cano (1977,pp.88-92); Cano (1985, pp.53-5) and Cano and Guimarães Neto (1986, p. 171).

53 For an analysis of the crisis that the Northeast faced by the end of the XIX century see Lyra (1981).

54 For a detailed analysis of the settlements of the North of Paraná and its great integration with São Paulo see Carvalho (1970).

Part III
The regions under the import substitution process

4 The real side of the regional economies in the import substitution phase

Introduction

This chapter analyses the real side of the regional question in Brazil in the import substitution model. However, as it is almost impossible to disentangle the real and financial spheres of a monetary economy, constant reference will be made to the financial elements of this economy. The chapter is organized as follows: in the first section we will analyse the main changes that were taking place in the Brazilian economy as a whole. This demonstrates that the policies used to intensify the import substitution process played a negative role in the peripheral regions of the country. In a second section we will establish the main structural characterisation of the regional economies of Brazil. After that we will analyse the action of the government in the regional economies. This section will be divided in three main sub-sections: the first one refers to the "implicit policies" carried out by the state in the regions, the second one refers to the explicit policies of the state to the regions and in the last section we will show how the accentuation of the inequalities between the regions led to the necessity of the creation of new directions to the action of the state in the main problematic region.

The beginning of the import substitution process, 1930-1960

Although there were some movements towards industrialisation in Brazil since the second half of the XIX century, they were mostly restricted to traditional industries, such as textiles, foodstuffs etc., and these industries were only appendices to the staple producer sector that had its dynamic determined by the conditions of the external markets from which all the dynamism of the economy was derived. Therefore, this period is still linked to the primary export model, since the dynamic of the economy was still determined by the primary exports of the country.

The Great Depression jointly with the internal conditions, marked the beginning of the import substitution model. According to Mello: "The transition from the 'model of growth toward outside' to the 'model of growth toward inside' in ECLA's paradigm is so absolutely determined: the dynamic of the economy is no longer external demand but endogenous investment. That is, as we used to say, the dynamic centre of the nation is determined inside the nation" (Mello, 1986, p. 92, our translation). Continuing this argument, Tavares notes: "The importance of exports as the main (exogenous) determinant of growth was substituted by the endogenous variable, investment" (Tavares, 1983, p. 34, our translation).

The constraints that the external sector put on the development of the national economy were overcome by quantitative and qualitative changes in the internal economy which resulted in successive changes in the external situation of dependence (Tavares, 1983, p. 41).

The process of industrial concentration in the Centre-South of the country which took place at the end of the XIX century and beginning of the XX century was greatly emphasised by the import substitution model. This was a consequence not only of the coincidence of the geographical dynamism of both primary export and import substitution models and of the natural external economies that the previous industrial concentration had generated, but also the industrialisation policy developed by the government, which strengthened the import substitution model. This resulted in accentuating the already important regional disparities (Tavares, 1983, p. 60), as we shall explain.

In the first period of industrialisation, import substitution took place mainly in the consumer goods sector, some intermediate sectors and some technologically simple capital goods sector. The second phase was one of "intensive" industrialisation or "heavy" industrialisation when import substitution included some technologically sophisticated consumer and capital goods (Mello, 1986, p. 93).

In the first phase, "restricted" industrialisation[1] there were both import substitution in the lighter industries and an increase in the imports of real capital. Thus, the development of the industrialisation process depended on the capacity to import, since industry did not have a developed capital goods producing sector (Aureliano, 1981, p. 94). Therefore, on the one hand, the limitation on the capacity to import created incentives for import substitution and, on the other, it limited its continuation. These two aspects of the role of the external sector were elements relevant to the structural changes which took place in the Brazilian economy during this period.

The conditions that allowed the beginning of the process of industrialisation by import substitution were described in Chapter 3 and are mainly related to the external constraint of the economy and to the programmes designed to stabilise the internal income, especially through devaluation of the national currency and purchase by the government of the coffee stock. In the 1930s, these policies were maintained in such a way as to allow the continuation of industrialisation.

After 1931, the monetary policy had clearly an expansionist character and with the revision of tariffs in the same year, the economic policy acquired a protectionist character (Aureliano, 1981, p. 131). During this period, the policy of protection of the coffee crops continued to be fundamental in the protection of internal income, which allowed the expansion of internal demand for domestically produced goods (Aureliano, 1981, p. 129). This period was marked by strong governmental intervention in the economy and this was reflected in the creation of new governmental organisations[2].

The structural changes in the Brazilian economy during the 30s can be observed in Table III.1 and Table III.2, where the increasing participation of the industrial sector is highlighted and the loss of agricultural production participation makes clear the new pattern of the economy.

Table III.1

Brazil: Average Yearly Growth Rates of the Economy, 1920-1939
(%)

	1920-29	1929-33	1922-39
Production by Sector			
Agriculture	4.0	2.5	1.6
Export Agr.	7.5	3.7	1.1
Industry	2.8	2.9	11.2

	1919	1939
Composition of Physical Output	100.0	100.0
Agriculture	79.0	57.0
Industry	21.0	43.0

Source: Villela and Suzigan (1975, p. 162).

The analysis of the composition of the industrial sector gives an idea of the magnitude of the structural changes that were taking place by that time. Analysing Table III.2 it is easily observed that the main dynamic sectors are the ones that are relatively new in the economy and which correspond to products that were previously imported, that is, industrialisation was really taking place in order to substitute imports, especially the ones to sectors that did not present complex technological processes[3].

Table III.2

Brazil: Yearly Rates of Growth of Industrial Output by Sector, 1933-1939

(%)

	1933-1939
Mining	8.1
Manufacturing	11.3
Non-Metallic Min.	19.9
Metallurgy	20.4
Paper and Cardboard	22.0
Leather Products	2.7
Chemical and Pharmaceutical	10.6
Perfumes, Soap and Candles	15.7
Textiles	11.1
Clothing and Footwear	9.8
Food Products	1.9
Beverages	8.4
Tobacco	5.2
Total	11.2

Source: Villela e Suzigan (1975, p. 194).

This rapid change in the structure of the economy put extra pressures on the financial institutions, since the financial needs of an agrarian economy are fundamentally different from the needs of an industrial economy when it is undergoing intensive changes to its structure. So in the agrarian export model, banks and the "comissários" were mainly responsible for financing production, and this did not constrain the economy because short term credit supplied by the banks was appropriated to the needs of this activity. However, the intense industrialisation that took place in the 1930s created new demands for new schemes of financing on a longer term basis. There was no developed capital market. Therefore, the banks had to cope with the burden of this new demand for credit. As Studart (1995) has explained fully this absence of a funding mechanism means that growth will leave banks in a progressively less liquid situation. As a consequence of these pressures, in 1932 the Caixa de Mobilização Bancária (CAMOB) was created within the Banco do Brasil. This institution acted mainly as a lender of last resort and its main objective was to avoid insolvency crises in the banking system. According to Villela and Suzigan, "This was the first attempt to supply medium- and long-term credit. However, the banks made little use of the CAMOB facilities" (Villela and Suzigan, 1975, p. 164).

A further attempt to extend credit on a long term basis was brought about by the change in legislation that allowed the Carteira de Crédito Agrícola e Industrial (CREAI) of Banco do Brasil to lend on a longer term basis. As Villela and Suzigan point out: "Although the country was still in need of a real development bank, the establishment of CREAI represented an important step forward in the country's financial markets. The areas covered by this new institution included: financing for interharvest periods, for acquisition of agricultural machinery and livestock, for purchase of raw materials, and for improvement of industrial machinery. Initially, CREAI could not participate in the new industrial establishment. This was later changed, however, and CREAI was enabled to finance new basic industries such as pulp and paper, aluminium, and steel" (Villela and Suzigan, 1975, pp. 169-70).

The structure of the agricultural sector was also undergoing rapid changes. During the period 1925-1943, coffee lost its importance in terms of the value of the main crops and cotton production gained relevance. This could have meant a recovery for the cotton producing regions, especially the Northeast, but this was not verified. As cotton began to present good prices, its culture was expanded to São Paulo where it assumed the role of a dynamic culture. The importance of cotton during this period can be observed in Table III.3. Another important process that took place during this period relates to the increasing importance of crops which were directed toward the internal markets. This can also be observed in Table III.3.

Table III.3
Brazil: Value of Agricultural Output by
Principal Crops, 1925-29/1939-43
%; Average for Period

Product	1925-29	1932-36	1939-43
Cotton	5.9	14.0	21.6
Rice	5.2	6.7	11.0
Cocoa	1.4	1.8	2.2
Coffee	48.0	29.5	16.1
Sugar Cane	3.5	5.7	7.5
Beans	5.4	3.8	5.5
Tobacco	2.9	2.6	2.2
Manioc	4.7	6.8	7.0
Corn	16.3	15.9	16.0
Wheat	0.9	0.8	1.3
Others	5.8	12.4	9.6
Total	100.0	100.0	100.0

Source: Villela and Suzigan (1975, p. 171).

The main effect of the Second World War was a positive balance of trade during the period. These surpluses were due to two reasons. The first one referred to the physical restriction of imports caused by the condition of war, and the second one referred to the increase in the international prices of the export products of Brazil (Villela and Suzigan, 1975, p. 201).

During this period, the government maintained a policy of free exchange rates (Villela and Suzigan, 1975, p. 210). This maintained the rate of exchange at its level during the 1930s. Considering that the rate of inflation did not follow the same tendency as the rate of exchange, the exchange rate remained strong. This was possible because war conditions created disguised quantitative constraints on imports. This can be observed in Furtado: "Between 1939 and 1944, for instance, import prices increased 64 per cent, whereas the domestic price level rose 98 per cent. In the following period, the disparity continued to be marked. Between 1944 and 1949, import prices rose 36 per cent whereas the domestic price level increased 70 per cent" (Furtado, 1963, p. 237).

The valuation of the exchange rate would be fundamental to the recovery of the economy, which during the war suffered an enormous constraint on its capacity to import the so necessary capital goods. This restriction was reflected in the reduction of the rhythm of growth of the economy during the war (Villela and Suzigan, 1975, p. 201).

During the period that we are analysing, there are basically three phases of the exchange policy which are fundamental to comprehend the acceleration of industrialisation in Brazil. In the period 1946-47, imports were free and the rate of exchange was at a level above that before the war. During the period 1947-53, a rationing of exchange was introduced, and imports were licensed. This system had an extremely restrictive character in relation to non-essential imported goods. During the period 1953-57, five categories of imports were established, and according to the category of the goods there was an over tax which had to be paid on the exchange rate (Ianni, 1971, p. 118 and Tavares, 1983, pp. 70-1).

These three phases of the exchange policy had an extraordinary effect on the import substitution process: since the main limit to import substitution was the absence of an internal sector that could produce capital goods, the exchange policies limited the internal supply of goods that had internal substitutes and made the import of capital goods cheaper. In this sense, Furtado observes: "The acceleration in the rate of growth in the postwar economy of Brazil was fundamentally connected with the exchange policy and the type of selective controls imposed on imports. By keeping the cost of imported equipment low while prices of domestically produced manufacturers were rising, there was obviously an increase in the marginal efficiency of industrial investments" (Furtado, 1963, pp. 246-7).

This policy had a concentrating character, as Furtado observes: "The relative decline in the prices of imported products, instead of benefiting every sector equally, was concentrated in the industrial sector for the simple reason that industry was the largest consumer of exchange (Furtado, 1963, p. 245). Later on, Furtado will observe, in his famous report, the regional concentrating character of this policy.

During 1951-1955, a new phase in the participation of the State in the economy began. Contrary to the post-war period, when the state reduced its intervention in the economy[4], this phase is marked by the intense intervention of the State in the economy (Ianni, 1971, p. 113). During 1951-1952, there was a concentrated import of capital goods which allowed a further diversification of the industrial sector and allowed the spread of the import substitution process to new boundaries (Tavares, 1983, p. 61). During 1947-1954, the public sector was responsible for 22 per cent of the Gross Formation of Fixed Capital (Bielschowsky, 1975, p. 40)[5].

In 1955, industrialisation by import substitution reached a new stage. It passed from the period of restricted or lighter industrialisation, when the dependence of the country from the imports of capital goods was almost total, to the stage when industrialisation reached this sector and some technologically sophisticated sectors. The mark of this period is the Target

Plan (1956) which was an audacious plan of intervention in the economy that had the principal objective of overcoming the main structural bottlenecks to the continuation and intensification of the import substitution process (Lessa, 1981, p. 19). According to Lessa, the Target Plan "Constituted the most solid conscious decision in favour of industrialisation in the economic history of the country" (Lessa, 1981, p. 27).

The main actions of the plan were centred in the direct government investment in basic sectors, such as energy, transport, steel, oil and other intermediary industries. Those sectors were not satisfactorily developed by the private sectors and began to represent a bottleneck to industrialisation (Lessa, 1981, p. 28). Public investment in transport and energy increased in the early 1950s, since these sectors in this period were largely observed at the time as actual bottlenecks (Lessa, 1981, p. 31).

However, the conception of the State investing in intermediary sectors of the productive structure was new, at least at the levels of the Target Plan. This intervention was absolutely necessary since the private sector gave no indication that it would invest in those sectors, nor did it have a structure to invest. So the only sector of the economy which could undertake the responsibility for the development of those essential sectors to industrialisation was the State (Lessa, 1981, p. 32)[6]. It is important to note that public investment during this period (1955-62) reached 25 per cent of the total gross formation of fixed capital of the country.

The financial side of the import substitution process

The extreme changes observed in the real side of the economy during the import substitution process were not followed or preceded by proportional changes in the financial mechanisms of the economy.

The banking system, which was the most important element in financing the productive process in the primary export model[7], was still the main support of the financing process in the import substitution model. However the needs of the economy had changed and this created an extra constraint to the continuation of this process. When the import substitution process reached its intensive phase, this problem was further accentuated, since the necessity for long term loans became more acute as the productive process lengthened and became more capital intensive[8].

As the banking system, due to its own characteristics, operates mainly on a short term basis, and as the main financial mechanism of the Brazilian economy in the 1950s was the banking system, the economy suffered an almost absolute constraint because of the need for long term loans and the absence of institutions able to supply those loans. As was observed previously, the CREAI since 1937 was able to extend credit on a long term basis, but this was not enough for the needs of the economy[9].

The transition from the extensive phase of the import substitution process to its intensive phase was supposed to be followed or preceded by structural changes in the financial system of the economy. However, when the economy passed from its agrarian export model to its extensive import substitution model this did not take place. So, the financial constraint which was a serious problem in the extensive phase became stronger during this new phase[10]. Basically, the mechanisms used to finance the Target Plan and all the structural changes that it caused were the inflationary mechanism and foreign capital (Lessa, 1981, pp. 33, 56)[11].

Thus, it is easily observed that the financial system of the country was not capable of allowing the continuation of the import substitution process by itself. Instead of creating new institutional arrangements that would give to the system the power to finance the industrialisation, mechanisms were created to make the enterprises and the government generate internal finance[12]. Based on those mechanisms the industrialisation was carried on, although in a very constrained way and generating an enormous series of imbalances in the whole economy.

To relieve the constraint the Banco Nacional de Desenvolvimento Econômico (BNDE) was created in 1952, a development bank that provided long term credit mainly to government industrial and infra-structural projects[13]. In 1952, a regional development bank was also created: the Banco do Nordeste do Brasil (BNB), which was to act as both a development and a commercial bank[14]. The creation of these two development banks was a recognition of the lack of adequate financial mechanisms was an important element in the constraints to industrialisation.

While the Brazilian economy was undergoing rapid and radical structural changes during this period it was observed that these transformations did not find domestic financial devices which allowed them to continue, and the external financial mechanism would not allow the development of the process at an adequate speed. The only way of overcoming the financial constraint was to generate new mechanisms which allowed the internal finance of the process. This was exactly what had been done since the beginning of the process of import substitution through government policies[15]. Tavares observes: "The incapacity of some of Latin American countries and, especially, of the Brazilian economy in establishing a financial structure capable of supporting and solving the appointed problems between the intersectoral transference of resources into the private sector and from this to the public sector has led the economic system to create hidden transference mechanisms, in particular via violent changes in the system of relative prices" (Tavares, 1983, p. 129, our translation).

These mechanisms, which lead to a change in relative prices and consequently to an increase in the margin of profits of the sectors that the governmental policy stimulated, were present in the majority of government policies. The more frequent ways of changing relative prices, as was previously mentioned, were through the exchange mechanism and inflation (Suzigan and Pereira, 1972, p. 49)[16].

Therefore, an analysis of the impact of the financial system on the regions must be undertaken. However, besides this, the way the policies of internal financing, through changes in relative prices, affected the regions is also relevant in order to assess how the internal financial mechanisms affected the regions differently. Thus, not only was the financial sector non-neutral, but the forms that were used by the State to increase the internal power of the private sector to finance industrialisation process was also not neutral. We will, thus, observe the effects of "implicit" regional policies which tended to accentuate a regional structure which by this time was already extremely uneven.

The characterisation of the regional economies in the period 1930-1960

The process of concentration of the dynamism of the economic activity in the Centre-South of the country, which we observed in Chapter 3 and which had its basis in the period before to the Great Depression, continued its pattern and accentuated its tendencies in the following years. To fully understand this phenomenon, an analysis of the general behaviour of the Brazilian economy during the period and its implications at the regional level is required. The uneven pattern of regional development was accentuated mainly as a consequence of certain policies adopted by the State with the explicit aim of intensifying and making possible the continuation of the import substitution process. The consequences of these policies were, obviously, not evenly distributed on a geographical basis and so its effects were concentrated in the regions which had a still more developed industrial basis. Our main aim now is to analyse the regional impact of these policies.

It is observed that countries which have industrialised through processes of import substitution tended to present more intense regional disparities, since the way that the import substitution processes tend to develop leads to industrial concentration and to the generation of "cumulative processes" which cannot be reversed by "natural forces". This element is observed as a consequence of the fact that in this kind of process the first goods to have their imports substituted by domestic production are consumer goods, and the production of these goods tends to be concentrated in regions which present a more developed consumer market. So, the location of such industries is determined more by the location of the market than by any other reason. But as the substituting industries are located there, they give dynamism to the economy of the region and tend to extend still more their internal market and so generate extra pressure for the location of new industries in that region. When the process of import substitution reaches the capital goods producing sector, a new element is introduced and generates still more concentration in the economic activity. Since the consumer goods industry is concentrated in the region that presents the most dynamic internal market and generates a cumulative growth within it, the capital goods producing industry will also locate in this region. Therefore, the import substitution process tends to intensify regional industrial concentration (PIMES, 1984, Vol.1, pp. 211-2).

The pattern of concentration of economic activity in specific regions can be demonstrated, in the first instance, by looking at the regional domestic income of different regions and their specific patterns through time[17]. From the analysis carried out in Chapter 3 and Table III.1.s.a., we see that concentration in the period before 1939 was much more intense than in the following period. However, given the intensity of concentration that had already taken place in the period before 1939, any small change towards further concentration had immense significance. In 1939, the Southeast participated with 63.22 per cent of the total income of the country, while the North only participated with 2.64 per cent and the Northeast with 16.71 per cent. The concentration was further limited at the regional level: São Paulo was responsible for the generation of 31.11 per cent of the total income of the country[18].

The tendency towards regional income concentration was even more accentuated in this phase and reached its maximum level, during the analysed period, in the middle of the 1950s. In 1953-1954, the North region was responsible for the generation of only 1.67 per cent of the total income of the country. The Northeast reached its minimum share in 1955, generating only 12.97 per cent. The South and Centre-West had reached their minimum levels previously, but their economies suffered different impacts from the development of the Southeast than the traditional peripheral regions (the North and Northeast). On the other hand, the Southeast reached its maximum level of concentration in 1954, being responsible for 66.53 per cent of the total income of the country.

Although a slight tendency toward deconcentration of the regional income is observed in the second half of the 1950s, this tendency was far from being capable of recovering the levels of the 1930s[19]. Moreover, the relatively rapid decline in the participation of the Southeast was not followed with the same speed by the State of São Paulo. This decline was much slower than that observed in the Southeast as a whole, which lets us assume that the decline in the Southeast was more the consequence of a decline in other states than of the most representative state in the region in terms of concentration of income. Some authors (Andrade and Haddad, 1974 and Semple and Gauthier, 1972) point out that the pattern of the differences in the rates of growth of the regional economies of Brazil present a U shape. That is, they are divergent in an initial period but after that they begin to converge. However, other authors observe that this tendency is not valid over a longer period (Magalhães, 1979 and PIMES, 1984). If we do so, these authors state that we would observe a S on its side. That is, at first there is divergence, then convergence and then divergence again. This can be observed in Table III.2.s.a.; São Paulo, which in 1939 was responsible for the generation of 49.21 pre cent of the total income of the Southeast, was by the 1960s generating 55.49 per cent of the regional income. In the second half of the 1950s, the tendency towards concentration of the income of the region in this state was accentuated. Hence the decline in the participation of the Southeast in the national income of the country can be better explained as a consequence of a rearrangement of the Southeast's internal stadual structure and the loss in importance of other states than as a consequence of a homogenous decrease in the participation of the region as a whole. The opposite regional pattern is observed in the peripheral regions: in the Southeast we observed a tendency toward concentration of the production in the most dynamic state, but in the periphery (Northeast) this tendency was in the opposite direction. The states in which the economic activity of the region concentrated (Pernambuco and Bahia) and which were responsible for the generation of more than 50 per cent of the total income of the region lost their position in terms of their participation in the generation of regional income. The minimum level for Pernambuco was reached in 1960 and, in that year, it had a participation that was still smaller than the one of 1939. The pattern of Bahia is, however, different. It tended to present a more erratic pattern and increased its participation in the regional income during this period. It probably absorbed part of the decrease in Pernambuco's participation. Some authors note that the convergence observed in the second half of the 1950s could be the result of a more intense growth of the agricultural income of the peripheral regions, such as the North and Northeast (PIMES, 1984, vol.1, p. 30).

The regional per capita income, however, presented a much more intense level of concentration. The analysis of this variable highlights the condition of the Northeast as the main problematic region of the country. Table III.4.s.a. presents the figures on the participation of each region in the national per capita income. In this table, again, we can observe that the per capita income of the Northeast suffered a drastic fall in the period 1947-1955, recovering its levels in the period 1956-1960. However, this cannot be observed as a redistribution of levels of the per capita income in terms of the main central region and the main traditional peripheral region, since the participation of São Paulo in the national per capita income remains relatively stable throughout all the analysed period, showing that economic activity still remained concentrated in this state and that this pattern had not changed.

Another important element to observe, which will be fundamental to our analysis of the financial system, is the stability of the pattern of growth in different regions. In order to do so we have analysed the behaviour of the real income of the North, Northeast and Centre-South[20]. Figure 1 shows the pattern of growth of the real income of the North, Northeast and Centre-South. The pattern of the rates of growth of the real income of these three regions can be seen in Figures 2 and 3. Figure 2 shows the behaviour of the rate of growth of real income in the North as opposed to the Centre-South, and Figure 3 shows the pattern of the rate of growth of the real income of the Northeast as opposed to the Centre-South. These figures show the comparative instability of the pattern of growth in the traditional peripheral regions. This impression is confirmed by the analysis of the variances of the rate of growth of the different regions which were calculated based on Table III.3.s.a. The calculated variances are: North: 0.0100; Northeast: 0.0024 and Centre-South: 0.0007[21]. The coefficients of variance are: North: 0.1612; Northeast: 0.0428 and Centre-South: 0.0120. The analysis of the instability of each region is fundamental in order to comprehend the behaviour of agents in what refers to their liquidity preferences in each region (see Chapter 2)[22]. The elements that lead to this intense instability will be analysed later on in the section on the dynamic sectors of each regional economy.

However, to understand the regional problem, we need to analyse the structure of each region to establish what were the dynamic sectors and the sectoral composition of each region. In this way we can observe the divergence and convergence of structural changes in different regional economies.

The sectoral composition of the regional economies

Agriculture The regional share of the total agricultural income can be observed in Table III.5.s.a. This table shows that the Southeast concentrates a great part of the agricultural product in the country. The concentration figures, however, do not just refer to the regions. If the State of São Paulo is separated from the Southeast, it will be observed that it was responsible for generating of more than 50 per cent of the regional agricultural income during the entire period (Table III.6.s.a.). São Paulo on its own generated an agricultural income larger than all the other regions of the country, including the rest of the Southeast.

Agriculture activity is also very concentrated in the Northeast, in the states of Bahia and Pernambuco. Together, these states generated almost 50 per cent of the total agricultural income of the region. The position of Pernambuco, though, was reducing, while the position of Bahia was advancing in a more or less stable pattern, reaching a peak in 1954.

In terms of patterns presented, it can be observed (Table III.5.s.a.) that agricultural activity intensified during the period 1939-1947. During this period, the Southeast and São Paulo increased their share of the total agricultural income, while the share of the North, Northeast and Centre-West was decreasing. This shift in the contribution made by agricultural activity persisted throughout the period in the traditional peripheral regions (North and Northeast). Only in the period 1959-1960 did the Northeast show a significant increase in its contribution; this was mainly due to favourable conditions in the external markets for sugar during this period (Furtado, 1964).

However, if we observe the figures for the Southeast and São Paulo, we can see that there was a relatively marked falling back in the position of the Southeast after 1949 and this regression reached São Paulo in 1952 and transformed its pattern into a declining one. This movement of deconcentration occurred in the so-called "new" peripheral areas, certain areas of the South (especially the State of Paraná) and of the Centre-West. In the South, we observe a gain in position compared even to 1939. The Centre-west, however, exceeded its figure of 1939 during the period 1953-1955, but after this period a relative decline can be observed.

Nevertheless, the dynamism of these new peripheral areas was mainly determined and stimulated by the economy of São Paulo, by the markets of this region or by the infrastructure that was available in regions close to this state[23].

The concentration of agricultural activity observed in the Southeast is attributed more to the extremely dynamic agriculture of this region, especially of São Paulo, than to the stagnant character of agriculture in other regions[24].

The agriculture of the Northeast was considered the main limitation to industrialisation in this region by the GTDN (Working Group for the Development of the Northeast). However, this is challenged by Castro (Castro, 1980, vol. II), who shows that during the period 1950-1960 agriculture was a highly dynamic activity in the Northeast, presenting a rate of growth of 6.1 per cent in real terms. Noting that the growth of the population of the region was 2.2 per cent during the same period, he observes that this accentuated growth was also reflected in the per capita agricultural product[25].

The contribution of the net agriculture production in the total income of the regions (Table III.7.s.a.) shows that for the periphery, as a whole, its income was heavily based in the agricultural sector[26]. Furthermore, except for the North, these seems to be a tendency for this activity to be concentrated in all peripheral regions (in terms of the composition of the regional income). Table III.7.s.a shows that the Northeast and the South, by the 1960s, contributed a larger share of agricultural income to the total regional income than in 1939. The North showed a stronger trend in reducing its share of agricultural income in the total regional income and this trend was followed by the Centre-West, which, although showing a decline in the pattern of its shared agricultural income in its total income, was the region which showed the largest contribution of agricultural income to its total income during the entire period analysed.

Therefore, the periphery as a whole presented a strong agriculture participation in its sectorial income composition along with the services sector.

Industry An analysis of the industrial concentration which took place in the country with the process of import substitution is fundamental to the understanding of the general concentrating pattern of the economy. As the main economic policies were directed toward intensification of the import substitution process, there was greater concentration of industrial production. The pattern of different regional industrial sectors and their contribution to the total net industrial product of the country can be seen in Table III.8.s.a.[27].

According to Table III.8.s.a. the process of industrial concentration in the Southeast extended over all the period of import substitution in both its phases: "restricted industrialisation" (1930-1955) and "heavy industrialisation" (1955-1960). The trend followed by the net industrial product in the Southeast was of an increasing concentration which reached its maximum level in 1955, showing a slight decrease in the following two years and recovering the concentration dynamic after 1957[28]. The minimum level of concentration shows by the Southeast was in 1939 at 71.74 per cent of the total industrial income, reaching a maximum of 77.65 per cent in 1955.

Contrary to what was taking place in the Southeast, which sometimes showed slight trends toward deconcentration of net industrial production, São Paulo showed a constant pattern of industrial concentration. São Paulo's contribution to the industrial production of Brazil rose steadily from 36.4 per cent in 1939 to 54.3 per cent in 1960. So, this state was solely responsible for a larger part of the industrial production than the whole of the rest of the country. In intra-regional terms also, São Paulo's position grew steadily, from representing 50.71 per cent of the net industrial product of the Southeast in 1939 to 70.07 per cent in 1960 (Table III.9.s.a.).

The trend observed in the peripheral regions is quite different from the one observed in the Southeast and especially in São Paulo. The North showed a strong decrease in its contribution to the total net industrial production. This region reached its minimum participation in 1951, with only 0.91 per cent of the total net industrial income. After this, the trend is erratic, but, in 1960, the participation of this region was still below the levels of 1939. The Northeast, which in 1939 was responsible for the generation of 12.09 per cent of the total net industrial production, showed a marked decrease in its participation to 7.6 per cent in 1954. A small recovery in the participation of the region was due to the development in Bahia of an industrial sector related to the production of oil and its derivatives which gave extra dynamism to this state at the end of the 50s (Magalhães, 1983, p. 266)[29].

The South showed a more or less stable participation in the total industrial income and the participation of the Centre-West fell sharply to a low of 0.44 per cent in 1954.

The participation of the industrial sector in the total income of each region can be seen in Table III.10.s.a. The Southeast is the region where the industrial sector is most important. And moreover, these figures show that this region showed a strong tendency to intensify the participation of the industrial sector. São Paulo showed a stronger tendency toward the industrial concentration of its activities than the Southeast as a whole, and great part of the industrial profile of the Southeast is due to the influence of São Paulo. In 1939, the industrial sector of this State contributed 22.38 per cent of the total income of the state and, in 1960, this contribution grew to 33.72 per cent. In the Centre-West the industrial sector was relatively less important than in other regions in terms of generation of regional industrial income and, in the South, the contribution of the industrial sector was more stable.

The growing importance of the industrial sector makes it necessary to look at the internal composition of this sector. We will focus on two regions: The Northeast and Southeast. The former because it is an example of a traditional peripheral region and is considered the main problematic region in Brazil; the Southeast because it is the central, dynamic region and the leading industrial region in the country.

Tables III.4 and III.5 show the regional composition and the participation of each region in the value of the industrial transformation. These figures establish the relevance of each sector in each region and give a more precise idea of what a certain level of contribution to the total industrial income means. We can see that the industries of the traditional periphery are mainly the so-called traditional industries, that is, industries which produce non-durable consumer goods and some intermediate goods. The importance of the capital goods and durable consumer goods sectors is negligible for the periphery throughout the period analysed and this sector is also not very representative of the industry of São Paulo. But when the country entered the period of "heavy" or "intensive" industrialisation, especially after 1955, this sector gained importance. However, as both tables show, this sector was concentrated mainly in the central region.

With relation to the participation of the periphery in non-durable consumer goods industries, we can see that it lost its position, and this loss of position was particularly significant to the Northeast, whose industrial basis mainly was concentrated in this group of industries (Table III.4), and which was the region that lost its position more strongly in the national sphere. São Paulo, on the other hand, went up the scale in this group of industries. Its participation rose from 37.60 per cent to 48.69 per cent of the national value of the industrial transformation in the non-durable goods industrial sector[30]. This sector in the peripheral regions was strongly linked to the natural available resources of those economies (Magalhães, 1983, p. 267).

The same effect observed for the non-durable consumer goods sector can be observed for the durable and capital goods sector. In this sector, we have the periphery losing position throughout the analysed period and São Paulo consolidating its position as leader in this sector. This was partly due to the policies which encouraged import substitution in the capital goods producer sector, which was mainly concentrated in the Southeast. This is a typical example of the policies present in the Target Plan. In addition, there were some cumulative processes (mentioned above) which tended to concentrate this new industry in the Southeast, since their main market was located there.

A further incentive for the installation of new industries in the Southeast, especially in São Paulo, was the role of economies of scale which this region presented to the industrial sector in general and to the capital goods sector in particular[31].

The only sector where the periphery gained position was the intermediate goods sector, and this occurred probably as a consequence of the natural basis of its economy. That is, these industries were closely linked to the natural resources available in those regions.

Table III.4

Regional Structure of the Industrial Sector, according to the Value of Industrial Transformation

(%)

Industry	Year	North	Northeast	São Paulo
non-durable consumer goods	1939	47.92	89.47	62.32
	1949	57.56	85.30	55.51
	1959	57.54	67.31	39.63
intermediate goods	1939	49.43	10.06	25.96
	1949	39.76	14.16	33.68
	1959	41.43	31.20	35.60
capital and durable consumer goods	1939	2.65	0.47	11.72
	1949	2.48	0.54	10.81
	1959	1.03	1.49	24.77

Source: Cano (1985, p. 96). Data computed from the census.

Table III.5
Participation of each Region in the Total Value of the Industrial Transformation
(%)

	Year	North	Northeast	São Paulo
Non-durable consumer goods	1939	0.79	14.46	37.60
	1949	0.70	12.82	44.65
	1959	1.19	10.26	48.69
Intermediate Goods	1939	2.12	4.24	40.85
	1949	0.93	4.07	51.89
	1959	1.03	5.66	52.02
Capital and durable consumer goods	1939	0.45	0.77	72.40
	1949	0.24	0.65	69.71
	1959	0.06	0.62	82.03

Some comments on the structural differences between the industry of the Northeast and the industry of São Paulo can be done based on Table III.6.

Table III.6
Comparison Between the Industry of the Northeast and the Industry of São Paulo

Indicator	Ratio Northeast/São Paulo				
	1907	1919	1939	1949	1959
(a)Number of Establishment	1.35	0.62	0.57	0.73	0.59
(b)Number of Employees	1.59	0.81	0.51	0.44	0.27
(c)Value of the Production	1.02	0.51	0.23	0.19	0.14
(d)Average Size(b)/(a)	1.18	1.29	0.89	0.61	0.46
(e)Productivity (c)/(b)	0.60	0.62	0.44	0.37	0.48

Source: Magalhães (1983, p. 264). Values calculated based on Census data.

From Table III.6, we can see an enormous reduction in the number of establishments of the Northeast in relation to São Paulo if we compare the series beginning in 1907. However, if we take the number of employees into account, this tendency is even more marked. A comparison between the value of the industrial production of the Northeast and São Paulo also shows also a tremendous concentration in the latter. The average size of the establishments shows that those in São Paulo tend to be bigger than the ones in the Northeast, which allowed them to incorporate economies of scale more easily. And, finally, we can see that the productivity of the industry of the Northeast was at much lower levels than the productivity of the industry of São Paulo. Table III.6 shows that this is not a new phenomenon: this fact was observed since 1907 and was still more accentuated during the period 1939-1949.

Finally, it is important to analyse the capacity of each regional industry to absorb labour. This is shown in Table III.7. There is an asymmetry between the industry of the Southeast and the industry of Northeast. While the industry of the Northeast has a great capacity to absorb labour per value of industrial transformation, the industry of the Southeast has a lower level of employment generation. This may be a consequence of the structure of the industrial sector of each region. The Northeast specialises in more labour intensive industries, whereas the Southeast specialises in more capital intensive industries. This can also be a consequence of the technology adopted in each region and/or the size of industrial establishments (Baer and Geiger, 1976, p. 21)[32]. As was observed in Tables III.4 and III.5, the industrial sector of the Northeast was concentrated in non-durable consumer goods. This sector is normally more labour intensive than the capital goods producing sector and the durable goods producing sector. On the other hand, as was shown in Table III.6, the average size of establishments in the Northeast is considerably smaller than those of São Paulo. This factor partly explains the larger absorption of labour by the industry of the Northeast.

Table III.7

Regional Distribution of the Value of Industrial Transformation (VIT) and the Employment (EMP)

	1940		1950		1960	
	VIT	EMP	VIT	EMP	VIT	EMP
North	1.1	1.5	0.7	1.4	1.1	1.1
Northeast	10.9	18.3	9.5	16.8	7.7	12.5
Southeast	73.6	65.5	75.6	66.4	77.9	70.4
South	14.0	14.1	13.7	14.9	12.5	15.1
Centre-West	0.4	0.6	0.5	0.5	0.8	0.9

Source: Baer and Geiger (1976, p. 20).

These elements characterise the regional diversity of the industrial sectors and give a general idea of their evolution during the analysed period. Thus, on the one hand, we have a region which has more diversified industrial production and in which was concentrated an enormous part of the industrial production of the country. This region was also the most dynamic and suffered fundamental changes in its productive structure and in the composition of its industrial sector. This process of diversification coincided with the installation of new industrial sectors which were more capital intensive and had a longer period of maturation. These radical changes put extra pressures on financing the structural changes which were occurring in this region. On the other hand, we have the peripheral regions, whose industries were linked strongly to traditional industries, mainly to the non-durable goods industries and intermediary goods industries. These industries put less pressure on the financial sphere of these economies and, as the changes that these economies were undergoing were much more related to the loss of participation in their industrial sector, the pressures on the financial mechanisms were weaker than those exerted by the central economy. However, this marks mainly a differential of intensity of the needs of finance, since there was growth in peripheral economies and consequently there was a need for further finance to cope with the financial needs that growth created in those economies.

The ways by which the economy of the Southeast was financed and the ways that were found to try to overcome the financial limits to the process of industrialisation were one of the chief factors responsible for the weakness of the peripheral economies and for the divergence in structural changes in the two economies. Thus, this could be considered a cumulative process in which causes and effects are difficult to differentiate and interact in a vicious circle.

Services The income generated by the service sector is also very concentrated in the central region. However, this is not reflected in a pattern similar to that of industrial income. The region which most generated income in this sector was the East. It is followed by the South and then by the Northeast. However, the degree of concentration in the Southeast was smaller than the one observed in relation to industrial production (Table III.11.s.a.)

The service sector plays a substantial role in the generation of income in Brazil. This sector is responsible for around 50 per cent of the total income of the country, as can be seen in Table III.12.s.a. The North, followed by the Southeast, is the region which that shows the strongest participation in the total income generated nationally by this sector (Table III.12.s.a.). It can also be seen that the greatest part of the income generated by this sector inside the Northeast in states of Pernambuco and Bahia. This follows the general trend of concentration observed with the other sectors. However, São Paulo, in spite of generating almost 50 per cent of the income of the service sector in the Southeast, does not show the same levels of concentration observed in the agriculture sector and especially in the industrial sector, as can be seen in Table III.13.s.a. Although the loss of importance of this sector to São Paulo, both in terms of the participation of this state in the total income generated by the service sector and of the importance of this sector in the total income generated in the state, it is necessary to point out that this is the more important sector to São Paulo in terms of generation of income. Compare Tables III.7.s.a, III.10.s.a. and III.12.s.a., in order to observe the stadual composition of income. The same thing can be observed in the other two states analysed (Pernambuco and Bahia).

In terms of the state's participation in the regional income generated by the services sector, we observe a tendency toward a decline in the participation of São Paulo and Bahia. However, Pernambuco advances its position in regional terms (Table III.12.s.a.).

It is normally assumed that the large contribution made by the service sector to the generation of income in developing countries and in less developed regions is a result of the needs to absorb labour in such economies. However, Baer and Geiger, observing the composition of the income and the sectorial absorption of labour, pointed out that this sector does not absorb a disproportionate amount of labour in relation to its capacity to generate income (Baer and Geiger, 1976, p. 47). This can be observed in Table III.14.s.a.

Therefore, we note that during the period analysed, the peripheral economies presented a composition of their incomes that was very close to the analysis which normally deals with centre/periphery models. That is, the periphery has a strong participation in its income of the agricultural sector whereas the centre has its dynamic sector focused on the industrial sector. However, agriculture in the centre was also very dynamic and made a much greater contribution to the total agricultural income than the periphery.

Inter-regional and international trade

The idea of the regional economies forming a semi-isolated "archipelago", in Brazil, was largely acceptable until the beginning of the XX century. In the 1920s, however, this situation began to change and opened up a new phase for economic relations between the regions. This new period is characterised by the commercial integration of the regional economies[33]. This new phase of the regional dynamic is fundamental to understanding the process of industrial concentration in São Paulo and of the decline of the traditional industries in the traditional periphery, which will be shown in this section. This phenomenon is relevant to the analysis of the distribution of finance and to the analysis of the latter sections, when we will deal specifically with the behaviour of the financial sector, because the outflows/inflows caused by the external sector of the regional economies are an important element in understanding the regional distribution of finance in the country and are also important to the analysis of the money multiplier in each region. Furthermore, when the external sector has the power to change the regional sectoral composition of income, this analysis becomes significant, as the new financial needs generated by this new sectoral composition are historically linked to the development of the external sector and to its dynamic.

Interregional commerce gained importance in the Brazilian economy only after the 1920s. As Guimarães Neto observes, before the 1920s, this was responsible for only a quarter of the total commerce of Brazil (Guimarães Neto, 1989, p. 84). The importance of interregional commerce was even less when we take into account the more remote regions, because distance and the higher cost of transportation between regions created substantive barriers to commerce (Cano, 1985, p. 154).

Since the beginning of the XX century, industry in São Paulo began to present rates of capital accumulation which were above the capacity of its own markets. This meant that, at some time, this economy would need to look for external markets for its products. The First World War, and the limits it imposed on imports, was a fundamental turning point in the relations of São Paulo with the rest of the country, when São Paulo began to extend its markets toward interregional commerce (Cano, 1985, pp. 158-9).

This tendency to over-accumulate by industry in São Paulo was still more accentuated in the 1920s. The solution to this problem was found in the markets of other regions. Increase in the interregional trade was observed everywhere during this phase; however, the exports of São Paulo to the rest of the country increased much more rapidly than the exports of the rest of the country to São Paulo (Cano, 1985, p. 160). Thus, it can be seen that the increase in trade between the regions began in answer to São Paulo's over-accumulation problems and continued to develop during the period.

This process of commercial integration began on the basis of complementarity between regions, based on the natural endowment of each region (Guimarães Neto, 1989, p. 85). However, the evolution of this process brought different results and had different patterns in different regions. In the traditional peripheral regions, instead of continuing their development based on complementary trade, this process soon give rise to products which were the basis of the industrial sector of the periphery (especially the North, Northeast and some parts of the South)[34]. Competition between these regions created barriers to the development of industrial sectors in these regions and later partially destroyed the industrial sector of these areas, which until then had been protected by the cost of transport (Guimarães Neto, 1989, p. 85 and Cano, 1985, p. 186).

This is one of the causes of the decrease in the participation of the North and Northeast in the total income generated by the industrial sector and the consequent increase in São Paulo's participation. The extra-regional markets allowed São Paulo to continue its path of industrial concentration and allowed it to develop beyond the capacity of its own markets and to take advantage of the economies of scale which this allowed.

The development of interregional trade had a completely different impact on the "new peripheral" economies. The creation of commerce between these areas and the dynamic region of the country allowed these economies to continue the complementary trend of growth previously developed. So the dynamism of São Paulo's economy, in a certain sense, had positive effects on these economies, since their productive structure was fundamentally different from São Paulo and the creation of commerce did not represent competition but complementarity (Guimarães Neto, 1989, p. 88).

This movement toward commercial integration was possible because of two fundamental elements. The first was the development of the transport network which made possible transportation by inland routes. The rail network lost its preeminence after 1920 and the roads became more important (especially after 1955), giving much more flexibility to the system of transport in the country (Guimarães Neto, 1989, pp. 94-5). However, until 1940, rail and shipping were still responsible for the greater part of interregional trade (Cano, 1985, p. 189). The second element responsible for intensification of trade between regions was the reduction and later elimination of the interstate tax barrier to trade. Elimination of these taxes began in 1938 and, in 1943, they were completely eliminated (Cano, 1985, p. 188).

There was a great and fundamental difference in the role that external markets (regional and foreign) played in each region. The relevance of these sectors to each economy according to its internal income can be seen in Table III.15.s.a. This table shows that the order of openness (in terms of exports) of the regional economies in 1947 is: North, South, Northeast, Southeast and Centre-West. However, in relation to its dependence on exports to foreign markets we can see that the most dependent region is the Northeast. The region most dependent on its imports from abroad is the Southeast. All regions, except the Southeast, present a surplus result in their commercial balances with abroad. Therefore, the result is that the surplus of all other regions in their foreign trade is used to cover the deficit of the Southeast[35].

In Table III.16.s.a. we can see that the Southeast showed a surplus in its trade with almost all regions in almost all the analysed years. However, the only year in which the Southeast had a total deficit was 1947. On the other hand the North and Northeast showed deficits through the analysed period.

However, the external sector played a fundamental role in peripheral economies, especially in the Northeast. The report of GTDN (Working Group for the Development of the Northeast) observed that the most important variable which had pushed the economy of the Northeast to its level of development was its external markets, and more precisely, the behaviour of the quantum exported by this economy (GTDN, 1978, p. 11). Nevertheless, it observed that the exports to the "Centre-South" of the country had a much more dynamic and stable pattern than the exports to foreign countries. This can be observed in Table III.8.

Table III.8
Index of Quantum of the Exports of the Northeast
(1948=100)

Years	To The Exterior	To the Centre-South	Total
1949	111.9	96.0	103.5
1950	108.9	98.9	101.2
1951	88.2	101.4	95.2
1952	55.1	83.7	70.2
1953	95.2	113.4	104.9
1954	99.5	122.5	111.5
1955	132.7	118.4	125.1
1956	115.8	146.8	132.1

Source: GTDN (1978, p. 36).

The constant deficit of the Northeast with the rest of the country is balanced by government transfers to the region (Baer and Geiger, 1976, p. 51 and GTDN, 1978). Government expenditure is considered by the GTDN as the other important variable in explaining the behaviour of the income of this region (GTDN, 1978, p. 12).

The deficits that the traditional periphery had mainly with the Southeast were increased by the integration of the national market. As was observed above, in contrast to the areas which can be considered "new peripheries", the traditional peripheries were particularly disadvantaged by the development of industry in São Paulo. This development established the dominance of São Paulo in the industrial sector of the country and created barriers to the industrial development of the traditional peripheral regions, even destroying part of the industrial sector of those regions.

As Cano points out, the industry of the Northeast and the economy of this region as a whole, presented other problems which made much more difficult any movement toward modernisation that would allow this economy to compete in better conditions with the industry of São Paulo. The elements that Cano observes as creating barriers to the development of this region are: "the crisis of the external markets of this economy, the backward and the less diversified agriculture of this region, the enormous concentration of land ownership in the region, low productivity and low diversification of industry in the region, weak capitalist production relations in the region, with predominance of the mercantile capital" (Cano, 1985, pp. 195-6, our translation).

The process of commercial integration "does not refer to only the partial loss of markets located in the Southeast and in the South which were traditionally reserved for enterprises from the Northeast, but, with the intensification of the 'invasion' of some segments of its market by extra-regional production, including non-durable consumer goods, to the loss of markets in the Northeast." (Guimarães Neto, 1978, p. 97, our translation).

However, these negative effects did not affect only the North and Northeast economies (although they were the most negatively affected). The regions of the South which had a more developed traditional industrial sector suffered also from the expansion of São Paulo. In this region, particularly in Rio Grande do Sul, the commercial integration of the regions had an inhibitory and, in some cases, destructive effect on its industrial sector. The participation of this state in the Total Value of the Industrial Transformation can be observed in Table III.9.

Table III.9

Participation of Rio Grande do Sul in the Total Value of the Industrial Transformation

(%)

	1919	1939	1949	1959
Non-durable consumer goods	10.76	9.46	8.36	8.81
Intermediary goods	11.07	9.42	7.89	6.63
Capital goods and durable consumer goods	3.00	3.82	4.09	2.77

Source: Cano (1985, p. 105).

In Rio Grande do Sul, the stronger negative effects of integration were perceived mainly after the 1950s. After this period, the economy of this state entered into a period of relative stagnation and lost its position in the national scenario. This was due to two elements. On the one hand, the competition of the industry of São Paulo produced negative effects on the local industry and on the local markets, which until this time were mainly supplied by the local industry. On the other hand, the exports of the regions to São Paulo faced a stronger competition from goods originating in the new peripheral regions (Paraná, Goiás and Mato Grosso) and this represented a decline in the position of this state in the total market of the country. As the dynamism that this state derived from its regional market and from its external market was not substituted by any other element, Rio Grande do Sul entered a new phase of relative stagnation (Castro, 1980, pp. 108-9).

Table III.17.s.a. shows the pattern of exports from the rest of the country to São Paulo and from São Paulo to the country. This table shows that, especially after 1955, the growth of São Paulo's exports was much more accentuated than the exports of the rest of the country to this state. And, as Cano observes, this can be considered a result of: "the greater diversification of the industrial structure of the 'Paulista' industry and of the greater expansion and modernisation of its productive capacity" (Cano, 1985, p. 211, our translation).

Therefore, Magalhães observes: "It is normally accepted that the existence of barriers to interregional trade, by protecting regional industry from competition from the rest of the country, allowed the survival of an obsolete industry in the Northeast. The collapse of these barriers since the 1940s showed the incapacity of an obsolete regional industry to survive in a national market which was more and more dominated by the efficient industry of São Paulo"(Magalhães, 1983, p. 270). These observations of Magalhães in relation to the industries of the Northeast are valid, on a smaller scale, to areas which can be considered traditional peripheries and where the collapse of trade barriers created competition with the industry of São Paulo and did not complementarity, as occurred in the new peripheral regions.

The action of the State on the traditional peripheral regions

"Implicit" policies

The non-functionality of the financial system to the rapid structural changes that the Brazilian economy was undergoing since the 1930s was pointed out in the first part of this chapter. As previously shown, the lack of adequate financial mechanisms to allow the continuation of the process of import substitution in its extensive phase and in its intensive phase was, in part, overcome by the creation of internal mechanisms of self-finance. These devices were the most important elements in financing the import substitution process[36]. The main forms that these devices assumed were: the exchange policy and inflation. Both mechanisms were analysed in the first part of this chapter; now we analyse their regional implications.

The policy adopted after the Second World War of maintaining an over-valued rate of exchange and adopting quantitative controls on the imports to make possible the cheap import of capital goods (which was the main constraint to the continuation of the import substitution process) and of creating barriers to the import of consumer goods which already had internal substitutes, in such a way as to create a protected market for the national industry, had serious implications at the regional level.

Castro points out that the main intention of this policy was to transfer resources from the traditional agricultural export sector to the dynamic industrial import sector (Castro, 1980, p. 149). However, as both the industrial and the export agricultural sectors presented different regional concentrations this policy ended by representing a strong mechanism of transference of surplus from the peripheral (agricultural export) regions to the central industrial region.

Furtado observes that the exchange policy adopted after the Second World War was one of the main mechanisms which allowed more intense deterioration of the economy of the Northeast. He notes that this region exported much more than it imported from abroad, that is, it presented a huge net surplus in its trade balance with abroad. However, on the other hand, it presented a huge deficit in its interior trade balance; this deficit was especially intense with the Southeast. Thus the exchange policy followed after the Second World War depreciated the value of exports and, hence, the value of the Northeast surplus, while there were quantitative controls over imports obliging the region to buy industrialised goods in the Southeast at higher prices than the same products in international markets (GTDN, 1978, p. 26). Therefore, this mechanism allowed the Northeast to contribute effectively to the industrialisation of the Southeast, since it supplied this region with "its most scarce resource: exchange "On the other hand, it extended the markets of this region, since it created barriers to imports and therefore redirected the demand of the market of the Northeast for industrialised goods to the industries of the Southeast (GTDN, 1978, p. 26, our translation). Therefore, Furtado states that "The protectionist policy, whose praiseworthy objective has to protect national industry, had provoked important internal transferences of resources to the detriment of the potentially poorest region, increasing, in this way, the disparities in development" (GTDN, 1978, p. 28; our translation).

Cano, however, points out that, as coffee was still the most important export product of Brazil and its production was concentrated in the Southeast and South, this product and this region would be the most affected by this kind of policy (Cano, 1985, p. 205). Whatever the negative effects this crop suffered[37], they can be understood as part of the normal transferences from the agricultural sector to the industrial sector, observed by Castro (Castro, 1980, vol.1). If this region was suffering losses in its main export agricultural product, it was also gaining from the development of its industrial sector and from the losses of all the other regions which based their economies on the agricultural export sector.

The second method of promoting internal finance in Brazil was the use of inflation as a mechanism of changing relative prices so as to increase profits of firms to allow the continuation of their process of accumulation. The inflationary mechanism of financing also showed a great regional character. This was because different sectors of the economy had different market power and the regional distribution of market power was not homogenous. The industries of the Southeast were more oligopolistic and had more market power, which allowed them to change relative prices in their favour. So it is fair to surmise that in Brazil inflationary finance has been used mainly by the industry of the Southeast to the detriment of the peripheral regions which had economies based on more competitive sectors.

Another important point which gave to inflationary finance a regional character is that, especially after the Target Plan, the government made successive efforts to avoid increases in prices of basic goods which were the main components of the cost side of the firms[38] (Lessa, 1981, p. 77). As these goods normally are relatively more important in the economies of the periphery, these efforts to maintain stable prices for basic goods really represented a drain of surplus from these peripheral regions which had these goods as their main economic activity.

Finally, concentration of investment in the infra-structure which the Target Plan aimed to complete took place mainly in the Southeast, thus giving this region further advantages compared with peripheral regions (PIMES, 1984, p. 255).

All these elements allow Galvão to confirm that the action of the State was one of the main reasons for the increase in regional inequalities in Brazil (Galvão, 1979 and Galvão, 1988).

Therefore, we can conclude that if the financial sector played a concentrating role in terms of regional disparities in Brazil, as will be observed later on, the main policies used to promote internal finance in the country, as a way of overcoming the lack of external financial mechanisms, also played an extremely imbalanced role in the process of regional development of the country.

"Explicit" policies

In this section, we analyse the government policies for the Northeast, which was considered the most problematic region in the country, and policies for the North.

The Northeast The Northeast is made up of three economic sub-regions characterised by completely different economic structures. The first is the "Zona da Mata", the humid coastal strip that is mainly dedicated to production of sugar cane, sugar and alcohol. The main industrial activity of the region is also located there. This is a region of relatively fertile soils, dominated by latifundia and plantations of sugar cane. The main urban centres of the region are concentrated in this sub-region, and, as a result, it is the biggest market of the region. The "Agreste" is an intermediate zone whose productive activity is mainly centred in the production of food for the main urban centres of Zona da Mata. In "Sertão", the semi-arid area, production is mainly centred on the production of "mocó" cotton, other xerophilous plants and cattle raising activities. Besides these more important activities, there is the subsistence activity which was always present in this region and gave to it a less developed monetary sector. These three economic systems are not properly integrated and present completely different problems.

The main Federal Government policies towards the Northeast were, until 1950, mainly directed to the semi-arid region that was subject to periodic droughts. Droughts were seen as the main problem to be fought in the Northeast[39]. The Federal policies to the regions were mainly based on assistance and were related to battling the droughts (GTDN, 1978, p. 13)[40].

The involvement of the Federal Government with the specific situation of the Northeast began after the drought of 1877-79 with the creation of the "Imperial Commission of Inquiry" (Hirschman, 1971, p. 22). With this commission began the "engineering" approach to the problem of the Northeast, with the construction of dams and reservoirs. Following this approach, a Federal agency IFOCS (Inspectory of Works Against the Drought) was created in 1909. In 1945, this organisation was transformed into DNOCS (National Department of Works Against the Droughts).

The actions of these agencies were mainly concerned with the problems of the bigger land owners and so it was an extra source of concentration of income in the region[41].

In 1948, the Federal Government created two new institutions for the region. They were CVSF (São Francisco Valley Commission) and CHESF (São Francisco's Hydroelectric Company). Hirschman observes that the creation of those two new institutions marked a new direction in the government intervention in the region, since they created a basic infra-structure, especially in the energy sector (Hirschman, 1971, p. 58).

In 1951, there was another drought in the region and, in 1952, the BNB (Bank of Northeast of Brazil) was created[42] as result of the drought. BNB was created with the main objective of extending credit to the agricultural sector of the semi-arid regions, later its main aim changed and incorporated the objective of offering extra incentives to the industrial sector of the region (Cohn, 1976, p. 62 and Hirschman, 1971, p. 62). Hirschman observes that the creation of BNB was further evidence of the change in the direction of government involvement in the region, which since 1948 had assumed a more interventionist character (Hirschman, 1971, p. 61).

The main source of the resources of BNB were funds that were allocated previously to Banco do Brasil by the constitution. That is, the constitution of 1946 had stipulated that one per cent of the total fiscal revenue must stay with Banco do Brasil for emergencies caused by droughts in the Northeast[43]. With the creation of BNB, these funds were transferred from Banco do Brasil to BNB. This bank acted both as a commercial bank and as an investment and development bank. However, the actual action of this bank restricted it to the functions of a commercial bank. Hirschman observes that in 1959 the short term credit amounted to three quarter of the total credit extended by the bank, an absolute contradiction of the aims which created the bank (Hirschman, 1971, p. 64).

All these Federal Government interventions in the region in reality did not represent much, especially because very often they were misused. They were very restricted in assistance and did not effectively intervene in the economic organisation of the region nor did they compensate for the effects which the implicit policies of the government were causing in the region.

The dominant class of the Northeast, especially the land owners, exploited the drought in order to have access to more funds from the Federal Government. This explains why the federal policies to the region were ever based on the fight against the drought (GTDN, 1978 and Furtado, 1964, p. 139). The clear objective of these policies was to maintain the status quo in the region and to divert attention from the main development problems of the region.

There was extreme misery both in the interior region and in the humid coastal strip. The sugar cane plantations did not allow their employees to have any form of labour contract and the conditions of exploitation in this region were beyond all imaginable limits. The problems of the region were far from being restricted to a climatic question.

The favourable conditions observed in the market for sugar, both internal and external, in the 50s caused a substantial expansion in its production. This expansion took the form of incorporation of new lands which were used previously for the self-subsistence of the workers in the plantations. At the same time, sugar cane plantations were absorbing lands previously used for commercial production of food for the region. This put extra pressure on prices of food in the region. On the other hand, competition from sugar production in the South increased the cost of sugar in the Northeast. In this scenario, expansion of sugar production in the region was attained with an extreme pressure on the levels of the wages paid to the workers who were no longer allowed to produce the food necessary for their subsistence. This resulted in deterioration in the living conditions of the rural population of the region which already lived in conditions of extreme poverty (Furtado, 1964, pp. 142-6)[44].

It is in this context of increasing misery of the rural workers that a series of new social movements began to take place. These movements had their origins mainly in the peasant sector, and the most important and representative of them was the Peasant League which began in 1955. This movement had its main base in the Zona da Mata[45]. This movement assumed great importance in the region, and, given its relative degree of organisation in relation to previous movements, it jeopardised the power of the dominant class in the region, especially the land owners.

It is in this context of deep regional disparities and increasing radicalisation aiming to change the established order that a new conception of State intervention in the region began to be developed.

The North In the North, which was not considered the main problematic region, the main action of the government was directed to protecting sectors linked to the production of rubber. The first effective intervention was very brief. In 1912, the Federal Government established the Plan for the Defence of Rubber. The main aim of this plan was to intervene in the external markets for rubber (Mahar, 1978, p. 10). However, given a series of problems, the National Congress denied financial support to the plan in 1914 and subsequently this plan was extinguished in this year (Mahar, 1978, p. 11).

During the Second World War, the Bank of Credit for Rubber was created. This Bank was founded on private (national and international) and public capital and was mainly linked to the production and sale of rubber (Mahar, 1978, p. 13).

In 1946, the new constitution allocated three per cent of the fiscal revenue to a plan for the development of the Amazon. This was supposed to be transferred to the region over 20 years. However, the law which had created this fund was only implemented in 1953, at the same time as the creation of a regional development plan whose main aim was to establish the infra-structural conditions for the development of agricultural, mineral and industrial production in the region (Mahar, 1978, p. 15). The agency responsible for the execution of this plan was SPVEA (Superintendency of the Plan of the Economic Valorization of the Amazon). The main objective of this institution was the agriculture development of the region.

This shows that the intervention of the government in the Amazon was based less on assistance than in the Northeast, however, this intervention did not provoke structural changes in the region, but, on the contrary, served to reinforce the way in which this region's economy was structured.

The new conception of governmental action in the regions

The first step towards establishing a new system of Government intervention in the Northeast was the creation of the GTDN (Working Group for the Development of the Northeast). This working Group prepared a report[46] on the economic conditions of the Northeast, which was the basis for the foundation of SUDENE (Superintendency for the Development of the Northeast).

This report marked a change in the official version of the problems of the Northeast. Instead of observing drought as the main cause of the poverty of the region, it pointed out other structural elements as the main source of the backward position of the region and proposed new fronts of action for the State to promote its development.

The report noted that the Northeast derived its economic dynamism from its external market; however, it observed that this source of dynamism was in a certain sense limited. The other main dynamic element of the region were

Federal Government expenditures. On the other hand, it pointed out that the region was unable to produce foodstuffs on an adequate scale and this was a by-product of the inadequate use of land and not a consequence of drought. It also noted that the main impediment to the development of its industrial sector was the relative inelasticity of the supply of foodstuffs[47]. The policy of industrialisation followed by the State, at the national level, was another element which intensified the regional inequalities in Brazil. As expansion of exports from the region was considered limited, one of the main suggestions of the report was diversification of the regional economy and further, this diversification was supposed to take place by restructuring the existent industrial sector, creating a new industrial sector and changing the structural character of the agriculture base of the region in order to allow this sector to answer the demand for foodstuffs that the new industrial sector, with its expansion, would generate in the region (GTDN, 1978).

The report pointed out that the backward position of this region could only be overcome through industrialisation of the region (GTDN, 1978, p. 12). Therefore, it established three main objectives for an industrialisation policy in the region. The first referred to stabilising the population in the region through expansion of employment; the second referred to the creation of an "enterprise class" which was committed to the "spirit" of development and the third was to retain in the region the capital generated there but which, at the time tended to flow out of the region (GTDN, 1978, p. 12).

Based on this report, SUDENE was created in 1959. The foundation of this institution did not have the support of the dominant class of the region, which had interests strongly linked to the traditional action of the State in the region and which especially found the action of the state against drought a profitable deal[48]. However, it received decisive support from industrialists in the South and from some of the region. This made possible the approval of the law in the National Congress in 15 December 1959 for the creation of this institution.

The creation of SUDENE marked a new conception of the role of the State in the economy in Northeast. From then on, the State played a fundamental role in the region, not only by having its expenditure as one of the main dynamic variables in the region, but as an institution that really intervenes in the economy and that has mechanisms to intervene and cause structural changes in the economy of the region.

Notes

1 For a more complex analysis of the restricted industrialisation see Mello (1986, p.110).

2 For a detailed analysis of the forms that this intervention assumed see

Mendes (1978, pp 80-4) and Baer, Kerstenetzky and Villela (1973).

3 However, this does not mean a decrease in the level of imports; on the contrary, there was a fundamental change in the structure of imports to the country.

4 However, some important initiatives were undertaken by the State in the post war period, such as the creation of the Companhia Siderúrgica Nacional (CSN), an important enterprise that produced steel and iron that was fundamental to the continuation of the process of import substitution. The company was created in 1946. But, although these elements represent a certain degree of intervention of the state in the economy, the general position was to maintain a minimal interference, at least if the interference is compared with the previous period. The position of the State in this period can be observed in Ianni (1971).

5 For a good analysis of this the role of the State in this period see Mendes (1978) and Baer, Kerstenetzky and Villela (1973).

6 A good description of the main aims of the Target Plan can be found in Lessa (1981,pp. 34-54).

7 As Tavares observes, the banking system was appropriate to the needs of financing the primary export model. But as the rapid changes of the economy toward industrialisation began to take place, the economy began to be constrained by the absence of an adequate mechanism of financing the new needs that an industrial economy presents (Tavares, 1983, p. 129).

8 A good analysis of the structural changes of the economy during the import substitution model and the new pressures on the financial side of the economy can be found in Suzigan (1972, pp.45-7). And a good analysis of the financial needs generated by rapid industrialisation can be found in Tavares (1983, pp.135-7).

9 For an analysis of the banking system as the main element in the financing process of the Brazilian economy see Suzigan (1972, pp. 230-231); and Bielschowsky (1975, p. 43).

10 For the more intense needs of funding mechanisms on the intense phase of the import substitution process and the lack of adequate mechanisms to cope with those needs in the Brazilian economy see Studart (1995).

11 There is a good discussion of inflation as a mechanism of promoting internal finance in Latin America in CEPAL (1975).

12 The mechanisms that led to the increased capacity of internal finance by firms in Latin America under the import substitution process are well explored in CEPAL, Chapter 4.

13 In the beginning, it only worked with government projects.

14 This bank also functions as a commercial bank.

15 Internal finance is a functional element in the accumulation process of many countries of Latin America, since it allows the self financing of firms and is a way of coping with the absence of adequate financial mechanisms in those economies.

16 For an excellent analysis of the inflation as an internal financial mechanism see Tavares (1983).

17 There are some important problems in working with the regional internal income, especially because the methodology used in the calculation of this variable presents some significant problems in regional terms. But given the absence of better indicators, we will work with it and try to develop a more detailed analysis looking to other alternatives and complementary indicators. The disadvantages and problems of the regional income are well developed in Andrade and Haddad (1974, p. 116).

18 To recall the reasons for treating the state of São Paulo separately: Chapter 3 dealt with the history of the formation of the regional question in Brazil. The section that explained the transition from the agrarian export model to the import substitution process dealt with elements which allowed the huge concentration of economic activity in that state. Because of the peculiarities settled in this phase of Brazilian economic history and their perpetuation a separate analysis of that state is necessary, as it dominates the Southeast region.

19 There are some studies on the convergence/divergence of the regional per capita income. However, there are some discrepancies between these studies: Andrade and Haddad (1974) and Semple and Gauthier (1972) observe a tendency toward convergence between states during the 1950s and they note that this convergence would extend in the following period. Magalhães (1979, p. 845) observes that over a longer period (1948-1973), the tendency is toward divergence between regions. Andrade (1976) citing Redwood, observes that the level of aggregation (states or regions) is important in terms of observing convergence or divergence in regional patterns of development.

20 We have aggregated the regions Southeast, South and Centre West and called this aggregate Centre-South. This was done to observe more easily the differences between the patterns of growth of the traditional periphery (North and Northeast) and of the Centre (Southeast) and the new periphery (Centre West and South).

21 Magalhães (1979, p. 842) develops this sort of calculus for a more extensive period and reach the same general patterns.

22 The correct analysis must use the instability of prices of financial assets, however, those data were not available for the Brazilian economy.

23 A good example of the stimulating position of São Paulo compared to these "new peripheral" regions can be seen in the analysis that Nicholls (1970) develops in the case of the State of Paraná.

24 This point can be observed in Cano (1985).

25 However, the GTDN was referring mainly to agriculture that produces foodstuffs, and Castro was referring to the agriculture sector as a whole.

26 This concentration in the agriculture sector is observed by Ladder (1976, p. 811) as the main cause for the huge instability of the peripheral regions in the Brazil's case.

27 We use data originated in the National Accounts as calculated by IBRE, but as industrial production is undervalued by this source, we use, for some periods, the value of the industrial transformation as calculated by the census. The point is to be aware that these two series are not compatible.

28 That is, after the Target Plan (1956).

29 The reasons for the falling back of the position of Pernambuco will be explained in the section where we will analyse the role of the regional integration of Brazil.

30 The reasons for this falling back of the Northeast and the ascendancy of São Paulo will be analysed later when we analyse the regional trade mechanisms.

31 The analysis of the importance of these scale and agglomeration economies can be observed in Baer and Geiger (1976, p. 35). Katzman (1974) adopts a different position and shows that these economies did not play a fundamental role in the case of Brazil.

32 O'Brien and Salm (1970) oppose this, showing the services sector as the main element responsible for the absorption of the labour force in the region.

33 This characterisation can be found in Cano and Guimarães Neto (1986); Cano (1985) and Guimarães Neto (1989).

34 Especially when trade reached sectors related to traditional industry which was rather developed in those peripheral regions.

35 This observation will be fundamental when we analyse the implicit regional policies of the state.

36 See Tavares (1983) and Lessa (1981).

37 Galvão (1979) denies the idea that coffee production was affected by these policies to the same extent as other agricultural export products, since, according to him, this product was protected by specific policies.

38 This was a result of their impact on wages.

39 However, some policies were directed to the Zona da Mata economy

and specially to the sugar cane producer sector. In this specific field, we can mention the fixation of quotes of production regionally by IAA (Institute of Sugar and Alcohol). This measure was intended to protect the production of sugar in the Northeast from competition with industries of the Centre-South (Cohn, 1976, p. 25).

40 Martins (1985), attempted to demonstrate that the policy of the Federal Government to the Northeast had a much more planned character than is normally observed. He based his argument on the action of IAA (Institute for Sugar and Alcohol) and of DNOCS to illustrate the international economic character of the action of the State in the period pre-1960.

41 The ways by which these organisations promoted the concentration of income in the region and aggravated the social situation can be seen in Hirschman (1971); Cohn (1976); GTDN (1978).

42 However, it only began its operation in 1954.

43 The constitution of 1946 gave three per cent of the fiscal revenue towards the combatting the droughts in the Northeast; one third of these funds was supposed to stay with Banco do Brasil.

44 On the conditions of misery of the working class in the region see Castro (1977).

45 For an analysis of the Peasant League see Cohn (1976) and Furtado (1964).

46 In 1953, another report was made on the general situation of the region, especially the drought polygon. This report was developed by Singer (1962) and focused on the scarcity of capital in the drought region. It tried to establish the necessity of investment in the area in order to overcome the backwardness of the region. This report was commissioned by BNDE. In 1963, another report was undertaken on the economic situation of the Northeast (Robock, 1963). This report was commissioned by the United States Foreign Aid Programme and it was in the general line of action of the Alliance for Progress.

47 Castro (1980) observes in this a Ricardian perspective of the problems of industrialisation and denies this position, affirming that the agriculture of the Northeast was quite dynamic in the period covered by the GTDN report. The important point is that the GTDN is referring to the agriculture which produced food in the region and the dynamic agricultural activity during the period was cane sugar, occupying the lands previously used in the production of foodstuffs. So the positions are, in a certain sense, compatible.

48 The opposition of the 'ruling class' to the creation of SUDENE is very well described in Hirschman (1971).

5 The financial system

Introduction

Chapter 4 analysed the process of import substitution and its impacts on the regional question in Brazil until the end of the 1950s. Although there were some references to the financial elements of the story, the emphasis was on the real side of the economy. In this chapter we will analyse the financial dynamic of this process at the regional level. This will be done in the light of the theoretical model analysed in Chapter 2. We will first discuss the different financial needs of an agrarian and an industrial economy and will observe that the transition from the first to the second creates further financial needs. The financial system of the Brazilian economy in this period was mainly based on banks. Therefore, we will analyse the behaviour of the banking system at the regional level, through the analysis of banks' balance sheets regionally aggregated. The full comprehension of these patterns will demand the joint analysis of real and financial aspects of the regional economic dynamic and, therefore, we will make frequent reference to the facts analysed in Chapter 4. This will allow us to demonstrate the role that the banking system has been playing in the regional question in the period 1930-1960.

Different economic structures and the financial system

This chapter examines the role of the financial system in an economy undergoing substantial and rapid economic changes in its basic structures: the Brazilian economy in the period of the import substitution process. The different impacts of the financial sphere on the real economy generated effects which created vicious circles which reinforced growth of the central economy and constrained the peripheral economies. Following the theoretical approach presented in Chapter 2, we will show that the behaviour of the banking system, especially the behaviour of private banks, is able to perpetuate and accentuate the situation of uneven regional development. We will analyse some aspects of the balance sheets of the regional banking system, especially aspects related to credit creation, the dynamic of redeposits and the decisions on reserves. However, those analyses are not complete without the observation of developments on the real side of the economy, since the same effect on the balance sheets of the banks can have multiple causes. In this way we will attempt to develop a joint analysis of the regional monetary production economies in order to find the elements that produce the pattern followed by the regional economies in Brazil.

The period analysed in this Part is marked by two fundamental shifts in the financial structure of the Brazilian economy. The first period is marked by the consolidation of the endogenization of the financial mechanisms of the Brazilian economy. In Chapter 3 we pointed out that the agrarian export model had its financial needs supplied from abroad. The dynamism of certain crops and the external markets determined jointly the central region in the country, and the foreign banks supplied the finance necessary to allow the full development of those activities. Both the real and financial activities mainly benefited the world centre and was a way of extracting surplus from the periphery. The coffee activity marked the beginning of the endogenization of the financial sphere of the economy. This activity was financed jointly by national banks, foreign banks and "comissários". The activities oriented towards the internal markets which rose with the first movements towards industrialisation in the end of the 19th Century were mainly financed by domestic sources. The international financial system had no interest in stimulating either the industrial sector in the periphery or the internal markets in the periphery.

The national financial system was, since its beginning, based on banks. Those banks grew, however, without the simultaneous support of a capital market to provide funding. In this way the short-term character of the whole system was accentuated and this, later on, put extra pressures on the possibilities of stable growth of the economy (Studart, 1995).

The second shift is the transition from an agrarian to an industrial economy. This shift had important effects on the financial needs of the economy, since an agrarian economy presents simpler and shorter-term financial needs[1] than an industrial economy. As the economy moves from one to the other, the extra pressure on the system tends to create financial mechanisms adequate to the new needs. If those mechanisms are not created, the financial element will probably constrain the real growth of the economy (Cameron, 1967).

In the first period analysed, when the economy was still in the agrarian export model the financial system was not the main determinant of the dynamic of the economy: this was determined by the conditions of the external markets and of the natural endowment of each region, but foreign finance supported the activities and contributed to the extraction of surplus by the world's central economies.

As the economy passed from the agrarian export model to the import substitution model of industrialisation, the financial system began to play a determining role in the economic development of the country and of the regions. At this time banks were still extremely concentrated in the Centre-South of the country, which allowed them to play a more positive role in this region than in the traditional peripheral regions[2].

Observing the non-neutral role that banking can play in the process of development, Gerschenkron (1962) analyses different historical experiences of development and observes that banking can play different roles according to the necessities imposed on different economies and by the way in which banking is regulated. So, in this section, we will try to make a bridge between the real side of the regional economies of Brazil, summarised in the previous section, and the behaviour of the financial sector, observing the roles that it may have played in the process of regional development during this period.

The banking system has played a more negative role than a positive one in the process of development in Brazil, since it did not create the necessary mechanisms of finance necessary in an economy suffering the rapid structural changes that Brazil was undergoing after the 1930s (Studart, 1995). In the peripheral regions, this role was much more negative, since the peripheral economies were not facing the structural changes that the central economies were confronting and the general scenario where the expectations were formed was much more unstable or negative than in the central economies. Therefore, the characteristics of the peripheral economies tended to emphasise the liquidity preference of agents and to create extra-financial constraints to their possibilities of growth. This fact was not only present in the decision making process of banks, but in the decision making process of all agents, which contributed to the drain of finance from these traditional peripheral regions to the central ones.

In his study on Industrialisation and Economic Concentration in São Paulo, Rattner observes: "The banking system, if it is not regulated in order to act in a different way, tends to transform itself into an instrument that spoils the poorest regions, draining its resources to the richer and more progressive regions, where the yield of the capital is higher and the political situation gives more stability and security to the investment. Commerce operates on the same basis, that is, in favour of the richest regions and against the poor regions, and the industries of the expanding centres avoid the implantation and development of them in other regions" (Rattner, 1972, p. 54, our translation).

This meets up with the main thread of our analysis and leads us to observe within the same framework the processes of trade, speculation and action of the banking system, both interacting in such a way as to make possible the analysis of the transferences of finance through the banking system.

The financial element in the analysis of regional growth has received a very limited treatment in Brazil. The main concerns have been on the real side and finance has had a small part in this question. Previous analyses of the Brazilian financial system from a regional perspective have been centred on the ratio of loans to deposits. This is the case of Bielschowsky, 1975; Albuquerque and Cavalcanti, 1976; Sayad, 1980; Chaloult, 1978 among others. Those authors observed this ratio higher in the periphery than in the centre, from which they concluded that the banking system has not played a concentrating role and has not contributed to the uneven pattern of development of Brazil. In each of the four studies the ratio loans/deposits has been chosen without any explicit theoretical reason. The authors have the view that deposits precede and limit credit creation. Those studies have been asserting that the banking system in Brazil has been an effective instrument of transference of real resources, savings, from central regions to the periphery. Therefore, their theoretical framework is based on stage 1 of banking development and the misconception of finance led them to misunderstand the role of banks in regional development. This misunderstanding is also a consequence of their partial analysis. In concentrating only on the ratio of loans to deposits they lost the elements that can fully explain the meaning of this ratio and concluded, without any basis for so doing, that the dynamic element in the whole story is the willingness of banks to extend loans to the periphery. This conclusion is the outcome of a limited analysis that does not present an appropriate monetary framework and observe the monetary dynamic isolated from the real dynamic.

Now we intend to analyse in a wider perspective the behaviour of the banking system, mainly after 1942 until 1960, and observe the various mechanisms of transference and creation of finance that it presented. First we will analyse the share of the financial sector in the regional income. This is an attempt to assess the relevance of this sector in each regional economy. Then, following the theoretical framework of Chapter 2, we analyse the distribution of credit and the implications for deposit creation. Recall that one problem of the periphery is retaining deposits so generated. The banking habit is not well developed and for those who do hold deposits, centre assets are often more attractive. Failure to attract and retain deposits creates balance sheet problems for peripheral banks, for as deposits leave the region as withdrawals of cash, regional banks also lose reserves, which is the real constraint in their lending. A further constraint is that peripheral banks, knowing they have higher cash drains and less certain loan repayments, also wish to keep proportionally higher reserve ratios.

Given this general framework, we will analyse the pattern followed by the deposits in order to identify possible problems in the regional dynamic of the deposit creation. Once we have a general picture of what is on the deposits side, we will observe the regional pattern of credit creation. Those two analyses prepare the ground for the comprehension of the meaning of the ratio of loans to deposits. On the real side of the economy we will demonstrate that the monetary dynamic begins with the creation of credit and that the financial bottleneck lies in the redeposits of the periphery. Then we examine the liquidity preference of banks. The higher instability of the peripheral regions and the less reliable bases of information result in higher liquidity preference among peripheral banks. This generates higher reserve to deposit ratios in the periphery. This constrains the credit creation process and depresses the money multipliers of those economies, which emphasises the financial constraint in the periphery. Once this analysis is developed, we will observe a tendency towards banking concentration in favour of the centre's banks since all the elements analysed above create comparative advantages to those banks in relation to peripheral banks.

The aggregation of the banking system

In the period of the import substitution process there are three aggregates of the banking system which should be analysed: a) the total of commercial banks (national and foreign). This group gives an idea of the role that the financial system as a whole played in the regional financial dynamic; b) Banco do Brasil. This bank should be analysed separately because it is government-owned and the most important bank in Brazil (see Table III.18.s.a.). During this period it was also the only bank that actually operated nationwide (Cano, 1985, p. 200); c) other national commercial banks. This group corresponds to the first group less foreign banks which had a declining role in the Brazilian economy since the First World War and Banco do Brasil. The analysis of this group attempts to eliminate the effects of Banco do Brasil in the Brazilian financial system.

The participation of the financial sector in the national/regional income

The first point to be analysed is the participation of banking in the total domestic income of the regions and of Brazil; this is shown in Table III.19.s.a.[3]. This analysis is relevant because it gives an idea of the different patterns followed by the financial system in each region in relation to the economy as a whole. However, the results obtained must be carefully analysed, since an increasing participation of the financial system in the income can mean more than just a positive role played by this sector in terms of its ability to extend finance. This will be the case when we analyse the period 1960-90 when an increase in such participation was more a consequence of the speculative behaviour of the financial sector associated with high inflation and internal debt than a result of its role as an element which allowed the financial expansion of the economy. The figures presented in this table show that the participation of banking in the Brazilian domestic income showed varying trends much more similar to the central regions's (East and South) than to those of the periphery. This is clearly because the banking system was much more concentrated in the central regions.

As can be observed, the participation of this sector varies between 4.4 per cent and 6.6 per cent in the national sphere and increases through the analysed period. The same can be observed with relation to the East and South. The East shows a great participation of the banking system in its total domestic income, followed by the South. São Paulo, however, shows a greater participation than the region in which it is included (The South) and shows a tendency to increase through out the analysed period. The traditional peripheral regions (The North and Northeast) shows a much smaller participation of the banking system in its total income and do not show a marked growth pattern in this sector. Its participation seems to be more or less stabilised at three or four per cent in both regions. This demonstrates the regional concentration of the banking system in the central regions and shows that probably the financial mechanisms of the peripheral economies were much more linked to internal finance than to the finance originated in the banking system, as this system plays a lesser role in these regions. This put more intense financial constraints on investment in peripheral regions than on the central ones. It is, notwithstanding, necessary to analyse other elements of the financial system in order to have the whole picture of the system and to make more complete statements on this question.

Deposits and credit

In this part, we will analyse the financial dynamic in Brazil. As the data are limited, we will basically work with the pattern of credit and deposits as opposed to other variables at the regional level. Here we will follow the monetary framework depicted in Chapter 2. According to that model, credit is the starting point in financial analysis. At the national level, credit creates deposits which allow further credit creation. However, at the regional level, there are financial leakages that break the credit/deposits circle. Therefore, for banks, it is essential to observe the behaviour of the redeposit ratio of the extended credit in order to decide about the credit policy for the region.

The regional share of deposits can be seen in Tables III.20.s.a., III.21.s.a., III.22.s.a. These tables differentiate between the total of the commercial banks, which includes foreign and national commercial banks, Banco do Brasil and the other national commercial banks. In Table III.20.s.a., we notice that there is a greater concentration of total deposits in the central region: East and South. The concentration of the South is mainly influenced by São Paulo (this can be seen by comparing São Paulo's share with that of the South as a whole). The participation of North and Northeast are declining, showing a small tendency towards recovery during the last phase of the period, but their levels are still lower than in 1942.

Comparing Table III.21.s.a. and III.22.s.a. we can see the relevance of each region to the generation of deposits in each class of banks. We can see the North, East and West representing a large potential source for capturing of deposits to Banco do Brasil (in relation to all the deposits of this bank) than to other national banks. In the Northeast, we observe the same pattern until 1954; after this period, other commercial banks show a greater participation in the deposits of the Northeast in relation to their total deposits than Banco do Brasil. This was probably because the BNB began operating which made the other commercial banks to present a more unconstrained behaviour in terms of extension of their branches for the capture of new deposits. The greater participation of Banco do Brasil in the deposits of peripheral regions is related to its less constrained behaviour in opening new branches in the periphery which gave the population of those regions easier access to the bank that manifests itself in the generation of deposits. In the South, however, the tendency was completely asymmetrical compared to other regions. Here, we observe a declining participation of the deposits in the region in Banco do Brasil and an increasing importance of other national commercial banks. This tendency probably is made possible because of the presence of São Paulo, which is the most expressive state in the generation of this pattern. This can be observed analysing the data of São Paulo and of the South in Tables III.21.s.a. and III.22.s.a. Therefore, the deposits of the periphery (except of the East) are relatively more important to Banco do Brasil than to other national commercial banks in each region. This can be considered a result of the bigger participation of this bank in the regional financial system.

The analysis of the deposits is important in order to observe the relevance that the banking system attributes to each region in terms of capturing deposits and the relevance that this region actually have in those terms. This, however, can be a self-fulfilling expectation, since, because the banking system expects that a certain region is unable to generate a certain amount of deposits it does not open branches in this region and so does not get deposits. Nevertheless, there are certain considerations on the cost of new deposits which are normally done more accurately and which are more important to the private banking system. This is probably the element that made the Banco do Brasil have a greater participation in the deposits of the periphery, since it acted less from a profit making motive and this allowed it to extend its branch network more easily in peripheral regions even though they presented a reduced potential for generation of deposits.

As we pointed out in the theoretical chapter, the real constraint on the monetary dynamic of the regions is the decision by banks to extend credit. The whole monetary/financial dynamic begins with the decision to extend credit by banks and then the deposits are generated. Therefore, deposits do not constrain nor precede loans. In stage 2 and after banks do not lend deposits, but deposits are created by the decision to extend loans. However, the behaviour of the deposits or the redeposit ratio will have some influence on the creation of new credit, not because they constrain credit in a fractional reserve system, but because banks do need deposits to balance their lending on their balance sheets. Hence, the observation of substantial losses of deposits will lead to changes of expectations in relation to the sector/region in which banks are extending credit. Therefore, financial/monetary leakages generate pessimistic expectations and consequently lead to the reduction of credit creation.

Tables III.23.s.a., III.24.s.a. and III.25.s.a. show the pattern of the total loans. Table III.25.s.a. presents data on the aggregate of the banking system. This shows a very concentrated location of credit creation in the East, South and especially in São Paulo. The North and West are almost negligible in importance in terms of their participation in the total loans. The Northeast represents a small parcel of the total loans created and did not undergo substantial changes in this pattern. The East shows a very unstable pattern of its participation in the total loans and, in 1960, it suffered a drastic decline which was caused probably by the transfer of the Capital from Rio de Janeiro to Brasília. This also explains the corresponding change in the pattern of the West (Brasília is in the West region). The South, although showing an oscillating pattern, increased its participation in the total share.

Tables III.24.s.a. and III.25.s.a. allow us to analyse the relative importance of each region in the credit creation of Banco do Brasil and of other national commercial banks and to observe the different patterns of these two sets of institutions. The periphery, as a whole, showed reduced importance in terms of credit creation in those two sets of institutions. However, its importance in the extension of loans by Banco do Brasil was much more significant than in other national commercial banks. This emphasises the fact that credit creation is restricted in peripheral regions. However, this restriction is weaker if we consider the behaviour of Banco do Brasil, which tends to extend credit more easily to the peripheral regions than other national commercial banks. This result was predicted by the model. Since government-owned banks take into account elements other than the profit making logic, they can extend loans more freely to the peripheral regions than private banks. Private banks, however, determine their credit creation for the perspective of profits and as assessment of the possibilities of profit is largely based on subjective elements, of which convention is very important, such banks tend to discriminate against peripheral regions.

When we observe the ratio total deposits/regional income (Table III.26.s.a.) we notice that it is lower in the most developed regions (East and South, especially São Paulo). However, this ratio does not allow us to make precise inferences on the relative liquidity preference between regions, since they are at very different levels of development of their financial system. Where the system is underdeveloped, people would tend to keep other liquid assets (like cash) instead of bank deposits for hoarding purposes and this can create serious distortions if we try to infer something using only the ratio deposits/income to evaluate the state of the liquidity preference of different regions. This demands more caution in inferring something from this ratio. In this case the best thing to do is not to take it in isolation, but look at it in a broader perspective observing other elements that characterise the monetary sphere of the regional economies. This is what we are pursuing with the analysis of a diverse range of variables. If we take the clearing of cheques as a proxy to the velocity of circulation of money[4] we will notice that it is superior in the central regions than in the peripheral regions, although acceleration of this variable has been observed during the whole period analysed in this book. This will be illustrated in Chapter 7.

Another element which could allow us to comment on the different levels of liquidity preference across regions is the ratio demand and short term deposits/total deposits (Table III.29.s.a.). However, as Dow points out: "A high ratio of demand deposits to saving deposits, for example, cannot necessarily be taken as an indication of a more liquid portfolio; the information has to be taken along with information on less liquid assets. Relatively low savings deposits could reflect a switch into bonds as much as a switch into demand deposits" (Dow, 1990, p. 86).

The need to be careful with this indicator is stressed when we are dealing with economic systems that present such a great degree of differentiation in their economic structure and in which the banking system shows such a great difference in participation in each regional economy, according to its development.

Another problem to be observed is associated with the open character of these economies. Since agents are allowed to speculate with assets of other regions, the liquidity preference of the regions cannot be measured only with assets that are supplied inside the region.

Observing these limits we can analyse Table III.29.s.a. According to this table, the North and West presented a higher level of the ratio demand and short term deposits/total deposits, throughout almost all the period observed, which could imply a bigger liquidity preference in those regions. However, the Northeast, one of the regions which presents great instability of income, presented smaller values of this ratio in relation to some Central regions (East, South or São Paulo) during a large part of the period observed. This shows the limitation that observing only this ratio can bring to a more accurate analysis. The development of the banking system and the access by the population to financial assets can interfere with this ratio. For instance, in extremely poor peripheries, such as the Northeast of Brazil, a great part of the population is kept out of the financial system, since they have not enough income to enter the system. Therefore, the "financial asset" used by this part of the population is cash. Those who do have enough income to enter the system also tend to demand more cash, since their economic relations with those who are out of the banking system are made in cash. Some of this population which does not have current accounts, can, however, have saving deposits, and this ends up by reducing slightly the ratio of short term deposits to total deposits in peripheral regions. Another point to observe is that the financial assets of the peripheral regions tend to be less liquid, for reasons given in Chapter 2, therefore, the liquidity preference of agents can take the form of other regions' assets and this can disturb the meaning of this ratio when analysed in regional terms as a proxy for the liquidity preference of agents.

The regional distribution of total deposits (Table III.20.s.a.) can also be compared with the regional distribution of population (Table III.27.s.a.). It will be seen that the regional share of total deposits is very different from the distribution of the regional population in the peripheral regions. However, the most dramatic case is the Northeast, which presents an enormous discrepancy between its distribution of the total population and its regional share of deposits. On the other hand, the central regions show a much greater share in the total deposits than in their share in the total population. This can be explained by the differences in the development of the financial system and the way that it operates in each region and, especially, by the diversity of the levels of income between regions. It is also an evidence of the extreme concentration of the financial system in the Central region.

On the other hand if we compare the regional share of the total loans (Table III.23.s.a.) with the share of the population (Table III.27.s.a.) we still observe a huge constraint on the per capita credit creation in the peripheral regions. Dow considers useless the comparison of the share of total loans with the share of regional income as an element that can indicate the discrimination of the banking system toward one region: "A benchmark that has been employed for assessing whether the initial allocation of credit was in some way 'fair' is the regional distribution of income. But the provision of credit is a major factor in determining that distribution since it partially determines the distribution of investment" (Dow , 1990, p. 91). Furthermore, "In the context of modern banking system, the interpretation should start rather with credit creation, and its effect on regional liquidity and economic activity.... The only benchmark, then, by which to measure credit creation is the regional distribution of population" (Dow, 1990, p. 76). Although considering the limitation of the analysis of these two variables as evidence of the credit limits imposed on some regions, it is interesting to observe the great difference that exists between the shares of the peripheral regions of total loans and their shares of national income (Table III.28.s.a.). In all peripheral regions (the North, Northeast and West), the share of income is bigger than the share of total loans. The Central region (the East and South), however, shows bigger shares in the total loans than in the total income. Special emphasis must be placed on São Paulo, which has a big advantage in its participation in the total loans in relation to its share in the national income. This criterion, notwithstanding all the problems that it has, is still a better indicator of the extension of credit than the comparison with the share of the population in countries that present regions with high levels of economic concentration, as is the case of Brazil.

There is, however, a problem of causality in this analysis. As was previously observed in Chapter 2, it is not income which generates deposits which, in their turn, allow the creation of credit. To the contrary, the extension of credit generates deposits. So credit creation, not being a restricted process, can promote the creation of income and so the comparison between credit and income shares is not appropriate for the analysis of the dynamic of the financial system. In order to make this sort of analysis coherent, it is fundamental to make it in a broad context.

The ratio loans to deposits and the regional financial and real linkages

The most common analysis of the role of financial systems in the regional spheres is the analysis of the ratio loans/deposits of each region and the comparison of this ratio to the national average. Normally it is assumed that the position of a specific region above the national average is a sign that it is a net receiver of financial resources. If this type of analysis is followed, it will be seen that in Brazil the peripheral regions have been, almost throughout the period studied and according to almost all the categories of banks, a net receiver of financial resources, and so there is no reason to think of these regions as suffering any financial constraints[5]. On the other hand, São Paulo throughout almost all the analysed period presents ratios that are below the national average, and this, according to these analyses means that this state was transferring net financial resources to the periphery (Tables III.30.s.a., III.31.s.a., III.32.s.a., III.33.s.a., III.34.s.a., III.35.s.a.).

Thus, it is necessary to highlight the fact that a larger ratio total loans/total deposits may imply that credit extended without any consideration to the deposits of the banks does not stay within the financial system of one specific region. Therefore, the determinant factor is not the higher capacity of a specific financial system in extending credit above its deposits nor the inflow of finance from one region to the other, but the incapacity of a particular region to keep the credit that is created there in the form of new deposits.

In this section, we will observe these ratios regarding the three groups of banks previously mentioned. Table III.30.s.a. shows the ratio loans/deposits to all banks and we can see that the Northeast and West are the regions that show the highest ratios during most of the analysed period, showing ratios above one. The South shows ratios above one after 1951 and São Paulo shows ratios above one after 1954, that is, one year before Brazil entered the intensive industrialisation phase. In Table III.31.s.a., these ratios are compared with the ratio for Brazil as a whole; then, if the region shows a ratio greater than one, this means that its ratio loans/deposit is above the national average[6]. According to this table, the Northeast presents ratios above the national average after 1945. The North is below the average throughout all the analysed period, with the exception of the period 1957-59. And the West is far above the national average throughout all the analysed period. The East is above average during 1943-50. South is below the average and only changes this situation in 1950. São Paulo, is also below the national average until 1954. This can demonstrate that the relative ease of credit was one more element that encouraged the phase of "heavy industrialisation" in Brazil.

This general trend undergoes some changes if we analyse only the ratios of Banco do Brasil. This institution shows a ratio loans/deposits (Table III.32.s.a.) below one throughout the period in the North region. In the Northeast, this ratio is far above one during all the analysed period. In the West, this ratio is also far above one. In the East, this ratio is more erratic and, in the South, it is far above one, especially 1954, that is, one year before the beginning of the intensive industrialisation process. Exactly the same tendency as seen in the South can be seen for São Paulo. This shows a relatively easier creation of liquidity in the Central region by this institution during the period of intensive industrialisation, and moreover, the ease of credit began before the process of intensive industrialisation started (1955). This ratio does not present any significant change during the period of intensive industrialisation, and this demonstrates the restricted regional character that it had presented.

In Table III.33.s.a., these ratios are seen in relation to the Brazilian average. The North is the only region that is below the national average during the period analysed. The Northeast and West are above the average during the analysed period. The East is above average only during 1948-50, after which it falls to a relatively low position in relation to the national average. This fall could have influenced the fall in the national average, given the relative importance of this region to the financial sector. The South is above average after 1951. São Paulo followed this general pattern of the South, but during 1951-52 it was very near the average, in 1953, it fell below average, and in the following period (1954), it increased its position with relation to Brazil very quickly. This shows again the regionally concentrated character that intensive industrialisation has had. And further, the behaviour of the ratios of the South and São Paulo demonstrates that easy credit was one of the elements used to implement and consolidate intensive industrialisation in the South and particularly in São Paulo, and especially that this easy credit preceded the period of intensive industrialisation, which shows that the financial system played an active role in this process. Therefore, given the greater degree of freedom of Banco do Brasil in relation to credit creation, it can be seen that it had an important role to play in the transition from extensive industrialisation to intensive/heavy industrialisation. This element was especially relevant to São Paulo.

The behaviour of the ratio loans/deposits to other national commercial banks is described in Table III.34.s.a. The North and West present an interesting pattern. Both regions present ratios above one during almost all the period covered[7]. The other regions however showed ratios below one throughout the period analysed (the Northeast in 1951 presented a ratio above one). This shows the more constrained action of the private sector, especially with relation to the action of Banco do Brasil, as was expected. In the Northeast, East and South we see a tendency for these ratios to fall, which illustrates the more conservative and restrictive behaviour of banks with relation to these regions.

In Table III.35.s.a. we can see the behaviour of the regional loan/deposit ratio of other national commercial banks in relation to the national average. This table shows the North and West ratios far above the national average. This is probably because the modest network of branches that those banks had in those regions, did not allow them to keep deposits on an adequate scale. In the great part of the period analysed the Northeast shows ratios just above the average. The South as a whole shows similar patterns, however, São Paulo, which is the most important state to characterise this region as a central region, is below average during almost all the period. However, the levels of its loan/deposit ratio are very near to the national average. São Paulo shows this ratio below one throughout the analysed period. This probably means that the redeposits due to loans extension are very high and that this state can receive deposits from other regions. Therefore, as the periphery tends to have outflows of finance from its banking system, these outflows represent inflows in the central economies, especially São Paulo, and these inflows of finance into its banking system are manifested through the smaller ratio total loans/total deposits. This, however, does not mean that other commercial banks have a restrictive policy with relation to extending loans to

São Paulo. Much to the contrary, this means that their capture of deposits in this state is above the national average and so this indicates to banks that loans must be extended towards this market. This sort of behaviour generates vicious circles which tend to make credit more easily available to this region and accentuate credit constraints within the periphery.

This illustrates successfully the main elements exposed in Dow's model. Here, clearly we have a problem of retaining deposits, or a problem of redeposits in the peripheral financial system. This can be explained by a joint analysis of the real and financial sides of these economies which demonstrates that the reasons for this problem are not related to the positive role that the financial system plays in the peripheral regions, but on the contrary, to the vicious circles which are generated by the interplay of real and financial forces which tend to cause huge leakages of finance from the peripheral regions and which manifest themselves in lower redeposit ratios.

Therefore, we have seen that the periphery mainly shows ratios loans/deposits above one and that the most important central state shows ratios below one. As Dow points out: "If we view the banking process as generating credit which then creates deposits, we want to look at bank assets first and then see how many deposits are generated, rather than the reverse" (Dow, 1990, p. 91). Referring to the specific case of Canada, she mentions, "The bank data show assets exceeding liabilities generally in all regions other than Ontario. This would imply that, when loans are extended outside Ontario, a significant proportion of the deposits thus created a flow into Ontario as capital flows or in payment for goods and services" (Dow, 1990, p. 91).

Therefore, the data analysed previously can also be interpreted according to this framework. On the one hand, we clearly have a constraint on the financial system in the peripheral regions, since both deposits and credit contributed to the national total much below the contribution of these regions to the total income or in the total population[8]. On the other hand, loans are normally greater compared to deposits in the peripheral regions than in the central regions. This is a consequence of the financial leakages observed in the peripheral regions; these leakages, as observed in Chapter 2, are the natural outcome of contact between economies that are structurally rather different and do not present barriers to the flow of trade and capital. These structural differences are manifested at diverse levels of the economy. There is an important differentiated development of the financial system which makes agents of the periphery choose to speculate with assets from the centre, as they are more liquid, because the markets are more active in that region and institutional development is more solid. On the other hand, the periphery tends to show a generalised higher instability both in its financial markets and in the real side of its economy which makes agents show higher liquidity preferences in this region. Further, the real causes for the leakage of finance from the periphery to the centre are the structural deficits which the first region presents and which represent a drain from its financial system. This general picture explains why the periphery shows a higher level of the ratio loans/deposits and shows that instead of it representing a positive role of the financial system in this region, it represents the leakages observed in these economies allowed by a nationally integrated financial system.

As was observed in Table III.15.s.a., peripheral regions tend to show high commercial deficits compared the central regions, especially São Paulo. This state which is the most dynamic state and the one which has been receiving more benefits from the opening of new channels of commerce between regions, shows lower ratios of loans to deposits compared to the national average. This clearly indicates that there is a transference of deposits which were supposed to be generated in the peripheral regions once credit was created. These newly created deposits, if retained, would allow the development of the money multiplier and would allow further credit creation in the region. In this case, what we are seeing is the creation of credit that through the deficits of the regions flows to the central region, thus creating a suitable environment for a faster expansion of credit in the central region. If the banking system is at a stage of development which permits it to extend credit above the level allowed by its reserves (stage 3 or higher) there will still be a constraint on the expansion of loans caused by the outflow of reserves, since the banking system will observe the permanent loss of reserves in a given region as an indication that credit extensions in this region must be cut back (see Chapter 2). So, probably, this is one of the reasons why loans extended to the periphery is such a small part of the total loans of the whole national financial system. This tendency is observed in all the categories of banks that we have been studying in this section.

Banco do Brasil is the most active bank in extending loans to the peripheral regions. It is the only bank that is not constrained by reserves, either at the national level or at the local level. However, as there is only a small capacity to retain as deposits the loans created in peripheral regions, the extension of credit to peripheral regions functions as an extension of financial capacity to central regions: through the growth of the deposits in these regions it allows further expansion of credit in the centre.

This, however, does not show any causality between reserves and credit. On the contrary, as was demonstrated and developed by Dow, creation of credit is the dynamic element in the whole story. Nevertheless, this credit creation must have a counterpart in new deposits, which perpetuates the process, this being the exact problem of the dynamic of credit creation in terms of regions.

The transference of funds from peripheral regions, especially from the traditional peripheral regions, however, did not take only the form of commercial deficits. The private sector also transfers finance in order to speculate or just hold more liquid and reliable assets in central regions. These transfers are due to the more reliable basis for the formation of expectations in the central economies, given their greater stability of those economies. The more volatile basis for the formation of expectations in the peripheral regions and the greater instability of peripheral regions leads to a greater liquidity preference of agents operating in those areas. However, the stronger liquidity preference of these economies is not necessarily manifested in the hoarding of local assets; it can also be manifested in the hoarding of assets of the central regions. These assets are normally more reliable and more liquid than those of the peripheral regions. This is an extra factor which does not allow us to use the ratio short term deposits/total deposits as the sole parameter for the analysis of the liquidity preference of the peripheral regions. As agents can use central assets to satisfy their liquidity preference, the analysis of the portfolios of the peripheral regions, as manifested by banks in the region, is not a reliable guide to observe the composition of the portfolios of the agents of the given region.

Analysing the case of the Northeast, Furtado observes that transfers of the private sector are balanced by transfers from the Federal Government. However, these two processes take place at different times. Normally, the government increases its transfers during years of drought and the private sector increases its transfers in years of good economic conditions in the region, because, during those years, the total available resources are greater (GTDN, 1978, pp. 10-1, our translation). Nevertheless, he observes that these two transfers are very different in their consequences in the Northeast. The government's transfers, according to him, will be spent, for the major part, in the Centre-South[9], so the transfers to the Northeast do not reduce the economic activity of the Centre-South, on the contrary, it probably increases it through the multiplier effect[10]. On the other hand, the transfers of the private sector represent a real decrease in the possibility of new investment in the economy of the region (GTDN, 1978, pp. 33-4)[11]. Therefore, the government transfer to the region, because they present a very reduced capacity of redeposits, end up by being a way of extending finance to the central regions.

Furtado is mainly concerned with the real limitation on investment that the transfers of capital to the South represented. However, if these transfers took the form of speculative activities in the Centre-South they still represented a leakage of finance from peripheral regions and will continue to contribute to the increase in the general level of deposits in those regions.

Cano observes that the transfers of capital from the Northeast to São Paulo and Rio de Janeiro did not stimulate those economies because these transfers were not directed to the productive sector but took the form of speculation, mainly in the housing market (Cano, 1985, p. 196). However, the mere transfer of finance caused by the creation of new deposits in the central regions and which represented a reduction in deposits and available liquidity in the peripheral regions is an element that has negative effects in the periphery and tends to generate cumulative effects, in the sense of further reducing the availability of liquidity in those regions. The leakage caused by the outflow of finance does not allow full development of the money multiplier, because deposits generated by loans do not tend to stay in regional banks. Thus, further expansion of credit is constrained. Additional credit creation will depend on the liquidity preference of the banks: if they are prepared to become less liquid, credit can still expand.

The ratio reserves to total deposits and the liquidity preference of the banks

The ratio reserves/total deposits is an indication of the state of liquidity preference of the banks. The structural characteristics of peripheral regions make banks accumulate higher reserves in these regions. This is a consequence of two elements: the first refers to the higher instability of these economies which subjects banks to a more uncertain environment when taking decisions on extending loans and this makes them more careful cautious in extending loans to the periphery; the second element refers to the higher levels of leakages that these regions present, which makes banks be aware of extending loans toward the periphery, since they will not get back a major part of those loans as redeposits. Table III.36.s.a. shows the ratio reserves/total deposits for all commercial banks by region. We can see that the periphery presented higher ratios reserves/total deposits, especially in the West. Table III.37.s.a. compares this ratio with the national level. We can see that the periphery tended to present ratios above one, which means that they had reserves above the national average. This is especially true in the West. The South after 1947 also showed ratios reserves/total deposits above the national average. Only the East showed this ratio below average throughout almost all the period. The Banco do Brasil had a great influence on the results shown by all the commercial banks. This can be observed in the change of pattern seen in 1960 when Banco do Brasil was transferred from the East to the Centre-West.

Table III.38.s.a. shows the behaviour of the ratio reserves/total deposits of Banco do Brasil. Here we see that the results of Table III.36.s.a., III.37.s.a. are greatly influenced by the action of Banco do Brasil. This bank maintained very high reserves in the periphery. The West was the region in which the reserves were higher in relation to the deposits; this region was followed by the Northeast and then by the North. In the centre, the reserve levels were at a lower level, but they were much lower in the East than in the South. However, it is important to highlight that São Paulo presented ratios below the East during the analysed period.

Comparison between the behaviour of Banco do Brasil in relation to its reserves in each region and the national average is shown in Table III.39.s.a. We can see clearly that there is a great variability in the level of this ratio among regions. The only region to show a lower ratio than the national average, throughout the analysed period, was the East. Other regions were all above the national average during the analysed period.

Nevertheless, the pattern followed by the other national commercial banks is completely different from the one of Banco do Brasil (Table III.40.s.a.). We can see that the region that presented the highest the ratio reserves/total deposits was still the West and it was followed by the North. However, the pattern changed drastically when we see that the East presented a higher ratio higher than the South and, what is more important, the Northeast shows lower levels of the ratio reserves/total deposits. The relative low levels of the ratio reserves/total deposits of the Northeast can be confirmed by analysing Table III.41.s.a. where the Northeast was below the national average throughout the period, with the exception of 1960.

This aggregation can cause some distortion in the data, since, after 1952, the BNB is also considered among the other commercial banks. This bank is very important in terms of its role in this region and presents a totally different policy of reserves for the region. As this bank is supposed to operate in the Northeast, its policy of reserves is assumed to benefit this region. That is, it is presumed that it will keep lower reserves in these regions as a form of amplifying its loan extension capacity. Also, as this bank is a government-owned bank its access to reserves at times of shortage of reserves is relatively easy and this allows it to keep the reserve/deposits ratio lower.

The behaviour predicted by the model analysed in Chapter 2 is confirmed by the analysis of the ratio reserves/deposits of the banks. It verified a tendency toward keeping higher levels of reserves in the periphery than in the centre, which was supposed to be a consequence of the higher degree of uncertainty to which banks are exposed in peripheral economies. There is also the problem that banks face in the periphery in relation to their redeposit levels. Banks that operate nationwide but that have a more restricted regional role tend to be more cautious of extending loans to the periphery since they know that there will be leakages in the credit extended and that they will not capture those deposits in other regions, since their participation in extra-regional markets is very restricted. On the other hand, nationwide banks that operate in a larger part of the country will be more wary of extending loans to the periphery because of the remoteness of those regions to assess the creditworthiness of a project which will accentuate the conventional mechanisms in the decision making process and so work against the region in terms of extension of loans. The higher redeposit ratios of banks from the centre end up by creating a concentrating tendency within the system, since they have a comparative advantage in capturing new deposits and in extending credit.

The regional distribution of the banking network

The distribution of the banking system in the East and South can be seen in Table III.42.s.a. and Table III.43.s.a. These tables, especially Table III.43.s.a., show a strong concentration of the head offices of banks in the East and South, especially in the East. For this phase, the analysis of the head offices is very important because until 1965 the banking system had limited operation at the local and regional level; that is why we observe a relatively small number of branches per head office[12]. The only bank that actually operated nationwide was Banco do Brasil. However, during this period, we can see a marked change in the concentration trend. In the first half of the analysed period, the East increased its share of the total head offices. This increase occurred mainly because of the decrease in the Northeast, since an equal increase is observed in the South. Thus, in the first half of the period, the head offices of the banking system were mainly concentrated in the central region. Nevertheless, after 1947, the East began to lose head offices and the South continued gaining them. However, the movement toward concentration in the South was strongly influenced by what was going on in São Paulo. An analysis of São Paulo's share of the total number of head offices shows a very rapid concentration both at national and at regional levels. These results, do not show precisely the increase in the concentration of the banking system, as, apart from the concentration of head offices in São Paulo there was still the factor of size of these banks which was not taken into account in the analysis of the number of head offices, as this type of analysis treats each head office as being identical to the rest, which is, of course, not the case.

With relation to the number of branches, we can see that the literature normally relates branches to the distribution of the population. If we compare Table III.43.s.a. and Table III.27.s.a. we will see that all peripheral regions have less branches compared to the population in the national total. The case of the Northeast is the most serious. Here the region has around 23-24 per cent of the national population and sharing only three or four per cent of the branches, which demonstrates a strong disparity between these two variables. This may be one more cause for the difficulties of retaining the deposits of these regions, or it could be a result of the inaccessibility to financial assets by the local population because of the lack of minimum income to give access to these assets. As this region's income is extremely concentrated in personal terms, the majority of the population does not have an income level that allows access to financial services. Given the lower level of income of those regions, banks do not extend their network in those directions and consequently do not get access to the deposits that (despite the lower level of incomes) can be generated in those regions. This explains why the Banco do Brasil has a greater participation in the deposits of the peripheral regions: as it has a more unconstrained policy for opening new branches, it can extend its network towards those regions and in doing so it can have access to the deposits generated there.

The East, on the other hand, at the beginning of the period of our analysis showed a higher share of branches compared to its share of the national population. However, this situation changed during the analysed period, and, towards the end of the period, its share of branches was less than its share of the total population. The opposite is seen in the South. This region's share was 31-34 per cent of the national population and shares 51-58 per cent of the total branches of banks. So we see an enormous concentration of branches in this region, and this tendency is accentuated during the analysed period. The concentration of branches in São Paulo is even stronger and the process of concentration is much more accentuated than that in the South.

Analysing the concentration of the banking system by size (in 1960), Rattner observes that the 43 biggest banks were distributed as follows:

Table III.10
Distribution of the 43 Biggest Banks
1960
(%)

Sao Paulo	46
Guanabara (R.J.)	20
Minas Gerais	4
Paraná	4
Rio Grande do	9
Sul	13
Others	

Source: Rattner (1972, p. 127).

Therefore, "this means that almost 90 per cent of the big banks have their head offices concentrated in the five richest states of the nation" (Rattner, 1972, p. 127, our translation). Thus, the figures of concentration are stronger when the banks are not treated as homogenous and their size is considered.

This general trend shows a strongly concentrated banking system not only in the distribution of credit and loans but also in the distribution of its network. This concentration is observed using the indicators of both regional population and regional income.

The analysis developed above shows a strong concentration of the financial system in the Centre-South of the country. This concentration can be observed both in the location of the head offices of the banks and in the operation of the banks through their extension of loans and their capture of deposits. This was a highly predicted result since there was a confluence of factors which gave advantages to the financial system of the centre and this tended to create and accentuate a process of banking concentration in this region. Among the factors that cause this bias we can mention the tendency of this part of the banking system to gain access to a larger part of the reserves of the system which allows it to amplify its operation[13]. The factors which allow the banks of the centre to do this are greatly related to the causes that lead to higher leakages in the monetary flows of the periphery, which allows the central banks to capture part of the credit that is extended to the periphery: or in the periphery through its action in these markets or in the centre through the deposits that credit extended in the periphery generates in the centre.

Therefore, we observed that the interplay of real and financial elements have created conditions for more constrained operation of the banking system in peripheral regions. The constraints put on the financial system in these regions originated in the profit maximizing logic of banks, firms and households that tend to present higher liquidity preferences in peripheral regions and manifest their higher liquidity preferences through assets from the central regions which causes larger leakages in the monetary flows of the peripheral regions and accentuates the relative disadvantage of the financial sector of these regions, thus stimulating a process of banking concentration in the central regions.

Notes

1 There are some elements that give a long term character to the financial needs of the agrarian export model (land, slaves, equipment etc.). However, those elements were in great part financed via internal accumulation and only in some cases by foreign banks. However, the financial needs of the agrarian export model were comparatively simpler and had a more intense short run character than the ones of the industrial economy.

2 When we mention the functionality (it had a well defined and adapted role to play) that the financial system has presented to the Centre-South of the country we are not saying that it played a functional role in the process of growth of the country, but that it has played a functional role in the centre compared with its role in the periphery. For an analysis of the disfunctional role of the financial system in the

process of industrialisation in the Brazilian economy as a whole, see Studart (1995).

3 The regional aggregation of the States is different in this section than in the previous section. This is because the regional banking data available were aggregated according to the political regional aggregation prior to 1970. The states are aggregated in this section as follows: North: Rondônia, Acre, Amazonas, Rio Branco, Pará, Amapá; Northeast: Maranhão, Piauí, Ceará, Rio Grande do Norte, Paraíba, Pernambuco, Alagoas; East: Sergipe, Bahia, Minas Gerais, Espírito Santo, Rio de Janeiro, Distrito Federal; South: São Paulo, Paraná, Santa Catarina, Rio Grande do Sul; West: Mato Grosso, Goias.

4 This variable is used very often by the Central Bank as a proxy for the measure of the velocity of circulation of money.

5 These are the conclusions of the main research concerned with this question in Brazil.

6 This sort of calculation is used by Sayad and Jatobá (1980).

7 This pattern is sometimes explained as a consequence of the limited volume of resources involved in these regions (Bielschowsky, 1975).

8 It is fundamental to bear in mind the limits to comparing the share of loans/deposits in relation to the share of income of one particular region, as previously observed.

9 This is so, because of the great deficits of the region with the Centre-South.

10 For the dynamic effect of extra-regional increased demand see the Kaldorian models presented in chapter 1.

11 Furtado is mainly concerned with the transference of resources that will be invested in the Centre-South, and not with resources that will be used for speculative purposes.

12 For a more detailed analysis of the local operation of banks before 1965 see Corrêa (1989).

13 To get this result it is not necessary to working within the boundaries of a fractionary reserves banking system, or put another way, being in an exogenous money approach. Banks also have to look at their level of reserves and their potential to have access to these reserves when extending loans, even if they are not absolutely constrained by these reserves.

Statistical appendix to Part III

Table III.1.s.a.
Regional Share of the Domestic Income (%)

Years	North	Northeast	Pernambuco	Bahia	Southeast	São Paulo	South	C. West	Total
1939	2.64	16.71	4.44	4.49	63.22	31.11	15.32	2.11	100.00
1947	2.35	15.53	4.05	4.34	63.75	32.46	16.70	1.68	100.00
1948	2.03	15.09	4.06	4.08	64.98	33.53	16.03	1.87	100.00
1949	1.77	14.40	3.83	3.79	65.86	34.38	16.17	1.80	100.00
1950	1.71	14.65	3.86	3.78	65.55	34.76	16.29	1.79	100.00
1951	1.83	14.09	3.92	3.60	66.12	35.01	15.94	2.02	100.00
1952	1.80	13.34	3.44	3.43	66.36	36.38	16.55	1.95	100.00
1953	1.67	12.66	3.34	3.59	65.47	35.09	17.69	2.52	100.00
1954	1.67	12.99	3.35	3.97	66.53	36.49	16.33	2.49	100.00
1955	1.68	12.56	3.18	3.77	65.33	35.93	17.92	2.51	100.00
1956	2.06	13.40	3.47	3.76	64.82	34.54	17.26	2.46	100.00
1957	2.41	13.61	3.58	3.87	64.55	34.87	17.16	2.27	100.00
1958	2.19	12.97	3.61	4.04	64.56	35.35	17.68	2.59	100.00
1959	1.99	14.43	3.51	4.18	63.20	34.95	17.93	2.45	100.00
1960	2.23	14.81	3.48	4.24	62.68	34.78	17.81	2.46	100.00

Source: Conjuntura Econômica, IBRE, FGV, 25(9), September, 1971.

Table III.2.s.a.
States Share of the Regional Income (%)

Years	Northeast	Pernambuco	Bahia	Southeast	São Paulo
1939	100.00	26.55	26.85	100.00	49.21
1947	100.00	26.10	27.96	100.00	50.91
1948	100.00	26.93	27.00	100.00	51.60
1949	100.00	26.59	26.32	100.00	52.20
1950	100.00	26.32	25.78	100.00	53.02
1951	100.00	27.80	25.53	100.00	52.94
1952	100.00	25.79	25.71	100.00	54.82
1953	100.00	26.36	28.38	100.00	53.60
1954	100.00	25.82	30.56	100.00	54.86
1955	100.00	25.29	30.00	100.00	55.00
1956	100.00	25.89	28.06	100.00	53.28
1957	100.00	26.34	28.43	100.00	54.01
1958	100.00	27.81	31.13	100.00	54.76
1959	100.00	24.30	28.98	100.00	55.30
1960	100.00	23.50	28.65	100.00	55.49

Source: Conjuntura Econômica, IBRE, FGV, 25(9), September, 1971 and Anuário Estatístico, IBGE.

Table III.3.s.a.
Annual Rate of Change in the Real Regional Income (%)

Years	North	Northeast	Centre - South
1948	-7,93	1.21	6.80
1949	3.71	8.34	6.56
1950	9.93	0.09	4.44
1951	8.21	4.31	10.19
1952	-4.94	-2.33	3.83
1953	7.57	10.06	7.34
1954	8.68	4.96	8.51
1955	20.05	7.93	0.40
1956	20.75	8.60	6.57
1957	-5.49	-0.17	5.44
1958	-5.38	13.62	2.51
1959	19.25	11.92	8.87

Source: Conjuntura Econômica, IBRE, FGV, 25(9), September, 1971.

Table III.4.s.a.
Regional Per Capita Income (in Relation to Brazil) (%)

Years	North	Northeast	Pernambuco	Bahia	Southeast	São Paulo	South	C. West	Total
1947	66.84	43.43	61.86	46.22	146.19	184.42	113.18	51.58	100.00
1948	56.80	43.43	62.03	43.49	149.42	190.36	107.69	57.00	100.00
1949	49.66	41.46	58.45	40.53	151.87	195.02	107.62	54.33	100.00
1950	48.29	42.36	59.03	40.60	152.06	197.61	107.82	53.64	100.00
1951	51.53	40.80	59.96	38.75	153.85	198.92	104.54	59.93	100.00
1952	50.95	38.71	52.68	37.06	154.90	206.63	107.52	57.19	100.00
1953	47.24	36.79	51.11	38.93	153.30	199.27	113.88	73.10	100.00
1954	47.23	37.82	51.41	43.14	156.29	207.17	104.16	71.51	100.00
1955	47.61	36.65	48.72	41.08	153.99	203.94	113.19	71.46	100.00
1956	58.52	39.16	53.22	41.10	153.32	196.02	108.01	69.21	100.00
1957	68.65	39.85	55.02	42.42	153.19	197.90	106.36	63.23	100.00
1958	62.24	38.00	55.44	44.44	153.77	200.70	108.51	71.66	100.00
1959	56.84	42.44	53.91	46.14	151.07	198.47	108.96	65.64	100.00
1960	63.74	43.68	53.59	47.00	150.38	197.59	107.15	66.73	100.00

Source: Conjuntura Econômica, IBRE, FGV, 25(9), September, 1971.

Table III.5.s.a.

Regional Share of the Agriculture Income (%)

Years	North	Northeast	Pernambuco	Bahia	Southeast	São Paulo	South	C. West	Total
1939	3.28	23.03	4.49	6.04	47.02	24.72	22.18	4.49	100.00
1947	2.44	19.95	3.84	5.96	51.66	28.15	23.18	2.78	100.00
1948	2.00	19.52	3.91	5.59	53.46	29.15	21.70	3.31	100.00
1949	1.66	18.65	3.48	5.13	54.23	30.12	22.16	3.30	100.00
1950	1.68	20.26	3.87	5.33	52.46	29.23	22.29	3.32	100.00
1951	1.90	19.01	4.00	4.90	53.98	29.66	21.15	3.96	100.00
1952	1.78	17.73	3.22	4.45	53.43	31.64	23.22	3.84	100.00
1953	1.64	16.72	3.37	4.98	50.65	27.33	25.76	5.24	100.00
1954	1.66	18.00	3.25	6.21	52.33	29.87	22.73	5.29	100.00
1955	1.60	16.56	2.87	5.15	48.95	28.57	27.60	5.29	100.00
1956	2.12	18.40	3.36	5.20	48.18	26.72	26.08	5.22	100.00
1957	2.12	18.49	3.68	4.99	49.42	27.77	25.41	4.56	100.00
1958	1.95	17.57	3.96	5.41	47.09	26.34	27.80	5.59	100.00
1959	1.70	21.00	3.70	5.74	43.68	23.80	28.82	4.80	100.00
1960	2.04	22.32	3.83	6.15	42.51	23.14	28.41	4.71	100.00

Source: Conjuntura Econômica, IBRE, FGV, 25(9), September, 1971.

Table III.6.s.a.
Agricultural States Participation in the Total Regional Agricultural Income (%)

Years	Pernambuco	Bahia	São Paulo
1939	19.50	26.24	52.58
1947	19.24	29.89	54.50
1948	20.02	28.62	54.52
1949	18.68	27.52	55.54
1950	19.11	26.31	55.72
1951	21.05	25.79	54.95
1952	18.14	25.09	59.23
1953	20.13	29.80	53.96
1954	18.05	34.53	57.09
1955	17.34	31.12	58.36
1956	18.24	28.25	55.46
1957	19.91	26.99	56.19
1958	22.55	30.78	55.94
1959	17.63	27.35	54.48
1960	17.17	27.57	54.42

Source: Conjuntura Econômica, IBRE, FGV, 25(9), September, 1971.

Table III.7.s.a.
Agriculture Participation in the Total Regional Income (%)

Years	North	Northeast	Pernambuco	Bahia	Southeast	São Paulo	South	C. West	Total
1939	35.49	39.35	28.90	38.46	21.23	22.68	41.31	60.88	28.55
1947	32.92	40.70	30.01	43.51	25.67	27.48	43.97	52.56	31.68
1948	31.29	41.03	30.50	43.48	26.10	27.57	42.95	56.04	31.72
1949	28.53	39.50	27.74	41.30	25.11	26.71	41.80	55.89	30.50
1950	30.09	42.55	30.88	43.42	24.62	25.87	42.09	56.95	30.77
1951	31.40	40.84	30.91	41.26	24.70	25.64	40.13	59.29	30.26
1952	28.91	38.90	27.37	37.95	23.57	25.46	41.09	57.67	29.27
1953	29.94	40.28	30.77	42.30	23.60	23.76	44.42	63.43	30.50
1954	29.60	41.18	28.79	46.52	23.38	24.33	41.37	63.16	29.72
1955	28.33	39.09	26.80	40.55	22.23	23.59	45.70	62.44	29.66
1956	28.29	37.70	26.56	37.95	20.40	21.24	41.47	58.33	27.45
1957	24.11	37.27	28.18	35.39	21.00	21.85	40.62	55.22	27.43
1958	23.44	35.67	28.93	35.27	19.21	19.62	41.41	56.79	26.34
1959	23.45	40.10	29.09	37.85	19.04	18.76	44.29	53.93	27.55
1960	25.12	41.35	30.20	39.78	18.61	18.25	43.77	52.50	27.44

Source: Conjuntura Econômica, IBRE, FGV, 25 (9), September, 1971.

Table III.8.s.a.
Regional Share of the Industrial Income (%)

Years	North	Northeast	Pernambuco	Bahia	Southeast	São Paulo	South	C. West	Total
1939	2.33	12.09	4.65	2.49	71.74	36.38	12.86	0.98	100.00
1947	1.33	9.95	4.25	1.78	74.61	44.38	13.43	0.68	100.00
1948	1.16	9.67	4.18	1.72	75.04	45.40	13.48	0.65	100.00
1949	1.02	9.45	4.11	1.68	75.39	46.39	13.53	0.61	100.00
1950	0.95	8.85	3.84	1.60	75.96	47.28	13.68	0.55	100.00
1951	0.91	8.32	3.57	1.55	76.44	48.10	13.83	0.50	100.00
1952	1.20	8.24	3.27	1.71	76.26	48.33	13.80	0.50	100.00
1953	1.11	7.60	3.00	1.62	76.88	49.25	13.94	0.46	100.00
1954	1.13	7.60	3.06	1.56	77.33	50.95	13.49	0.44	100.00
1955	1.18	7.69	2.90	1.94	77.65	51.14	12.98	0.50	100.00
1956	1.36	8.47	3.24	2.17	76.75	51.37	12.90	0.51	100.00
1957	2.26	8.57	3.07	2.43	76.19	51.25	12.35	0.62	100.00
1958	2.03	7.95	2.69	2.58	77.03	52.36	12.36	0.64	100.00
1959	1.70	8.32	2.56	2.70	76.87	53.34	12.34	0.77	100.00
1960	1.89	8.03	2.54	2.38	77.47	54.29	12.60	0.74	100.00

Source: Conjuntura Econômica, IBRE, FGV, 25 (9), September, 1971.

Table III.9.s.a.
Industrial States Participation in The Total Regional Industrial Income (%)

Years	Pernambuco	Bahia	São Paulo
1939	38.48	20.61	50.71
1947	42.69	17.91	59.48
1948	43.24	17.74	60.50
1949	43.53	17.74	61.53
1950	43.39	18.10	62.24
1951	42.90	18.63	62.92
1952	39.71	20.70	63.37
1953	39.40	21.27	64.05
1954	40.24	20.50	65.89
1955	37.74	25.19	65.87
1956	38.26	25.59	66.93
1957	35.77	28.31	67.27
1958	33.88	32.42	67.98
1959	30.81	32.52	69.39
1960	31.64	29.66	70.07

Source: Conjuntura Econômica, IBRE, FGV, 25(9), September, 1971.

Table III.10.s.a.
Industrail Participation in the Total Regional Income (%)

Years	North	Northeast	Pernambuco	Bahia	Southeast	São Paulo	South	C. West	Total
1939	16.65	13.63	19.75	10.46	21.38	22.03	15.80	8.79	18.84
1947	9.38	10.63	17.39	6.81	19.41	22.68	13.34	6.69	16.59
1948	10.54	11.84	19.01	7.78	21.33	25.01	15.54	6.42	18.47
1949	11.57	13.12	21.48	8.85	22.91	27.00	16.75	6.76	20.01
1950	11.34	12.39	20.42	8.70	23.75	27.88	17.21	6.32	20.50
1951	9.70	11.52	17.77	8.41	22.55	26.80	16.92	4.84	19.51
1952	13.84	12.88	19.84	10.37	23.97	27.71	17.40	5.32	20.86
1953	13.89	12.50	18.69	9.37	24.44	29.21	16.40	3.79	20.81
1954	14.90	12.82	19.98	8.60	25.46	30.58	18.10	3.92	21.91
1955	15.12	13.16	19.63	11.05	25.54	30.59	15.57	4.27	21.49
1956	14.28	13.70	20.24	12.49	25.66	32.23	16.20	4.52	21.67
1957	19.85	13.34	18.12	13.28	24.99	31.12	15.23	5.80	21.17
1958	20.04	13.20	16.08	13.75	25.71	31.92	15.06	5.30	21.55
1959	18.39	12.40	15.72	13.91	26.16	32.82	14.80	6.74	21.50
1960	18.35	11.71	15.76	12.12	26.70	33.72	15.29	6.48	21.60

Source: Conjuntura Econômica, IBRE, FGV, 25(9), September, 1971.

Table III.11.s.a.
Regional Share of the Services Income (%)

Years	North	Northeast	Pernambuco	Bahia	Southeast	São Paulo	South	C. West	Total
1939	2.40	14.93	4.33	4.35	68.96	32.69	12.49	1.21	100.00
1947	2.62	14.61	4.12	4.17	67.68	31.27	13.78	1.32	100.00
1948	2.37	14.28	4.12	3.99	68.58	31.92	13.36	1.41	100.00
1949	2.14	13.79	3.93	3.82	69.17	32.15	13.54	1.36	100.00
1950	2.06	13.54	3.85	3.71	69.44	32.98	13.61	1.35	100.00
1951	2.14	13.36	4.00	3.60	69.43	33.14	13.63	1.44	100.00
1952	2.07	12.90	3.64	3.55	69.81	34.16	13.77	1.45	100.00
1953	1.93	12.28	3.46	3.57	69.87	33.90	14.24	1.70	100.00
1954	1.91	12.35	3.55	3.68	70.36	34.02	13.68	1.69	100.00
1955	1.94	12.29	3.48	3.74	69.86	33.71	14.20	1.71	100.00
1956	2.33	12.80	3.63	3.66	68.72	31.58	14.36	1.79	100.00
1957	2.63	13.07	3.74	3.86	67.83	31.90	14.18	1.72	100.00
1958	2.37	12.73	3.81	3.95	68.24	32.87	14.77	1.89	100.00
1959	2.27	13.45	3.80	3.96	67.98	33.22	14.40	1.89	100.00
1960	2.48	13.65	3.69	4.01	67.27	32.79	14.63	1.98	100.00

Source: Conjuntura Econômica, IBRE, FGV, 25(9), September, 1971.

Table III.12.s.a.
Services Participation in the Total Regional Income (%)

Years	North	Northeast	Pernambuco	Bahia	Southeast	São Paulo	South	C. West	Total
1939	47.86	47.02	51.34	51.07	57.39	55.29	42.88	30.34	52.62
1947	57.70	48.67	52.60	49.68	54.92	49.84	42.69	40.75	51.74
1948	58.17	47.13	50.49	48.73	52.57	47.42	41.51	37.54	49.81
1949	59.90	47.38	50.78	49.85	51.98	46.29	41.45	37.35	49.49
1950	58.57	45.06	48.69	47.88	51.63	46.25	40.69	36.73	48.74
1951	58.89	47.64	51.31	50.34	52.75	47.56	42.95	35.87	50.24
1952	57.25	48.22	52.79	51.68	52.46	46.83	41.51	37.01	49.87
1953	56.17	47.21	50.55	48.34	51.96	47.04	39.18	32.78	48.68
1954	55.51	46.00	51.24	44.88	51.16	45.09	40.53	32.93	48.37
1955	56.55	47.76	53.56	48.41	52.23	45.82	38.73	33.29	48.85
1956	57.43	48.61	53.20	49.56	53.95	46.53	42.33	37.15	50.88
1957	56.04	49.38	53.71	51.33	54.01	47.03	42.47	38.97	51.40
1958	56.52	51.13	54.99	50.99	55.08	48.45	43.53	37.91	52.11
1959	58.16	47.50	55.19	48.24	54.80	48.42	40.92	39.33	50.95
1960	56.54	46.94	54.03	48.10	54.69	48.03	41.84	41.02	50.96

Source: Conjuntura Econômica, IBRE, FGV, 25(9), September, 1971.

Table III.13.s.a
States' Services Participation in the Regional Total Services Income
(%)

Years	Pernambuco	Bahia	São Paulo
1939	28.99	29.16	47.40
1947	28.20	28.53	46.20
1948	28.84	27.92	46.54
1949	28.50	27.69	46.48
1950	28.45	27.39	47.50
1951	29.94	26.97	47.73
1952	28.23	27.55	48.94
1953	28.22	29.06	48.53
1954	28.76	29.81	48.35
1955	28.36	30.41	48.25
1956	28.34	28.61	45.96
1957	28.64	29.55	47.03
1958	29.91	31.04	48.17
1959	28.24	29.43	48.87
1960	27.05	29.36	48.74

Source: Conjuntura Econômica, IBRE, FGV, 25(9), September, 1971.

Table III.14.s.a.
Sectorial Distribution of Income and Employment

	Agriculture				Industry			
	1950		1960		1950		1960	
	Income	Employment	Income	Employment	Income	Employment	Income	Employment
North/C.W.	43.82	72.8	39.49	62.8	8.77	7.5	12.12	9.1
Northeast	42.55	73.8	41.35	69.6	12.39	8	11.71	8
Southeast	24.62	47.1	18.61	38.8	23.75	19	26.7	18.4
South	42.09	63.3	43.77	59.4	17.21	12.6	15.29	10.2

	Services			
	1950		1960	
	Income	Employment	Income	Employment
North/C.W.	47.4	19.7	48.39	28.1
Northeast	45.06	18.2	46.94	22.4
Southeast	51.63	33.9	54.69	42.8
South	40.69	24.1	41.84	30.4

Source: for income: Conjuntura Econômica, IBRE, FGV, 25(9), September, 1971 ; for Employment: Baer and Geiger, 1976.

Table III.15.s.a.

Total Exports and Imports at Current Prices as Percentage of the Domestic Income

	Southeast				Northeast			
	XT	MT	XA	MA	XT	MT	XA	MA
1947	25.2	30.88	15.03	21.05	35.27	32.44	17.16	8.85
1950	-	-	11.14	10.81	-	-	10.3	4.79
1952	-	-	7.94	13.06	-	-	4.9	7.22
1955	-	-	7.86	11.21	-	-	11.98	4.47
1957	-	-	5.3	10.52	-	-	7.89	4.77
1958	-	-	4.03	11.15	-	-	9.46	4.02
1959	-	-	5.95	13.42	-	-	8.82	3.62

	West				North			
	XT	MT	XA	MA	XT	MT	XA	MA
1947	23.49	28.52	0.7	0.27	47.92	51.49	15.32	9.24
1950	-	-	0.26	0.43	-	-	8.82	5.42
1952	-	-	0.14	0.27	-	-	4.23	6.72
1955	-	-	0.57	0.21	-	-	7.85	9.23
1957	-	-	1.13	0.35	-	-	11.43	6.42
1958	-	-	0.25	0.49	-	-	11.57	4.93
1959	-	-	0.68	0.12	-	-	14.29	6.26

To be continued next page

Table III.15.s.a. (Continuation)

South	XT	MT	XA	MA
1947	38.45	25.16	13.69	6.09
1950	-	-	9.69	4.38
1952	-	-	9.54	6.41
1955	-	-	6.73	4.36
1957	-	-	5.89	3.96
1958	-	-	6.58	3.78
1959	-	-	7.62	4.11

XT and MT refer to the Total Exports and Imports
XA and MA refer to the Exports and Imports from abroad

Source: Galvão, 1980, p.205.

Table III.16.s.a.
Brazil: Balances of Interregional Trade by Inland Routes – CR$ 1000000 (at current prices)

Region of origin	Years	Region of Destination North	N.East	S.East	South	C.West	Balances
North	1943	*	0.4	-8.7	-2.3	-2	-12.6
	1947	*	-4.5	-31.3	-4.9	-23.1	-63.8
	1961	*	-520	-3483	-521	-64.1	-4588
	1969	*	-88313	-358715	-36006	-4977	-488011
Northeast	1943	-0.4	*	-185.7	-7.1	-21.3	-214.5
	1947	4.5	*	-249.3	-8.1	-25	-277.9
	1961	520	*	-27485	-2484	-70.7	-29519.5
	1969	88313	*	-2048330	-316232	2936	-2273313
Southeast	1943	8.7	185.7	*	69.7	146.2	410.3
	1947	31.3	249.3	*	-675.5	175.1	-219.8
	1961	3483	27485	*	20859	-910.8	50915.5
	1969	358715	2048330	*	-189559	834917	3052403
South	1943	2.3	7.1	-69.7	*	0.3	-60
	1947	4.9	8.1	675.5	*	2.4	690.9
	1961	521	2483.7	-20859	*	1219.9	-16633.8
	1969	36006	316232	189559	*	88764	630561
C. West	1943	2	21.3	-146.2	0.3	*	-123.2
	1947	23.1	25	-175.2	-2.4	*	-129.4
	1961	64.1	70.7	910.8	-1220	*	-174.4
	1969	4977	-2936	-834917	-88764	*	-921640

Source: Galvão, 1988, p. 80 - 1969 includes costal shipping trade.

Table III.17.s.a.
External and Inter-Regional Trade
1928=100

Years	Exports to Abroad S.P.	Exports to Abroad Other States	Interregional Exports S.P.	Interregional Exports Other States	Imports from Abroad S.P.	Imports from Abroad Other States
1939	149	140	191	141	137	139
1950	161	184	302	339	164	142
1955	143	226	316	388	263	184

Source: Cano, 1985, p. 210.

Table III.18.s.a.
Participation of Banco do Brasil in the Total of the Banks Operating in Brazil (%)

Years	Total Loans	Total Deposits
1948	31.82	33.45
1949	34.19	29.27
1950	38.28	28.74
1951	40.33	33.69
1952	44.76	39.76
1953	46.99	39.12
1954	50.96	40.56
1955	50.61	41.81
1956	53.18	43.23
1957	55.11	42.43
1958	51.99	35.98
1959	45.92	33.46
1960	49.70	35.58

Source: Movimento Bancário do Brasil, CIEF.

Table III.19.s.a.
Participation of Banking in the Regional Income (%)

Year	North	Northeast	East	South	São Paulo	West	Total
1947	3.00	3.10	6.00	4.20	4.40	3.50	4.70
1948	3.00	3.00	5.60	3.90	4.10	2.90	4.40
1949	3.90	3.00	5.70	4.00	4.20	2.70	4.50
1950	4.30	3.00	6.50	4.50	4.70	2.90	5.00
1951	4.20	3.30	6.80	4.80	5.00	2.60	5.30
1952	3.80	3.20	6.40	4.90	5.10	2.80	5.20
1953	4.10	3.60	6.40	5.00	5.50	2.30	5.30
1954	4.10	3.70	6.60	5.10	5.40	2.50	5.40
1955	4.00	4.10	6.90	5.00	5.40	2.70	5.50
1956	3.20	3.60	7.10	5.00	5.40	2.60	5.50
1957	3.30	3.80	7.10	5.40	5.80	3.30	5.80
1958	3.90	4.90	8.00	6.20	6.70	3.50	6.60
1959	4.30	3.80	7.90	5.90	6.30	3.80	6.20
1960	3.80	4.00	8.50	6.30	6.80	4.90	6.70

Source: Conjuntura Econômica, FGV, IBRE, September 1971.

Table III.20.s.a.
Participation of Each Region in the Total Deposits (%)
All Commercial Banks

Years	North	Northeast	East	South	São Paulo	West	Brazil
1942	1.90	4.80	53.80	38.60	30.00	0.60	100.0
1943	1.90	4.60	56.30	36.50	29.30	0.70	100.0
1944	1.60	5.20	50.20	42.30	33.80	0.80	100.0
1945	1.60	4.90	55.60	43.50	34.90	0.70	100.0
1946	1.40	4.20	51.00	42.70	34.10	0.60	100.0
1947	1.10	4.60	52.20	41.50	33.40	0.60	100.0
1948	1.40	4.80	51.80	41.50	33.20	0.60	100.0
1949	1.30	4.60	50.90	42.50	34.30	0.70	100.0
1950	1.00	4.10	50.90	43.40	34.40	0.70	100.0
1951	0.80	3.70	53.00	41.90	33.40	0.70	100.0
1952	0.80	3.80	51.80	43.00	34.30	0.70	100.0
1953	0.80	3.70	55.10	39.60	30.30	0.70	100.0
1954	1.00	3.60	56.20	38.50	27.90	0.70	100.0
1955	0.90	3.80	56.50	38.20	27.80	0.60	100.0
1956	1.00	4.40	57.00	36.90	27.00	0.70	100.0
1957	1.00	4.30	55.90	37.90	23.70	1.00	100.0
1958	1.00	4.40	52.70	40.90	32.40	1.00	100.0
1959	0.90	4.50	48.50	44.80	35.50	1.30	100.0
1960	1.10	4.60	35.50	43.40	34.40	15.40	100.0

Source: Movimento bancário do Brasil, CIEF.

Table III.21.s.a.
Participation of Each Region in the Total Deposits (%)
Banco do Brasil

Years	North	Northeast	East	South	São Paulo	West	Brazil
1948	1.84	5.37	61.44	30.58	23.27	0.77	100.00
1949	1.62	5.80	60.02	31.65	24.87	0.91	100.00
1950	1.77	4.74	64.92	27.61	21.16	0.96	100.00
1951	1.03	3.93	69.43	24.88	19.40	0.72	100.00
1952	0.95	4.25	65.27	28.94	23.44	0.60	100.00
1953	1.10	3.59	72.65	22.01	21.20	0.65	100.00
1954	1.55	3.42	76.56	17.88	14.03	0.59	100.00
1955	1.07	3.10	79.36	15.95	11.92	0.51	100.00
1956	1.25	3.54	80.43	14.21	9.49	0.57	100.00
1957	1.11	3.30	79.14	15.62	8.30	0.84	100.00
1958	1.12	3.27	74.85	19.99	15.49	0.76	100.00
1959	1.23	3.63	71.31	22.95	18.08	0.88	100.00
1960	1.45	3.56	33.40	21.37	16.05	40.21	100.00

Source: Movimento Bancário do Brasil, CIEF.

Table III.22.s.a.
Participation of Each region in the Total Deposits (%)
Other Commercial Banks

Years	North	Northeast	East	South	São Paulo	West	Brazil
1948	0.94	3.97	47.75	46.80	36.87	0.55	100.00
1949	0.97	3.68	47.94	46.84	37.05	0.58	100.00
1950	0.47	3.41	45.31	50.25	39.12	0.57	100.00
1951	0.41	3.19	45.08	50.64	39.49	0.73	100.00
1952	0.43	3.23	43.10	52.46	40.38	0.79	100.00
1953	0.45	3.52	44.00	51.14	34.03	0.89	100.00
1954	0.64	3.56	42.78	52.18	36.57	0.84	100.00
1955	0.76	4.23	40.14	54.06	38.25	0.80	100.00
1956	0.75	5.02	38.88	54.44	39.64	0.91	100.00
1957	0.81	4.98	38.63	54.46	34.48	1.13	100.00
1958	0.91	5.17	40.17	52.51	41.36	1.23	100.00
1959	0.78	5.01	36.78	55.84	43.90	1.58	100.00
1960	0.94	5.22	36.41	55.69	44.23	1.74	100.00

Source: Movimento Bancário do Brasil, CIEF.

Table III.23.s.a.
Participation of Each Region in the Total Loans (%)
All Commercial Banks

Years	North	Northeast	East	South	São Paulo	West	Brazil
1942	0.79	4.47	50.70	42.80	32.68	1.24	100.00
1943	0.76	4.27	60.19	33.84	26.64	0.94	100.00
1944	0.74	4.92	60.87	32.14	25.35	1.33	100.00
1945	0.84	6.26	55.70	35.32	27.69	1.88	100.00
1946	0.90	6.23	52.73	38.28	29.33	1.86	100.00
1947	0.84	6.00	52.85	38.70	29.69	1.62	100.00
1948	0.83	6.19	52.47	39.12	30.39	1.38	100.00
1949	0.64	6.10	53.19	38.85	30.02	1.22	100.00
1950	0.53	5.72	53.18	39.53	30.34	1.04	100.00
1951	0.67	6.33	48.17	43.52	33.16	1.03	100.00
1952	0.72	6.29	46.93	44.87	33.48	1.19	100.00
1953	0.71	5.84	48.79	43.36	26.77	1.30	100.00
1954	0.67	5.58	46.43	45.99	29.78	1.33	100.00
1955	0.78	5.70	42.23	49.94	32.75	1.35	100.00
1956	0.86	5.62	46.70	45.55	30.88	1.27	100.00
1957	0.99	4.97	49.76	43.00	27.55	1.27	100.00
1958	1.09	5.34	46.11	46.02	33.62	1.43	100.00
1959	1.08	5.83	42.52	48.96	34.21	1.61	100.00
1960	1.06	5.21	25.98	45.53	32.05	22.22	100.00

Source: Movimento Bancário do Brasil, CIEF.

Table III.24.s.a.
Participation of each Region in the Total Loans (%)
Banco do Brasil

Years	North	Northeast	East	South	São Paulo	West	Brazil
1948	0.97	9.20	61.97	25.05	18.76	2.80	100.00
1949	0.45	9.18	65.53	22.59	16.12	2.25	100.00
1950	0.40	7.77	68.35	21.85	15.53	1.64	100.00
1951	0.51	9.56	56.20	32.19	23.27	1.53	100.00
1952	0.63	9.31	54.95	33.95	24.73	1.71	100.00
1953	0.59	8.11	56.75	32.76	18.99	1.78	100.00
1954	0.48	7.27	50.70	39.77	22.04	1.78	100.00
1955	0.45	7.11	45.83	44.89	27.18	1.73	100.00
1956	0.47	6.20	54.40	37.48	23.42	1.45	100.00
1957	0.45	4.79	61.02	32.38	20.06	1.38	100.00
1958	0.58	5.20	54.44	38.14	25.15	1.65	100.00
1959	0.77	6.65	50.70	39.88	23.50	2.01	100.00
1960	0.72	5.47	17.41	33.03	17.81	43.36	100.00

Source: Movimento Bancário do Brasil, CIEF.

Table III.25.s.a.
Participation of Each Region in the Total Loans (%)
Other Commercial Banks

Years	North	Northeast	East	South	São Paulo	West	Brazil
1948	0.55	4.12	48.92	45.65	34.90	0.76	100.00
1949	0.54	3.94	47.84	46.97	36.10	0.71	100.00
1950	0.48	3.73	44.81	50.29	38.29	0.69	100.00
1951	0.61	3.64	43.82	51.16	38.84	0.76	100.00
1952	0.65	3.42	41.60	53.47	39.28	0.86	100.00
1953	0.70	3.47	42.42	52.46	31.99	0.95	100.00
1954	0.90	3.56	42.35	52.25	37.02	0.94	100.00
1955	1.14	4.06	38.68	55.07	37.35	1.04	100.00
1956	1.34	4.88	37.76	54.87	38.69	1.14	100.00
1957	1.70	5.16	35.81	56.11	36.08	1.23	100.00
1958	1.70	5.55	37.21	54.26	41.99	1.28	100.00
1959	1.35	5.16	35.39	56.74	42.81	1.35	100.00
1960	1.40	4.92	34.06	58.21	46.03	1.42	100.00

Source: Movimento Bancário do Brasil, CIEF.

Table III.26.s.a.
Ratio Total Deposits/Income
All Commercial Banks

Years	North	Northeast	East	South	São Paulo	West	Brazil
1948	0.236	0.155	0.487	0.284	0.336	0.109	0.339
1949	0.239	0.148	0.460	0.272	0.322	0.117	0.323
1950	0.213	0.142	0.521	0.305	0.355	0.134	0.359
1951	0.159	0.140	0.568	0.312	0.361	0.127	0.379
1952	0.156	0.151	0.569	0.303	0.351	0.126	0.373
1953	0.182	0.154	0.572	0.269	0.309	0.105	0.358
1954	0.203	0.140	0.538	0.240	0.253	0.093	0.330
1955	0.167	0.140	0.517	0.218	0.238	0.079	0.308
1956	0.148	0.146	0.501	0.216	0.238	0.090	0.304
1957	0.132	0.153	0.547	0.243	0.226	0.141	0.333
1958	0.141	0.164	0.486	0.240	0.285	0.121	0.311
1959	0.154	0.151	0.475	0.274	0.329	0.171	0.324
1960	0.166	0.151	0.357	0.272	0.326	2.061	0.330

Source: Movimento Bancário do Brasil, CIEF.

Table III.27.s.a.

Participation of the Regional Population in The Total of the Country (%)

Years	North	Northeast	East	South	São Paulo	West	Brazil
1941	3.67	24.19	37.61	31.47	17.46	3.05	100.00
1942	3.59	24.21	37.48	31.64	17.50	3.09	100.00
1943	3.59	24.20	37.32	31.78	17.52	3.12	100.00
1944	3.58	24.19	37.16	31.92	17.54	3.15	100.00
1945	3.58	24.18	37.00	32.06	17.56	3.18	100.00
1946	3.57	24.17	36.83	32.21	17.58	3.22	100.00
1947	3.48	24.87	36.35	32.07	17.45	3.22	100.00
1948	3.57	24.13	36.51	32.51	17.62	3.28	100.00
1949	3.56	24.13	36.34	32.65	17.63	3.32	100.00
1950	3.56	24.11	36.17	32.80	17.64	3.35	100.00
1951	3.56	24.09	36.01	32.95	17.65	3.39	100.00
1952	3.55	24.07	35.84	33.11	17.67	3.42	100.00
1953	3.55	24.05	35.67	33.27	17.68	3.46	100.00
1954	3.49	24.05	35.52	33.45	17.70	3.50	100.00
1955	3.54	24.01	35.33	33.59	17.69	3.53	100.00
1956	3.54	23.98	35.16	33.75	17.70	3.56	100.00
1957	3.53	23.96	34.99	33.92	17.70	3.60	100.00
1958	3.53	23.99	34.79	34.06	17.69	3.64	100.00
1959	3.52	23.90	34.64	34.26	17.71	3.68	100.00
1960	3.52	23.87	34.47	34.43	17.71	3.71	100.00

Source: Censos Demongráficos, IBGE and Anuário Estatístico , IBGE.

Table III.28.s.a.

Regional Participation in the National Income (%)

Years	North	Northeast	East	South	São Paulo	West	Total
1947	2.35	10.61	36.21	49.15	32.46	1.68	100.00
1948	2.03	10.46	36.08	49.56	33.53	1.87	100.00
1949	1.77	10.05	35.83	50.55	34.38	1.80	100.00
1950	1.71	10.39	35.06	51.05	34.76	1.79	100.00
1951	1.83	9.91	35.30	50.95	35.01	2.02	100.00
1952	1.80	9.35	33.97	52.93	36.38	1.95	100.00
1953	1.67	8.53	34.50	52.78	35.09	2.52	100.00
1954	1.67	8.55	34.47	52.82	36.49	2.49	100.00
1955	1.68	8.36	33.60	53.85	35.93	2.51	100.00
1956	2.06	9.15	34.54	51.80	34.54	2.46	100.00
1957	2.41	9.25	34.04	52.03	34.87	2.27	100.00
1958	2.19	8.43	33.76	53.03	35.35	2.59	100.00
1959	1.99	9.72	33.02	52.83	34.91	2.45	100.00
1960	2.23	10.06	32.78	52.48	34.71	2.46	100.00

Source: Conjuntura Econômica, IBRE, FGV, 25 (9), September, 1971.

Table III.29s.a.
Ratio Demand and Short Term Deposits/ Total Deposits
All Commercial Banks

Years	North	Northeast	East	South	São Paulo	West	Brazil
1942	0.886	0.769	0.695	0.699	0.733	0.799	0.703
1943	0.808	0.747	0.722	0.707	0.748	0.789	0.720
1944	0.831	0.746	0.672	0.727	0.771	0.775	0.702
1945	0.817	0.696	0.653	0.704	0.750	0.738	0.722
1946	0.817	0.710	0.676	0.691	0.732	0.768	0.687
1947	0.796	0.766	0.731	0.707	0.732	0.779	0.723
1948	0.793	0.768	0.740	0.680	0.690	0.805	0.718
1949	0.846	0.775	0.753	0.680	0.688	0.823	0.725
1950	0.814	0.785	0.795	0.749	0.757	0.852	0.775
1951	0.828	0.810	0.839	0.806	0.816	0.861	0.824
1952	0.839	0.855	0.858	0.847	0.852	0.883	0.853
1953	0.877	0.839	0.873	0.848	0.855	0.937	0.862
1954	0.879	0.836	0.895	0.842	0.845	0.942	0.873
1955	0.865	0.831	0.923	0.865	0.856	0.956	0.897
1956	0.903	0.840	0.938	0.884	0.876	0.961	0.914
1957	0.928	0.833	0.948	0.898	0.901	0.974	0.924
1958	0.903	0.809	0.942	0.908	0.908	0.970	0.922
1959	0.941	0.837	0.950	0.926	0.923	0.984	0.935
1960	0.963	0.849	0.945	0.907	0.896	0.999	0.932

Source: Movimento Bancário do Brasil, CIEF.

Table III.30.s.a.
Ratio Total Loans/Total Deposits
All Commercial Banks

Years	North	Northeast	East	South	São Paulo	West	Brazil
1942	0.360	0.779	0.796	0.938	0.922	1.716	0.845
1943	0.371	0.844	0.973	0.845	0.827	1.182	0.911
1944	0.469	0.964	1.225	0.768	0.757	1.748	1.010
1945	0.530	1.323	1.031	0.836	0.818	2.786	1.030
1946	0.584	1.364	0.959	0.833	0.798	2.659	0.928
1947	0.668	1.174	0.910	0.837	0.798	2.611	0.898
1948	0.527	1.159	0.903	0.841	0.816	2.048	0.891
1949	0.476	1.284	1.011	0.885	0.847	1.796	0.968
1950	0.540	1.440	1.078	0.940	0.910	1.604	1.031
1951	0.864	1.712	0.902	1.030	0.985	1.500	0.992
1952	0.912	1.593	0.871	1.005	0.940	1.748	0.962
1953	0.918	1.735	0.965	1.193	0.963	1.913	1.090
1954	0.749	1.767	0.949	1.373	1.224	2.187	1.148
1955	0.911	1.603	0.798	1.396	1.257	2.246	1.067
1956	0.946	1.405	0.902	1.358	1.258	1.928	1.100
1957	1.107	1.250	0.951	1.211	1.245	1.417	1.068
1958	1.226	1.332	0.971	1.249	1.151	1.570	1.109
1959	1.092	1.228	0.835	1.041	0.917	1.186	0.952
1960	0.969	1.167	0.753	1.081	0.960	1.488	1.030

Source: Movimento Bancário do Brasil, CIEF.

Table III.31.s.a.
Ratio Total Loans/Total Deposits (in Relation to Brazil)
All Commercial Banks

Years	North	Northeast	East	South	São Paulo	West	Brazil
1942	0.426	0.922	0.942	1.110	1.091	2.030	1.000
1943	0.407	0.927	1.068	0.928	0.908	1.297	1.000
1944	0.464	0.954	1.213	0.760	0.749	1.731	1.000
1945	0.514	1.284	1.001	0.812	0.794	2.705	1.000
1946	0.629	1.469	1.033	0.898	0.859	2.864	1.000
1947	0.743	1.307	1.013	0.931	0.889	2.906	1.000
1948	0.591	1.301	1.014	0.943	0.916	2.298	1.000
1949	0.491	1.327	1.044	0.914	0.875	1.855	1.000
1950	0.524	1.396	1.046	0.912	0.882	1.555	1.000
1951	0.871	1.727	0.909	1.038	0.994	1.513	1.000
1952	0.948	1.656	0.905	1.045	0.977	1.816	1.000
1953	0.842	1.592	0.885	1.094	0.883	1.754	1.000
1954	0.652	1.539	0.826	1.196	1.066	1.904	1.000
1955	0.853	1.501	0.748	1.308	1.178	2.104	1.000
1956	0.860	1.277	0.820	1.234	1.143	1.752	1.000
1957	1.036	1.170	0.890	1.133	1.165	1.326	1.000
1958	1.105	1.201	0.875	1.126	1.037	1.415	1.000
1959	1.147	1.290	0.877	1.093	0.963	1.246	1.000
1960	0.941	1.133	0.731	1.050	0.933	1.446	1.000

Source: Movimento Bancário do Brasil, CIEF.

Table III.32.s.a.
Ratio Total Loans/Total Deposits
Banco do Brasil

Years	North	Northeast	East	South	São Paulo	West	Brazil
1948	0.446	1.454	0.855	0.694	0.683	3.099	0.848
1949	0.314	1.789	1.234	0.807	0.733	2.794	1.130
1950	0.306	2.250	1.446	1.087	1.008	2.344	1.374
1951	0.583	2.885	0.961	1.536	1.423	2.519	1.187
1952	0.726	2.372	0.912	1.271	1.143	3.095	1.083
1953	0.704	2.956	1.023	1.950	1.173	3.579	1.310
1954	0.446	3.070	0.956	3.209	2.267	4.355	1.443
1955	0.539	2.964	0.746	3.636	2.946	4.374	1.292
1956	0.507	2.370	0.916	3.572	3.339	3.441	1.354
1957	0.559	2.012	1.070	2.876	3.353	2.286	1.388
1958	0.824	2.545	1.166	3.059	2.604	3.465	1.603
1959	0.819	2.395	0.929	2.270	1.698	2.974	1.306
1960	0.715	2.207	0.750	2.223	1.596	1.550	1.438

Source: Movimento Bancário do Brasil, CIEF.

Table III.33.s.a
Ratio Total Loans/Total Deposits (in Relation to Brazil)
Banco do Brasil

Years	North	Northeast	East	South	São Paulo	West	Brazil
1948	0.526	1.715	1.009	0.819	0.806	3.656	1.000
1949	0.278	1.583	1.092	0.714	0.648	2.472	1.000
1950	0.223	1.638	1.053	0.791	0.734	1.707	1.000
1951	0.491	2.430	0.809	1.294	1.199	2.122	1.000
1952	0.670	2.190	0.842	1.173	1.055	2.857	1.000
1953	0.538	2.257	0.781	1.489	0.895	2.733	1.000
1954	0.309	2.128	0.662	2.224	1.571	3.018	1.000
1955	0.417	2.294	0.577	2.814	2.280	3.385	1.000
1956	0.374	1.751	0.676	2.638	2.467	2.542	1.000
1957	0.403	1.450	0.771	2.073	2.417	1.648	1.000
1958	0.514	1.588	0.727	1.908	1.624	2.161	1.000
1959	0.627	1.833	0.711	1.737	1.300	2.276	1.000
1960	0.498	1.535	0.521	1.546	1.110	1.078	1.000

Source: Movimento Bancário do Brasil, CIEF.

Table III.34.s.a.
Ratio Total Loans/Total Deposits
Other Commercial Banks

Years	North	Northeast	East	South	São Paulo	West	Brazil
1948	0.552	0.974	0.961	0.915	0.888	1.300	0.938
1949	0.513	0.980	0.912	0.917	0.891	1.127	0.914
1950	0.928	0.990	0.896	0.907	0.887	1.105	0.906
1951	1.336	1.020	0.869	0.903	0.879	0.935	0.894
1952	1.391	0.965	0.879	0.928	0.886	0.993	0.911
1953	1.509	0.958	0.936	0.996	0.912	1.040	0.971
1954	1.344	0.953	0.943	0.954	0.964	1.071	0.952
1955	1.371	0.877	0.881	0.931	0.893	1.192	0.914
1956	1.620	0.885	0.884	0.918	0.889	1.149	0.911
1957	1.762	0.870	0.777	0.864	0.878	0.908	0.839
1958	1.559	0.892	0.770	0.859	0.844	0.865	0.832
1959	1.334	0.795	0.742	0.784	0.752	0.658	0.771
1960	1.192	0.756	0.750	0.838	0.834	0.653	0.801

Source: Movimento Bancário do Brasil, CIEF.

Table III.35.s.a.
Ratio Total Loans/Total Deposits (in Relation to Brazil)
Other Commercial Banks

Years	North	Northeast	East	South	São Paulo	West	Brazil
1948	0.589	1.038	1.025	0.975	0.946	1.385	1.000
1949	0.561	1.072	0.998	1.003	0.974	1.232	1.000
1950	1.023	1.092	0.989	1.001	0.979	1.219	1.000
1951	1.495	1.142	0.972	1.010	0.984	1.046	1.000
1952	1.527	1.059	0.965	1.019	0.973	1.090	1.000
1953	1.555	0.987	0.964	1.026	0.940	1.071	1.000
1954	1.411	1.001	0.990	1.001	1.012	1.124	1.000
1955	1.499	0.959	0.964	1.019	0.977	1.304	1.000
1956	1.780	0.972	0.971	1.008	0.976	1.262	1.000
1957	2.101	1.037	0.927	1.030	1.046	1.082	1.000
1958	1.875	1.072	0.926	1.033	1.015	1.040	1.000
1959	1.730	1.030	0.962	1.016	0.975	0.853	1.000
1960	1.488	0.943	0.935	1.045	1.041	0.815	1.000

Source: Movimento Bancário do Brasil, CIEF.

Table III.36.s.a.

Ratio Voluntary Reserves in Cash/Total Deposits

All Commercial Banks

Years	North	Northeast	East	South	São Paulo	West	Brazil
1952	0.109	0.090	0.045	0.074	0.072	0.136	0.060
1953	0.104	0.087	0.049	0.076	0.065	0.165	0.063
1954	0.089	0.095	0.040	0.075	0.065	0.156	0.057
1955	0.087	0.100	0.041	0.077	0.073	0.187	0.058
1956	0.077	0.089	0.035	0.070	0.070	0.143	0.051
1957	0.066	0.079	0.030	0.059	0.060	0.109	0.044
1958	0.112	0.085	0.039	0.064	0.058	0.140	0.053
1959	0.092	0.081	0.040	0.058	0.053	0.131	0.052
1960	0.080	0.078	0.051	0.056	0.051	0.012	0.049

Source: Movimento Bancário do Brasil, CIEF.

Table III.37.s.a.

Ratio Total Voluntary Reserves in Cash/Total Deposits (in Relation to Brazil)

All Commercial Banks

Years	North	Northeast	East	South	São Paulo	West	Brazil
1952	1.809	1.485	0.745	1.232	1.194	2.254	1.000
1953	1.664	1.389	0.789	1.213	1.036	2.647	1.000
1954	1.560	1.672	0.712	1.312	1.136	2.734	1.000
1955	1.492	1.707	0.698	1.328	1.256	3.207	1.000
1956	1.505	1.731	0.681	1.356	1.373	2.780	1.000
1957	1.504	1.797	0.681	1.331	1.371	2.469	1.000
1958	2.115	1.608	0.743	1.198	1.090	2.637	1.000
1959	1.757	1.550	0.776	1.119	1.024	2.512	1.000
1960	1.649	1.592	1.044	1.152	1.048	0.244	1.000

Source: Movimento Bancário do Brasil, CIEF.

Table III.38.s.a.
Ratio Total Voluntary Reserves in Cash/ Total Deposits
Banco do Brasil

Years	North	Northeast	East	South	São Paulo	West	Brazil
1952	0.142	0.127	0.025	0.066	0.057	0.209	0.043
1953	0.143	0.124	0.033	0.092	0.036	0.258	0.052
1954	0.111	0.151	0.020	0.099	0.050	0.279	0.041
1955	0.109	0.169	0.020	0.133	0.093	0.323	0.046
1956	0.079	0.125	0.012	0.085	0.068	0.200	0.028
1957	0.059	0.119	0.009	0.064	0.074	0.141	0.023
1958	0.110	0.154	0.014	0.071	0.056	0.284	0.033
1959	0.088	0.141	0.016	0.065	0.049	0.237	0.035
1960	0.073	0.123	0.030	0.067	0.055	0.006	0.032

Source: Movimento Bancário do Brasil, CIEF.

Table III.39.s.a.
Ratio Voluntary Reserves in Cash/Total Deposits (in Relation to Brazil)
Banco do Brasil

Years	North	Northeast	East	South	São Paulo	West	Brazil
1952	3.287	2.934	0.576	1.519	1.325	4.821	1.000
1953	2.740	2.375	0.638	1.765	0.693	4.942	1.000
1954	2.700	3.653	0.477	2.393	1.204	6.765	1.000
1955	2.387	3.718	0.449	2.928	2.034	7.090	1.000
1956	2.798	4.469	0.420	3.013	2.419	7.121	1.000
1957	2.556	5.160	0.399	2.781	3.229	6.144	1.000
1958	3.310	4.636	0.429	2.125	1.672	8.545	1.000
1959	2.535	4.063	0.469	1.860	1.422	6.817	1.000
1960	2.258	3.839	0.947	2.075	1.721	0.175	1.000

Source: Movimento Bancário do Brasil, CIEF.

Table III.40.s.a.
Ratio Voluntary Reserves in Cash/Total Deposits
Other Commercial Banks

Years	North	Northeast	East	South	São Paulo	West	Brazil
1952	0.095	0.056	0.065	0.078	0.079	0.093	0.072
1953	0.079	0.060	0.067	0.072	0.078	0.117	0.070
1954	0.053	0.060	0.068	0.070	0.070	0.092	0.069
1955	0.065	0.060	0.071	0.066	0.071	0.120	0.068
1956	0.082	0.068	0.074	0.068	0.072	0.114	0.070
1957	0.076	0.058	0.063	0.059	0.059	0.089	0.061
1958	0.114	0.061	0.068	0.064	0.060	0.086	0.066
1959	0.089	0.058	0.065	0.058	0.055	0.099	0.062
1960	0.085	0.060	0.063	0.054	0.051	0.096	0.059

Source: Movimento Bancário do Brasil, CIEF.

Table III.41.s.a.
Ratio Voluntary Reserves in cash/Total Deposits (in Relation to Brazil)
Other Commercial Banks

Years	North	Northeast	East	South	São Paulo	West	Brazil
1952	1.316	0.772	0.904	1.086	1.089	1.291	1.000
1953	1.129	0.850	0.962	1.030	1.107	1.667	1.000
1954	0.774	0.880	0.983	1.019	1.018	1.343	1.000
1955	0.945	0.884	1.042	0.967	1.037	1.754	1.000
1956	1.164	0.965	1.045	0.959	1.017	1.612	1.000
1957	1.240	0.950	1.034	0.967	0.962	1.459	1.000
1958	1.727	0.925	1.030	0.964	0.909	1.309	1.000
1959	1.447	0.941	1.058	0.943	0.889	1.614	1.000
1960	1.445	1.020	1.069	0.926	0.862	1.637	1.000

Source: Movimento Bancário do Brasil, CIEF.

Table III.42.s.a.
Number of Banks
31December

Years	North Head	Branches	N.East Head	Branches	East Head	Branches	South Head	Branches
1941	7	9	135	52	239	508	126	542
1942	8	9	141	57	248	569	145	715
1943	10	14	154	65	289	652	165	789
1944	7	18	153	70	314	767	180	898
1945	7	20	66	67	291	663	136	774
1946	5	22	45	66	280	689	135	814
1947	5	22	44	67	256	733	129	917
1948	5	22	45	68	242	730	125	993
1949	5	22	45	71	235	787	125	1090
1950	5	23	44	73	232	820	124	1222
1951	5	24	44	79	227	863	121	1269
1952	5	26	44	89	224	922	127	1526
1953	5	29	43	96	213	962	125	1761
1954	5	30	41	101	209	985	122	1866
1955	5	33	40	115	191	1039	125	1926
1956	5	35	38	122	189	1071	125	2002
1957	5	54	38	157	184	1269	125	2300
1958	5	55	38	158	181	1303	127	2348
1959	5	57	38	189	172	1464	123	2605

Source: Movimeno Bancário do Brasil, CIEF.

Table III.42.s.a. (Continuation)

Years	S.Paulo Head	Branches	C.West Head	Branches	Brazil Head	Branches
1941	98	303	5	23	512	1134
1942	97	362	6	30	548	1380
1943	118	420	7	36	625	1556
1944	128	502	9	43	663	1796
1945	114	526	9	41	509	1565
1946	112	554	12	43	477	1634
1947	106	602	10	44	444	1783
1948	103	641	9	42	426	1855
1949	103	702	8	42	418	2012
1950	102	801	8	45	413	2141
1951	100	832	8	45	405	2280
1952	105	988	8	56	408	2619
1953	104	1137	8	61	394	2909
1954	102	1219	8	63	385	3045
1955	104	1235	5	79	366	3192
1956	104	1291	5	84	362	3314
1957	103	1495	5	97	357	3877
1958	105	1527	5	102	356	3966
1959	100	1704	5	110	343	4425

Source: Movimento Bancário do Brasil, CIEF.

Table III.43.s.a.
Regional Participation in the Number of Banks (%)
31 December

Years	North		N.east		East		South	
	Head	Branches	Head	Branches	Head	Branches	Head	Branches
1942	1.46	0.65	25.73	4.13	45.26	41.23	26.46	51.81
1943	1.60	0.90	24.64	4.18	46.24	41.90	26.40	50.71
1944	1.06	1.00	23.08	3.90	47.36	42.71	27.15	50.00
1945	1.38	1.28	12.97	4.28	57.17	42.36	26.72	49.46
1946	1.05	1.35	9.43	4.04	58.70	42.17	28.30	49.82
1947	1.13	1.23	9.91	3.76	57.66	41.11	29.05	51.43
1948	1.17	1.19	10.56	3.67	56.81	39.35	29.34	53.53
1949	1.20	1.09	10.77	3.53	56.22	39.12	29.90	54.17
1950	1.21	1.07	10.65	3.41	56.17	38.30	30.02	57.08
1951	1.23	1.05	10.86	3.46	56.05	37.85	29.88	55.66
1952	1.23	0.99	10.78	3.40	54.90	35.20	31.13	58.27
1953	1.27	1.00	10.91	3.30	54.06	33.07	31.73	60.54
1954	1.30	0.99	10.65	3.32	54.29	32.35	31.69	61.28
1955	1.37	1.03	10.93	3.60	52.19	32.55	34.15	60.34
1956	1.38	1.06	10.50	3.68	52.21	32.32	34.53	60.41
1957	1.40	1.39	10.64	4.05	51.54	32.73	35.01	59.32
1958	1.40	1.39	10.67	3.98	50.84	32.85	35.67	59.20
1959	1.46	1.29	11.08	4.27	50.15	33.08	35.86	58.87

Source: Movimento Bancário do Brasil, CIEF.

Table III.43.s.a. (continuation)

Years	S.Paulo Head	Branches	C.West Head	Branches	Brazil Head	Branches
1942	17.70	26.23	1.09	2.17	100.00	100.00
1943	18.88	26.99	1.12	2.31	100.00	100.00
1944	19.31	27.95	1.36	2.39	100.00	100.00
1945	22.40	33.61	1.77	2.62	100.00	100.00
1946	23.48	33.90	2.52	2.63	100.00	100.00
1947	23.87	33.76	2.25	2.47	100.00	100.00
1948	24.18	34.56	2.11	2.26	100.00	100.00
1949	24.64	34.89	1.91	2.09	100.00	100.00
1950	24.70	37.41	1.94	2.10	100.00	100.00
1951	24.69	36.49	1.98	1.97	100.00	100.00
1952	25.74	37.72	1.96	2.14	100.00	100.00
1953	26.40	39.09	2.03	2.10	100.00	100.00
1954	26.49	40.03	2.08	2.07	100.00	100.00
1955	28.42	38.69	1.37	2.47	100.00	100.00
1956	28.73	38.96	1.38	2.53	100.00	100.00
1957	28.85	38.56	1.40	2.50	100.00	100.00
1958	29.49	38.50	1.40	2.57	100.00	100.00
1959	29.15	38.51	1.46	2.49	100.00	100.00

Source: Movimento Bancário do Brasil, CIEF.

Part IV
State intervention and the regions: the period 1960-1990

6 Structural changes in the real side of the regional economies

Introduction

In this chapter we analyse the real side of the regional economies in the period 1960-1990. As was previously mentioned, the choice of this period was marked by the shift of the action of the State to the peripheral regions. Consequently, the chapter begins with an overview of the main lines of action of the State agencies for the peripheral regions (mainly the Northeast). Some of these policies concerned funding and finance. However, we decided to treat them in this chapter for the financial actions of the State in the regions influenced the structural changes underwent by these economies. Furthermore, an appreciation of the specificities of each of these mechanisms will help to explain the relative lack of success in capturing all the potential for the regions that these mechanisms could have generated.

After analysing the mechanisms of State intervention we shall observe how the private sector reacted to them and the consequent structural changes. In so doing we will prepare the ground for the financial analysis of this whole process that will be carried out in Chapter 7.

The creation of SUDENE and its main lines of action

In Chapter 4, we observed the general state of crisis surrounding the foundation of SUDENE (Superintendency of Development of the Northeast). The creation of this institution had the explicit aim of transforming the action of the State in the Northeast from one of assistance to operating directly in transforming the economic structure of the region and affecting the roots of the economic problems of the region.

The action of SUDENE was mainly inspired by the report which originated it (GTDN)[1]. This report identified some important bottlenecks to the development of the region, among them the limits that agriculture put on development and the "triangular" commercial relations that this region developed with the Centre-South of the country (GTDN, 1978 and Furtado, 1962, p. 47)[2]. Furthermore, the report pointed out that three-quarters of the population of this region was only in the "margin" of the monetary economy, that is, the model of development followed by this region excluded the main part of its population from access to the monetary economy (Furtado, 1962, p. 47).

The report suggested that industrialisation and land reform were the two main ways of overcoming the backward position of this region (GTDN, 1978 and Furtado, 1962, p. 49). With this aim it proposed a strong scheme of State intervention in the region in order to change the structure of its economy.

Some authors point out that the actual course of the State intervention in the regional economy[3] eliminated the peculiarities that characterise the Northeast as an economic region, since it encouraged the action of extra-regional firms in the region and these firms assumed the dynamic of the capital accumulation (Oliveira, 1981, p. 113). Notwithstanding, homogenisation at the national level led to a process of heterogenisation at the regional level, since the new dynamic sectors were not linked to the old traditional sectors and this accentuated the intra-regional structural differences. However, the homogenisation of the process of accumulation of capital has some peculiarities which make it difficult to accept the idea of the destruction of the concept of region in the Brazilian case. Extra-regional firms were the leading element in capital accumulation in peripheral region since the 1960s and the periphery underwent this whole process in a dependent way. However, this does not mean the complete elimination of the peculiarities of the regional economy. The relation between the extra-regional firms and the local economy and the particularities that this relation generates are sufficient elements to characterise an economic region. The homogenisation observed by these authors is closer to the ideas which Cardoso develops on the new forms that dependence assumes in the Third World. However, the peculiarities of the periphery are still maintained as also its dependent situation.

SUDENE's objectives and instrument of economic policy were determined in its four medium term plans (Planos Diretores). SUDENE, in its creation, was supposed to have a wide range of action in the regional economy. It was supposed to "supervise, coordinate and control the elaboration and execution of projects under the responsibility of other federal agencies" (Goodman and Albuquerque, 1974, p. 163). Its action and the expenditure of the resources allocated to it out of federal tax revenue were supposed to take place through medium and long term Plans which were subject to approval by the National

Congress (Goodman and Albuquerque, 1974, p. 163).

The first (1961-63) and second (1963-66)[4] Plans followed the same approach as the creation of this institution. In both, the emphasis was on the creation of infra-structure and in reformist measures which allowed diversification of the economic structure of the region. The tax credit scheme was created in the first plan and widened in the second one. However, the military coup of 1964 changed completely the approach of SUDENE and this was reflected in its Plan. Thus, the third and fourth[5] plans abolished the reformist measures undertaken by this institution and put emphasis on the financing of private investment in the region.

Following the lines of SUDENE and BNB in 1966, the Bank of Development of the Amazon (BASA) was created with the Law 5122 of 28/09/1966 and the Superintendency for the Development of the Amazon (SUDAM) with Law 5173 of 27/10/1966). The latter began by formulating two plans, the first five year plan and the first "Plano Diretor". In both plans, the main areas of concern were the regional import substitution process and the geopolitical purpose of the occupation of the Amazon (Mahar, 1978, p. 26).

The tax credit scheme

SUDENE presented a wide range of actions. But the element that gained most attention was the tax credit scheme known as article 34/18 as a reference to the articles of the Law which established this mechanism[6].

The tax incentive mechanism was established by article 34 of Law No. 3995 of 1961, which approved the first "Plano Diretor" of SUDENE. In this article, this tax incentive mechanism was only available to national corporations. The scope of the scheme was extended by article 18 of Law No. 4239 of 1963 which approved the second "Plano Diretor" of this agency. In 1974, the Decree-Law No. 1376 of 12/12/1974 changes the 34/18 mechanism by the FINOR (Fundo de Investimento do Nordeste). Nevertheless, the main lines of this scheme were maintained. For this reason, we will refer to this mechanism as 34/18/FINOR.

The tax incentive mechanism made available, for use in industrial and agricultural projects approved by SUDENE, funds that otherwise would be expended in taxes. Firms were permitted to transform half of their tax liabilities in investments in projects approved by SUDENE in the Northeast of Brazil. This scheme represented a joint action of SUDENE and BNB. In the first instance, the funds available from the tax credit scheme were deposited in a blocked account at BNB. These deposits were supposed to be used in SUDENE-approved projects within three years; otherwise they would revert to the Federal Treasury. The available funds could be converted into preferential non-voting stocks which were not negotiable for five years, or they could be invested in a project of the corporation that used this scheme[7].

In the second case, the corporation was supposed to provide fresh funds for the total implementation of the projects; that is, the tax credit scheme established a ceiling for the use of funds. Article 34 established this ceiling at 50 per cent. However, in 1966 this ceiling was extended to 75 per cent, which meant that the corporation only needed to contribute 25 per cent of fresh funds for the implementation of a new project. There were other facilities which made the real need for fresh funds less than those established by article 34/18. The Bank of Northeast (BNB) created a special line of credit for industrial projects in the region. These credits offered a very attractive interest rate, about 12 per cent when the commercial bank rate was around 30 or 40 per cent. These credits could finance up to 50 per cent of the capital needed for the project. Therefore, if a project reached the ceiling of 75 per cent of article 34/18 funds and got this special credit of BNB, the need for fresh funds was reduced to 12.5 per cent. Other credit facilities were available from state banks which wanted to attract new projects to their states, reducing further the need for own funds (Hirschman, 1968-69, p. 6).

The Amazon also had its own tax credit scheme on the same lines as the 34/18/FINOR mechanism. The tax credit incentive was extended to this region in 1966 and the funds of this scheme were deposited in BASA. The projects which could receive these funds had to be projects for the development of the Amazon and had to be approved by SUDAM. The tax credit mechanism for the Amazon is FINAM (Fundo de Investimento da Amazônia).

The tax credit mechanism is said to have created a "captive capital market" for the Northeast and, later on, for the Amazon, since funds could only be used to buy shares of approved projects which would be developed in the region. Thus, although, there is an opportunity cost involved in any decision taken by the investor, this opportunity cost refers only to projects in the region, the investor had to make his choice between projects available in the region, and, in this sense, it was a "captive market" (Magalhães, 1983, pp. 47-8). This was clearly a recognition that funding was a constraint to the economic growth of the region. Since this mechanism facilitated the access of firms to funds, it alleviated the effects that the shortage of adequate funding mechanisms had on the growth of the region.

The demand for and effective disbursement of the 34/18 funds in the first years of the implementation of this tax credit scheme lagged behind the deposits made on the blocked account of BNB. Hirschman observes that this is a consequence of the intrinsic characteristics of this scheme, but this did not have perverse effects as was suggested by some authors. According to Hirschman, the availability of these funds in BNB made it possible to extend the activities of this bank as a commercial bank in the Northeast, and this made more liquidity available in the form of working capital to firms which were already operating in the region. Therefore, despite the fact that these funds were not being used as they were supposed to be, and were apparently idle when the country was suffering a huge shortage of liquidity resulting from the monetary policy adopted in the period 1961-67, they contributed to the development of the region by allowing the extension of credit by BNB (Hirschman, 1968-69, p. 12). Furthermore, the BNB's idle balances were maintained in a deposit account in Banco do Brasil. These resources were used on a nationwide scale, since the Banco do Brasil could extend credit without any regional constraint (Hirschman, 1968-69, p. 13).

The division between funds from 34/18/FINOR and fresh funds of a project was made according to criteria established by SUDENE, and this institution was also responsible for allowing access by firms to those funds. The criteria of allocation of resources of 34/18 followed a system of points which each project received according to its characteristics.

The 34/18 mechanism financed between 30 and 75 per cent of the capital of the projects, the percentage depending on the priority of the project according to SUDENE. The most important characteristics of a project being assessed for funding were: "location, the kind of goods that would be produced, use of regional inputs, import substitution and promotion of exports". (Goodman and Albuquerque, 1974, p. 201, our translation). The criteria for location tended to encourage the decentralization of investment, especially in the location in Recife and Salvador. The criteria for the kind of goods to be produced encouraged the production of capital goods and intermediate goods, some extra points being given to industries which would reduce the dependence of the region on the supply of intermediate goods from other regions. The problem of employment, a major problem in the region, received little attention in the criteria for allocation of funds[8]. This tended to intensify the problems of employment and underemployment in the region.

The criteria followed by SUDAM (the federal agency for the development of the Amazon) for the establishment of the priorities of a project were related mainly to the population and economic occupation of the region, use of regional raw material and use of local labour force (Cardoso and Muller, 1977, p. 118). There are some differences in these criteria compared to the ones followed by SUDENE; these differences refer mainly to the peculiarities of this region, especially its lower population density.

The tax credit mechanism is normally considered a subsidy for the industries which were created in the Northeast and which had access to these funds. However, as Magalhães observes, it is a subsidy for the investor, who transforms his taxes into stocks, but not for the firm which receives the funds, since this firm is supposed to pay dividends for its stocks. However, the mechanism makes it easier for firms in the peripheral regions to have access to funding and allows them to present smaller expected rates of return; therefore, it may be a disguised expenditure of the government (Haddad, 1989, p. 81), but it is not a subsidy per se to the firm (Magalhães, 1983, p. 48). The creation of this mechanism is a recognition of the difficulties in funding the investment in the region according to market interest rates.

This sort of tax concession is a great incentive towards concentration, since big firms have more tax to pay and consequently more to transform into deposits, and this is the actual source of subsidy. Furthermore, as the larger firms are more concentrated in the Centre-South than elsewhere, this region dominates in terms of the volume of deposits that resulted from this mechanism. So we have a large number of firms which show small values of their 34/18 deposit and big firms which keep an enormous value of the total deposits. This can be seen in Tables IV.1 and IV.2 (Oliveira, 1981, p. 119 and Oliveira, 1984, p. 59 , Magalhães, 1983, p. 53).

The predominance of extra-regional firms in terms of deposits in this scheme weakens its potential. Extra-regional firms prefer to apply their funds in projects that have a higher integration with their original region. This is because these projects normally demand more inputs from these regions, thus increasing the demand for their products and because the bases for the formation of expectation are more reliable, given the reduced remoteness, in firms from the same region as the firms that will invest their funds. This tends to encourage firms which present higher leakages, both financial and real in regional terms. Therefore, the potential to retain gains for the target region are reduced and the capacity of the region to create a self-perpetuating process of growth is also reduced. These elements have important implications in financial terms: the higher leakages that these projects entail reduce the money multipliers in the target region and, at the same time, reduce the multiplicand, and, in this way, prevent the region from retaining the benefits of the funding mechanism.

Table IV.1

FINOR- 1976: Distribution of Deposits According to the Number of Depositors and Value of the Deposit

Class of Value Cr$ 1000 of 1976	Number of Depositors	Value of Deposits
Less than 1	41.4	1.3
1 to 5	32.3	5.9
5 to 100	24.7	35.7
100 to 300	1.2	14.6
300 to +	0.4	42.5

Source: Magalhães (1983, p. 54).

Table IV.2
FINOR: Regional Source of Deposits
(Deposits over Cr$ 300000,00)
(%)

Region	Depositor	Deposit
North	0	0
Northeast	17	13
Centre-West	1	2
South	7	7
Southeast	75	78
Total	100	100

Source: Magalhães (1983, p. 55).

The extra-regional concentration of the deposits can also be observed in the case of the Amazon (see Table IV.3).

Table IV.3
SUDAM: Origin of the Fiscal Credit and Investment of Enterprises
(%)

	North	N.East	S.East	South	C.West
1968	3.1	0.4	77.2	14.2	5.1
1969	4.2	0.4	74.6	14.6	6.2
1970	3.7	0.5	77.1	13.9	4.8
1971	4.0	1.6	77.5	10.9	6.0
1972	4.6	0.4	75.4	13.9	5.7
1973	3.5	0.4	76.9	12.7	6.5
1974	4.3	0.3	76.3	12.9	6.2
1975	3.7	0.3	73.2	14.9	7.9

Source: Mahar (1978, p. 116).

As previously pointed out, the tax credit scheme was originally created to encourage the economic development of the backward regions. First it was implemented in the Northeast and later on it was extended to the Amazon (1965). Nevertheless, in the seventies it was transformed from a regional programme into a sectorial programme and in this moment it lost part of its importance in regional terms since the dispersion of resources was too large and the resources allocated to the regions were dissipated in the middle of plenty of other sectorial incentives[9]. As can be observed in Table IV.4 (Mendonça de Barros, 1984, p. 389 and PIMES, 1984, vol.3,p.XLI).

Table IV.4

Tax Incentive Mechanism According to Options

(%)

Fund/Programme	1962	1965	1970	1975	1980	1985*
SUDENE	100.0	93.0	56.0	25.6	19.9	51.86
SUDAM	-	7.0	20.4	8.1	8.3	15.7
SUDEPE	-	-	13.7	1.0	0.4	0.3
EMBRATUR	-	-	4.2	1.2	1.0	0.7
IBDF	-	-	6.7	13.2	18.4	24.7
PIN	-	-	-	28.7	28.6	-
PROTERRA	-	-	-	19.1	19.0	-
FUNRES (ES)	-	-	-	0.4	0.4	1.2
EMBRAER	-	-	-	1.6	1.8	3.57
MOBRAL	-	-	-	1.1	3.0	-

* The increase in the values of SUDENE and SUDAM is a consequence of the values of PIN and PROTERRA being incorporated in these figures.

Source: Guimarães Neto (1989, pp. 140-2). For 1985, Coordenação do Sistema de Informações Econômico Fiscais - Receita Federal - Ministério da Fazenda.

Regional and national impacts of the reation of 34/18 The reasons for the creation of a tax credit scheme such as 34/18 are the subject of a long controversy. Of course, overcoming of the backward position of the Northeast is the first reason which appears in anyone's mind; however it is not so simple, especially when we see who has received the main benefits of such a scheme, as we will do later on.

On the one hand, Oliveira, Cano and Guimarães Neto note that the creation of this mechanism was one more element which intensified homogenisation of the economic space in the country. That is, this mechanism was created when the dynamic of accumulation of the oligopolist capital of the Centre-South was extending to the backward regions, dominating the dynamic of the accumulation of capital in the backward regions (Oliveira, 1981, 1984, Cano, 1985, Guimarães Neto, 1989, Galvão, 1987). Cano and Guimarães Neto (1986) called this the "productive integration" of the regions.

On the other hand, Moreira argues that the tax credit incentive had as its first aim the development of the industrial sector of the Northeast; in this sense, it could have been considered originally as a regional development policy. However, it really gained importance because of a conjunctural element: the crisis that the country underwent in the period 1961-1967 (Moreira, 1979), which was, to a great extent, a result of the limits of the import substitution model of industrialisation. The intensity of the crisis can be observed in Table IV.5:

Table IV.5
Rates of Growth of Real Income

Years	Real Income Per capita	Total Investment
1950-55	2.4	13.4
1955-60	2.6	7.6
1960-64	0.8	-
1960-61	4.1	1.6
1961-62	2.0	-2.0
1962-63	-1.6	-3.7
1963-64	-1.2	-

Source: Moreira (1979, p. 66).

Moreira observes that the tax credit mechanism cannot be considered a consequence of the crisis because it was created just before the beginning of the crisis (1961) and if it was created as a mechanism to overcome the crisis, it could have been created in any other sector or region. However, he observes that the effective use of this mechanism by firms of the Centre-South only took place after the beginning of the crisis and this, according to him, is evidence that it allowed the maintenance of the rate of profit in this region, or at least, made investment worthwhile in the Northeast, through the mechanism of subsidising funds for new investment. Araújo followed the same reasoning as Moreira, observing that the most intensive use of the tax credit scheme took place in the period 1965-69, which was a period of crisis for the economy of the Centre-South. She also observes that the dispersion of the resources of the 34/18 took place exactly at the end of the 1960s, when the crisis was overcome; after this period, it assumed a much more sectorial character rather than a regional character (Araújo, 1981, p. 18).

By contrast, Guimarães Neto argues that the conjunctural cause of industrial decentralisation began with the crisis and its continuation was determined by structural causes: the oligopolistic capital of the Centre-South made use of tax credit incentives to continue its accumulation now involving the backward regions. That is, he observes this process receiving the benefits at a crisis but continuing because of structural needs. In this way, he tries to conciliate the positions of Moreira and Oliveira (Guimarães Neto, 1989).

The common point to observe in the analyses of the determination of the importance of the 34/18/FINOR mechanism is the dependent character shown by the structural change in the Northeast of Brazil. On the one hand, Oliveira attributes the homogenisation of the national economic space to the need of the oligopolistic capital to continue its expansion by incorporating peripheral regions; homogenisation is dominated by capital from the central regions. On the other hand, Moreira shows that 34/18 was used mainly to overcome the crisis which the central economy was facing. In either explanation, 34/18 was used according to the needs of the central economy rather than for the development of an independent process of industrialisation in the peripheral economies.

The dominant position of firms from the Centre-South in the process of industrialisation led by governmental policies toward the Northeast has important consequences in the whole process of regional growth. The extra-regional origin of the firms makes them more integrated with their original region than with the host economy, since the strategy of the firms is determined in the central economy, and therefore they present higher import coefficients than local firms. These firms also present higher leakages in relation to their financial behaviour, since they tend to hold more assets of their original region than assets of the host region. Thus, the sort of industrialisation followed by the Northeast does not allow the region to keep the majority of the benefits from the incentives which were created in order to industrialise the region.

Structural changes in the regional economies

In Part III we observed that the structure of the regional economies followed the typical centre/periphery model. The policies for the peripheral regions changed the sectorial composition of these economies; however, the change was just a transformation of the relations of dependence of the peripheral regions, since the main elements that characterise dependence and create the sort of relation between central and peripheral regions which allow the full play of vicious circles were maintained and, in a certain sense, deepened.

Government intervention in the traditional peripheral regions, especially in the Northeast, caused important transformations in these economies. However, these structural transformations cannot be observed only by analysing the data on the distribution of the gross regional product which indicate that the concentration of the product has not suffered significant changes since the 1950s. We only begin to observe a process of deconcentration after 1975, especially in the Southeast. The process of deconcentration, however, was directed more toward new peripheral areas than to the traditional periphery[10] (PIMES, 1984, Vol.I, p. 62). This is more marked in the improved relative position of the Centre West, as can be seen in Tables IV.1.s.a. to IV.3.s.a.

The main structural changes in the traditional peripheral areas, especially in the Northeast, can be observed when we analyse the sectorial composition of the gross regional product and especially when we analyse the data on the structural composition of the sectors of this economy[11]. The participation of each region in the total production of agriculture, industry and services can be observed in Tables IV.4.s.a., IV.7.s.a. and IV.10.s.a.

In relation to agriculture, we can notice a certain increase in the participation of the North and Northeast; in this case, it is important to emphasise the relative growth of Bahia and Southeast. However, the growth of the Southeast in the last five years represents a change from the previous pattern of this region's relative decline in agricultural product. On the other hand, the decrease observed in the South and Centre West also corresponds to a change of the historical tendency towards increasing participation of those regions in the whole agricultural product of Brazil. Observing Table IV.5.s.a. we also notice a strong concentration of the agricultural production inside the regions.

In terms of the share of agriculture in the total product of the region, we can observe a tendency toward the homogenisation of the participation of this sector (Table IV.6.s.a.). The only region which really presents a much smaller participation of this sector in its gross regional product is the Southeast and this is much more accentuated when we analyse the composition of the product of São Paulo, as can be observed in Table IV.6.s.a.

The industrial product, on the other hand, is still extremely concentrated in the Southeast and in São Paulo, despite a slight tendency toward development in peripheral regions of the Northeast and North: see Table IV.7.s.a. Within the peripheral regions, the concentration is very marked: we can see in Table IV.8.s.a. that Bahia and Pernambuco account for almost 50 per cent of the whole industrial production of the Northeast and almost 70 per cent of the whole industrial production of the Southeast is concentrated in São Paulo. A process of homogenisation of the industrial participation in the regional product also occurred during the analysed period. The only region that really presents a marked difference in relation to the others is the Centre West, which shows a much smaller participation of the industrial sector in its whole product. This can be observed in Table IV.9.s.a.

The services sector also appears extremely concentrated in the central regions, especially in the Southeast. This sector plays a fundamental role in peripheral economies, being responsible for the largest part of the regional product (Tables IV.10.s.a. and IV.11.s.a.). This sector was of the greatest importance to these economies around the 70s and, after that, underwent a relative decline and was, in part, substituted by the industrial sector (Table IV.9.s.a.). Intra-regional concentration is also observed in this sector (see Table IV.12.s.a.).

Thus, we can notice a certain tendency toward the homogenisation of the composition of the regional product during this period. However, in order to understand the process taking place it is necessary to analyse more carefully the changes in the composition of the industrial sector of each region and see what are the main specialisation tendencies of this sector.

Observing the composition of the value of the industrial transformation (Table IV.14.s.a.)[12] we notice an extremely concentrated industrial sector. An analysis of the number of industrial establishments also shows a huge concentration; however, this concentration is far below the levels of concentration of the value of the industrial transformation, which demonstrates that the size of the establishments in the Southeast tends to be larger than in other regions, especially in the Northeast, South and Centre West (Table IV.15.s.a.). Analysing Table IV.16.s.a. we see a relatively bigger participation of the workers in Northeast and South, compared to the value of the industrial transformation, which may imply a smaller productivity of these regions, or it may be due to the smaller size of the establishments in these regions which does not allow them to attain gains of scale. In terms of the internal composition of the industrial sector, Tables IV.17.s.a., IV.18.s.a. and IV.19.s.a. show that, in the analysed period, there was a significant change in the composition of the industrial sector of peripheral regions. In the specific case of the Northeast, we can observe a change in the concentration of industrial activities from traditional industries to modern industries, especially in intermediary goods and goods related to the natural base of the region.

Thus, observing the sectors that grew more during the period, we note that the principal sectors which received the benefits of the tax credit scheme were sectors related to the dynamic industries of the Centre-South of the country, especially those which have an oligopolic market structure. Thus, industrialisation or the intensification of the industrialisation of the Northeast proceeded as an extension of the industrialisation which took place in the

Centre-South and was led by industries that operated and had their head offices in that region.

This pattern intensified leakages from the Northeast to the Centre-South of the country, since the extra-regional industries, which were the main element in the process of industrialisation of the region, had greater links with the central economy than with the Northeast. This intensified the two types of leakages observed by the theoretical model analysed in Chapter 2: a) trade deficits and b) financial leakages caused by speculative movements of money. The intensification of these two elements tended to magnify the results predicted by the model: a constrained capacity for credit creation in peripheral regions resulting from the smaller redeposit ratios in the peripheral region.

We can also examine a process of concentration in the large industries of the peripheral regions. This can be seen in Table IV.6 and IV.24.s.a.

Table IV.6

Regional Distribution of the 1000 Biggest Firms According to Region and Sector - 1977-1987

	North		Northeast		Southeast	
	1977	1987	1977	1987	1977	1987
Agriculture	2	1	0	0	23	16
Mining and Manufacturing	10	23	67	96	416	330
Building	2	1	5	5	67	37
Commerce	0	1	4	5	41	43
Services	1	1	6	20	122	174
Public Services	8	6	25	25	41	27
Transport and Storage	3	0	0	2	17	13
Total	26	33	107	153	727	640

Source: Guimarães Neto (1990, p. 160).

The relevance of the tax credit scheme to the location of new industries in the Northeast can be seen from the analysis of the results of BNB/SUDENE research from 1977 where we see the main factors which determined the location of new industries in the region. The result of the research are shown in Table IV.7.

Table IV.7
Factors Determining the Location of New Firms in the Northeast: Number of Firms, Fixed Investment and Employment
(%) According to The First Option
1977

Factors	No. of firms	Fixed Investment	Employment
Tax Credit Scheme	47.2	45.3	45.9
Raw Material	21.8	36.8	22.8
Market	5.8	2.0	3.5
Labour	1.1	0.3	1.1
Entrepreneur From Northeast	19.7	8.6	20.6
Other	4.4	7.0	6.0

Source: Magalhães (1983, p. 66).

Table IV.7 shows that the main factor which defines the location of a new industry in the Northeast is the tax credit mechanism, and this is more important when we observe the number of firms involved. These results show that this mechanism was fundamental to the structural changes which took place over the region during this period. The relevance of the existence of raw materials in the region, especially in terms of fixed investment, tends to determine the kind of industries which were created in this region, particularly in relation to the extra-regional capital which had been installed in the region. Another important factor is the regional origin of the entrepreneur. We can see that this element is important to the number of firms and the amount of employment in these firms. This highlights the fact that firms with entrepreneurs from the region tend to be smaller, and that these same firms tend to adopt more labour-intensive technologies than firms from other regions.

This situation changes when we look at the 1988 data of SUDENE/BNB.

Table IV.8
Primary Factors Determining the Location of New Firms in the Northeast - 1988 (%)

Factors	% of Firms
Market	13.7
Regional Raw Material	29.2
Labour	2
Tax Credit Scheme	28.2
Origin of The Entrepreneur(Northeast)	23.4
Special Lines of Credit	0.3
Other	3.2

Source: SUDENE/BNB (1992, p. 36).

Table IV.8 shows a change in the relative position of the motives which led to the location of new firms in the Northeast in 1988. During this period, the more important element is regional availability of raw material and this is followed by the tax credit mechanism. This may be due to the dispersion of this kind of incentive to other sectors and the loss of the regional character of this kind of incentive, as was previously emphasised.

The regional origin of the entrepreneur continues to be an important element which lead to the creation of new firms in the region. This is in accordance with the model developed in Chapter 2, since a local entrepreneur has a more reliable base for the formation of expectations on conditions in the regional economy. Put another way, although the higher instability of the peripheral regions drives entrepreneurs from the region to invest in other regions, the tendency of these entrepreneurs to quit from the region is less than the tendency of extra-regional entrepreneurs, since the conventions and the bases for the formation of expectations of the state of these economies are more solid for the local entrepreneur than for the extra-regional entrepreneur. On the contrary, in the case of an entrepreneur from the periphery it is the central economies which are remote in terms of the basis of information.

The motives which make firms invest their funds from 34/18/FINOR in a specific project have been investigated by Oliveira. He points out that banks tend to apply their funds to firms or projects that have a close relation with them, are in the same economic group of the bank or these firms are important in terms of generation of deposits to this bank and so on. Other firms tend to apply their funds from 34/18/FINOR in projects which would demand inputs from these firms, thus creating advantages for them (Oliveira, 1984, p. 55). This type of behaviour tends to accentuate the tendency towards leakage of these funds to other regions, since the majority of the funds of the 34/18/FINOR is for extra-regional firms, as can be seen in Table IV.2. This constrains the money multipliers of the periphery and also reduces the multiplicand of these regions, since it tends to accentuate the leakages of these economies. Even if we assume that the banking system is at later stages of banking development, this will still constrain the capacity of credit creation in the regions, since banks will observe smaller redeposit ratios in the periphery and will reduce the credit supply to these regions.

The technological profile of the new industry of the Northeast tends to generate larger import coefficients and lower job creation, both of which are major problems of the economy of the Northeast. The extra-regional origin of the head offices or the capital origin of the majority of the industries that have migrated to the Northeast after the creation of the tax credit mechanism and the characteristics of this mechanism tend to create a technological profile that is rather different from that of the industries which were installed in this region during the period before tax credit incentives.

The main characteristic of the technology adopted by the incentivated[13] industries is its capital intensity. There are basically two positions for the causes of this intensity. On the one hand, we have analysts who believe that the tax credit mechanism brings with it a subsidy for capital. This tends to encourage the adoption of capital intensive technology (Guimarães Neto, 1982, Goodman and Albuquerque, 1974, Albuquerque and Cavalcanti, 1976).

On the other hand, we have the position adopted by Magalhães and Ferreira. Magalhães observes that the technological profile of the incentivated industry in the Northeast is much more due to the sectorial composition of the industry and of the integration of this industry at the national level than to any kind of subsidy to capital (Magalhães, 1983, p. 9). Ferreira observes that the technological profile of the project is determined by the competition between firms at the national level. This makes industry in the Northeast adopt technological processes that are very close to those used in the Centre-South, since the products of both industries will be competing in the same markets. Furthermore, this competition is responsible for the homogenisation of the technological processes at the national level and consequently for the capital intensity of technologies adopted by the incentivated industries in the Northeast (Ferreira, 1983a, pp. 221-2; Ferreira, 1983b).

The capital intensity of the technological processes adopted by the incentivated industry is, however, mainly a characteristic of the extra-regional industries. The industries owned by entrepreneurs of the Northeast tend to present a more labour intensive technological profile compared to those that are extra-regional. Projects whose ownership is intra-regional tend to be smaller and use more labour intensive technologies (Magalhães, 1983, p. 10). In a certain sense, these two elements are interconnected, since these projects are normally associated with sectors that allow more labour intensive technologies and small plants. Therefore, this can demonstrate a regional division of labour where the extra-regional capital stays in the dynamic sectors and the intra-regional capital stays in the traditional sectors. On the other hand, not being linked to extra-regional head offices gives them more autonomy and freedom in the determination of the technology to be adopted. The size and the number of establishments and the control of these establishments is shown in Tables IV.9 and IV.10.

Table IV.9

New Industry in the Northeast: Origin and Control of Social Capital in the Firm - 1977

(%)

Origin of the Control of the Social Capital	Firm	Fixed Invest-ment	Employment	Social Capital
1-Private Groups From the Northeast	57.1	29.1	48.5	36.6
2-Private Groups of Rest of the Country	38.2	59.1	45.4	55.1
São Paulo	22.1	27.8	26.1	29.8
Other States	16.1	31.3	19.3	25.3
3-Private Groups From Abroad	1.9	3.6	1.4	2.1
4-Government	2.8	8.2	4.7	6.2

Source: Magalhães (1983, p. 108).

Table IV.10

New Industry in the Northeast: Origin and Control of Social Capital in the Firm – 1986 (%)

Northeast	66.0
North/Centre-West	1.0
Southeast	28.0
South	4.0
Abroad	1.0
Total	100.0

Source: SUDENE/BNB (1992, p. 96).

Table IV.20.s.a. shows that there is a certain type of regional division of labour. Extra-regional capital tends to specialise in sectors that are considered more dynamic while regional capital tends to be more concentrated in sectors that are more traditional. This regional division of labour could be one of the features which explain the larger capacity for labour absorption in the industries whose capital is controlled by local entrepreneurs, as observed earlier.

Another important element to be examined in the new industrial sector, created since the implementation of the 34/18/FINOR mechanism, is the regional integration of these industries. In this sense, it is also important to point out the differences in the control of capital compared to the regional integration of this industry or in terms of the regional linkages that these industries represent.

Table IV.11

New Industry in the Northeast: Origins of Inputs According to the Origin of the Control of Social Capital - 1977 (%)

Origin of The Input / Origin of The Capital	Northeast	São Paulo	Rest of the Country	Abroad
Northeast	66.5	17.4	13.0	3.1
São Paulo	38.1	24.0	19.7	18.2
Rest of The Country	47.0	14.7	16.0	22.3
Abroad	19.5	54.8	24.6	1.1
Government	27.3	15.0	21.9	35.8
Total	52.5	18.9	16.0	12.6

Source: Magalhães (1983, p. 148).

Tables IV.11, IV.21.s.a. and IV.22.s.a. show that firms that have their capital controlled by local entrepreneurs are much more integrated in the local economy than those that have their capital controlled by extra-regional entrepreneurs. This could also be due to the fact that local entrepreneurs tend to have their projects in sectors that are considered traditional, as seen in Table IV.20.s.a. Both traditional and local projects have greater linkages with the local economy than extra-regional firms. This is due to the general policy of the extra-regional firms which have more general targets than regional ones. As these extra-regional firms operate in a broader environment, their level of integration is restricted by their general policy and is not dictated by local plants[14]. The degree of integration of firms in the local economy is not only important in terms of the income multipliers but also in terms of the money multipliers, as demonstrated in Chapter 2. Therefore, if a certain kind of mechanism creates incentives to industries that show less linkages with the local economy it will have just partial results, since its multiplier effects will be reduced and it will end up by reducing the money multipliers of the region, as a consequence of the real and financial leakages that it allows, and will intensify the financial constraints to the region.

Another indicator of local integration is the destination of the sales of the new industries of the Northeast. This can be observed in Tables IV.12 and IV.23s.a.

Table IV.12
New Industry in the Northeast: Destination of Sales
(%)

Destination	Northeast	São Paulo	Rest of the Country	Abroad
Sector of The Industry				
Non Durable Consumer Goods	38.7	19.9	17.2	24.2
Intermediate Consumer Goods	48.2	27.7	18.0	6.1
Durable Consumer Goods and Capital Goods	33.1	35.7	20.2	11.0
Mineral Extractive Industry	7.0	38.1	43.0	11.9

Source: Magalhães (1983, p. 150).

Tables IV.12 and IV.23.s.a. show that extra-regional markets play an important role in the demand for products of the new industry in the Northeast especially in sectors such as mineral extractive industry, durable consumer goods and the capital goods. The huge import of inputs and the extra-regional character of the demand of the new industry of the Northeast made Furtado states that the industrialisation of the Northeast proceeded as an "enclave" economy (Furtado, 1982). He observes that as the new industry of the Northeast is fundamentally composed by branches of central or multinational firms, there is a great volatility in the re-investment of the surplus generated by these plants. This is what made him point out that these industries do not differ substantially from mining and agriculture activities of the colonial era, since the only elements which create links between these activities and the region are payment of wages and the creation of taxes for the local governments. However, these elements cannot be a source of change for the local economy because there are no inter-sectorial relations of production which allow an increase in the monetary income of the region to be translated into increases in the demand for local products: the increases in monetary incomes show themselves through the increase in the demand for imports (Furtado, 1982, p. 140). However, this sort of "enclave" economy does not have only real effects, it also has financial consequences which result in real constraints to growth. Since there are no mechanisms to retain the finance which enters the region or which is created in the region to finance these projects, it leaks to the central region in its first round. In this sense, the multiplier effects that this creation of liquidity can present are extremely reduced.

As observed before, one of the most important characteristics of the industrialisation led by the 34/18/FINOR mechanism was its intra-regional concentration. New industry tended to locate its new plants in states which were more industrialised, that is Pernambuco and Bahia and more recently Ceará[15]. This was due to the external economies which these states had already established. The mechanism tried to avoid this tendency, attributing more points (which put the project in a better position to get more funds from 34/18/FINOR) to projects that were not located in these states, but this was not enough to counteract this tendency (Goodman and Albuquerque, 1974, pp. 200-10 and 280). This emphasised the existent tendency toward intra-regional inequalities in the Northeast (Araújo, 1981 and 1994). The intra-regional concentration of the industry of the Northeast can be seen in Table IV.13. The intra-regional concentration which this mechanism made easier created sub-peripheral regions within the region. This reproduces the results of the theoretical model inside the region, that is, we begin to observe sub-peripheral regions which are constrained twice: first in relation to the central economy and then by the peripheral economy which is its sub-central economy. All the mechanisms that create vicious circles in financial and real terms are present in these sub-systems and, what is worse, they are intensified further.

Table IV.13

New Industry in the Northeast: Number of Firms According to Location (%)

State	1977	1986
Maranhão	1.7	2.9
Piauí	1.9	2.4
Ceará	17.0	19.8
Rio G. do Norte	8.0	7.4
Paraíba	12.5	10.2
Pernambuco	26.6	24.3
Alagoas	3.1	3.6
Sergipe	3.6	3.5
Bahia	20.8	19.5
Minas Gerais	4.8	6.5

Source: Magalhães (1983, p. 283) and SUDENE/BNB (1992, p. 31).

The industrialisation generated by the tax credit mechanism in the North was also extremely concentrated in states that exhibited a more developed industrial base. This can be noticed in Table IV.14. Projects related to cattle raising and services are also very concentrated, in spite of the fact that cattle raising projects followed a different pattern, being very concentrated in Mato Grosso.

Table IV.14
Amazônia: Projects Given Incentive by the Tax Credit Mechanism According to Location (%)
1975

	Industry	Cattle	Services	Total
Rondonia	0.8	0.4	0.2	0.5
Acre	0.3	2.4	0.8	1.2
Amazonas	23.9	3.6	45.4	20.2
Roraima	-	-	-	-
Pará	54.1	26.5	31.5	39.5
Amapá	2.3	-	15.2	3.8
Maranhão	7.8	1.5	1.8	4.3
Mato Grosso	7.9	61.2	5.1	27.6
Goiás	2.8	4.4	0.1	2.9
Amazônia	100.0	100	100	100

Source: Mahar (1978, p. 125).

The structural change in the regional economies, in particular, the changes in peripheral economies which were led by the tax credit scheme, brought with it a tendency to homogenise their sectorial composition. These changes were supposed to have had some impact on the productivity of the region and on the differentials in productivity observed in the country. Analysing this, Boisier noticed that differential productivity in Brazil was mainly explained by sectorial differentials rather than differences in the location of projects. He observes a reduction in the productivity differential between Brazilian states in the period 1965-69 and attributes this to changes in the sectorial composition of each state (Boisier, 1975). On the other hand, he observes that, in Brazil, the spatial element is fundamental to the explanation of wage differentials and this element is more important than the sectorial element, showing an opposite situation than that observed for the explanation of the differential in productivity (Boisier, 1975, p. 80).

In spite of the huge efforts toward the industrialisation of the Northeast since 1960, we can see that the economy of this region as a whole still continued to be less dynamic than the Brazilian economy overall. This could be due to the concentration of government policies in the industrial sector and the characteristics of the industrial sector which was incentivated. This produced minimal linkage effects in the regional economy and, in doing so, created smaller income multipliers than intended. On the other hand, the industrial sector of the region was far more dynamic than in the rest of the country and this dynamism was mainly a consequence of the economic policies developed in the region. This differential behaviour can be observed in Table IV.15. As previously observed, the main elements of economic policy for the region were centred on the industrial sector. Later on, the tax credit scheme was extended to agricultural projects and credit for agriculture became an important element in dynamising this activity. However, most of the credit went towards cattle raising, which in the Northeast has an extensive character and has very limited labour absorption power. Thus, its ability to increase the income of this sector was very weak (Rebouças, 1979, pp. 260-4).

Table IV.15

Income Geometric Averaged Rates of Growth

Period	Northeast				Brazil	
	Total	Agric	Ind.	Serv.	Total	Ind.
1950-60	6.4	5.9	8.1	6.4	6.4	8.7
1961-70	4.9	1.6	7.4	6.6	5.1	5.8
1971-80	8.3	3.3	10.4	9.8	7.8	8.3
1961-80	6.9	3.6	8.9	8.2	7.6	8.5

Source: Magalhães (1983, p. 174).

Government policy for the region was important in reducing the instability which characterised this economy until the 60s. As observed in Chapter 4, the economies of both the North and the Northeast were more unstable than the economy of the rest of the country. Analysing the behaviour of regional income and national income in the period 1965-90 we found a reduction in the instability of the economy of the Northeast in relation to Brazil. This can be observed in Figure 1 and Table IV.13.s.a.[16]. Nevertheless, the economy of the Northeast is still more unstable than the economy of Brazil as a whole. If we compare the variance of the yearly rate of growth of the Brazilian economy (0.002) and the variance of the rate of growth of the Northeast (0.003) in the period 1966-90, and the coefficient of variation of Brazil (0.042) and of the Northeast (0.063), we will see that instead of a relative stabilisation in the latter, compared to the previous period analysed in Part III, it is still more unstable than the economy of Brazil. A reduced instability of the Northeast after the 1960s compared with the previous period was observed by Guimarães Neto (1989, p. 171), Magalhães (1983, p. 176), Harber Jr. (1982, p. 706) and Gomes (1988). This change in the behaviour of the economy is normally attributed to the government intervention in the region.

Harber Jr. observes a more stable behaviour of the economy of the Northeast compared to the rest of the country and attributes this to smaller income multipliers for the region (although we have observed only a reduction in the level of instability, compared to the period of Part III, which does not imply that this economy is more stable than the economy of Brazil as a whole, as Harber Jr. proposes). The theoretical explanation for these smaller income multipliers comes from the larger leakages from this economy and this is also related to the reduced money multipliers observed in this region. However, this argument is not enough to explain why this region was more unstable than the central region before the 1960s. The point seems to centre on the fact that instead of the argument that this economy showed smaller income multipliers than the central economy which gave it a tendency towards stability, the multiplicand in this region was more unstable than in the central region before the 1960s and this was the element responsible for the great instability. After the1960s, when government action was stronger, the multiplicand was more stable (especially for government expenditure) and attained higher levels. This seems to be the element responsible for stabilising the level of income in the region. Another important element for stabilising this region is the important role played by the local services sector. As this sector is mainly linked to the action of the State, and as such action attained a more stable pattern for the region, this tended to contribute to the stabilisation of the economy of the region (Gomes, 1988, p. 396).

Inter-regional and international trade

In Chapter 4, we saw that peripheral regions tended to have substantial deficits in their commercial relations with other regions of the country and that this was especially true in relation to São Paulo. Industrialisation led by the tax credit mechanism did not change this tendency. As previously observed, new industry was overwhelmingly integrated with the industry in the Centre-South of the country and a large part of its inputs and capital were imported from the central region, for technological or strategic reasons. Thus, the tendency toward deficits increased instead of decreasing in this period. The behaviour of inter-regional trade can be observed in Table IV.16.

Table IV.16
Balance of Inter-Regional Trade

States	Balances		
	1975-Cr$Millions	1980-Cr$Thousand	1985-Cz$ Thousand
North	-2,170.5	-27,978.5	-5,587,470
N. East	-12,609.4	-210,095.1	-23,469,719
PE	-2,270.5	-50,841.5	-3,415,009
BA	-3,627.3	-7,850.9	-1,227,149
C.West	-8,182.9	-140,022	-19,037,802
S.East	34,294.4	532,787.6	43,566,334
SP	37,818.5	699,227.7	29,764,621
South	-11,331.6	-154,692	4,528,657

Source: Revista de Finanças Públicas.

Table IV.16 illustrates the tendency towards a reduction in the deficits in the trade balances of the peripheral regions[17]. The Northeast instead of still presenting deficits reduced these deficits compared to other regions. If we observe the states that are responsible for generation of these positive results, we see that those states which have an important productive base for generation of raw materials, such as petroleum (Bahia, Northeast) and minerals (North, especially Pará[18]), and in Amazônia where we observe the formation of Zona Franca de Manaus[19], that instead of having deficits in its commerce abroad, shows positive results in its commerce with other regions. These states have received important stimuli to create industrial poles that could dynamise the region; they also had natural resources which allowed the creation of an industry to produce important raw materials for the Southeast. These characteristics made it possible to reverse the tendency towards deficits in their trade balances, and this tendency brought positive results in the trade balance of the region as a whole. However, São Paulo, still maintaining its dominant position, shows surpluses in relation to all other regions.

Table IV.17
Ratio Trade Balance/Regional Income

	1975	1980	1985
North	-0.12	-0.07	-0.09
Northeast	-0.13	-0.14	-0.12
Pernambuco	-0.09	-0.16	-0.10
Bahia	-0.11	-0.01	-0.02
Southeast	0.06	0.07	0.05
São Paulo	0.11	0.15	0.06
South	-0.07	-0.07	0.02
C. West	-0.22	-0.21	-0.22

Source: Revista de Finanças Públicas and Anuário Estatistítico, IBGE.

An analysis of Table IV.17 shows that the regions which have more marked deficits in their trade balances compared to their GDP are the Centre-West, Northeast and North. The large deficit of the Centre-West can be explained by the presence of Brasília in this region which has a small productive base and represents a great consumption pull which is satisfied with imports from other regions. The Northeast and North also exhibit critical values in their relation between deficits and GDP. The higher import coefficients of the peripheral regions was assumed as one of the characteristics of these regions in the theoretical chapter. This results in reducing the income and money multipliers of these regions, since the impacts of exogenous expenditure and of expansion of money and credit leak from the region through the imports. These leaks, determined by trade deficits, add to the leaks caused by the speculative behaviour of agents in such a way as to reduce considerably the money multipliers in peripheral regions.

The external commercial relations of Brazil were very important for understanding some of the changes in the dynamics in the regional development of Brazil over this period. After 1964, the government began to show a clear interest in the diversification of Brazilian exports. This was due to the necessity to extend the import substitution process to new sectors, highlighting the need for more foreign exchange. At the same time, economic policy began to stimulate export of industrial products, which until this period, were mainly produced for the domestic market. This led to a strong reduction in the participation of exports of the less developed regions in total Brazilian exports and consequently this led to a reduction in growth of these economies (Galvão, 1979, pp. 162-8). On the other hand, the stimulus given to the export of non-industrialised goods, mainly agricultural goods, was also concentrated in the Centre-South of the country, as the newly stimulated crops were located mainly in South and Centre-West (Galvão, 1979, p. 173; Guimarães Neto, 1989, p. 135 and Hess, 1987). Nevertheless, with the inclusion of new products in the exports of Brazil, products that had a strong natural basis, such as minerals and fuel, the incentives to export began to be absorbed by some peripheral regions and not just the centre. That is, the new peripheral regions got part of the benefits of the incentives to primary product exports. However, these policies had negative effects on the traditional peripheral regions, since they did not produce the products which received the incentives of these policies and, consequently, they were relatively disadvantaged by these policies.

Linkages of the new industry of the Northeast

The relevance of analysing the propensity of the new industry in the Northeast to import both capital goods and inputs is due to the multipliers which this industry can present and the degree of linkages that it can generate. Thus, this analysis allows us to observe the capacity of the adopted policy to reverse to a greater or lesser extent, the backward position of the region.

The analysis of linkages in one specific sector cannot be carried out by only keeping in mind the technological determinant of these linkages or by extrapolating the analysis of these linkages from the national level to the regional level[20]. As Weiskoff and Wolff observed "an intensively linked sector in an industrialised country, contrary to all expectations, may prove singularly shorn of linkages on transplantation to a developing region" (Weiskoff and Wolff, 1977, p. 609). Furthermore, "linkages once thought to be 'capturable' on the basis of historical and comparative industrial studies may be persistently neutralised by the leakages of imported or by immediate export of the intermediate outputs" (Weiskoff and Wolff, 1977, p. 611).

Based on these observations, we can try to examine the possible linkages that a process of industrialisation, such as the one in the Northeast of Brazil led by the tax credit scheme, can generate. Firstly, the main projects of the new industry of the Northeast were developed by branches of firms that have their head offices out of the region. These projects tend to present weaker linkages with the host economy. This is because some of the commercial relations of the firm are established at the national level and not particularized by branches[21]. This tends to create strong leakages in the form of imports of inputs for the firm. On the other hand, the depositors of the 34/18/FINOR system tend to invest their funds in projects they can relate to economically. In this sense, as the extra-regional depositors represent the larger part of total deposits, the commercial and financial relations generated by the system tend to be stronger with the extra-regional economy. However, all these observations refer to backward linkages, whereas, the sort of industrialisation produced in this region also presents problems in relation to forward linkages. This is because the newly created sectors do not principally aim to sell to the regional markets, but produce mainly intermediate goods to be re-exported to the Centre-South of the country. Thus, the capacity to stimulate and generate new sectors in this economy is very restricted (Haddad, 1989, p. 85). This is a consequence of the enclave character which the new stimulated industry presents in the region (Guimarães Neto, 1983, p. 14 and Furtado, 1982).

Another source of leakage to the income flow is the larger propensity to import of peripheral regions. This was verified when we observed the trade balances of the regions. In this sense, a larger part of the income generated in the region is spent outside it, which substantially reduces the income and money multipliers of the region.

Leakages in the flow of income seem to be the main elements responsible for the smaller income multipliers estimated by Harber Jr. (1982). A region which has low income levels tends to present higher multipliers than a region which has higher levels of income as a consequence of the larger marginal propensity to consume verified in poorer regions. However, leakages from the poorer economy can compensate the larger marginal propensity to consume and can result in smaller multipliers. The elements that lead to smaller income multipliers also induce smaller money multipliers. However, there are reasons for the income multipliers being higher in peripheral regions than in central regions. This, however, does not occur with money multipliers, since, as observed in Chapter 2, the main elements that determine money multipliers are leakages in the income flow, especially trade and capital leakages, and the liquidity preference of agents. Both elements reduce the money multipliers of peripheral regions. So, for policy making purposes, it is important to analyse the capacity of creating both forward and backward linkages in the activities to be stimulated by policies which act on the financial side, since these linkages are responsible for the retention of the finance created in the specific region. Otherwise, this mechanism will finance just the first round of the investment process, but will exit in the second round, financing the exports of other regions.

Industrialisation, leakages and effects on employment in peripheral regions

All of the leakages which reduce the income multiplier also reduce the employment multiplier. In the case of employment, we have an extra problem, for the 34/18 mechanism incentivated capital intensive industries. The Northeast is an economy with fundamental problems of misery, underemployment and unemployment among a great part of its population. Thus it is important to analyse how the incentives extended to this region have affected employment.

Open unemployment, historically, does not constitute the major problem in the Northeast. This can be seen in Tables IV.19 to IV.23, where the unemployment rates do not seem to present a huge problem. For the region as a whole, the major problems are underemployment and disguised unemployment (Guimarães Neto, 1978, p. 218). However, unemployment shows up in the urban labour force (Table IV.19).

Table IV.18
Disguised Unemployment
4th Term 1972
(%)

	Less Than 0.5 Minimum Wage	Less Than 1 Minimum Wage
Urban	16.48	38.77
North	-	25.92
Northeast	33.11	61.92
Southeast	12.07	32.10
South	12.00	34.92
C. West	6.75	20.74
Rural	46.98	75.51
North	37.26	45.91
Northeast	67.99	91.36
Southeast	35.23	69.82
South	20.54	52.94
C.West	29.63	54.32

Source: PNAD, IBGE, 4th term, 1972.

Table IV.19
Open Unemployment
4th Term 1972

Regions	Total Unemployment	Urban Unemployment	Rural Unemployment
All Regions	3.1	4.8	0.7
Region I	4.6	4.9	2.3
Guanabara	3.5	3.5	-
Rio de Janeiro	5.7	7.5	2.3
Region II	3.1	3.5	1.1
São Paulo	3.1	3.5	1.1
Region III	2.3	4.8	0.5
Paraná	1.2	3.0	0.3
Rio Grande do Sul	3.1	5.7	0.5
Region IV	3.8	6.0	0.8
Minas Gerais	4.0	6.3	0.8
Region V	2.7	5.8	0.7
Bahia	3.0	5.8	0.9
Pernambuco	4.4	7.4	1.0
Region VI	4.9	5.0	2.4
Distrito Federal	4.9	5.0	2.4

Source: PNAD, IBGE,4th. term (1972).

Regions
Region I- Guanabara, Rio de Janeiro
Region II- São Paulo
Region III- Paraná, Santa Catarina and Rio Grande do Sul
Region IV- Minas Gerais and Espírito Santo
Region V- Maranhão, Piauí, Ceará, Rio Grande do Norte, Paraíba, Pernambuco,

Alagoas, Sergipe and Bahia.
Region VI- Distrito Federal
Region VII- Amazonas, Acre, Pará, Amapá, Roraima, Rondonia, Goiás and Mato Grosso.

Table IV.20
Disguised Unemployment
1985 (%)

	Less Than 0.5 Minimum Wage	Less Than 1 Minimum Wage
Urban	8.54	19.64
North	-	-
Northeast	13.58	26.77
Southeast	7.22	17.84
South	6.89	17.47
C. West	7.78	18.85
Rural	13.98	28.15
North	-	-
Northeast	19.41	35.11
Southeast	11.36	26.87
South	7.55	17.54
C. West	6.49	18.60

Source: PNAD, IBGE (1985).

Table IV.21
Unemployment
1990

Brazil	3.7
North	3.7
Northeast	3.3
Southeast	4.2
South	3.0
C.West	2.9

Source: Anuário Estatistico, IBGE (1992).

Table IV.22
Disguised Unemployment (%)

	Less than 0.5 Minimum Wage	Less than 1 Minimum Wage
Urban	4.86	15.09
North	-	-
Northeast	9.54	24.17
Southeast	3.42	12.35
South	3.69	12.45
Centre West	4.27	14.26
Rural	10.64	24.86
North	-	-
Northeast	15.22	30.98
Southeast	7.49	22.65
South	6.3	16.73
Centre West	4.80	17.07

Source: Anuário Estatistico, IBGE (1992).

We can see from these tables IV.19 to IV.23 that open unemployment remains relatively stable. However, disguised unemployment was high in peripheral economies over the period, especially in the Northeast. This can be seen as a result of the great capacity of peripheral economies to generate employment in informal activities, which provide lower levels of remuneration[22].

The policies of the government for the region did not reach all sectors of the economy. One of the main problems of the Northeast is the large participation in the labour force of under-paid and under-employed labour. These two elements are strictly linked to the informal activities developed in this economy and play an important role in the absorption of labour. Guimarães Neto observes that, in 1973, 30 per cent of those employed in the manufacturing industry declared that they were self-employed, giving their employment relations an informal character. In 1972, 43 per cent of people interviewed by PNAD (National Research by Household Sample) who worked in non-agriculture activities did not have any kind of formal contract of employment. A greater percentage probably exists since the number of employed was only 61 per cent of the total number of people in non-agriculture activities (Guimarães Neto, 1982, p. 467)[23]. These data give us an idea of the importance of informal activities for the absorption of labour in the Northeast. This non-formal character of a great part of Northeastern economic activity, mainly in the urban areas, highlights two points. The first concerns the functionality of the existence of the informal sector in relation to the accumulation of capital by the formal and large firms in terms of the downward pressure that it puts on wages paid in the economy as a whole. The second point is that the informal segment is not provided for the economic policies of the State. That is, the sector that is responsible for the most absorption of labour does not receive any of the stimuli given by the government (Guimarães Neto, 1982, p. 495). The relevance of the informal sector to the economy of the Northeast can be observed in Table IV.23. This is one of the causes for the persistence of underemployment in the region, in spite of all the efforts made to encourage structural changes in this economy.

Table IV.23

Self-Employment

(%) of People Aged 10 or Over Employed

	1985	1990
Brazil	22.69	22.77
North	23.91	25.49
Northeast	29.89	31.79
Southeast	18.33	16.83
South	23.74	23.54
Centre-West	20.44	23.37

Source: Anuário Estatístico, IBGE.

The higher participation of the informal sector and of disguised unemployment in the periphery has important consequences on the financial dynamic of the region. The higher participation of the informal sector results in excluding a greater part of the population and of the economic activity from the formal mechanisms of finance, mainly the banking system, as the informal sector, almost by definition, is out of the sphere of the formal mechanisms of finance. On the other hand, disguised unemployment is characterised by lower level of payments and this also excludes workers in this segment from the banking system. They are totally excluded. However, not only they are the excluded, a greater part of the workers in the lower strata of payment which could formally be considered employed do not attain the minimum income to enter the banking system. As the peripheral regions are the ones in which the higher proportion of the labour force is in these lower strata, a greater part of their population is excluded from the banking system. The main consequence of this is the restricted penetration of the banking system into the social tissue which reduces the spread of the effects of the effects of the extension of credit. On the other hand, this also contributes to the economy as a whole to present a higher relation cash/deposits, which also reduces the money multipliers.

The great role the informal sector plays in the absorption of labour in the peripheral economies presents another problem with relation to access of these sector to government policies, as previously observed. That is, the segment of the economy capable of creating the most jobs did not receive any kind of government incentives, incentives which played a huge role in the structural changes in the Northeast since the 1960s. Thus, the economic policies developed for the region were not properly concerned with the nature of employment or underemployment. This particular aspect of the labour market seems to be one of the fundamental reasons for poverty in the region.

The inadequacy of government policy in dealing with the problems of employment in peripheral regions, especially in the Northeast, is related not just to policies for the industrial sector which tend to be of an urban character, but also to agricultural policies. The main tool used to reach the agriculture sector was government credit. However, this credit, instead of being directed toward activities which require a high level of labour absorption were mainly directed towards cattle raising activity in its worst form, that is, extensive cattle raising activity which has an extremely low capacity for labour absorption. Instead of reducing the problem of disguised unemployment and underemployment in rural areas, government policy increased it, since it allowed a change of activities that were more labour intensive for ones that are less labour intensive. This not only aggravated the problem in rural areas but had extremely negative effects in urban areas because of the consequent migration of the population which had lost its employment to the cities (Furtado, 1982, pp. 140-1).

The weakness of the labour market and its informal character can be observed in Table IV.24 where we see the proportion of the employed labour force which did not pay compulsory social security and therefore did not have a formal labour contract.

Table IV.24

Proportion of The Employed Aged 10 or More which Did Not Pay Compulsory Social Security (%)

	1985	1990
Brazil	52.78	49.91
North	49.52	52.12
Northeast	73.61	71.05
Southeast	40.45	36.32
South	51.84	50.22
C. West	55.81	55.62

Source: Anuário Estatístico, IBGE (1992).

The opinion of many authors (Furtado, 1982, Mendonça de Barros, 1984 and others) that the policies for the development of the Northeast were based on the ideas of the Growth Pole of Perroux (1967) and Hirschman (1958), seem valid. However the implementation of these policies included some characteristics which did not allow the development of the type of dynamism expected by the theory of Perroux, and did not create strong forward and backward linkages able to change the conditions of underdevelopment of the economy of the Northeast.

Therefore, the industrialisation that the Northeast underwent after the 1960s was mainly characterised by two elements: "dependency and complementarity" (Araújo, 1981). As Araújo points out, dependency could be observed in the origin of resources which financed this process, in the origin of the capital of the main firms, in the origin of the inputs that were used by the new industry and in the destination of the production of such industry[24]. Complementarity can be observed in the sectors in which new industry acts. That is, the main sectors of this new industry are complementary to the industrial centre located in the Centre-South of the country. The new industry created in the Northeast thus did not compete with the industry of the Centre-South but complemented it (Araújo, 1981).

The transformation of peripheral regions which took place after 1960 created a new regional division of labour, where the Northeast became responsible for the supply of industrial inputs to the Centre-South of the country and represented a strong demand for capital goods from the Southeast. In this process, the Centre-South retained most of the benefits of the incentives given to peripheral regions (Araújo, 1979).

These elements provide the base for a wider analysis of the financial dynamic of the monetary production economies. An isolated analysis of the financial system may disguise important elements which can only be understood with a joint analysis of the real and financial spheres of the regional economies.

Notes

1 Some of the policies adopted by SUDENE were inspired by the Italian experience. For a good analysis of the Italian case see Allen and MacLennan (1970) and for the comparison between the Brazilian case and the Italian experience see Carvalho (1979).

2 The way in which these commercial relations developed were extensively analysed in Chapter 4.

3 The regional economy can only be considered if, when we analyse it, it presents specific forms of production and reproduction of capital, that is, the regional economy is supposed to present a specific pattern of accumulation of capital. According to Oliveira, this is what gives relevance to the concept of region (Oliveira, 1981a, pp. 25-29 and Pedrão, 1984).

4 See SUDENE (1961 and 1966).

5 See SUDENE (1966b and 1968).

6 A good analysis of this mechanism can be found in Hirschman (1968-69) and in Goodman and Albuquerque (1974).

7 Later on (1966), this was modified and the funds of 34/18 were made available as loan capital and were supposed to be repaid within a maximum period of five years. A further liberalisation was to allow the use of these funds to reinforce the working capital of the enterprises of Northeast. This was allowed in 1966.

8 The small role that the criterion of absorption of labour played was determined by the practice of the institution. The original idea of the criteria was to stimulate industries with a large capacity for job creation.

9 The resources available for the tax credit mechanism were also reduced as a consequence of the Decree Law No.1106 of 16/06/1970 which created PIN (Programa de Integração Nacional, National Integration Programm) and Decree Law No. 1179 of 6/07/1971 which created PROTERRA (Programa de Redistribuição de Terras e Estímulo à Agroindústria do Norte e Nordeste, Programm of Land Redistribution and Incentive to Agroindustry of North and Northeast). These two special programmes absorbed 50 per cent of the resources of the tax credit scheme, 30 per cent going to PIN and 20 per cent to PROTERRA (SUDENE, 1979).

10 Frick (1991) observes that there was not a proper reversal of polarisation in regional terms, but this reversal could only be observed in terms of the metropolitan region of the city of São Paulo.

11 Boisier observes that the regional development plans tend to treat the regional question as a spatial question and not as a sectorial matter, and this, according to him, is a mistake because the main differential of

productivity and capacity of generating dynamic elements refers to the sectorial element and not to the spatial element (Boisier, 1975, p. 60). However, in the Brazilian case, we observe that the sectorial problem has a spatial dimension, since sectorial composition is normally regionally distinctive. This was one of the elements which seems to have been considered when the plans gave extreme importance to the changes in the sectorial composition of particular regions, as was the case of the Northeast.

12 The value of the industrial transformation tends to stress the concentration of the industrial sector and differs from the values observed in the data from the national account because of different methodologies.

13 We will refer to the industries that are in the system of 34/18/FINOR as incentivated industries because that is the closest term in English to the Portuguese term "indústrias incentivadas".

14 For a more extensive discussion on this topic see Weisskoff and Wolff (1977).

15 Brandão (1985) developed an excellent analysis on the main peculiarities of the industrialisation of Bahia and Pernambuco and the differences between these two states.

16 Sarmento (1980), develops a model which explains the differential in the level of development between the Northeast and the Centre-South of the country as a consequence of the differences in the level of uncertainty and risk aversion of the agents. However, this model has an orthodox basis and deals with uncertainty as risk and not with uncertainty in the Post-Keynesian sense.

17 However, this is extremely concentrated in some states inside the peripheral regions.

18 Guimarães Neto (1994) observed more recently that Para has developed a strong export character which has its base in mineral activities. However, the positive results that this state has achieved are contrasted, in terms of the region, by the negative results for the Zona Franca de Manaus, which presents a strong deficit in its trade balance abroad.

19 Zona Franca de Manaus is a free trade zone located in Manaus, the capital of the state of Amazon, and was conceived as a centre for processing imported inputs for sale in the internal and external markets.

20 Prado, 1981, has analysed the degree of linkage as a way of observing which sectors should be incentivated by government policies in order to attain bigger results in terms of generating poles of growth in a particular region. However, he observed the degree of linkages using

the input-output matrix of Brazil and extrapolated these results to the regional level, which is not strictly correct, since the possibilities of a sector generate linkages vary regionally as was observed previously. Therefore, the most appropriate procedure would have been to use a regional input-output matrix. This, however, was not available in the time of the research of Prado. Recently BNB (1992), produced an input-output matrix for the Northeast and now more accurate anlysis can be made in this field.

21 This tendency is also observed by Guimarães Neto (1994).

22 Macedo observes that the equalization of the minimum wage in all the regions of Brazil was an inefficient way of reducing poverty in the peripheral regions, since the increase in the value of the minimum wage in these regions amplified the part of the population that receive less than the minimum wage (Macedo, 1982).

23 We used the self employment as an indication for the informal activity, however, not all self-employment is related to the informal sector.

24 Furtado (1981) also observes that the relations of dependency of the industry of the Northeast to the economy of the Centre-South of the country; these relations of dependency were also analysed by Haddad, 1989, p. 85).

7 The financial system: 1960-1990

Introduction

The regional economies in the period 1960-1990 underwent significant real structural changes which were mainly led by governmental policies that had as one of their main supports a tax credit scheme that provided funding for investment in peripheral regions. Now we shall analyse the effects of those structural changes and of the governmental policies on the banking system and its joint dynamic with the real side of the economy. The banking system is still the most important financial element in the Brazilian economy. We shall analyse the balance sheets of the banks regionally aggregated and then make a joint analysis of what was happening in the real and financial spheres.

The chapter begins with an analysis of the financial reform that took place in 1964. This indicates the changes that were taking place at the national level. In a second section we will analyse the process of banking concentration that was observed in Brazil after 1965 and its effects on the regional financial system. Then we will analyse the balance sheets of the banks at the regional level, to establish patterns of behaviour and by making comparisons with the previous period, assess the impacts of the structural changes of this period on the financial variables and vice-versa.

The financial reform

The financial system underwent important transformations between 1960 and 1990 as a result of the financial reform and other policy changes. The reforms applied to Brazil as a whole but also had differentiated regional impacts. They began in 1964 when Brazil suffered a military coup and they were the consequence of the economic thinking of the group that assumed power. The main lines of the financial reforms can be seen from the following economic policy measures: Law 4357 of 16/07/1964 created a new indexed government bond. This marked the introduction of indexation in the Brazilian financial market. Later on, indexation was extended to almost all financial titles or contracts. The indexed government bond was introduced with a series of incentives for purchase, e.g. fiscal incentive, allowing agents to use 20 per cent of their income tax to purchase these bonds. Law 4320 of 21/08/1964 created the Financial Housing System. This Law also created the National Housing Bank which centralized and organized the operations of other banks that operated in the housing sector. Law 4595 of 31/12/1964, also known as the Law of Banking Reform, created the National Monetary Council and the Central Bank of Brazil, which replaced the Superintendency of Money and Credit (SUMOC). This Law was necessary, according to the theoretical framework of the policy makers, to control more tightly the liquidity of the economy. Liquidity was considered one of the main elements determining the high level of inflation. Law 4728 of 14/07/1965, also known as the Law of the Capital Market Reform, regulated the market for private securities and created new financial institutions like investment banks. The main aim of this Law was to create conditions for the development of capital markets in Brazil. According to the analysis developed by the policy makers, these markets were underdeveloped because of an excessive level of regulation and because of the underdevelopment of institutional arrangements within which these markets could operate.

The banking concentration process and its regional impact

Besides these reforms, another important process was taking place in the banking system during this period. This was the creation of new regulations whose explicit aim was to promote an intense process of banking concentration so that banks could achieve returns of scale, and to create a more "solid" banking system, where the risk of institutional insolvency was more remote. This policy reinforced the rapid conglomeration led by the commercial banks in Brazil at the same time. For an extensive analysis of this see Perdigão, 1983.

These policies were controversial since some studies have sought to show that there were no gains from scale involved in the process of banking concentration that the Brazilian economy underwent after 1965[1]. Furthermore, this process was followed by an increase in interest rates, which in one way were the result of more ample economic policies of the government, but in another could represent an increase in the mark-ups charged by banks as they increased their market power with concentration. It has been argued that the entire process had a negative impact on the economic system as a whole (Mendes, 1988).

Banking concentration in the Brazilian economy was accentuated with the economic policies that had this aim. The process began after the Second World War as a consequence of the dispute for deposits by the existing banks. However, the dimension and velocity that it assumed after 1965 was far from natural: the levels of banking concentration achieved by the Brazilian banking system in the 1970s and 1980s were fundamentally the result of governmental policies that had stimulated the incorporation of smaller banks with bigger banks (Mendes, 1988; Marques 1982 and 1985; Moreira, 1984).

Banking concentration brought substantial changes in the structure of the Brazilian banking system. Until economic policy began to stimulate the natural process of concentration that had been taking place since the Second World War, we had a banking system that basically operated at local or regional levels. Banking concentration made banks assume a nationwide character which until then was seen only in Banco do Brasil[2].

Some evidence of this process can be seen in Table IV.25.s.a. These data show that there was tremendous concentration, especially in terms of the net worth and deposits of those banks[3]. However, when we analyse the participation of the four to seven biggest banks in the total amount of credit extended, we observe that this concentration is significantly less. This shows that these big banks do not play such an important role in extending credit and this makes the aim of concentration still more problematic since great incentives were given to the larger banks and to concentration of banking at the same time when it seemed that the small banks, which were disappearing, were the more important element in the creation of liquidity through the creation of credit.

Banking concentration[4] can also be observed when we analyse the number of head offices that existed in 1970 and compare this with the number in 1984. This is done in Table IV.25.

Table IV.25

Number of Private National Commercial Banks

	Head	Branches
1970	144	5541
1975	69	5655
1980	67	7285
1984	64	8843
Rate of Change 1984-1970 (%)	-55.6	59.6

Source: Mendes (1988, p. 67).

The main government policies that intensified banking concentration can be divided into two groups: on the one hand, we have those that had a general aim based on restrictions on the opening new branches and on financial and fiscal incentives to incorporate smaller banks with larger banks[5]; on the other hand, we have another set of measures which had an explicit regional aim, that is, they created restrictions for extending new branches in central regions and allowed their creation in peripheral regions; consequently, they greatly encouraged the expansion of the network of branches of the banks in these areas[6] (Mendes, 1988, p. 74). The action of the government was directed first at the number of bank branches and later this action extended to financial and fiscal incentives for the merger of banks. Controlling the number of branches stimulated banking concentration: as there was a limit on the number of branches that a bank could have and as new deposits represented the main source of profits to these banks, especially during periods of growing inflation, these banks could only increase their participation in total deposits by incorporating other banks and their branches.

Nevertheless, this process did not affect all regions with the same intensity. Analysing Tables IV.26.s.a. and IV.27.s.a. we can see that it was much more intense in central regions than in peripheral regions. This does not contradict the prediction of the model developed in Chapter 2, because the model ignores the discretionary action of the State, which in the Brazilian case was fundamental. As was previously seen, the Central Bank regulations that stimulated banking concentration discriminated (positively) between regions, since restriction on opening new branches was limited to "first order" cities and there was an explicit stimulus to open new branches in the "second order" cities[7]. This allowed the banking system which was operating on a more restricted basis in those areas, to continue operating and not undergo the mergers and incorporations which were taking place in the central regions. However, the other form of stimulus toward banking concentration reached all the regions and this was the main cause for concentration seen in the peripheral regions, which despite not reaching the same levels as the central regions, was still very intense[8].

Observing the relative participation of each region in the total number of head offices and branches we can see less developed regions advancing both in terms of the number of head offices and of branches. The increase in head offices participation in the periphery was, however, much less than the increase in the participation in the total of the branches. The increased participation in the number of head offices in the periphery results from the easy policy of opening new branches in these regions. As banks could open branches in these regions, they did not need to incorporate other banks to extend their network, as was happening in the centre. Therefore, the process of banking concentration was less intense in the periphery than in the centre and so the participation of the periphery in the number of head offices increased in relation to the national total. At the same time, as these policies made easier the opening of new branches in the periphery than in the centre, the branches network was extended towards these regions.

From Table IV.28.s.a. we can see that in central regions the growth of the number of branches was mainly due to the action of government-owned banks, as they had a greater degree of freedom compared to the restrictive character of the regulation on the number of branches. However, in the periphery we can note that, until 1976, government-owned banks had an important role in the installation of new branches. Nevertheless, in the period 1976-85 this pattern changed and the private national banks increased their share of new branches in the peripheral regions. This can be seen as a consequence of the legislation which made the process of opening branches in the periphery easier and the increase in inflation which made banks compete harder for new deposits.

Banking concentration can also be seen in Table IV.26, which shows the pattern of concentration of net worth, deposits and credit creation. Net worth shows the higher concentration. If we analyse the deposit/credit ratio we see that the banks that have their head offices in São Paulo have a greater capacity to capture deposits than those that have their head offices out of São Paulo.

Table IV.26
Share of 50 Biggest Banks According to Deposits
(%)

		Net Worth	Deposits	Credit
São Paulo	1980	-	63.23	-
	1985	-	65.87	-
	1990	77.81	68.61	66.18
Rest of the Country	1980	-	36.76	-
	1985	-	34.12	-
	1990	22.18	31.38	33.81

1980- Private Commercial Banks.
1985- Public and Private Commercial Banks Except Banco do Brasil.
1990- The 41 biggest multiple private banks.

Source: Balanço Anual, Gazeta Mercantil, September, 1980;
Ranking , Balanço Financeiro, April, 1986;
Balanço Anual, Gazeta Mercantil, September, 1991.

The aggregation of the banking system

It is now important to analyse the pattern followed by the financial sector in the regional economies and to differentiate regional phenomena within the wider process. Here we will be working with a different level of bank aggregation from the one of Part III. This was possible because the data is more disaggregated after 1968, and this gives us a more precise idea of the kind of behaviour by type of institution. Again, we will be treating the general total of the banks in order to have an idea of the full role of banks in the regional economies. Banco do Brasil is analysed separately[9] because of its government-owned character, and because of the immense importance of this institution in the Brazilian economy as a whole and in some regional economies in particular (North, South and Centre-West). The significance of this institution in the Brazilian economy and in the regional economies, both in terms of deposits and credit, can be seen in Tables IV.31.s.a. and IV.32.s.a. We will also analyse the Federal Official banks with a regional character (BNB/BASA) and finally we will analyse the private banks (after 1968). This will allow us to establish more precise patterns for each sector of the financial system and how each sector interacts with the dynamic of the economy as a whole.

The analysis of the financial system must be undertaken within a general framework that is made up of elements such as the regional concentration of the banking system; the behaviour of deposits; the behaviour of credit; the ratio of credit to deposits; the liquidity preference of banks and some elements of the real side of the economy.

The participation of the financial sector in the national/regional income

Now, we will analyse some regional aspects of the banking system and make some comments on the effect of regional incentives especially the tax credit scheme on the banking system, in order to see if governmental policies directed toward the periphery had any effect on the role of the banks in the regions.

The regional participation of banking at the national level can be seen in Table IV.29.s.a. This table shows a relative increase in the participation of banking in peripheral regions at the expense of the central region (Southeast). However, as frequently emphasised, it is more important to analyse São Paulo separately than to consider the Southeast as a whole. If we do so, we can see that the participation of banks in this state was not reduced significantly; on the contrary, it was relatively stable throughout the analysed period. When we consider the participation of banking in GDP, as is shown in Table IV.30.s.a., we see a much more intense growth in the share of this activity in peripheral regions than in central ones, although it did grow in all regions. This may be due to two combined elements: a) the initial base of peripheral regions was very small, therefore, any movement towards increased participation really represents a significant growth and b) the policy of promoting of new branches in peripheral regions made banks to extend their activities in those regions more easily and this increased the participation of this sector in GDP[10]. The intense growth observed in banking in the period 1980-85 in all regions is due to increased inflation and the financial disintermediation process suffered by the Brazilian economy. This process allowed banks to retain large profits and increased their participation in GDP. However, this increase in the participation of banking in regional and national income was not followed by an increase in the availability of finance in the economy. On the contrary, this process was related to the increasingly speculative behaviour of banks associated with the increasing indebtedness of the public sector and to the higher interest rates paid to refinance the public debt.

Deposits and credit

We observed in Chapter 5 that the analysis of the deposits at the regional level is important not because deposits precede credit extensions, but to observe what is going on in the regional financial systems after credit is extended. Put another way, deposits tend to show the capacity of particular regions to retain or capture from other regions credit that was created. Banks expectations of how much of extended credit will come back as redeposit is an important variable in their decision to extend credit towards specific regions or sectors.

Tables IV.33.s.a., IV.34.s.a., IV.35.s.a., IV.36.s.a. and IV.37.s.a. show the pattern followed by deposits according to the kind of bank. At a more aggregate level, in Table IV.33.s.a., we can see that there was not a significant change in the regional generation of deposits from the one analysed in Chapter 5. What is important to observe is that, apart from some peaks, the participation of São Paulo increased slightly throughout the period analysed. However, this pattern is not followed by the Southeast as a whole, which may imply an internal regional redistribution of the generation of deposits in favour of São Paulo. For Banco do Brasil (see Table IV.34.s.a.) we can observe an increasing participation of the Northeast in the generation of deposits. The South participation is also increasing. The data for the Centre-West is biased by the location of Brasília in this region in 1960 and this causes a significant jump in the level of deposits, since this institution is the financial institution of the Federal Government. This general pattern of Banco do Brasil has relation with the policy followed by this bank of extending new branches towards the periphery, which ended up by allowing this bank to capture a large amount of deposits in the localities where it extended new branches.

The relevance of deposits in peripheral regions to BNB/BASA is great in the analysed period, as can be observed in Table IV.35.s.a. The generation of deposits from outside the regions that these banks were supposed to operate in was only marginal. Finally, we should analyse the regional pattern of deposit generation compared to other kinds of national banks (until 1967) and to the private banks (after 1968) (Table IV.36.s.a.). Here, we can see the marginal role that peripheral regions play in generating deposits to this category of banks. The Southeast, and inside it São Paulo, is the main source of deposits to this category of banks. This tendency is maintained when we analyse the aggregate of the banks, except Banco do Brasil (Table IV.37.s.a.). The reduced importance of the peripheral regions in generating deposits to private banks is predictable since the network of the private banks is much more developed in central regions than in peripheral regions. The higher capacity which government-owned banks have in retaining deposits in the periphery is in contrast to private banks and is explained by the more extensive network that these banks have in these regions. On the other hand, the periphery has an inherent problem in retaining deposits, because of the real and financial leakages observed in these regions.

As was mentioned in Chapter 5, the regional distribution of deposits was supposed to follow the distribution of the population. In the Brazilian case, this cannot be observed for the analysed period, as can be seen in Tables IV.32.s.a. and IV.38.s.a. Again, we can see an enormous concentration of deposits in São Paulo in relation to the population of this state. The inverse can be observed for peripheral regions, with the exception of the Centre-West where the presence of Brasília creates a bias and pushes up the value of deposits. This discrepancy is due to the enormous difference in the levels of income of these regions (Table IV.1.s.a.). There is also an enormous discrepancy between the share of the national GDP between the regions and the share of deposits, however, this discrepancy is less than that of the share of population. Therefore, the share of the GDP explains better the share of deposits than the share of the population.

We pointed out in Chapter 2 and Chapter 5 that the characteristics of the periphery lead agents to show higher liquidity preference in those regions. This is basically because the periphery tends to be more unstable, both in real and financial terms. We also pointed out that the more developed financial markets of the central regions give higher liquidity to central assets than peripheral assets and so agents prefer assets from central economies to manifest their liquidity preference. Therefore, just analysing the composition of portfolios through the analysis of bank balance sheets we cannot have a precise idea of the liquidity preference of agents, since they could be holding liquid assets of the centre and this is shown in the balance sheet of banks of the centre and not in the peripheral banking system. Another problem is the retention of cash, that is, the maximum limit to the manifestation of the liquidity preference that cannot be measured, given the non-availability of data. Given the characterisation of the centre and the periphery, we expect a higher ratio cash/deposits in the periphery. This is a result of the reduced income level of the population in these regions as well as the relatively less developed banking network which results in making agents to use more cash than agents in the centre. Another important element that contributes to this tendency, and is particularly accentuated in Brazil, is the higher participation of the informal markets in the whole economic structure of the peripheral regions. Nevertheless, apart from the inaccuracies that need to be taken into account, we can observe the balance sheet of the banking system to have an idea of the behaviour of agents in relation to diverse assets with different degrees of liquidity supplied by the banking system.

The short term deposit to total deposit ratio must be analysed with some caution, as observed in Chapter 5, since we are dealing with financial systems that are operating in economies that are structurally rather different and this may mean that the relations of local populations to their respective financial systems are also different. For instance, in an economy such as that of the

Northeast, a large part of the population cannot maintain any kind of current account in banks since they do not have the minimum level of income/wealth to allow them to participate in this system. The banking system has a reduced network, which does not allow the population easy access to banks, which reduces, in relative terms, the liquidity of the deposits (banking money). Furthermore, the informal sector, which is highly important in these economies, does not have access to the financial system, which sets apart an important segment of the economy and compels this segment to use more cash compared to deposits. Therefore, their retention and use of cash is much larger than in regions with higher levels of income. On the other hand, as Dow observes (Dow, 1990, p. 86), this ratio can only be considered a measure of the liquidity preference of the agents if their manifestation of liquidity in other liquid assets were the same across regions. Analysing Table IV.39.s.a., we see a higher ratio of short term deposits to total deposits in peripheral regions, with the exception of the Northeast. However, the case of the Northeast can be biased by the presence of BNB, which receives long term deposits. So if we consider all banks except BNB we can have a more precise picture of the behaviour of the region. Analysing Table IV.40.s.a., we see that the results expected by the model are still valid in this region. This ratio oscillates across the analysed period, but underwent a reduction in the 1980s. This is due to the increase in inflation (especially after the 1980s), which caused a significant loss in the real value of money and so, the third attribute of liquidity of this asset was reduced (see Chapter 2). In 1990 we see a great fall in the ratio demand deposits to term deposits and this is clearly a consequence of the intensification of inflation and of the diversification of non-money financial assets, especially with indexation, that made the liquidity preference of agents to be expressed more in these assets. This explains the fall in the demand deposit levels (as shown for 1990) and the consequent rise in the level of term deposits.

As the peripheral economies are more unstable than the central ones, the liquidity preference of agents tends to be higher in the former than in the latter. However, as the financial system of the centre is more developed than that of the periphery, agents tend to manifest their higher liquidity preference in the centre's assets. This causes leakages of liquidity from the periphery to the centre. At the same time, the periphery presents higher deficits in its trade balance with the centre which causes extra leakages for real reasons. Therefore, there are causes related to the higher liquidity preference of agents in the periphery and to the financial leakages from the periphery to the centre that end up by reducing the possibility of money creation in the periphery and therefore create monetary constraints to growth in those areas.

The reduced absorption of new deposits by the periphery in Brazil was observed both in relation to the distribution of the population and of the income. Therefore, there will be constraints to growth in this economy.

As was observed in Chapter 2, the relevant decision is the credit extension.

The direction of causality goes from credit to deposits and, therefore, the relevant element is credit creation. Observing Tables IV.41.s.a., IV.42.s.a., IV.43.s.a., IV.44.s.a. and IV.45.s.a. we get an idea of the distribution of credit between regions in Brazil, according to the kind of institution extending it. Table IV.41.s.a. shows a change in the pattern of extension of loans toward the periphery. In contrast with the previous period analysed (Chapter 5), after 1970, we observe a greater participation in total loans than in total income in the Northeast, the peripheral region par excellence. This tendency is also observed in the South. The North, however, maintained its participation in total loans at a lower level than its participation in the total income. The Southeast and especially São Paulo also showed a smaller participation in total loans than in the total income. Nevertheless, it is important to comment on the reasons for the change in this situation. That is, it is fundamental to identify the new possibilities of credit creation in the peripheral regions in order to see if this change of pattern follows a private logic or if it is the result of the State's action. Analysing Tables IV.42.s.a., IV.43.s.a., IV.44.s.a. and IV.45.s.a., we can see that extension of new loans towards the periphery is mainly due to public banks (Banco do Brasil and BNB/BASA). That is, the change of trend observed earlier is much more due to the discretionary policy of the State which extended credit toward the periphery, than a real result of a change in the behaviour of private institutions. On the contrary, comparing the data in Chapter 5 with the data in Chapter 7, we can see that other commercial banks and private banks maintained their pattern of regional credit extension. However, if we consider only São Paulo, we can see that private banks increased their concentration of credit provision to this state.

Thus the private banking system concentrates its creation of credit in the central regions. This is in accordance with the model analysed in Chapter 2, since banks have a more reliable basis of information in these regions because of the higher stability and easier access to information for the decision making process. Furthermore, these regions present higher redeposit ratios than the periphery and this is one more element which encourages banks to extend credit to these regions. The government-owned banks, however, extend credit more easily to peripheral regions than private banks. However, given the higher leakages in the periphery, the liquidity created by the government-owned banks is not kept in the periphery but leaks very soon to the central regions.

The ratio loans to deposits and the regional financial and real linkages

Another important indicator normally used to assess the financial position of the regions is the ratio total loans to total deposits for each region. The analysis of this indicator is done using a comparison of this variable with the national average. As was mentioned in Chapter 5, the result of this kind of analysis normally leads to the conclusion that the region is a net receiver of resources from the banking system if it presents a ratio above one. However, as we mentioned in Chapter 5, this analysis must be more detailed and specific in order to give it analytical relevance[11].

Table IV.46.s.a. shows that the ratios of total loans to total deposits for all banks are higher in peripheral regions than in central ones, including São Paulo. This result can be seen better in Table IV.47.s.a., where the regional level of this ratio is compared with the national average. Here, we can see that peripheral regions tend to present ratios far above their levels in the centre, especially São Paulo. This is particularly true for the Northeast and South.

These data give an idea of the total leakages that each region is subject to. The analysis of type of institution shows the differences in terms of degree of leakage that each institution is exposed to.

Analysing the ratio of loans to deposits for the Banco do Brasil (Table IV.48.s.a.), we can see that this ratio is above one for almost all regions. The regions where this ratio is lower are the North, Southeast (São Paulo presents a different result) and the Centre-West. The Centre-West again has problems due to Brasília which captures deposits in all regions, but whose deposits are registered there. Thus, we see much more unconstrained behaviour by the Banco do Brasil compared to other banks. If we compare the regional average with the national average (Table IV.49.s.a.) we notice that the main points observed in Chapter 5 are maintained. That is, the North still shows ratios far below average, the Northeast is above average, the Southeast is below average, and São Paulo is above average over a great part of the analysed period[12]; the South is well above average (probably because of the importance that rural credit plays in Banco do Brasil and in this region, in particular). The change in the pattern of the Centre-West is due to the introduction of Brasília in this region which made the level of deposits grow without any relation to the level of credit extended by the region. This last point is especially true for Banco do Brasil.

Table IV.50.s.a. shows the ratios of total loans to total deposits for the Federal official banks, BNB and BASA. This table shows that these banks lent more freely, as they were supposed to do, in peripheral regions than in the centre. However, they show an even more unconstrained lending policy in peripheral regions where they were not supposed to operate, that is in the South and Centre-West (the action in the Centre-West is partly explained by the inclusion of part of the Centre-West in what is considered Legal Amazon). Comparing this data with the national average (Table IV.51.s.a.), we can see the effect of this above mentioned tendency, that is, this ratio was much higher in peripheral regions where they were not supposed to operate. This is due to their smaller participation in the total deposits of these regions, that allows the great part of the credit extended by these banks in these regions to be captured by other banks, and, in this way, does not generate new deposits. The opposite situation is taking place in the regions where there is greater participation in the market (the North and Northeast).

The ratio of total loans to total deposits for other commercial banks (until 1968) and private banks (after 1968) (Table IV.52.s.a.) is much more constrained than all the other groups of banks we have analysed. Comparing this ratio with the national average (Table IV.53.s.a.), we can see that peripheral regions are still above average as is the case with the North, Northeast, South and Centre-West. However, this ratio does not present a stable pattern as the previous categories of banks showed. When we observe this ratio for all the banks except the Banco do Brasil for the most recent period (Table IV.54.s.a.) we can see a less constrained pattern in this ratio in all regions. Table IV.55.s.a. compares this ratio regionally with the national average and here the previous tendency of presenting higher ratios in peripheral regions is maintained and the lower ratio is observed in the more developed region (Southeast).

As noted above, there is a tendency for the ratio of total loans to total deposits to be higher in peripheral regions. On the real side of the economy peripheral regions exhibited substantial deficits with the central regions (especially São Paulo) over the whole period. This tends to create the sort of pattern observed in Brazil. That is, credit is extended in a peripheral region, but the resulting deposits almost instantaneously leak to the central region, decreasing the level of the ratio of loans to deposits in the centre at the same time indicating to the centre banks that the redeposit ratio is higher in the centre and, so, it is worth extending credit to this region[13].

As previously observed the government-owned banks used an easier credit policy for peripheral regions than for the central ones. This broke the vicious circle created by the financial system only partially, as the role played by the extension of finance to these peripheral region is not complete. That is, new liquidity was not retained in the region, but played its role only once or twice in the system and then flowed to the central regions where it played its role fully.

We observe that the main elements characteristic of the banking system in regional terms during 1942-60 were maintained in the period 1960-90. The operation of the state, as an exogenous element, eased the availability of credit to the peripheral regions. But the endogenous element continued to play its role and drained the newly created liquidity from these peripheral regions to the central ones. Therefore, the higher ratio loans to deposits observed in the periphery of Brazil compared to the central region has some specific causes. First of all there are substantial differences in the way that the financial system penetrates in and integrates with different regional economic systems. In the periphery, due to various causes, e.g. lower level of income, higher participation of the informal sector etc., the integration of the financial system is more tenuous. This reduces the potentialities of the money multipliers in these regions. Given the smaller banking network and its lower degree of integration in these regions the capacity of capturing deposits is diminished.

The hypothesis that the institutional differences between the central and the peripheral financial systems make agents prefer to manifest their liquidity preferences in assets from the centre is also confirmed by the higher ratio of loans to deposits in the peripheral regions. The deficits in the trade balance of the periphery reinforces this tendency. In the Brazilian case, we saw that the policies of industrialisation pursued in the periphery resulted in intensifying real and financial leakages, since the industrialisation was based on extra-regional capital which was much more integrated with its original region than with the peripheral economic system. This enforced the tendency towards higher ratios of loans to deposits in the periphery since it increased leakages from the periphery. Therefore, the policies of easy credit to the periphery, followed by the government-owned banks, did not have a significant effect because leakages in the peripheral economies ended up by redirecting the newly created liquidity to the central economies. This general analysis of the data conforms to the main ideas of the model presented by Dow and summarized in Chapter 2. That is, peripheral regions are constrained in terms of availability of credit. This constraint is due to the interaction of financial and real forces which end up creating vicious circles that can be broken only partially by the action of the State. This is because the State is exogenous only to a certain extent and is normally captured by private mechanisms, as seems to be the case in Brazil. This experience demonstrates that a mechanism that seemed to be appropriated to tackle the regional problem ended up by reinforcing it and by diverting part of the benefits to the centre regions. This was a consequence of the diversion of the original targets of the mechanism by the interplay of State and private firms of the centre.

The ratio of reserves to deposits and the liquidity preference of the banks

Now, it is important to analyse the behaviour of banks in terms of their level of reserves. As the banking system evolved, this variable lost its relevance as a limit to the extension of loans. This variable is fundamental in stage 2 of banking development; however, after this stage, it is relevant only in the sense that banks still look to it as a way of indicating their capacity to acquire new deposits resulting from previous extensions of credit. Therefore, though it is yet another element that banks take into account when extending credit, it is no longer the main limit to this decision.

The level of reserves that banks keep has two main components: one is legally determined and the other has a voluntary character. In this section we will analyse these two elements.

Legislation on banking reserves began in Brazil in 1932 and, since then it has developed a regional character[14]. Later, this regional character became more emphasised. In 1962, the regional character of the legislation on reserves was recovered with Instruction No. 225 of SUMOC of 18/05/1962. This instruction established that the compulsory reserves of the banks in SUMOC must be of 22 per cent of the total demand deposits and short term deposits (less than 90 days) and 14 per cent of the long term deposits. Banks that operated in the states of Amazonas, Pará, Maranhão, Piauí, Ceará, Rio Grande do Norte, Paraíba, Pernambuco, Alagoas, Sergipe, Bahia, Espírito Santo, Goiás and Mato Grosso only required 14 per cent of their demand and short term deposits and seven per cent of the long term deposits. Thus, we can see a clear policy for differentiating the level of reserves according to the level of development of the regions, allowing thus banks of peripheral regions to act in a more unconstrained manner[15]. This instruction was altered by Resolution No. 10 of the Central Bank of 26/11/1965, but the regional differentiation was still maintained. Resolution No. 30 of the Central Bank of 20/07/1966 established at 21 per cent the level of reserves to demand deposits and short term deposits and at 14 per cent their level in the incentivated areas. Resolution No. 382 of the Central Bank of 21/07/1976 increased from 33 per cent to 35 per cent the level of compulsory reserves on demand deposits in non-incentivated areas and maintained a level of 18 per cent in incentivated areas.

Resolution No.652 of the Central Bank of 17/12/1980 established, for the first time, differentiation between big, medium and small banks for the regulation of reserves. In non-incentivated areas big banks must maintain 35 per cent of their demand deposits as reserves, medium banks 31 per cent and small banks 28 per cent. In incentivated areas, big banks must maintain 18 per cent of their total demand deposits as reserves; medium banks, 14 per cent and small banks, 11 per cent. This resolution gave an extra incentive to peripheral regions relative to the asymmetric distribution of banks according to their size. As the participation of medium and small banks is bigger in peripheral regions, these regions tend to benefit from these differentiated reserve policy according to size of bank. Resolution No. 762 of the Central Bank of 14/09/1982 raised the compulsory reserves of non-incentivated areas of medium banks to 40 per cent and of big banks to 45 per cent. Resolution No.833 of the Central Bank of 09/06/1983 raised the compulsory reserve ratio of big banks to 50 per cent and of medium banks to 45 per cent in the non-incentivated areas, maintaining the ratio for incentivated areas. Resolution No. 1632 of the Central Bank established that deposits in pioneer branches must not be computed for reserves purposes. This gave extra incentive to the opening of new agencies, since it allowed a reduction in the level of reserves. Circular No. 1601 of the Central Bank of 18/03/1990 changed the ratio for compulsory reserves; however, it maintained the structure of differentiation.

We can see a clear concern by the policy makers to differentiate the policy of compulsory reserves with the aim of stimulating extension of credit in peripheral regions (incentivated areas). However, it is important to observe the banks' voluntary reserves, in order to see what the "natural" policy of the banks would be if there were no exogenous intervention in this sphere.

Observing the ratio of total voluntary reserves to total deposits (Table IV.56.s.a. and IV.57.s.a.) we notice that banks in the periphery tend to maintain larger ratios of voluntary reserves to total deposits than banks in the centre. This is in accordance with the model developed in Chapter 2 which predicted this tendency as a consequence of the greater instability of the peripheral regions. This is an extra element which constrains extension of credit to the peripheral regions. The policy of allowing lower ratios of compulsory reserves to deposits by banks which operate in the periphery is a way of balancing this tendency. Although banks after stage 2 are not constrained by their volume of reserves, this variable is still analytically important, because it reflects the liquidity preference of banks and their confidence in their expectations in each region. Banks that have lower confidence in their expectations, because of remoteness of the basis of information or because of the degree of uncertainty that the economy is submitted to, tend to keep higher ratios of voluntary reserves to deposits and be more cautious in terms of extending credit. At the same time, banks that expect lower levels of redeposit, that is, higher levels of leakages of reserves, will also limit their extension of credit. As observed earlier, banks in the periphery are confronted by the two types of situations and, therefore, are supposed to present high ratios of voluntary reserves to deposits as was shown by the data. The high ratios of voluntary reserves to deposits that banks keep in the periphery have important effects on the money multipliers. As well as the liquidity preference of other economic agents, the high liquidity preference of banks reduces the regional money multiplier putting monetary limits to growth. Even if banks are at a further stage of banking development, the tendency of banks in the periphery to show higher levels of reserves depresses those regions since this puts limits to further credit extensions and consequently to investment.

The Banco do Brasil holds lower ratios of voluntary reserves to deposits than the general total of the banks (Tables IV.59.s.a. and IV.60.s.a.). This is due to the role this institution played over a large part of the analysed period, operating jointly with the Central Bank as Monetary Authority. However, the same tendency to maintain larger ratios of voluntary reserves to deposits in peripheral regions than in the central region is still observed. Table IV.59.s.a. compares the values of this ratio for each region and the Brazilian average. The same tendency to maintain lower ratios of voluntary reserves to deposits in relation to the general total can be seen in BNB/BASA in Table IV.60.s.a. Again this can be considered a result of the public character of these banks which permits them to have easier access to funds when there is a shortage of liquidity. Table IV.61.s.a. shows that these banks have lower ratios of voluntary reserves to deposits in peripheral regions than in the central regions. This ratio stayed at levels below the average of Brazil in great part of the analysed period. This is because the target of these banks was exactly the peripheral regions, so they were supposed to have a policy of easier extension of credit to these regions than to the central ones.

All banks except the Banco do Brasil had a higher ratio of total voluntary reserves to total deposits (until 1968) than the general total, as can be seen in Table IV.62.s.a., IV.63.s.a., IV.64.s.a., IV.65.s.a. These tables also show the position of private banks (after 1968). The higher ratio of reserves to deposits is due to the greater difficulties these banks had in gaining access to funds when there was a shortage of reserves, and this forced them to maintain more liquid positions.

Tables IV.63.s.a. and IV.65.s.a. show that banks (all national banks except Banco do Brasil until 1968 and private banks after 1968) in peripheral regions tend to maintain higher ratios of voluntary reserves to deposits than banks in central regions, which made them achieve higher ratios than the national average. This is in accordance with the model developed in Chapter 2 since the great instability of peripheral regions tends to make banks maintain more liquid portfolios. This pattern was indicated when we dealt with the results of the general total of the banks (public and private). Therefore, this is also a valid result for private banks, which are really motivated by the private logic of profit maximization and do not have exogenous elements which force them to act against this logic, as is the case for government-owned banks.

Therefore, the characteristics of the periphery make banks keep higher reserves of deposits in the periphery than in the centre. This is due to the greater instability of these economies and of the more remote bases of information compared to banks of the centre. The higher liquidity preference of banks results in reduced credit creation in these regions and depressed economies. Government-owned banks, on the other hand, do not follow the logic of the private sector to determine their level of voluntary reserves and, in this way, can keep lower levels of reserves in the periphery. Consequently, they are much more important to these regions for credit creation than private banks. However, the dynamic financial role that they play in these areas results in reduced effects due to real and financial leakages that these regions present.

It is now important to consider the velocity of circulation of money in the regions. Our model predicted that peripheral regions are supposed to exhibit a smaller velocity of circulation because of their less developed financial system and their higher liquidity preference. Table IV.66.s.a. gives a proxy for the relative velocity of circulation of money using the number of cleared cheques in relation to the Brazilian total. What we observe from this table is a relative acceleration in the velocity of circulation of money in peripheral regions in contrast with a decrease in the centre. However, the loss of the relative position of the Southeast is greater than the loss of the relative position of São Paulo, which shows that this phenomenon was much more intense in other states of the region than in the state which can be considered the core of the central region. The increase in the velocity of circulation of money, however, was not homogenous across peripheral regions. We can see that there was a greater increase in this variable in the South and Centre-West than in the traditional peripheral regions. This is due to the higher level of development of the first region and of the presence of Brasília in the second.

BNDES and the regions

The BNDES system is and was one of the most important elements in funding industrial investment and infra-structural investment in Brazil since 1952, as observed in Chapter 4. However, it is important to mention that it does not take part in the Brazilian monetary system, as the commercial banks do. Nevertheless, BNDES still plays an important role in the government-owned banking system, since there are some banks that mainly relend funds of BNDES, as is the case with BNB/BASA and of the state banks. Therefore, the funds of BNDES are fundamental to the capacity to extend loans of BNB/BASA.

Table IV.67.s.a. shows the regional distribution of funds of the BNDES through time. This table clearly demonstrates the importance of this institution at the time of the intensive industrialisation of Brazil, analysed in Chapter 4. During this period, however, the funds of BNDES were extremely concentrated in the Southeast and especially in São Paulo. Notwithstanding, after the 70s we observe a relative deconcentration of these funds, especially in direction of Northeast and South, which was intensified after 1985. However, this was led by economic policy, not by private profit-seeking.

Regional interest rate differentials

The model developed in Chapter 2 showed that peripheral and central economies are characterised by very different economic structures. The outcome of these structures can be summarized as: a) central economies are more stable than peripheral ones; b) peripheral economies present a less reliable base for the formation of expectation because of their remoteness in relation to the decision making centres and of their higher levels of uncertainty; c) peripheral agents present higher liquidity preference as a consequence of the more intense level of uncertainty; d) agents in the periphery prefer to manifest their higher liquidity preference in the assets of central economies, since these markets are more active and give higher liquidity to their assets; e) as there is a generalised higher liquidity preference in the periphery and there is also a leakage of finance from the periphery toward the centre, this region tends to present higher interest rate levels. In the case of Brazil it is not easy to observe the differentiation of interest levels across regions, since data are very rudimentary.

Nevertheless, there are some indicators that we can employ. First, we can use the special enquiry of the census of 1970[16] to observe the ratio of proceeds on loans to total loans as a proxy for the interest rate charged by banks. However, this presents problems since government banks are considered together with private banks and this does not allow us to make definitive statements on the private tendency. These data show that peripheral regions have higher levels of interest, as predicted by the model.

Another indicator of the level of interest charged in peripheral regions can be found by observing the margin allowed by BNDES to be charged by banks that are responsible for the relending of its funds. Though the interest charged by BNDES is determined by economic policy to the regions and not by private mechanisms, the margin allowed to be charged by banks that relend these funds reflects the incentive to relend these funds and is a reflexion of the degree of uncertainty faced by banks in doing so[17]. As expected, higher spreads are allowed in peripheral regions (Tables IV.68.s.a. and IV.69.s.a.). We can also see that this tendency is contrasted with the lower interest rates charged by BNDES, which result in lower levels of total interest.

The rates of interest on institutional credit[18] to agriculture demand attention due to the fact that these rates are fixed by government (Table IV.70.s.a.). This obliges the banks to charge lower interest rates in peripheral regions and, so the lower interest rates in this sector are much more a result of a deliberate measure of economic policy than the result of the private considerations of the banks.

The general characterisation of regional interest differentials which was analysed up to now emphasised the regional power of discrimination by banks. However, inside the regions, banks also have the power to discriminate against certain groups and sectors and especially against the combination of these two. The rate of interest is an instrument of this discrimination. Makler (1982) observed that in Bahia the Banco do Brasil has a special role to play in the availability of short term finance and the Bank of Northeast has a special role to play in the extension of long term loans, local industrialists paid lower interest rates for short term finance compared to extra-regional or foreign industrialists, and the opposite situation was observed for long term finance, where foreign or extra-regional capital achieved lower interest rates than regional capital. The local industrialists operating in traditional sectors received favourable interest rates on short term loans from Banco do Brasil. On the other hand, the sectors that received more favourable interest rates for long term loans, especially from BNB, were those that associate extra-regional capital with dynamic sectors. Moreover, he observes that BNDES acts mainly in a restricted way, with extra-regional capital acting in dynamic sectors and the local banks, like Banco Econômico, tend to act and give favourable interest rates to projects that join extra-regional capital and dynamic sectors. The same pattern is followed by private banks who have their head offices in the Centre-South of the country. Therefore, we can see that the banking structure, public and private, discriminates through the interest rate in accentuating the regional division of labour that was established mainly since 1960. This stimulates the participation of native capital in traditional sectors and creates long term finance, which makes possible installation of extra-regional capital in the dynamic sectors.

Finally, credit restriction to peripheral regions cannot be analysed only in terms of price (interest), but must also be analysed in terms of quantity. This sort of analysis is far more complex, since this constraint cannot be measured only in terms of refused applications for credit, but must also incorporate the applications that were not made because the applicant knew "ex-ante" that the application would be refused. This is particularly true when we analyse the case of traditional peripheral regions where the informal sector is very strong; by definition, the informal sector is out of the sphere of the formal financial system. As has been seen, these sectors are extremely important in peripheral economies, especially in terms of labour absorption, and as they do not have access to the financial system they are under a permanent financial constraint. So the poorer the region is, the more it is under this type of disguised credit constraint which cannot be measured but which is extremely important and perverse. So if we take only the applications for credit that were not accepted, we may have a situation where the credit constraint is greater in the centre than in the periphery, when the real situation is exactly the opposite. Unfortunately, in Brazil, we do not have available data that can give us any idea of the quantitative constraints of credit. What we can do is suggest that, given the real conditions of the regional economies, the type of disguised quantitative limits to credit are greater in peripheral economies than in central ones.

Therefore, we can see that there was not a significant change in the banking system for regions in the periphery. The dynamic role was played much more by the funding mechanism created by the government in 1961, which promoted a fundamental change in the structure of peripheral regions. There was also government stimulus through financial agencies like the Banco do Brasil and the regional development banks. However, we can observe some small changes in the role played by the private banking system in the regions although some natural tendencies were counteracted by the deliberate action of the state, as was the case in the banking concentration process.

The inefficiency of government policies in attaining significant results in the reduction of regional disparities (in terms of income) and in deepening the results of the funding mechanism created by the state was a result of the type of industrialisation that was led by the state in peripheral regions. Thus, we can see an interplay between state and oligopolistic central capitals which has tended to create vicious circles in which the main benefits of the stimulus generated to peripheral regions was attained by the central regions. That is, the structural changes observed in peripheral regions, especially the sectorial changes that those economies underwent with the tax credit scheme, had characteristics which made it easier for finance to leave those regions for the central ones. Among the characteristics of this process of industrialisation we must emphasise the origin of the capital which was responsible for this process and the kind of industry responsible for its dynamic. The principal source of capital for this process came from the Centre-South of the country. As mentioned before, the origin of the capital can create completely different relations and linkages depending on which region it comes from. Extra-regional capital has a much greater degree of leakage, both of real resources and of financial resources, since it leads to fewer linkages with the regional economy than local capital and because it leads to higher degrees of capital leakages through portfolio and speculative flows. Therefore, extra-regional capital tends to lead to smaller degrees of regional financial linkages, which is one of the reasons for the reduction of the money multipliers observed in Chapter 2. Thus, the kind of stimulated industrialisation which took place in the traditional peripheral regions of Brazil since 1960 was the main reason for the lesser gains achieved by those regions in terms of the relative level of income. It was also responsible for the maintenance of the pattern of the financial behaviour of the private sector observed in the period before state intervention.

Therefore, what can be observed in the Brazilian experience is very close to the model developed by Cardoso (Cardoso, 1972) and by Dow for the financial sphere. Clearly, we observe a tendency toward the deepening of the relation of dependence of the peripheral regions led by a governmental mechanism and by the oligopolist capital of the central region. Nevertheless, this allowed the peripheral economies to undergo significant structural changes and to grow, without altering the relations of dependency. However, this accentuated income distribution problems, did not solve the main problems of these economies in terms of the generation of employment, and finally, did not alter the financial behaviour of the system as a whole, which did not allow the self-perpetuation of the growth process, since the main elements that cause the intensive leakages in the flow of finance and liquidity from the periphery to the centre were still present and in some cases were accentuated.

The character of state intervention in the regional economies underwent significant changes in the period 1960-1990. Mechanisms were created which were responsible for fundamental structural transformations in peripheral regions. However, the transformations only produced small results for the regional gross product and in the overcoming of the main social problems of the peripheral regions. This is basically due to the sort of industrialisation which was stimulated in those peripheral regions. The process stimulated mainly capital intensive extra-regional industries, which accentuated the unemployment/under-employment and exacerbated leakages of income.

On the financial side, we saw that the incentives for the industrialisation of the peripheral regions have not been able to change the behaviour of the private financial sector. We continue to observe the fundamental problem of retaining finance in these regions. This puts extra limits on the extension of new loans for the banks operating in the region. This ended up creating vicious circles that put further limits on finance for investment.

Notes

1 See Bouzan (1973) and Mendes (1988).

2 For a good analysis of this change of structure of the banking system see Corrêa (1989).

3 This can be a consequence of the way banks are formed and operate. But any way is an important element to be considered when analysing banking concentration.

4 Carvalheiro (1982) using the variance of logarithms of the size of the banks concluded that this variance decreased during 1964-76 and this demonstrated the reduction of the level of concentration in the banking system. However, we are dealing with another notion of concentration. Our idea of concentration deals with the behaviour of the banking system over time and tries to analyse the level of oligopolization of this sector.

5 The measures of general character were: Circular n. 18 of the Central Bank (07/12/1965), Portaria GB 281 (28/08/1971, Decree Law 1182 (16/07/1971), Resolution n. 201 of the Monetary Council (20/12/1971) and Resolution n. 204 of the Monetary Council (20/12/1971).

6 The main measures with explicit regional character were: Resolution n. 43 of the Central Bank (28/12/1966), Circular n. 67 of the Central Bank (28/12/1966), Resolution 107 of the Monetary Council (03/02/1969), Resolution n. 141 of the National Monetary Council(23/03/1970), Resolution n. 266 of the National Monetary Council (15/12/1973).

7 The definition of first order and second order cities followed a joint criterion of economic importance and population.

8 This analysis is taking only the number of head offices into account and not the size of the banks that those head offices represent. This can hide a process of banking concentration in terms of the relative size of

banks. This process that certainly took place in Brazil, but that cannot be observed with this kind of data.

9 The reduced participation of Banco do Brasil in the credit extension in the 1980s is a result of the restrictions imposed on this institution by economic policies (Almeida, 1988, p. 21).

10 The increase in the participation of Banking in the Centre West is due to the location of Brasília in this region, and of the action of the government in the financial system of this city.

11 An extensive analysis of this point can be found in Chapter 2 and Chapter 5.

12 In this case, the fact that this ratio is above one in São Paulo could be because this bank has a disproportionately small participation in the market of São Paulo as seen in Table IV.30.s.a. where we noticed that this bank does not have a significant participation in this market, compared with its participation in the peripheral regions. This give a smaller redeposit ratio to this bank, which allows this ratio to be above the national average.

13 The sort of industrialization induced in the Northeast and North was mainly responsible for the deepening of this sort of tendency since it was mainly led by extra-regional firms that are much more integrated with the central economies than with the regional economies. This integration generated leakages for commercial flows and for capital flows.

14 There is an alternation of periods of regional differentiation and non-regional differentiation as well as of the intensity of those differentiations.

15 Although this is a compensatory policy, since the banks in the periphery tend to maintain higher levels of voluntary reserves, as was observed in chapter 2, as an answer to the more unstable pattern of growth and the consequent higher level of uncertainty of those economies that make the banks to present a more intense liquidity preference.

16 Despite the existence of data for the banking system in the Commercial census of 1950, 1975, 1980 we cannot establish a proxy for the interest rate because interest appears as a flow in the census and loans appear as a stock.

17 This is in accordance with the model presented in Chapter 2; however, it applies also to the case of governmental regulation in terms of the operations of the private sector with public funds.

18 Institutional credit is regulated and corresponds to a certain amount of the demand deposits of the banks which is assigned, by law, to credit for agriculture.

Statistical appendix to Part IV

Table IV.1.s.a.
Regional Share of the Domestic Income (%)

Years	North	Northeast	Pernambuco	Bahia	Southeast	São Paulo	South	C. West	Total
1960	2.23	14.81	3.48	4.24	62.68	34.78	17.81	2.46	100.00
1961	2.48	14.12	3.50	3.72	63.02	35.16	17.23	3.16	100.00
1962	2.05	14.99	3.62	3.66	61.45	34.40	17.72	3.80	100.00
1963	2.00	14.59	3.86	3.44	63.32	35.75	16.81	3.27	100.00
1964	1.95	15.03	3.76	3.90	62.40	34.01	18.54	3.62	100.00
1965	2.05	14.75	3.73	4.10	61.60	34.06	17.60	3.49	100.00
1966	2.04	14.31	3.50	4.08	63.04	35.32	17.49	3.13	100.00
1967	1.93	15.03	3.63	4.21	62.16	34.11	17.67	3.21	100.00
1968	2.08	14.43	3.39	4.22	62.89	35.23	17.34	3.27	100.00
1970	2.14	11.65	3.04	3.51	65.46	39.29	17.14	3.60	100.00
1975	2.10	11.30	2.72	3.78	64.22	39.19	18.11	4.27	100.00
1980	3.09	11.98	2.54	4.35	62.42	37.49	17.00	5.52	100.00
1985	4.08	13.64	2.39	5.16	59.15	35.44	17.15	5.98	100.00
1990*	3.48	13.18	2.56	4.79	60.79	35.70	16.63	5.92	100.00

Source: Conjuntura Econômica, IBRE, FGV, September, 1971 and July, 1977; Anuário Estatístico, IBGE and Kasznar, 1990.
*Estimated by Programa de Estudos dos Estados EBAP/FGV-RJ.

Table IV.2.s.a.

States' Share of the Regional Income (%)

Years	Northeast	Pernambuco	Bahia	Southeast	São Paulo
1960	100.00	23.50	28.65	100.00	55.49
1961	100.00	24.77	26.34	100.00	55.80
1962	100.00	24.18	24.44	100.00	55.98
1963	100.00	26.48	23.57	100.00	56.45
1964	100.00	25.03	25.95	100.00	54.50
1965	100.00	25.28	27.82	100.00	55.30
1966	100.00	24.49	28.53	100.00	56.03
1967	100.00	24.14	28.01	100.00	54.87
1968	100.00	23.47	29.24	100.00	56.02
1970	100.00	26.06	30.12	100.00	60.02
1975	100.00	24.10	33.40	100.00	61.03
1980	100.00	21.18	36.27	100.00	60.06
1985	100.00	17.52	37.79	100.00	59.92
1990*	100.00	19.45	36.34	100.00	58.73

Source: Conjuntura Econômica, IBRE, FGV, September, 1971 and July, 1977; Anuário Estatístico, IBGE and Kasznar, 1990.

*Estimated by Programa de Estudos dos Estados EBAP/FGV-RJ.

Table IV.3.s.a.
Regional Per Capita Income (in Relation to Brazil) (%)

Years	North	Northeast	Southeast	São Paulo	Southeast	C. West	Total
1960	60.86	46.87	143.24	190.26	106.45	58.14	100.00
1961	67.46	45.11	143.99	191.77	101.77	72.94	100.00
1962	55.67	48.34	140.41	187.10	103.46	85.84	100.00
1963	54.42	47.51	144.72	193.97	97.00	72.33	100.00
1964	52.84	49.44	142.65	184.12	105.71	78.28	100.00
1965	55.44	49.00	140.89	184.04	99.09	73.81	100.00
1966	55.13	48.01	144.26	190.47	97.22	64.84	100.00
1967	52.21	50.97	142.36	183.64	96.96	65.19	100.00
1968	56.07	49.44	144.15	189.41	93.95	64.98	100.00
1970	55.34	38.60	152.99	205.92	96.78	66.16	100.00
1975	48.22	38.03	148.67	194.65	107.76	72.04	100.00
1980	55.76	40.95	143.53	178.23	106.18	96.63	100.00
1985	65.60	46.89	137.26	166.83	110.23	99.08	100.00
1990*	58.90	46.29	139.43	162.32	109.84	86.13	100.00

Source: Conjuntura Econômica, IBRE, FGV, September, 1971 and July, 1977; Anuário Estatístico, IBGE and Kasznar, 1990.
*Estimated by Programa de Estudos dos Estados EBAP/FGV-RJ.

Table IV.4.s.a.
Regional Share of the Agriculture Income (%)

Years	North	Northeast	Pernambuco	Bahia	Southeast	São Paulo	South	C.West	Total
1960	2.04	22.32	3.83	6.15	42.51	23.14	28.41	4.71	100.00
1961	2.45	21.42	3.98	4.82	42.29	24.24	27.73	6.11	100.00
1962	1.67	23.56	4.20	5.10	40.00	21.56	27.87	6.90	100.00
1963	1.80	23.86	4.86	5.07	40.39	22.93	27.25	6.69	100.00
1964	1.83	23.52	4.35	5.85	40.86	20.38	26.80	6.99	100.00
1965	1.87	23.20	4.25	5.92	40.99	22.40	27.45	6.49	100.00
1966	1.90	23.09	4.25	6.50	41.80	22.68	27.07	6.14	100.00
1967	1.79	24.78	4.28	6.74	38.89	20.89	28.50	6.03	100.00
1968	2.07	24.59	3.96	6.93	37.94	19.51	28.68	6.72	100.00
1970	3.59	20.26	3.25	6.66	33.78	17.71	35.36	7.02	100.00
1975	0.00	19.81	2.83	6.46	32.09	15.79	36.14	8.27	100.00
1980	4.96	19.49	2.73	6.90	34.68	14.25	29.51	11.36	100.00
1985	6.47	20.61	2.75	8.11	38.31	16.67	27.10	7.50	100.00

Source: Conjuntura Econômica, IBRE, FGV, September, 1971 and July, 1977 and Anuário Estatístico, IBGE.

Table IV.5. s.a.

Agricultural Sates' Participation in the Regional Agricultural Income (%)

Years	Pernambuco	Bahia	São Paulo
1960	17.17	27.57	54.42
1961	18.60	22.49	57.32
1962	17.81	21.63	53.91
1963	20.35	21.24	56.78
1964	18.51	24.86	49.87
1965	18.30	25.53	54.65
1966	18.42	28.15	54.26
1967	17.28	27.19	53.72
1968	16.11	28.17	51.44
1970	16.02	32.88	52.43
1975	14.29	32.64	49.21
1980	13.99	35.38	41.09
1985	13.34	39.37	43.50

Source: Conjuntura Econômica, IBRE, FGV, September, 1971 and July, 1977 and Anuário Estatístico, IBGE.

Table IV.6.s.a.
Agriculture Participation in the Total Regional Income (%)

Years	North	Northeast	Pernambuco	Bahia	Southeast	São Paulo	South	C. West	Total
1960	25.06	41.34	30.20	39.78	18.61	18.25	43.77	52.50	27.44
1961	25.90	39.65	29.76	33.86	17.54	18.02	42.09	50.51	26.14
1962	23.21	44.79	33.00	39.65	18.55	17.86	44.83	51.73	28.49
1963	22.09	40.15	30.86	36.19	15.66	15.75	39.78	50.18	24.55
1964	25.08	41.82	30.92	40.05	17.50	16.02	38.63	51.60	26.73
1965	25.13	43.32	31.36	39.77	18.33	18.11	42.96	51.32	27.54
1966	22.24	38.46	28.93	37.95	15.80	15.30	36.89	46.78	23.83
1967	22.24	39.59	28.33	38.44	15.02	14.70	38.73	45.13	24.00
1968	22.18	37.90	26.01	36.51	13.42	12.32	36.78	45.75	22.24
1970	18.73	19.45	11.95	21.23	5.77	5.04	23.06	21.77	11.18
1975	-	21.64	12.84	21.15	6.17	4.98	24.64	23.93	12.35
1980	16.11	16.32	10.78	15.92	5.57	3.81	17.41	20.66	10.03
1985	16.66	15.87	12.08	16.53	6.80	4.94	16.60	13.17	10.50

Source: Conjuntura Econômica, IBRE, FGV, September, 1971 and July, 1977 and Anuário Estatístico, IBGE.

Table IV.7.s.a.

Regional Share of the Industrial Income (%)

Years	North	Northeast	Pernambuco	Bahia	Southeast	São Paulo	South	C. West	Total
1960	1.89	8.03	2.54	2.38	77.47	54.29	12.60	0.74	100.00
1961	1.96	7.49	2.50	1.98	78.44	55.54	11.41	0.70	100.00
1962	1.85	6.69	2.46	1.47	79.35	56.71	11.49	0.63	100.00
1963	1.53	6.99	2.51	1.46	79.64	57.16	11.19	0.65	100.00
1964	1.40	7.47	2.57	1.55	79.57	57.29	10.87	0.68	100.00
1965	1.35	6.66	2.20	1.52	68.13	47.98	9.61	0.71	100.00
1966	1.42	6.43	2.16	1.60	79.94	55.65	11.51	0.70	100.00
1967	1.34	6.46	2.43	1.45	80.59	55.01	10.83	0.79	100.00
1968	1.43	6.26	2.32	1.52	80.89	56.85	10.76	0.65	100.00
1970	1.08	5.79	2.05	1.55	80.26	57.02	11.97	0.91	100.00
1975	1.33	7.49	2.22	2.60	75.21	54.95	14.83	1.14	100.00
1980	3.00	9.49	2.07	4.05	69.05	47.23	16.24	2.22	100.00
1985	4.05	12.04	2.00	5.22	65.80	44.00	15.70	2.40	100.00

Source: Conjuntura Econômica, IBRE, FGV, September, 1971 and July, 1977 and Anuário Estatístico, IBGE.

Table IV.8.s.a.
States' industrial Participation in the Total Regional Industrial Income (%)

Years	Pernambuco	Bahia	São Paulo
1960	31.64	29.66	70.07
1961	33.37	26.42	70.80
1962	36.74	22.03	71.48
1963	35.91	20.92	71.78
1964	34.37	20.70	72.00
1965	33.06	22.77	70.43
1966	33.66	24.88	69.62
1967	37.65	22.40	68.27
1968	37.00	24.19	70.27
1970	35.37	26.71	71.05
1975	29.67	34.71	73.06
1980	21.82	42.70	68.41
1985	16.63	43.34	66.87

Source: Conjuntura Econômica, IBRE, FGV, September, 1971 and July, 1977 and Anuário Estatístico, IBGE.

Table IV.9.s.a.
Industrial Participation in the Total Regional Income (%)

Years	North	Northeast	Pernambuco	Bahia	Southeast	São Paulo	South	C. West	Total
1960	18.35	11.71	15.76	12.12	26.70	33.72	15.29	6.48	21.60
1961	17.23	11.56	15.58	11.60	27.13	34.42	14.43	4.84	21.79
1962	19.13	9.48	14.40	8.54	27.42	35.01	13.77	3.49	21.23
1963	17.72	11.16	15.14	9.91	29.30	37.25	15.51	4.64	23.30
1964	15.65	10.86	14.92	8.66	27.86	36.80	12.81	4.11	21.84
1965	15.73	10.82	14.15	8.86	26.48	33.72	13.08	4.87	23.94
1966	16.24	10.48	14.40	9.14	29.59	36.77	15.36	5.25	23.33
1967	15.40	9.56	14.92	7.65	28.86	35.90	13.65	5.45	22.26
1968	16.90	10.63	16.76	8.80	31.49	39.51	15.19	4.90	24.48
1970	15.30	15.12	20.53	13.41	37.31	44.17	21.25	7.66	30.43
1975	20.04	20.95	25.79	21.77	37.03	44.33	25.89	8.46	31.62
1980	37.21	30.32	31.23	35.70	42.33	48.21	36.56	15.37	38.27
1985	39.82	35.41	33.60	40.61	44.62	49.80	36.73	16.09	40.11

Source: Conjuntura Econômica, IBRE, FGV, September, 1971 and July, 1977 and Anuário Estatístico, IBGE.

Table IV.10.s.a.

Regional Share of the Service Income (%)

Years	North	Northeast	Pernambuco	Bahia	Southeast	São Paulo	South	C. West	Total
1960	2.48	13.65	3.69	4.01	67.27	32.79	14.63	1.98	100.00
1961	2.71	13.23	3.67	3.90	66.97	32.11	14.39	2.71	100.00
1962	2.35	13.63	3.79	3.78	66.04	32.25	14.59	3.39	100.00
1963	2.31	13.62	4.00	3.55	66.82	32.21	14.41	2.83	100.00
1964	2.25	13.83	3.96	3.89	66.29	31.20	14.51	3.12	100.00
1965	2.34	14.06	3.92	4.07	65.70	31.70	14.95	2.95	100.00
1966	2.37	13.82	3.76	4.09	65.16	32.05	15.80	2.84	100.00
1967	2.25	14.22	3.83	4.22	64.93	31.35	15.66	2.95	100.00
1968	2.38	13.94	3.64	4.33	65.03	31.85	15.63	3.03	100.00
1970	2.42	13.06	3.51	3.93	63.82	34.18	16.35	4.36	100.00
1975	2.18	11.58	2.98	3.85	65.10	35.46	15.99	5.15	100.00
1980	2.79	12.36	2.85	4.07	62.89	34.79	15.13	6.82	100.00
1985	3.60	13.46	2.63	4.47	58.17	32.47	16.20	8.57	100.00

Source: Conjuntura Econômica, IBRE, FGV, September, 1971 and July, 1977 and Anuário Estatístico, IBGE.

Table IV.11.s.a.
Services Participation in the Total Regional Income (%)

Years	North	Northeast	Pernambuco	Bahia	Southeast	São Paulo	South	C. West	Total
1960	56.54	46.94	54.03	48.10	54.69	48.03	41.84	41.02	50.96
1961	56.87	48.79	54.66	54.55	55.33	47.56	43.48	44.65	52.07
1962	57.65	45.73	52.60	51.81	54.03	47.13	41.40	44.78	50.27
1963	60.19	48.68	54.00	53.90	55.04	47.00	44.71	45.18	52.16
1964	59.26	47.32	54.16	51.28	54.64	47.19	40.25	44.29	51.43
1965	59.15	49.36	54.49	51.38	55.20	48.16	43.96	43.81	51.76
1966	61.52	51.06	56.67	52.91	54.61	47.93	47.75	47.96	52.83
1967	62.45	50.85	56.75	53.92	56.13	49.40	47.62	49.42	53.74
1968	60.91	51.47	57.22	54.70	55.09	48.17	48.03	49.35	53.28
1970	65.97	65.43	67.52	65.36	56.92	50.79	55.69	70.57	58.38
1975	58.19	57.41	61.37	57.08	56.80	50.69	49.47	67.60	56.03
1980	46.68	53.36	57.99	48.38	52.09	47.97	46.03	63.96	51.70
1985	43.52	48.72	54.32	42.86	48.57	45.26	46.66	70.75	49.39

Source: Conjuntura Econômica, IBRE, FGV, September 1971 and July 1977 and Anuário Estatístico, IBGE.

Table IV.12.s.a.

States' Service Participation in the Regional Income (%)

Years	Pernambuco	Bahia	São Paulo
1960	27.05	29.36	48.74
1961	27.74	29.45	47.96
1962	27.81	27.69	48.83
1963	29.37	26.10	48.20
1964	28.65	28.12	47.07
1965	27.91	28.96	48.25
1966	27.18	29.56	49.18
1967	26.94	29.69	48.29
1968	26.09	31.08	48.98
1970	26.89	30.09	53.56
1975	25.76	33.21	54.48
1980	23.03	32.89	55.31
1985	19.53	33.25	55.82

Source: Conjuntura Econômica, IBRE, FGV, September, 1971 and July, 1977 and Anuário Estatístico, IBGE.

Table IV.13.s.a.
Rate of Change of the real Gross Domestic Product (%)

Years	Brazil	Northeast
1966	6.70	-1.00
1967	4.20	12.60
1968	9.80	0.90
1969	9.50	4.10
1970	10.40	-4.20
1971	11.30	25.40
1972	12.10	5.90
1973	14.00	11.30
1974	9.00	1.60
1975	5.20	8.50
1976	9.80	7.00
1977	4.60	8.90
1978	4.80	10.50
1979	7.20	7.20
1980	9.20	2.90
1981	-4.50	-0.70
1982	0.50	10.50
1983	-3.50	3.80
1984	5.30	8.60
1985	7.90	8.20
1986	7.60	14.40
1987	3.60	2.00
1988	-0.10	3.00
1989	3.30	2.30
1990	-4.40	-2.80

Source: For Brazil: (1961-1980) Estatísticas Históricas do Brasil, IBGE; (1981-1990); Anuário Estatístico do IBGE and for the Northeast: Produto e Formação Bruta de Captial, SUDENE.

Table IV.14.s.a.
Value of the Industrial Transformation (%)

	1960	1970	1975	1980	1985
North	1.11	1.00	0.00	2.48	2.78
Northeast	7.64	5.76	6.64	7.36	8.05
Pernambuco	2.55	2.10	2.24	1.83	0.64
Bahia	2.42	1.53	2.12	3.06	3.57
Southeast	78.14	79.49	76.28	72.84	66.78
São Paulo	54.51	56.64	55.89	52.76	47.40
South	12.42	11.90	14.75	15.37	15.43
Centre West	0.69	0.81	1.04	1.23	1.34
Brazil	100.00	100.00	100.00	100.00	100.00

Source: Censos Industriais, IBGE.

Table IV.15.s.a.
Number of Industrial Establishments (%)

	1960	1970	1975	1980	1985
North	1.64	1.94	2.62	3.41	3.86
Northeast	19.15	18.84	17.16	16.44	19.71
Pernambuco	3.26	3.58	3.58	3.19	4.05
Bahia	5.37	4.88	4.51	2.90	5.64
Southeast	54.22	51.79	51.89	53.61	49.80
São Paulo	32.73	30.68	32.42	32.76	28.65
South	22.53	23.04	23.03	21.00	21.21
Centre West	2.46	4.38	5.29	5.54	5.42
Brazil	100.00	100.00	100.00	100.00	100.00

Source: Censos Industriais, IBGE.

Table IV.16.s.a.
Workers of the Industry (%)

	1960	1970	1975	1980	1985
North	1.12	1.49	0.00	2.55	2.67
Northeast	12.43	10.23	10.13	10.44	10.77
Pernambuco	4.00	3.31	2.98	2.68	2.70
Bahia	2.78	2.20	2.31	2.53	2.64
Southeast	70.46	69.73	67.72	66.45	64.16
São Paulo	46.20	47.99	47.55	46.84	45.06
South	15.16	16.92	18.68	18.51	20.00
Centre West	0.83	1.38	1.73	2.01	2.18
Brazil	100.00	100.00	100.00	100.00	100.00

Source: Censos Industriais, IBGE.

Table IV.17.s.a.

Value of the Industrial Transformation-1959 (%)

	North	Northeast	Southeast	Sao Paulo	South	C. West	Brazil
Manufacturing	0.94	6.99	78.97	55.18	12.46	0.64	100.00
Nonmetallic Minerals	0.61	8.50	78.15	50.54	11.14	1.60	100.00
Metallurgy	0.23	1.20	91.46	43.80	7.04	0.08	100.00
Machinery	0.00	0.31	9.39	78.25	6.97	0.00	100.00
Electrical and Communication Mat.	0.00	0.17	96.19	80.00	3.64	0.00	100.00
Transport Equipment	0.04	0.70	96.87	86.86	2.33	0.06	100.00
Wood	1.84	3.59	34.44	20.56	57.97	2.17	100.00
Furniture	0.58	5.08	79.30	58.51	14.23	0.81	100.00
Paper and Cardboard	0.08	5.73	78.68	59.78	15.50	0.01	100.00
Rubber	2.27	0.67	93.79	84.17	2.85	0.42	100.00
Leather Products	18.32	14.51	54.60	29.76	28.47	0.59	100.00
Chemicals	2.22	11.91	76.71	64.45	9.04	0.12	100.00
Pharmaceuticals	0.09	0.85	97.36	51.05	1.68	0.01	100.00
Perfumes, Soaps and Candles	2.56	7.19	83.39	47.90	57.00	0.37	100.00
Plastics	0.00	0.23	96.82	51.30	2.96	0.00	100.00
Textiles	1.27	13.79	78.88	57.22	6.03	0.03	100.00
Clothing, Footwear and Woven Articles	0.40	4.32	76.75	54.65	17.81	0.71	100.00
Food Products	1.17	12.42	61.31	40.77	23.03	2.07	100.00
Beverage	1.97	7.22	75.26	46.44	15.07	0.48	100.00
Tobacco	3.14	16.51	29.73	38.26	18.29	0.00	100.00
Printing and Publishing	0.82	4.34	85.54	50.38	8.89	0.41	100.00
Others	0.12	1.57	87.07	70.85	11.11	0.12	100.00

Source: Censos Industriais, IBGE.

Table IV.18.s.a.

Value of the Industrial Transformation-1970 (%)

	North	Northeast	Southeast	São Paulo	South	C.West	Brazil
Extractive Industry and Manufacturing							
Extractive industry	6.97	6.89	38.76	6.31	9.44	1.64	100.00
Manufacturing	0.82	5.73	80.68	58.11	11.98	0.79	100.00
Nonmetallic Minerals	0.90	10.95	76.47	49.88	9.86	1.82	100.00
Metallurgy	0.18	2.48	89.29	52.73	7.84	0.21	100.00
Machinery	0.18	1.49	88.41	68.48	9.69	0.24	100.00
Electrical and Communication Equip.	0.06	2.69	92.45	78.92	4.72	0.09	100.00
Transport Equipment	0.14	0.81	94.28	81.07	4.65	0.12	100.00
Wood	4.09	3.66	30.58	18.81	58.89	2.79	100.00
Furniture	0.69	5.10	76.26	54.91	17.14	0.80	100.00
Paper and Cardboard	0.12	1.87	80.45	16.84	17.44	0.12	100.00
Rubber	2.06	0.99	91.19	83.93	5.12	0.65	100.00
Leather Products	1.87	5.89	52.00	27.88	39.51	0.72	100.00
Chemicals	1.30	8.39	80.11	54.13	10.08	0.11	100.00
Pharmaceuticals	0.00	0.74	97.49	66.38	1.69	0.00	100.00
Perfumes, Soaps and Candles	1.37	3.11	91.95	675.27	3.46	0.11	100.00
Plastics	0.00	1.87	85.33	68.29	12.55	0.00	100.00
Textiles	1.01	7.96	80.10	61.66	10.52	0.41	100.00
Clothing, Footwear and Woven art.	0.25	6.26	74.81	56.65	18.31	0.37	100.00
Food Products	1.24	12.37	65.12	43.95	18.37	2.90	100.00
Beverage	1.69	11.54	67.31	41.70	18.72	0.74	100.00
Tobacco	2.14	14.00	68.08	36.54	15.78	0.01	100.00
Printing and Publishing	0.80	3.75	86.41	52.51	7.86	1.20	100.00
Others	1.09	1.21	88.89	70.45	8.65	0.15	100.00

Source: Censos Industriais, IBGE.

Table IV.19.s.a.

Value of the Industrial Transformation-1980 (%)

	North	Northeast	Southeast	São Paulo	South	C.West	Brazil
Extractive Industry and Manufacturing	2.57	8.05	72.18	52.42	15.64	1.27	100.00
Extractive Industry	10.98	7.89	51.66	6.96	10.51	6.27	100.00
Manufcturing	2.39	8.06	72.63	53.43	15.76	11.60	100.00
Nonmetallic Minerals	1.90	11.34	66.81	39.84	15.69	4.26	100.00
Metallurgy	0.67	3.93	85.48	54.04	9.50	0.43	100.00
Machinery	0.74	3.72	82.77	66.39	12.42	0.35	100.00
Electrical and Communication Equip.	0.00	3.03	76.36	64.59	7.30	0.00	100.00
Transport Equipment	2.10	0.81	89.77	68.48	7.03	0.29	100.00
Wood	10.60	6.10	26.16	19.50	51.33	5.81	100.00
Furniture	1.55	6.20	58.03	44.83	32.25	1.97	100.00
Paper and Cardboard	2.73	4.47	73.16	53.38	19.54	0.11	100.00
Rubber	3.59	3.34	0.00	74.91	9.54	0.00	100.00
Leather Products	1.52	8.46	42.63	27.55	46.72	0.67	100.00
Chemicals	0.63	14.85	69.00	54.23	15.33	0.19	100.00
Pharmaceuticals	0.16	1.62	0.00	65.18	2.92	0.00	100.00
Perfumes, Soaps and Candles	2.26	0.00	86.96	69.54	4.98	0.00	100.00
Plastics	0.9	0.00	74.87	59.57	17.31	0.00	100.00
Textiles	0.0	13.68	69.91	53.71	13.69	0.00	100.00
Clothing, Footwear, and Woven Material	0.53	8.77	59.69	42.37	30.69	0.32	100.00
Food Products	1.91	13.51	57.62	39.46	23.25	3.79	100.00
Beverage	5.35	12.22	54.38	33.23	25.29	2.76	100.00
Tobacco	0.00	0.00	41.72	21.96	45.12	0.04	100.00
Printing and Publishing	0.86	5.44	83.69	50.04	7.56	2.45	100.00
Others	0.00	0.00	84.53	67.87	9.98	0.14	100.00

Source: Censos Industriais, IBGE.

Table IV.20.s.a.
Participation of the Region and Abroad in the Control of Capital of Firms According to the Kind of Industry - 1988 (%)

	N.East	North/C.W	Southeast	South	Abroad	Total
Northeast	66	1	28	4	1	100
Extractive Ind.	-	50	50	-	-	100
Mannufacturing	66	1	28	4	1	100
Kind of Industry						
Extract. Minerals	-	50	50	-	-	100
Non Metallic Minerals	76	-	21	1	1	100
Metallurgy	50	2	44	5	-	100
Machinery	45	5	45	5	-	100
Elect. Material						
Electronic amd Comp.	41	-	50	9	-	100
Transport Equip.	60	-	-	40	-	100
Wood	100	-	-	-	-	100
Furniture	86	-	7	7	-	100
Paper and Cardboard	83	3	11	6	-	100
Rubber	40	-	60	-	-	100
Leather Prod.						
Travel Goods	87	-	7	7	-	100
Chemical	56	1	36	4	2	100
Pharmaceuticals	75	-	25	-	-	100
Perfumes, Soaps						
And Candles	80	-	20	-	-	100
Plastics	58	-	38	4	-	100
Textiles	64	1	32	2	-	100
Cloting, Footwear						
amd Woven Aticles	78	-	13	9	-	100
Food Products	81	-	18	-	-	100
Beverage	27	9	55	9	-	100
Tobacco	50	-	-	-	50	100
Printing and Publ..	71	-	14	-	14	100
Other	50	-	38	13	-	100
Auxiliar Activities						
and Industrial Services	67	-	-	33	-	100

Source: Direcet Reserch,BNB/SUDENE, 1992.

Table IV.21.s.a.
Participation of the Regions in the Value of the Equipment of the New Industry of the Northeast – 1988 (%)

	Northeast	Southeast	North/C.W.	South	Abroad	São Paulo
Maranhão	15.2	56.3	0	4.4	23.8	81.6
Piauí	9.8	59	0	2.1	29	98.6
Ceará	7.9	55.6	0.1	8.2	28.2	90
Rio G. do Norte	7	53.9	0.4	4.4	34.3	76.6
Paraíba	14.9	47.9	1.2	12	24	75.1
Pernambuco	6.2	51.7	2	5.6	34.5	82.7
Alagoas	4.1	68.3	3.1	2	22.5	67.6
Sergipe	0.9	45.1	0	6.9	47.1	67.3
Bahia	13.4	40.5	2.2	6	37.9	83.5
Minas Gerais	0.6	80.7	1.8	5.6	11.3	51.9
Total	9.9	48.9	1.6	6.2	33.4	80

Source: Direct Rersearch BNB/SUDENE, 1992.
1-The participation of São Paulo refers to its participation inside the Southeast.

Table IV.22.s.a.
Participation of the Regions and Abroad in the Supply of Raw Material for the New Industry of The Northeast According to the Kind of Industry
1988 (%)

	Northeast	North/C.W	Southeast	South	Abroad	São Paulo
Kind of Industry	66	3	17	5	9	66
Extractive	100	-	-	-	-	-
Mannufacturing	66	3	17	5	9	66
Kind of Industry						
Extract. Mineral	100	-	-	-	-	-
Non-Metallic Minerals	83	6	10	-	-	64
Metallurgy	36	9	23	8	24	30
Machinery	8	1	89	2	-	85
Elect. Material						
Electronic and Comp.	20	4	56	10	10	83
Transport Equip.	6	-	81	13	-	65
Wood	93	-	-	7	-	-
Furniture	10	12	78	1	-	20
Paper and Cardboard	74	10	12	4	-	45
Rubber	44	-	55	1	-	45
Leather Prod.						
Travel Goods	87	5	8	-	-	25
Chemical	87	-	4	-	9	82
Pharmaceuticals	53	3	31	9	4	77
Perfumes, Soaps						
and Candles	34	21	42	3	-	78
Plastics	90	-	9	1	-	70
Textiles	60	5	24	10	1	91
Clothing, Footwear						
and Woven Articles	29	1	60	8	1	72
Food Products	84	3	7	5	1	33
Beverages	15	7	21	30	27	84
Tobacco	100	-	-	-	-	-
Printing and Publ.	14	-	84	2	-	40
Other	21	-	53	18	8	91
Auxiliary Activities						
and Industrial services	100	-	-	-	-	-

Source: Direct Research BNB/SUDENE, 1992, p. 56.

Table IV.23.s.a.
Destination of the Industrial Production of the Northeast According to the Regions- 1986 (%)

	Northeast	North/C.W.	Southeast	South	Abroad	São Paulo
Maranhão	51	10	23	2	14	65
Piauí	42	9	40	4	5	56
Ceará	38	4	40	4	14	71
R.G.Norte	28	4	52	14	3	53
Paraíba	37	6	33	13	11	52
Pernambuco	45	7	35	5	8	71
Alagoas	52	1	23	5	18	82
Sergipe	32	3	52	7	5	81
Bahia	33	1	49	4	12	76
M. Gerais	11	8	59	2	20	34
Northeast	36	4	44	5	11	71

Source: BNB/SUDENE, 1992, p.47.

Table IV.24.s.a.
Regional Distribution of the 1000 Biggest Firms (Acording to the Revenue and the Number of Firms) (%)

	1975		1980		1990	
	Firms	Revenue	Firms	Revenue	Firms	Revenue
North	0.9	0.4	1.8	1	3	2.2
Northeast	6.3	3	8.1	4.7	10.5	7.9
Pernambuco	2.4	1.2	2.5	1.2	1.9	1.4
Bahia	2.7	1.4	4.4	2.9	4.9	4.8
Southeast	80.3	88.3	73.8	83	68.2	73.1
São Paulo	21	48.6	47.2	39.2	43	37
South	10.9	6.7	14	8.3	15.4	11.7
C.West	16	1.6	2.3	3	2.9	5

Source: Araújo, 1994.

Table IV.25s.a.
Participation of the Biggest Commecial Banks*in the Market (%)

Years	The Four Biggest Deposits	Loans	Net Worth	The Seven Biggest Deposits	Loans	Net Worth
1965	15	14	11	22	22	17
1970	17	12	12	24	17	18
1975	29	23	22	40	32	30
1980	30	15	27	40	22	36
1984	24	15	40	35	21	52

*All banks except Banco do Brasil
Source: Marques, 1982, p. 161.

Table IV.26.s.a.
Number of Banks

Years	North Head	North Branch	N.east Head	N.east Branch	Pern. Head	Pern. Branch	Bahia Head	Bahia Branch	S.east Head	S.east Branch	S.Paulo Head	S.Paulo Branch
1960	5	59	58	409	10	82	13	189	247	3115	124	2732
1961	6	62	55	452	9	84	11	222	241	3280	100	1860
1962	6	67	56	507	9	93	12	240	236	3665	102	2019
1963	6	73	56	588	9	102	12	275	229	3877	102	2164
1964	6	87	58	672	10	119	12	306	226	4097	102	2290
1965	7	96	58	751	11	135	11	338	217	4299	101	2409
1966	7	106	56	786	11	141	11	347	198	4510	93	2548
1967	6	112	50	824	8	149	9	347	162	4594	84	2618
1968	6	121	46	873	7	164	9	349	136	4693	73	2737
1969	7	131	41	889	6	171	7	344	119	4734	65	2781
1970	7	132	38	902	6	177	6	341	107	4712	60	2802
1971	8	137	34	898	5	181	5	333	87	4695	49	2793
1972	6	149	30	909	6	184	4	328	72	4675	44	2785
1973	5	165	25	937	4	185	3	335	72	4796	44	2836
1974	5	162	24	903	4	182	3	327	58	4440	37	2659
1975	5	170	24	940	4	182	3	327	62	4540	39	2760
1985	6	703	22	3340	4	530	3	927	64	6932	44	3809
1990*	6	422	9	1548 -		194	2	493	29	2507	18	885
1990**		344	10	1416	3	389	2	380	140	6152	79	4148

*Commercial banks
** Multiple banks
Source: Movimento Bancário do Brasil, CIEF; 1985: Sistema Financeiro Nacional, Banco Central; 1990 – Banco Central.

Table IV.26.s.a. (Continuation.)

Years	South Head	South Branch	C.West Head	C.West Branch	Brazil Head	Brazil Branch
1960	22	946	6	132	338	4661
1961	23	1002	7	153	332	4949
1962	26	1101	8	221	332	5561
1963	27	1170	8	259	326	5967
1964	29	1239	9	294	328	6389
1965	30	1315	8	328	320	6789
1966	28	1386	8	322	297	7110
1967	23	1495	8	332	249	7357
1968	21	1548	8	352	217	7587
1969	17	1544	8	358	192	7656
1970	13	1564	7	365	172	7675
1971	9	1574	7	375	145	7679
1972	9	1593	6	386	123	7712
1973	7	1618	6	415	115	7931
1974	7	1617	6	417	100	7539
1975	6	1680	6	464	103	7794
1985	9	2991	6	1401	107	15367
1990*	2	1154	4	602	50	6233
1990**	14	2249	2	841	166	11002

*Commercial banks
**Multiple banks

Table IV.27.s.a.

Regional Participation in the Number of Banks (%)

Years	North		N.East		Pernamb.		Bahia		S.East		S.Paulo	
	Head	Branch	Head	Branch	Head	Branch	Head	Branch	Head	Branch	Head	Branch
1960	1.48	1.27	17.16	8.77	2.96	1.76	3.85	4.05	73.08	66.83	36.69	58.61
1961	1.81	1.25	16.57	9.13	2.71	1.70	3.31	4.49	72.59	66.28	30.12	37.58
1962	1.81	1.20	16.87	9.12	2.71	1.67	3.61	4.32	71.08	65.91	30.72	36.31
1963	1.84	1.22	17.18	9.85	2.76	1.71	3.68	4.61	70.25	64.97	31.29	36.27
1964	1.83	1.36	17.68	10.52	3.05	1.86	3.66	4.79	68.90	64.13	31.10	35.84
1965	2.19	1.41	18.13	11.06	3.44	1.96	3.44	4.98	67.81	63.32	31.56	35.48
1966	2.36	1.49	18.86	11.05	3.70	1.98	3.70	4.88	66.67	63.43	31.31	35.84
1967	2.41	1.51	20.08	11.20	3.21	2.03	3.61	4.72	65.06	62.44	33.73	35.59
1968	2.76	1.59	21.20	11.51	3.23	2.16	4.15	4.60	62.67	61.86	33.64	36.07
1969	3.65	1.71	21.35	11.61	3.13	2.23	3.65	4.49	61.98	61.83	33.85	36.32
1970	4.07	1.72	22.09	11.75	3.49	2.31	3.49	4.44	62.21	61.39	34.88	36.51
1971	5.52	1.78	23.45	11.69	3.45	2.36	3.45	4.34	60.00	61.14	33.79	36.37
1972	4.88	1.93	24.39	11.79	4.88	2.39	3.25	4.25	58.54	60.62	35.77	36.11
1973	4.35	2.08	21.74	11.81	3.48	2.33	2.61	4.22	62.61	60.47	38.26	35.76
1974	5.00	2.15	24.00	11.98	4.00	2.41	3.00	4.34	58.00	58.89	37.00	35.27
1975	4.85	2.18	23.30	12.06	3.88	2.34	2.91	4.20	60.19	58.25	37.86	35.41
1985	5.61	4.57	20.56	21.73	3.74	3.45	2.80	6.03	59.81	45.11	41.12	24.79
1990*	12.00	6.77	18.00	24.84	0.00	3.11	4.00	7.91	58.00	40.22	36.00	14.20
1990**	0.00	3.13	6.02	12.87	1.81	3.54	1.20	3.45	84.34	55.92	47.59	37.70

*Commercial banks

**Multiple banks

Source: Table IV.26.s.a.

Table IV.27.s.a. (Continuation)

Years	South		C.West		Brazil	
	Head	Branch	Head	Branch	Head	Branch
1960	6.51	20.30	1.78	2.83	100.00	100.00
1961	6.93	20.25	2.11	3.09	100.00	100.00
1962	7.83	19.80	2.41	3.97	100.00	100.00
1963	8.28	19.61	2.45	4.34	100.00	100.00
1964	8.84	19.39	2.74	4.60	100.00	100.00
1965	9.38	19.37	2.50	4.83	100.00	100.00
1966	9.43	19.49	2.69	4.53	100.00	100.00
1967	9.24	20.32	3.21	4.51	100.00	100.00
1968	9.68	20.40	3.69	4.64	100.00	100.00
1969	8.85	20.17	4.17	4.68	100.00	100.00
1970	7.56	20.38	4.07	4.76	100.00	100.00
1971	6.21	20.50	4.83	4.88	100.00	100.00
1972	7.32	20.66	4.88	5.01	100.00	100.00
1973	6.09	20.40	5.22	5.23	100.00	100.00
1974	7.00	21.45	6.00	5.53	100.00	100.00
1975	5.83	21.56	5.83	5.95	100.00	100.00
1985	8.41	19.46	5.61	9.12	100.00	100.00
1990*	4.00	18.51	8.00	9.66	100.00	100.00
1990**	8.43	20.44	1.20	7.64	100.00	100.00

*Commercial banks
** Multiple Banks

Table IV.28.s.a.

Creation of New Branches

	Oficial Banks Banco do Brasil		Other Federal		State		Private		Total	
	Branches	Change	Branches	Change	Branches	Change	Branches	Change	Branches	Change
North										
1968	20		38		26		57		143	
1985	136	184.8	79	102.6	104	131.3	378	372.5	969	225.2
N.East										
1968	158		72		159		543		939	
1985	810	143.2	196	130.6	726	158.4	1577	218.6	3316	176.1
S. East										
1968	315		6		664		3849		4852	
1985	789	96.8	123		1272	36.3	4645	26.2	6850	35.9
South										
1968	162		1		293		1124		1586	
1985	525	113.4	254		818	73.7	1369	13.6	2973	54
C. West										
1968	64		14		89		202		371	
1985	193	91.1	42	200	213	57.9	743	178.2	1393	135.7
Total										
1968	719		131		1231		5775		7891	
1985	2448	117.2	694694	359.6	3130	88	8912	53.7	15228	69.6

Source: Mendes, 1988, P.84.

* Change in %

Table IV.29.s.a.
Regional Share of Banking (%)

Years	North	Northeast	Pernambuco	Bahia	Southeast	São Paulo	South	C. West	Brazil
1960	1.28	9.19	2.61	2.87	73.92	35.34	13.80	1.81	100.00
1961	1.00	8.87	2.37	3.30	74.82	35.40	13.89	1.41	100.00
1962	1.00	9.11	2.37	3.51	73.53	34.20	14.92	1.45	100.00
1963	1.08	9.75	2.59	3.31	72.08	33.80	14.60	2.49	100.00
1964	1.09	9.76	2.59	3.31	72.06	33.78	14.60	2.49	100.00
1965	1.09	9.76	2.59	3.31	72.03	33.73	14.63	2.49	100.00
1966	1.97	13.30	2.92	4.71	62.21	29.33	19.68	2.84	100.00
1967	2.02	13.52	2.94	4.80	61.80	28.82	19.77	2.89	100.00
1968	2.02	13.40	2.90	4.75	61.96	29.00	19.70	2.92	100.00
1970	2.14	14.31	3.80	4.55	61.19	35.09	18.66	3.70	100.00
1975	0.65	8.35	2.61	2.98	69.94	38.48	15.84	5.22	100.00
1980	1.25	9.02	2.15	2.90	65.60	34.62	12.70	11.43	100.00
1985	1.93	12.09	2.11	4.43	56.70	35.27	17.46	11.82	100.00

Source: Conjuntura Econômica, IBRE, FGV, September, 1971 and July, 1977 and Anuáio Estatístico, IBGE.

Table IV.30.s.a.

Banking Participation in the Total Regional Income (%)

Years	North	Northeast	Pernambuco	Bahia	Southeast
1960	3.84	4.16	5.02	4.53	7.90
1961	2.69	4.20	4.52	5.94	7.93
1962	3.40	4.25	4.57	6.72	8.38
1963	3.76	4.65	4.67	6.70	7.92
1964	4.08	4.75	5.04	6.21	8.45
1965	4.42	5.51	5.77	6.72	9.72
1966	8.64	8.30	7.44	10.31	8.81
1967	9.59	8.25	7.44	10.46	9.12
1968	8.79	8.40	7.74	10.18	8.91
1970	6.29	7.73	7.87	8.16	5.88
1975	2.35	5.58	7.23	5.97	8.23
1980	3.23	5.98	6.74	5.30	8.35
1985	5.21	9.76	9.75	9.46	10.56

Source: Conjuntura Econômica, IBRE, FGV, September, 1971 and July, 1971 and Anuário Estatístico, IBGE.

Table IV.31.s.a.
Participation of Banco do Brasil in the Total of the Banks (Deposits) (%)

Years	North	Northeast	Southeast	São Paulo	South	C. West	Brazil
1960	46.00	26.47	25.21	16.62	20.96	93.09	35.58
1961	53.20	30.14	33.55	22.34	24.02	95.07	43.72
1962	54.55	33.25	37.35	29.29	26.69	96.23	50.17
1963	38.47	30.68	33.92	22.41	23.62	96.38	47.99
1964	48.98	32.02	32.52	18.63	27.66	98.20	59.28
1965	46.82	33.69	30.79	18.30	27.37	98.51	62.46
1966	47.47	32.30	28.21	19.57	30.39	96.84	50.92
1967	32.49	24.64	26.74	18.11	28.30	94.20	43.36
1968	30.65	24.43	24.51	16.30	28.56	92.20	37.69
1969	34.09	25.37	29.07	20.26	31.14	90.69	39.42
1970	39.48	27.20	28.34	18.88	35.94	88.31	38.55
1971	27.94	30.08	29.29	20.05	34.19	87.70	37.74
1972	22.22	20.13	22.37	12.42	22.88	85.81	31.02
1973	25.42	24.40	24.53	12.01	28.31	81.51	32.09
1974	28.40	35.61	51.99	48.60	50.28	82.72	52.96
1975	34.66	45.54	48.31	47.78	47.61	85.23	52.01
1980	22.62	23.65	17.00	-	18.29	79.41	26.57
1990	24.81	16.38	6.63	-	13.28	20.67	9.69

Source: Movimento Bancário do Brasil, CIEF and Banco Central do Brasil.

Table IV.32.s.a.
Participation of Banco do Brasil in the Total of the Banks (Loans) (%)

Years	North	Northeast	Southeast	São Paulo	South	C. West	Brazil
1960	33.97	47.09	29.87	27.62	56.10	96.97	49.70
1961	39.82	50.23	33.51	31.23	55.54	98.44	59.88
1962	34.43	51.61	34.01	32.22	55.03	98.47	64.31
1963	27.32	53.92	34.14	33.47	56.09	98.59	65.15
1964	28.06	50.27	35.59	36.93	55.55	98.98	72.20
1965	24.41	48.64	26.59	26.43	45.33	98.98	71.44
1966	27.86	40.01	29.80	28.88	52.18	97.12	55.23
1967	18.60	36.64	26.73	23.58	50.17	94.91	50.08
1968	20.55	28.80	25.99	23.57	51.38	91.28	42.90
1969	18.80	29.69	27.91	24.53	54.56	89.18	41.78
1970	21.55	30.17	28.78	25.61	60.09	86.77	41.74
1971	25.94	36.32	28.71	25.21	58.07	82.64	40.64
1972	25.36	35.24	27.17	23.55	53.74	76.74	37.38
1973	25.72	37.52	27.41	22.02	53.39	69.50	36.99
1974	26.50	42.65	32.79	27.45	59.73	69.79	42.10
1975	28.08	48.46	34.85	29.54	57.81	71.33	44.09
1980	41.25	45.66	30.65	-	50.86	66.66	38.80
1990	20.74	17.59	12.93	-	19.87	16.05	14.62

Source: Movimento Bancário do Brasil and Banco Central do Brasil.

Table IV.33.s.a.
Participation of Each Region in the Total Deposits (%)
General Total

Years	North	Northeast	Southeast	São Paulo	South	C. West	Brazil
1960	1.12	6.96	67.53	34.36	9.02	15.37	100.00
1961	1.10	6.65	65.41	31.68	8.91	17.94	100.00
1962	0.99	6.66	60.66	30.32	8.26	23.43	100.00
1963	0.83	7.26	60.73	29.87	7.17	24.02	100.00
1964	1.07	5.99	46.14	21.68	5.85	40.95	100.00
1965	0.86	5.94	40.25	20.40	6.33	46.62	100.00
1966	1.30	10.48	48.90	25.74	7.46	31.86	100.00
1967	1.36	10.67	54.90	29.95	8.40	24.66	100.00
1968	1.51	10.57	59.88	32.57	9.24	18.80	100.00
1969	1.69	10.94	60.10	32.75	10.31	16.96	100.00
1970	1.63	10.70	61.72	34.18	10.33	15.61	100.00
1971	2.25	8.98	64.01	36.07	11.32	13.44	100.00
1972	2.14	8.49	64.70	37.25	10.83	13.85	100.00
1973	2.04	8.70	65.12	37.43	11.67	12.48	100.00
1974	1.42	7.00	71.64	45.20	11.33	8.61	100.00
1975	1.50	5.67	69.73	42.98	11.88	11.21	100.00
1980	2.36	12.14	60.63	-	11.29	13.59	100.00
1990	1.27	7.94	69.86	-	11.93	9.00	100.00

Source: Movimento bancário do Brasil, CIEF and Banco Central do Brasil.

Table IV.34.s.a.

Participation of Each Region in the Total Deposits (%)

Banco do Brasil

Years	North	Northeast	Southeast	São Paulo	South	C. West	Brazil
1960	1.45	5.17	47.85	16.05	5.32	40.21	100.00
1961	1.33	4.59	50.19	16.19	4.89	39.00	100.00
1962	1.08	4.41	45.17	17.71	4.40	44.95	100.00
1963	0.66	4.64	42.93	13.95	3.53	48.24	100.00
1964	0.88	3.23	25.32	6.81	2.73	67.83	100.00
1965	0.65	3.21	19.84	5.98	2.77	73.53	100.00
1966	1.21	6.65	27.09	9.89	4.45	60.60	100.00
1967	1.02	6.07	33.86	12.51	5.48	53.58	100.00
1968	1.23	6.85	38.94	14.09	7.00	45.99	100.00
1969	1.46	7.04	44.33	16.83	8.15	39.03	100.00
1970	1.67	7.55	45.38	16.74	9.63	35.77	100.00
1971	1.66	7.16	49.68	19.16	10.26	31.24	100.00
1972	1.53	5.51	46.66	14.92	7.99	38.31	100.00
1973	1.62	6.61	49.79	14.01	10.29	31.69	100.00
1974	0.76	4.71	70.32	41.49	10.76	13.45	100.00
1975	1.00	4.97	64.78	39.49	10.88	18.37	100.00
1980	2.01	10.81	38.79	11.47	7.78	40.62	100.00
1985	2.73	9.96	39.43	14.34	14.64	33.24	100.00
1990	3.24	13.42	47.79	19.34	16.36	19.19	100.00

Source: Movimento Bancário do Brasil, CIEF and Banco Central do Brasil.

Table IV.35.s.a.
Participation of Each Region in the Total Deposits (%)
BNB/BASA

Years	North	Northeast	Southeast	São Paulo	South	C. West	Brazil
1968	7.91	70.52	18.23	12.12	2.20	1.15	100.00
1969	7.39	69.77	18.81	14.27	2.42	1.61	100.00
1970	4.51	71.96	19.41	14.35	2.33	1.79	100.00
1971	28.21	66.54	4.35	2.40	0.38	0.53	100.00
1972	25.32	64.16	8.66	4.72	0.66	1.21	100.00
1973	23.22	64.92	9.17	6.12	1.31	1.38	100.00
1974	24.78	64.97	7.49	4.06	1.47	1.29	100.00
1975	23.77	41.61	27.27	10.71	3.75	3.59	100.00
1990	47.73	45.03	4.96	-	0.30	1.98	100.00

Source: Movimento Bancário do Brasil, CIEF and Banco Central do Brasil.

Table IV.36.s.a.
Participation of Each Region in the Total Deposits
Private Banks

Years	North	Northeast	Southeast	São Paulo	South	C. West	Brazil
1960	0.94	8.01	77.85	44.23	11.47	1.74	100.00
1961	0.91	8.37	76.60	43.68	12.46	1.66	100.00
1962	0.91	9.04	75.61	42.90	12.58	1.87	100.00
1963	0.99	9.92	76.43	44.46	10.90	1.75	100.00
1964	1.36	10.28	75.68	43.40	10.79	1.90	100.00
1965	1.21	10.77	73.48	44.25	12.62	1.92	100.00
1966	1.39	14.63	70.99	41.97	10.87	2.12	100.00
1967	1.59	14.43	70.54	43.08	10.84	2.60	100.00
1968	1.11	8.34	78.47	48.72	10.23	1.84	100.00
1969	1.22	8.91	76.02	47.36	11.85	2.00	100.00
1970	1.23	8.22	77.12	49.55	11.18	2.26	100.00
1971	1.21	6.90	77.73	51.37	11.90	2.25	100.00
1972	1.21	6.76	77.82	52.10	11.84	2.37	100.00
1973	1.15	7.05	76.59	52.79	12.45	2.77	100.00
1974	1.09	7.04	61.89	53.90	27.42	2.55	100.00
1975	1.19	5.00	79.03	52.03	11.95	2.83	100.00
1990	0.45	6.98	83.15	65.50	8.66	0.77	100.00

Source: Movimento Bancário do Brasil, CIEF and Banco Central do Brasil.

Table IV.37.s.a.
Participation of Each Region in the Total Deposits
All Banks Except Banco do Brasil

Years	North	Northeast	Southeast	São Paulo	South	C. West	Brazil
1980	2.49	12.62	68.53	44.73	12.57	3.81	100.00
1990	1.05	7.35	72.23	-	11.46	7.90	100.00

Source: Separata of the Boletim Mensal of Banco Central do Brasil, June 1985 and Banco Central do Brasil.

Table IV.38.s.a.
Regional Share of the Population (%)

Years	North	Northeast	Southeast	São Paulo	South	C. West	Brazil
1960	3.67	31.60	43.76	18.28	16.73	4.24	100.00
1961	3.67	31.31	43.76	18.34	16.93	4.33	100.00
1962	3.68	31.01	43.76	18.38	17.12	4.43	100.00
1963	3.68	30.70	43.76	18.43	17.33	4.52	100.00
1964	3.69	30.40	43.74	18.47	17.54	4.62	100.00
1965	3.69	30.10	43.72	18.51	17.76	4.72	100.00
1966	3.70	29.79	43.70	18.54	17.99	4.82	100.00
1967	3.70	29.49	43.67	18.57	18.22	4.92	100.00
1968	3.71	29.18	43.63	18.60	18.46	5.03	100.00
1969	3.71	28.86	43.56	18.61	18.75	5.13	100.00
1970	3.87	30.18	42.79	19.08	17.71	5.45	100.00
1975	4.35	29.72	43.20	20.14	16.81	5.92	100.00
1980	5.54	29.26	43.49	21.03	16.01	5.71	100.00
1985	6.22	29.09	43.09	21.24	15.56	6.04	100.00

Source: Anuário Estatístico, IBGE and Censo Econômico, IBGE.

Table IV.39.s.a.
Ratio Short Term Deposits /Total Deposits
General Total

Years	North	Northeast	Southeast	São Paulo	South	C. West	Brazil
1960	0.963	0.873	0.921	0.896	0.948	0.999	0.932
1961	0.971	0.895	0.941	0.921	0.951	0.999	0.950
1962	0.973	0.888	0.950	0.974	0.963	1.000	0.959
1963	0.984	0.887	0.952	0.970	0.970	1.000	0.960
1964	0.994	0.871	0.943	0.980	0.976	1.000	0.964
1965	0.995	0.835	0.980	0.988	0.987	1.000	0.981
1966	0.963	0.728	0.961	0.954	0.962	0.999	0.949
1967	0.939	0.701	0.951	0.944	0.948	0.996	0.935
1968	0.955	0.740	0.956	0.951	0.946	0.994	0.939
1969	0.947	0.740	0.954	0.949	0.949	0.992	0.937
1970	0.941	0.754	0.943	0.936	0.947	0.990	0.931
1971	0.644	0.803	0.913	0.906	0.944	0.992	0.911
1972	0.698	0.821	0.890	0.889	0.904	0.991	0.896
1973	0.751	0.827	0.906	0.893	0.939	0.991	0.910
1974	0.726	0.867	0.936	0.943	0.967	0.992	0.937
1975	0.899	1.397	0.893	0.943	0.960	0.992	0.941
1980	0.777	0.647	0.779	-	0.828	0.969	0.869
1990	0.617	0.324	0.162	-	0.208	0.208	0.190

Source: Movimento Bancário do Brasil, CIEF and Banco Central do Brasil.

Table IV.40.s.a.
Ratio Short Term Deposits/Total Deposits
General Total Except BNB/BASA

Years	North	Northeast	Southeast	São Paulo	South	C. West	Brazil
1968	0.974	0.974	0.966	0.964	0.956	0.996	0.972
1969	0.972	0.970	0.966	0.966	0.959	0.995	0.971
1970	0.969	0.966	0.954	0.949	0.955	0.994	0.962
1971	0.956	0.986	0.913	0.905	0.944	0.992	0.933
1972	0.942	0.938	0.890	0.888	0.904	0.991	0.910
1973	0.968	0.952	0.905	0.893	0.938	0.991	0.925
1974	0.972	0.967	0.936	0.943	0.967	0.992	0.947
1975	0.965	1.435	0.894	0.943	0.960	0.992	0.943

Source: Movimento Bancário do Brasil, CIEF.

Table IV.41.s.a.

Participation of Each Region in the Total Loans (%)

General Total

Years	North	Northeast	Southeast	São Paulo	South	C. West	Brazil
1960	1.06	7.77	55.47	32.05	13.48	22.22	100.00
1961	0.94	6.78	45.63	26.01	11.93	34.73	100.00
1962	0.83	6.81	39.85	23.17	10.93	41.58	100.00
1963	0.93	7.75	39.02	23.13	9.79	42.51	100.00
1964	0.73	6.28	31.19	18.64	7.90	53.90	100.00
1965	0.76	6.31	27.65	16.12	7.05	58.23	100.00
1966	1.47	10.44	44.53	25.16	10.98	32.58	100.00
1967	1.71	12.08	45.84	25.91	11.67	28.69	100.00
1968	1.94	13.08	51.10	28.45	13.70	20.17	100.00
1969	1.84	12.76	53.98	30.40	15.72	15.71	100.00
1970	1.97	13.14	54.79	31.17	17.01	13.09	100.00
1971	1.74	12.77	56.37	33.93	19.14	9.98	100.00
1972	2.07	13.26	57.28	35.06	19.14	8.25	100.00
1973	2.04	13.83	57.17	35.99	19.43	7.53	100.00
1974	1.94	13.55	56.96	37.11	20.90	6.65	100.00
1975	1.94	15.40	55.10	35.47	20.52	7.04	100.00
1980	2.50	14.76	59.84	-	16.32	6.58	100.00
1990	0.93	9.50	66.63	-	11.61	11.31	100.00

Source: Movimento Bancário do Brasil, CIEF and Banco Central do Brasil.

Table IV.42.s.a.

Participation of Each Region in the Total Loans (%)

Banco do Brasil

Years	North	Northeast	Southeast	São Paulo	South	C.West	Brazil
1960	0.72	7.36	33.34	17.81	15.22	43.36	100.00
1961	0.62	5.69	25.54	13.57	11.07	57.09	100.00
1962	0.45	5.46	21.07	11.61	9.36	63.66	100.00
1963	0.39	6.41	20.45	11.88	8.43	64.32	100.00
1964	0.29	4.37	15.37	9.54	6.08	73.90	100.00
1965	0.26	4.29	10.29	5.96	4.47	80.68	100.00
1966	0.74	7.56	24.03	13.16	10.37	57.30	100.00
1967	0.64	8.84	24.47	12.20	11.69	54.37	100.00
1968	0.93	8.78	30.96	15.63	16.41	42.93	100.00
1969	0.83	9.07	36.05	17.85	20.52	33.53	100.00
1970	1.02	9.50	37.79	19.12	24.49	27.21	100.00
1971	1.11	11.41	39.82	21.05	27.36	20.30	100.00
1972	1.40	12.50	41.64	22.10	27.52	16.94	100.00
1973	1.42	14.03	42.35	21.42	28.05	14.15	100.00
1974	1.22	13.73	44.37	24.20	29.66	11.02	100.00
1975	1.24	16.93	43.54	23.77	26.90	11.40	100.00
1980	2.66	17.38	47.27	20.48	21.39	11.30	100.00
1985	1.29	11.23	43.05	21.58	31.27	13.16	100.00
1990	1.32	11.43	58.90	35.90	15.77	12.41	100.00

Source: Movimento Bancário do Brasil (CIEF) and Banco Central do Brasil.

Table IV.43.s.a.
Participation of Each Region in the Total Loans (%)
BNB/BASA

Years	North	Northeast	Southeast	São Paulo	South	C. West	Brazil
1968	16.60	71.03	7.76	2.87	0.27	4.33	100.00
1969	16.71	69.82	8.21	2.27	0.53	4.72	100.00
1970	15.75	72.90	6.69	0.99	0.51	4.14	100.00
1971	14.70	70.93	9.43	2.57	1.33	3.61	100.00
1972	15.08	66.48	11.88	4.17	2.27	4.29	100.00
1973	14.24	65.53	12.99	4.76	2.41	4.82	100.00
1974	13.40	67.40	11.73	3.83	2.30	5.17	100.00
1975	13.61	67.87	10.49	2.97	2.15	5.89	100.00
1990	11.18	57.23	27.82	-	0.39	3.39	100.00

Source: Movimento Bancário do Brasil, CIEF and Banco Central do Brasil.

Table IV.44.s.a.
Participation of Each Region in the Total Loans (%)
Private Banks

Years	North	Northeast	Southeast	São Paulo	South	C. West	Brazil
1960	1.40	8.13	76.87	46.03	12.18	1.42	100.00
1961	1.41	8.43	75.09	44.53	13.66	1.41	100.00
1962	1.55	9.27	73.13	43.82	14.19	1.86	100.00
1963	1.97	10.37	73.15	43.92	12.71	1.81	100.00
1964	1.92	11.28	71.78	42.25	12.96	2.05	100.00
1965	2.01	11.41	70.57	41.04	13.84	2.17	100.00
1966	2.37	14.16	69.35	39.51	11.95	2.16	100.00
1967	2.79	15.76	66.64	39.37	11.81	3.00	100.00
1968	1.12	9.47	75.29	45.72	11.90	2.21	100.00
1969	1.02	8.71	75.72	47.46	12.59	1.97	100.00
1970	1.14	8.90	76.04	47.56	11.93	1.99	100.00
1971	1.08	7.91	74.90	49.75	14.08	2.03	100.00
1972	1.05	7.82	74.60	50.39	14.61	1.92	100.00
1973	1.00	7.32	73.98	52.16	15.41	2.30	100.00
1974	0.92	6.92	74.05	55.21	15.83	2.27	100.00
1975	0.89	7.78	72.43	53.54	16.35	2.55	100.00
1990	0.74	10.09	77.65	25.85	10.04	1.48	100.00

Source: Movimento Bancário do Brasil, CIEF and Banco Central do Brasil.

Table IV.45.s.a.
Participation of Each Region in the Total Loans (%)
All Banks Except Banco do Brasil

Years	North	Northeast	Southeast	São Paulo	South	C. West	Brazil
1980	2.40	13.11	67.81	47.26	13.10	3.58	100.00
1990	0.87	9.17	67.95	-	10.89	11.12	100.00

Source: Separata of the Boletim Mensal of Banco Central do Brasil, June, 1985 and Banco Central do Brasil.

Table IV.46.s.a.
Ratio Total Loans/Total Deposits
General Total

Years	North	Northeast	Southeast	São Paulo	South	C. West	Brazil
1960	0.969	1.150	0.846	0.960	1.539	1.488	1.030
1961	0.922	1.100	0.753	0.886	1.446	2.091	1.080
1962	0.849	1.032	0.663	0.771	1.335	1.790	1.009
1963	1.163	1.108	0.666	0.803	1.416	1.835	1.037
1964	0.714	1.091	0.703	0.895	1.404	1.370	1.040
1965	0.783	0.941	0.609	0.701	0.988	1.108	0.887
1966	0.915	0.803	0.734	0.788	1.186	0.824	0.806
1967	1.126	1.008	0.743	0.770	1.237	1.036	0.890
1968	1.118	1.076	0.742	0.759	1.289	0.933	0.869
1969	1.072	1.154	0.888	0.918	1.507	0.916	0.989
1970	1.263	1.285	0.929	0.955	1.724	0.878	1.047
1971	0.850	1.564	0.968	1.034	1.860	0.816	1.100
1972	1.095	1.768	1.002	1.066	2.001	0.675	1.132
1973	1.146	1.825	1.007	1.103	1.911	0.693	1.147
1974	1.313	1.866	0.766	0.791	1.778	0.744	0.964
1975	1.411	2.965	0.863	0.902	1.887	0.686	1.092
1980	2.057	2.360	1.915	-	2.803	0.939	1.941
1990	1.575	2.555	2.037	-	2.077	2.684	2.136

Source: Movimento Bancário do Brasil, CIEF and Banco Central do Brasil.

Table IV.47.s.a.
Ratio Total Loans/ Total Deposits
General Total (in Relation to Brazil)

Years	North	Northeast	Southeast	São Paulo	South	C. West	Brazil
1960	0.941	1.117	0.821	0.933	1.494	1.446	1.000
1961	0.854	1.019	0.698	0.821	1.339	1.936	1.000
1962	0.841	1.023	0.657	0.764	1.323	1.774	1.000
1963	1.121	1.068	0.643	0.774	1.366	1.770	1.000
1964	0.687	1.049	0.676	0.860	1.349	1.316	1.000
1965	0.883	1.061	0.687	0.790	1.114	1.249	1.000
1966	1.135	0.996	0.911	0.977	1.472	1.022	1.000
1967	1.264	1.132	0.835	0.865	1.389	1.163	1.000
1968	1.286	1.238	0.853	0.874	1.483	1.073	1.000
1969	1.085	1.167	0.898	0.928	1.524	0.926	1.000
1970	1.206	1.228	0.888	0.912	1.647	0.838	1.000
1971	0.773	1.422	0.881	0.941	1.691	0.742	1.000
1972	0.967	1.562	0.885	0.941	1.767	0.596	1.000
1973	0.999	1.590	0.878	0.961	1.666	0.604	1.000
1974	1.363	1.936	0.795	0.821	1.845	0.772	1.000
1975	1.292	2.714	0.790	0.825	1.727	0.628	1.000
1980	1.060	1.216	0.987	-	1.445	0.484	1.000
1990	0.737	1.197	0.954	-	0.973	1.257	1.000

Source: Movimento Bancário do Brail, CIEF and Banco Central do Brasil.

Table IV.48.s.a.
Ratio Total Loans/Total Deposits
Banco do Brasil

Years	North	Northeast	Southeast	São Paulo	South	C. West	Brazil
1960	0.715	2.046	1.002	1.596	4.117	1.550	1.438
1961	0.690	1.833	0.752	1.239	3.344	2.165	1.479
1962	0.536	1.602	0.603	0.848	2.752	1.832	1.293
1963	0.826	1.947	0.671	1.199	3.363	1.877	1.408
1964	0.409	1.713	0.769	1.774	2.819	1.381	1.267
1965	0.408	1.358	0.526	1.012	1.636	1.113	1.014
1966	0.537	0.994	0.775	1.163	2.037	0.827	0.874
1967	0.645	1.498	0.743	1.003	2.192	1.044	1.028
1968	0.750	1.268	0.786	1.098	2.319	0.923	0.989
1969	0.591	1.350	0.852	1.111	2.640	0.901	1.048
1970	0.689	1.425	0.944	1.295	2.883	0.862	1.133
1971	0.789	1.888	0.949	1.301	3.158	0.769	1.184
1972	1.249	3.095	1.217	2.021	4.699	0.603	1.364
1973	1.159	2.806	1.125	2.022	3.604	0.591	1.323
1974	1.225	2.235	0.483	0.447	2.112	0.628	0.766
1975	1.143	3.155	0.623	0.557	2.291	0.574	0.926
1980	3.750	4.557	3.453	5.058	7.794	0.788	2.834
1985	0.636	1.522	1.473	2.031	2.881	0.534	1.349
1990	1.316	2.744	3.972	5.982	3.107	2.084	3.223

Source: Movimento Bancário do Brasil, CIEF and Banco Central do Brasil.

Table IV.49.s.a.

Ratio Total Loans/ Total Deposits (in Relation to Brazil)

Banco do Brasil

Years	North	Northeast	Southeast	São Paulo	South	C. West	Brazil
1960	0.498	1.423	0.697	1.110	2.863	1.078	1.000
1961	0.467	1.240	0.509	0.838	2.261	1.464	1.000
1962	0.414	1.239	0.467	0.656	2.128	1.416	1.000
1963	0.586	1.383	0.476	0.852	2.388	1.333	1.000
1964	0.323	1.352	0.607	1.400	2.225	1.089	1.000
1965	0.402	1.339	0.519	0.997	1.613	1.097	1.000
1966	0.614	1.137	0.887	1.330	2.330	0.946	1.000
1967	0.627	1.457	0.723	0.975	2.131	1.015	1.000
1968	0.758	1.282	0.795	1.110	2.344	0.933	1.000
1969	0.564	1.288	0.813	1.060	2.519	0.859	1.000
1970	0.608	1.257	0.833	1.142	2.543	0.761	1.000
1971	0.667	1.595	0.802	1.099	2.667	0.650	1.000
1972	0.916	2.269	0.892	1.481	3.445	0.442	1.000
1973	0.877	2.122	0.851	1.529	2.725	0.447	1.000
1974	1.600	2.918	0.631	0.583	2.757	0.819	1.000
1975	1.234	3.407	0.672	0.602	2.474	0.620	1.000
1980	1.323	1.608	1.219	1.785	2.750	0.278	1.000
1985	0.472	1.128	1.092	1.505	2.135	0.396	1.000
1990	0.408	0.852	1.232	1.856	0.964	0.647	1.000

Source: Movimento Bancário do Brasil ,CIEF and Banco Central do Brasil.

Table IV.50.s.a.
Ratio Total Loans/Total Deposits
BNB/BASA

Years	North	Northeast	Southeast	São Paulo	South	C. West	Brazil
1968	2.250	1.080	0.456	0.254	0.130	4.034	1.072
1969	2.573	1.138	0.496	0.181	0.250	3.342	1.138
1970	4.234	1.228	0.418	0.084	0.265	2.808	1.212
1971	0.681	1.393	2.834	1.395	4.647	8.961	1.307
1972	0.979	1.704	2.257	1.454	5.694	5.830	1.645
1973	1.219	2.006	2.815	1.545	3.665	6.933	1.987
1974	1.346	2.582	3.899	2.348	3.899	9.958	2.489
1975	2.506	7.142	1.684	1.214	2.507	7.184	4.379
1990	1.935	10.497	46.356	-	10.820	14.107	8.261

Source: Movimento Bancário do Brasil, CIEF and Banco Central do Brasil.

Table IV.51.s.a.
Ratio Total Loans/ Total Deposits (in Relation to Brazil)
BNB/BASA

Years	North	Northeast	Southeast	São Paulo	South	C. West	Brazil
1968	2.099	1.007	0.426	0.237	0.121	3.764	1.000
1969	2.261	1.001	0.436	0.159	0.220	2.938	1.000
1970	3.493	1.013	0.345	0.069	0.219	2.316	1.000
1971	0.521	1.066	2.169	1.068	3.556	6.858	1.000
1972	0.595	1.036	1.373	0.884	3.462	3.545	1.000
1973	0.613	1.009	1.417	0.777	1.844	3.489	1.000
1974	0.541	1.037	1.567	0.944	1.567	4.001	1.000
1975	0.572	1.631	0.385	0.277	0.572	1.641	1.000
1990	0.234	1.271	5.612	-	1.310	1.708	1.000

Source: Movimento Bancário do Brasil, CIEF and Banco Central do Brasil.

Table IV.52.s.a.
Ratio Total Loans/Total Deposits
Private Banks

Years	North	Northeast	Southeast	São Paulo	South	C. West	Brazil
1960	1.192	0.814	0.791	0.834	0.851	0.653	0.801
1961	1.202	0.778	0.757	0.788	0.847	0.660	0.773
1962	1.244	0.746	0.704	0.743	0.821	0.725	0.727
1963	1.386	0.731	0.669	0.691	0.815	0.720	0.699
1964	1.010	0.785	0.679	0.697	0.860	0.774	0.716
1965	1.119	0.712	0.646	0.624	0.738	0.759	0.673
1966	1.263	0.715	0.722	0.696	0.812	0.751	0.739
1967	1.379	0.860	0.744	0.720	0.859	0.911	0.788
1968	0.715	0.805	0.680	0.665	0.824	0.850	0.709
1969	0.701	0.823	0.839	0.844	0.895	0.829	0.842
1970	0.814	0.946	0.862	0.839	0.933	0.770	0.874
1971	0.833	1.074	0.903	0.907	1.108	0.845	0.937
1972	0.801	1.061	0.880	0.888	1.133	0.744	0.918
1973	0.813	0.973	0.905	0.925	1.159	0.779	0.937
1974	0.880	1.023	1.245	1.066	0.601	0.924	1.041
1975	0.803	1.677	0.987	1.108	1.474	0.970	1.077
1990	1.501	1.329	0.858	0.363	1.065	1.777	0.919

Source: Movimento Bancário do Brasil, CIEF and Banco Central do Brasil.

Table IV.53.s.a.
Ratio Total Loans/Total Deposits (in Relation to Brazil)
Private Banks

Years	North	Northeast	Southeast	São Paulo	South	C. West	Brazil
1960	1.488	1.016	0.988	1.041	1.062	0.815	1.000
1961	1.555	1.007	0.980	1.019	1.096	0.854	1.000
1962	1.710	1.025	0.967	1.021	1.129	0.997	1.000
1963	1.983	1.045	0.957	0.988	1.166	1.030	1.000
1964	1.411	1.097	0.949	0.973	1.202	1.082	1.000
1965	1.664	1.059	0.960	0.928	1.097	1.128	1.000
1966	1.709	0.968	0.977	0.941	1.100	1.016	1.000
1967	1.751	1.092	0.945	0.914	1.090	1.156	1.000
1968	1.009	1.135	0.959	0.938	1.163	1.200	1.000
1969	0.833	0.977	0.996	1.002	1.062	0.984	1.000
1970	0.931	1.082	0.986	0.960	1.068	0.881	1.000
1971	0.889	1.146	0.964	0.968	1.183	0.902	1.000
1972	0.872	1.156	0.959	0.967	1.234	0.811	1.000
1973	0.868	1.039	0.966	0.988	1.238	0.832	1.000
1974	0.845	0.983	1.197	1.024	0.577	0.888	1.000
1975	0.745	1.557	0.916	1.029	1.368	0.901	1.000
1990	1.634	1.446	0.934	0.395	1.159	1.934	1.000

Source: Movimento Bancário do Brasil, CIEF and Banco Central do Brasil.

Table IV.54.s.a.
Ratio Total Loans/Total Deposits
All Banks Except Banco do Brasil

Years	North	Northeast	Southeast	São Paulo	South	C. West	Brazil
1980	1.561	1.680	1.600	1.709	1.686	1.521	1.617
1990	1.660	2.518	1.899	-	1.920	2.840	2.019

Source: Separata of Boletim Mensal of Banco Central do Brasil, June 1985 and Banco Central do Brasil.

Table IV.55.s.a.
Ratio Total Loans/Total Deposits (in Relation to Brazil)
All Banks Except Banco do Brasil

Years	North	Northeast	Southeast	São Paulo	South	C. West	Brazil
1980	0.965	1.039	0.989	1.056	1.042	0.940	1.000
1990	0.822	1.247	0.941	0.000	0.951	1.407	1.000

Source: Separata of Boletim Mensal of Banco Central do Brasil, June 1985 and Banco Central do Brasil.

Table IV.56.s.a.
Ratio Total Voluntary Reserves/Total Deposits
General Total

Years	North	Northeast	Southeast	São Paulo	South	C. West	Brazil
1960	0.200	0.231	0.209	0.203	0.218	0.075	0.190
1961	0.202	0.246	0.200	0.207	0.226	0.067	0.181
1962	0.217	0.215	0.146	0.152	0.184	0.016	0.124
1963	0.260	0.248	0.174	0.189	0.190	0.014	0.143
1964	0.229	0.266	0.171	0.200	0.202	0.007	0.112
1965	0.205	0.251	0.158	0.185	0.183	0.005	0.094
1966	0.186	0.233	0.143	0.152	0.173	0.012	0.114
1967	0.162	0.153	0.131	0.141	0.155	0.016	0.107
1968	0.118	0.116	0.076	0.080	0.106	0.025	0.074
1969	0.122	0.104	0.072	0.080	0.087	0.030	0.070
1970	0.106	0.078	0.065	0.067	0.080	0.023	0.062
1971	0.070	0.123	0.075	0.083	0.090	0.020	0.073
1972	0.081	0.136	0.097	0.106	0.089	0.017	0.088
1973	0.077	0.130	0.098	0.112	0.078	0.023	0.089
1974	0.065	0.105	0.067	0.074	0.072	0.059	0.070
1975	0.105	0.161	0.047	0.055	0.084	0.017	0.055

Source: Movimento Bancário do Brasil, CIEF.

Table IV.57.s.a.

Ratio Total Voluntary Reserves/Total Deposits (in Relation to Brazil)

General Total

Years	North	Northeast	Southeast	São Paulo	South	C. West	Brazil
1960	1.053	1.214	1.096	1.067	1.145	0.394	1.000
1961	1.113	1.358	1.100	1.142	1.248	0.371	1.000
1962	1.752	1.729	1.179	1.224	1.486	0.126	1.000
1963	1.826	1.740	1.218	1.322	1.334	0.097	1.000
1964	2.039	2.370	1.525	1.779	1.799	0.066	1.000
1965	2.178	2.667	1.680	1.970	1.947	0.050	1.000
1966	1.635	2.047	1.260	1.337	1.521	0.109	1.000
1967	1.512	1.422	1.218	1.319	1.446	0.153	1.000
1968	1.598	1.560	1.026	1.085	1.429	0.342	1.000
1969	1.738	1.475	1.015	1.135	1.241	0.420	1.000
1970	1.698	1.248	1.051	1.076	1.289	0.364	1.000
1971	0.959	1.681	1.018	1.133	1.224	0.275	1.000
1972	0.921	1.551	1.101	1.211	1.014	0.191	1.000
1973	0.868	1.465	1.106	1.264	0.879	0.259	1.000
1974	0.928	1.503	0.964	1.065	1.040	0.851	1.000
1975	1.887	2.894	0.853	0.990	1.508	0.301	1.000

Source: Movimento Bancário do Brasil, CIEF .

Table IV.58.s.a.
Ratio Total Voluntary Reserves/Total Deposits
Banco do Brasil

Years	North	Northeast	Southeast	São Paulo	South	C. West	Brazil
1960	0.073	0.111	0.037	0.055	0.101	0.054	0.052
1961	0.075	0.105	0.025	0.033	0.091	0.052	0.043
1962	0.088	0.075	0.019	0.024	0.102	0.004	0.019
1963	0.124	0.123	0.025	0.033	0.114	0.003	0.023
1964	0.071	0.150	0.041	0.080	0.115	0.002	0.020
1965	0.057	0.081	0.020	0.032	0.089	0.001	0.010
1966	0.039	0.051	0.019	0.027	0.078	0.002	0.013
1967	0.050	0.047	0.027	0.040	0.048	0.003	0.017
1968	0.042	0.033	0.007	0.010	0.022	0.010	0.012
1969	0.027	0.045	0.008	0.009	0.037	0.009	0.014
1970	0.027	0.036	0.010	0.017	0.028	0.012	0.015
1971	0.024	0.030	0.009	0.017	0.021	0.004	0.010
1972	0.033	0.054	0.007	0.014	0.037	0.005	0.012
1973	0.024	0.048	0.006	0.013	0.023	0.005	0.011
1974	0.033	0.034	0.002	0.001	0.011	0.055	0.012
1975	0.024	0.032	0.002	0.002	0.011	0.004	0.005

Source: Movimento Bancário do Brasil, CIEF.

Table IV.59.s.a.
Ratio Total Voluntary Reserves/Total Deposits (in Relation to Brazil)
Banco do Brasil

Years	North	Northeast	Southeast	São Paulo	South	C. West	Brazil
1960	1.405	2.156	0.715	1.070	1.957	1.049	1.000
1961	1.728	2.435	0.580	0.759	2.113	1.207	1.000
1962	4.621	3.919	0.994	1.240	5.323	0.210	1.000
1963	5.509	5.463	1.100	1.454	5.029	0.126	1.000
1964	3.501	7.337	2.017	3.948	5.625	0.100	1.000
1965	5.800	8.169	1.988	3.225	9.043	0.075	1.000
1966	2.872	3.769	1.422	1.989	5.751	0.121	1.000
1967	2.994	2.822	1.622	2.423	2.882	0.171	1.000
1968	3.608	2.805	0.619	0.886	1.922	0.843	1.000
1969	1.978	3.291	0.575	0.688	2.745	0.669	1.000
1970	1.856	2.481	0.655	1.138	1.905	0.841	1.000
1971	2.302	2.939	0.836	1.629	2.025	0.411	1.000
1972	2.818	4.668	0.592	1.189	3.214	0.435	1.000
1973	2.200	4.461	0.582	1.235	2.180	0.489	1.000
1974	2.826	2.920	0.143	0.111	0.945	4.749	1.000
1975	4.569	6.033	0.441	0.321	2.146	0.737	1.000

Source: Movimento Bancário do Brasil, CIEF.

Table IV.60.s.a.
Ratio Total Voluntary Reserves/Total Deposits
BNB/BASA

Years	North	Northeast	Southeast	São Paulo	South	C. West	Brazil
1968	0.102	0.082	0.070	0.069	0.009	0.147	0.081
1969	0.192	0.055	0.073	0.047	0.037	0.108	0.069
1970	0.323	0.048	0.106	0.103	0.043	0.115	0.073
1971	0.054	0.145	0.577	0.686	0.054	0.514	0.140
1972	0.073	0.166	0.184	0.256	0.032	0.246	0.144
1973	0.095	0.125	0.331	0.368	0.177	0.209	0.139
1974	0.059	0.092	0.370	0.292	0.080	0.545	0.110
1975	0.226	0.168	0.220	0.138	0.297	0.174	0.201

Source: Movimento Bancário do Brasil, CIEF and Banco Central do Brasil.

Table IV.61.s.a.
Ratio Total Voluntary Reserves/ Total Deposits (in Relation to Brazil)
BNB/BASA

Years	North	Northeast	Southeast	São Paulo	South	C. West	Brazil
1968	1.260	1.019	0.869	0.851	0.112	1.816	1.000
1969	2.779	0.799	1.056	0.677	0.536	1.567	1.000
1970	4.434	0.662	1.450	1.416	0.593	1.574	1.000
1971	0.387	1.037	4.139	4.915	0.384	3.685	1.000
1972	0.505	1.153	1.274	1.778	0.224	1.708	1.000
1973	0.683	0.902	2.384	2.650	1.273	1.509	1.000
1974	0.530	0.836	3.353	2.647	0.723	4.944	1.000
1975	1.123	0.836	1.096	0.685	1.478	0.867	1.000

Source: Movimento Bancário do Brasil and Banco Central do Brasil.

Table IV.62.s.a.
Ratio Total Voluntary Reserves/Total Deposits
Private Banks

Years	North	Northeast	Southeast	São Paulo	South	C. West	Brazil
1960	0.280	0.268	0.267	0.235	0.247	0.355	0.267
1961	0.311	0.297	0.285	0.179	0.265	0.358	0.285
1962	0.352	0.279	0.221	0.203	0.209	0.311	0.227
1963	0.311	0.298	0.247	0.232	0.208	0.305	0.250
1964	0.381	0.308	0.229	0.225	0.227	0.299	0.241
1965	0.313	0.331	0.220	0.222	0.214	0.261	0.233
1966	0.313	0.320	0.192	0.183	0.210	0.336	0.217
1967	0.214	0.179	0.168	0.165	0.194	0.235	0.175
1968	0.171	0.180	0.101	0.098	0.123	0.182	0.112
1969	0.189	0.168	0.099	0.096	0.101	0.129	0.107
1970	0.137	0.130	0.089	0.079	0.113	0.108	0.096
1971	0.124	0.162	0.103	0.103	0.108	0.106	0.108
1972	0.116	0.141	0.120	0.120	0.079	0.079	0.115
1973	0.107	0.171	0.132	0.141	0.086	0.087	0.127
1974	0.075	0.155	0.154	0.135	0.052	0.061	0.123
1975	0.073	0.275	0.095	0.000	0.103	0.039	0.103
1990	0.000	0.000	0.003	0.003	0.000	0.000	0.002

Source: Movimento Bancário do Brasil, CIEF and Banco Central do Brasil.

Table IV.63.s.a.

Ratio Total Voluntary Reserves/Total Deposits (in Relation to Brazil)

Private Banks

Years	North	Northeast	Southeast	São Paulo	South	C. West	Brazil
1960	1.049	1.006	1.002	0.883	0.927	1.331	1.000
1961	1.091	1.042	1.000	0.627	0.932	1.257	1.000
1962	1.548	1.228	0.971	0.891	0.917	1.366	1.000
1963	1.243	1.191	0.991	0.928	0.834	1.219	1.000
1964	1.583	1.281	0.953	0.934	0.943	1.244	1.000
1965	1.340	1.418	0.944	0.954	0.916	1.121	1.000
1966	1.442	1.473	0.882	0.842	0.969	1.549	1.000
1967	1.220	1.025	0.961	0.941	1.107	1.345	1.000
1968	1.530	1.605	0.900	0.879	1.101	1.625	1.000
1969	1.773	1.577	0.923	0.897	0.943	1.209	1.000
1970	1.428	1.361	0.925	0.828	1.177	1.127	1.000
1971	1.145	1.496	0.954	0.952	1.001	0.985	1.000
1972	1.005	1.217	1.038	1.036	0.685	0.687	1.000
1973	0.841	1.340	1.036	1.106	0.673	0.683	1.000
1974	0.611	1.267	1.253	1.105	0.422	0.499	1.000
1975	0.706	2.662	0.922	0.000	0.998	0.380	1.000
1990	0.001	0.023	1.201	1.499	0.000	0.000	1.000

Source: Movimento Bancário do Brasil, CIEF and Banco Central do Brasil.

Table IV.64.s.a.
Ratio Total Voluntary Reserves/Total Deposits
All Banks Except Banco do Brasil

Years	North	Northeast	Southeast	São Paulo	South	C. West	Brazil
1980	0.061	0.085	0.079	0.093	0.051	0.085	0.076
1990	0.000	0.009	0.011	-	0.011	0.052	0.014

Source: Separata of Boletim Mensal of Banco Central do Brasil, June, 1985 and Banco Central do Brasil.

Table IV.65.s.a.
Ratio Total Voluntary Reserves/Total Deposits (in Relation to Brazil)
All Banks Except Banco do Brasil

Years	North	Northeast	Southeast	São Paulo	South	C. West	Brazil
1980	0.804	1.125	1.038	1.228	0.668	1.122	1.000
1990	0.001	0.636	0.792	-	0.766	3.715	1.000

Source: Separata of Boletim Mensal of Banco Central do Brasil, June, 1985 and Banco Central do Brasil.

Table IV.66.s.a.

Cleared Cheques, Number (%)

Year	North	Northeast	Pernambuco	Bahia	Southeast	São Paulo	South	C. West	Brazil
1941	0.10	4.43	3.49	0.21	94.05	52.66	1.42	0.00	100.00
1950	0.10	7.41	6.11	0.65	89.44	49.14	3.05	0.00	100.00
1955	0.12	7.07	4.92	1.30	87.20	46.57	5.61	0.00	100.00
1960	0.26	6.71	3.79	1.71	84.40	51.01	7.49	0.93	100.00
1965	0.43	6.52	2.51	2.32	59.66	48.51	1.06	2.93	100.00
1970	0.69	7.29	2.44	2.82	74.08	45.98	13.62	4.33	100.00
1975	0.64	7.34	2.30	2.72	70.76	48.37	16.52	4.73	100.00
1980	0.72	6.95	1.85	2.59	66.59	44.86	20.12	5.63	100.00
1990	1.20	8.61	1.85	3.30	61.42	40.52	21.12	13.06	100.00

Value (%)

Year	North	Northeast	Pernambuco	Bahia	Southeast	São Paulo	South	C. West	Brazil
1941	0.28	5.98	4.70	0.50	92.09	38.99	1.66	0.00	100.00
1950	0.14	9.25	7.76	1.02	86.90	47.60	3.71	0.00	100.00
1955	0.24	6.63	4.44	1.61	86.75	47.98	6.38	0.00	100.00
1960	0.39	6.28	3.02	2.06	85.30	50.11	7.11	0.87	100.00
1965	0.73	7.15	2.73	2.54	54.69	46.83	8.87	1.86	100.00
1970	0.96	7.11	2.52	2.67	80.47	44.34	9.42	2.03	100.00
1975	0.42	4.41	1.09	1.40	86.26	36.01	7.40	1.51	100.00
1980	0.97	6.23	1.69	2.39	74.25	38.42	13.18	5.36	100.00
1990	1.95	7.28	1.65	2.55	75.58	46.53	10.84	4.37	100.00

Source: Anuário Estatístico, IBGE and Banco Central do Brasil.

Table IV.67.s.a.
Authorised Loans of BNDES (%)

	1952/65	1970	1985	1990
North	0.93	0.58	6.59	9.93
Northeast	3.83	14.55	20.33	21.77
Southeast	86.40	67.07	52.49	44.89
São Paulo	53.35	37.98	25.69	22.17
South	2.57	16.12	14.27	19.75
C. West	3.16	1.67	6.32	3.67
Other	0.10	0.00	0.00	0.00
Brazil	100.00	100.00	100.00	100.00

Source: Anuário Estatístico, IBGE.

Table IV.68.s.a.
Interest Rates on the Repass of BNDES Funds for Industrial Purposes
1980, (% Per Year)

Small and Medium Firms

Region	BNDE	Spread	Final Cost
I	0.5	3	3.5
II	5	2.5	7.5
III	6	2.5	8.5

Big Firms

Region	BNDE	Spread	Final Cost
I	8	3	11
II	9.5	2.5	12
III	9.5	2.5	12

Region I- AM, PA, AC, RO, MA,PI,CE,RN,PB, PE,AL,SE,BA,ES,MT,MS,GO, Minas Polígono das Secas, Território Amapá, RO, Fernando de Noronha.
Region II- Other States.
Region III-São Paulo.
Source: BNB/DESIN.

Table IV.69.s.a.
Interest Rates on the Repass of BNDES Funds for Industrial Purposes
1985, (% Per Year)

Investment and Financial Adjustment

Region	BNDES	Bank	Final Cost
I	1	4	5
II	4	3	7
III	6.5	2.5	9

Working Capital

Region	BNDES	Bank	Final Cost
I	3.5	3	6.5
II	6	2.5	8.5
III	8	2	10

Region I-AM, PA, AC, RO, MA,PI,CE,RN,PB, PE, AL, SE, BA, ES, MT, MS, GO, Minas Polígono das Secas, Territórios do Amapá, RO and Fernando de Noronha.
Region II-Other States.
Region III-São Paulo.

Source: BNB/DESIN.

Table IV.70.s.a.
Interest Rates on Rural Credit (Institutional)
1982, (% Per Year)

	SUDAM/SUDENE ES/Vale Jequit	Other Regions
Working Capital	35	45
Investment Machines	35	-
Machines and Equipments for Irrigation	35	45

Rural Credit
1987
(% Per Year Plus Monetary Correction)

		SUDAM/SUDENE ES/Vale Jeq	Other Regions
Working Capital			
	Small Farmers	3	10
	Cooperatives I		
	Medium Farmers	6	10
	Big Farmers	8	10
	Cooperatives II		
Investment		3	6
	Pre-Commercial	10	10
	Commercial		
	Federal Govern.		
	Raw Products	10	10
	Manuf.Prod.	15	15
Agro Business		8	10

Source: BNB/DERUR.

Conclusion

This book analysed the regional question in Brazil under a monetary production approach. We departed from a relatively well developed real analysis and tried to integrate in it monetary and financial aspects, so arriving at a more general and complete picture of the problem. The theoretical framework on which we based our analysis was the one developed by Dow for financial systems from a regional perspective.

Some points of the general theoretical model of Dow deserved further attention for the application to the Brazilian case. These concern the analysis of the integration of each region in the national economy and the impact of this integration over the linkages, real and financial, that these regional economies could generate. This is especially important in order to assess the policy implications of the model that suggested the action of the State in order to break the financial and real vicious circles that encourage growth in the centre and constrain the periphery. We claim that for State policies fully to achieve their expected results, they have to act both on the financial and on the real spheres of the economy and these two spheres must be compatible; otherwise, policies of easy credit by government-owned banks or monetary expansions, if extended to problematic sectors, can have a reduced effect. A reduced effect is better than nothing, but the credit/money created in the periphery will just play its first round in these economies and soon will leak to the central regions. In this way, it can have a more positive effect in the central economies (where it will fully play its role) than in peripheral economies.

A further element emphasised in the model is the problem relating the definition of the stages of banking development at the regional level. We pointed out that the institutional differences in the banking system at the regional level make difficult it to establish a stage for the banking system as a whole. What we have is banks of the centre, which operate nationwide, advancing in the stages of banking development while the peripheral banks lag behind them. This accentuates still more the relative advantages that centre's banks present and restricts the action of the peripheral banking system, which has important impacts on the regional financial dynamic.

In the specific case of Brazil we observed that the regional problem has its origins in earlier periods of the economic history of the country and that the settlement of the centre/periphery relation generated a series of vicious circles which perpetuated the situation of uneven regional development throughout the various phases of Brazilian economic history. The financial element began to play a key role in the regional question when the dynamic of accumulation was endogeneized in the transition from the agrarian export model to the import substitution period. At this period we observed that the regional dynamic was well depicted by a traditional centre/periphery model and the financial system had constraining effects on the peripheral economies, for two main reasons. First, the general characteristics of these economies resulted in higher liquidity preference in these regions. Second, these economies presented higher leakages, both financial and real, which resulted in drains of reserves from the periphery to the centre. This created a relative advantage to the financial system of the centre and constrained the possibilities of growth of the periphery.

At this period we have government-owned banks extending credit more easily to the periphery. However, the leakages that these economies presented made this mechanism of finance innocuous, since the newly created finance leaked very soon to the central economies. Private banks, on the other hand, fully conformed to the results predicted by the theoretical model. Therefore, government-owned banks have an important role to play in reducing the financial constraints of the periphery. However, the impacts of the reduction of these constraints are reduced because of the leakages of those economies.

We reached these results for the period of import substitution when the State had no well-defined policy for the periphery, offering mainly emergency aid. We asked what could have changed in the phase of strong State intervention after the 1960s. We concluded that although State intervention has caused important structural changes in these economies, a great part of the potential benefits drained away to the central region, since the kind of industrialisation promoted in the periphery accentuated the leakages that peripheral economies already presented. Thus although the traditional characterisation of centre/periphery had changed its form, its essence was retained. The dynamic of the financial system continued to be one of reinforcing growth in the centre and restricting it in the periphery.

This illustrated well our point made in the theoretical part where we emphasised that State policies (fiscal and financial) must have very well defined targets and these targets should be defined observing the degree of linkages, real and financial, that stimulated sectors can generate within the regional economies. Since one of the main problems with the industrialisation of the periphery (mainly the Northeast) of Brazil was to create mechanisms which stimulated a certain ownership structure and sectorial composition that enforced the leakages that this economy already presented.

We began our analysis (Chapter 1) reviewing heterodox models of regional economic development which suggest the existence of cumulative processes in regional development. For this, we analysed Dependency Theory, its main streams, Myrdal's model and Kaldorian models. These models suggest different sources for the vicious circles observed at the regional level and give different explanations for the feedback effects of these circles. However, there is one common point to all them: they observe the market dynamic as the logic behind these vicious circles. Therefore, market mechanisms are unable to break these vicious circles. On the contrary, the logic of the free market originates and develops cumulative processes which are responsible for the intensification of the original regional disparities.

These models are mainly concerned with real causes for regional uneven patterns of development. Financial elements are not taken into account properly and their power to generate and reinforce vicious circles is analysed only marginally. The reason for this varies according to the school of thought, but we can mention three main reasons for the lack of monetary analysis within the heterodoxy: a) the lack of an adequate monetary theoretical framework; b) the misconception of finance and its confusion with saving (in common with orthodoxy) and c) the adoption of a "horizontalist" position which considers the money supply as absolutely endogenous and so considers the supply of finance as a mere accommodating variable.

In Chapter 2 we worked with the idea of monetary production economies and demonstrated that within this conception money is non-neutral. Therefore, it is not possible to separate real and financial elements in the analysis of the pattern of growth, since these two spheres interplay in the determination of growth in the economy.

Since we adopted a general framework in which money plays such a relevant role, it is not reasonable to think of it as a neutral element in regional terms. So we analysed the model developed by Dow which successfully attempted to conciliate the theories that work with vicious circles at the real level and the Post Keynesian monetary framework, showing how each element which leads to the non-neutrality of money at the general level operates when referring to economies which are structurally rather different and which are in close contact, without barriers to monetary or trade flows.

The models developed by Dow assume a central region that has more solid institutions, has the economic structure concentrated in the industrial sector, has more developed financial markets, has a more integrated economy which originates a lower propensity to import, has an endogenous growth dynamic and has a more stable pattern of growth. On the other hand, peripheral economies present less developed markets, especially financial markets, a less developed institutional framework, the economic structure concentrated in primary sectors, an export led pattern of growth and a more unstable trend of growth. As a consequence of these elements we have higher degrees of uncertainty in the periphery than in the centre and the bases for the diffusion of information are more volatile in the periphery than in the centre. This is especially true when we observe the degree of uncertainty which institutions of other regions are submitted to when operating in peripheral regions, since for these institutions, the uncertainty of the periphery is emphasised by the more remote bases of information that those regions present. Therefore, the conventional element in the decision making process is emphasised in these regions. As the conventional element of the decision making process tends to act against peripheral regions, this creates constraints to the economic expansion of these regions.

In the periphery, as a consequence of higher instability, agents are supposed to present higher liquidity preferences than in the centre. This creates limits to investment in peripheral regions. As the financial markets of the centre are more developed, their assets are more liquid. This makes agents prefer to use assets from the centre to manifest their liquidity preference which causes leakages in the financial flows in the periphery. Therefore, the money multiplier is reduced in the periphery as a consequence of two elements of the financial behaviour of agents: a) the higher liquidity preference of agents in the periphery (i) as a consequence of the instability, (ii) as a consequence of the lower level of income that made the ratio cash/deposits higher in the periphery than in the centre, iii) as a consequence of the larger reserves/deposits ratio which banks keep because the higher instability of the periphery and b) leakages caused by the preference of agents in manifesting their liquidity preference in assets of the centre than in assets of the periphery. Another element that reinforces the tendency to constrain credit creation in the periphery is the higher leakages that these regions show in terms of their trade balances.

However, financial restrictions to money creation in the periphery do not come only from the action of the money multipliers. As the economy overcomes stage 2 of banking development, banks begin to have an important role in the creation of money. As peripheral economies are under greater uncertainty, banks tend to keep larger reserve/deposit ratios, which constrain credit creation and new deposits. Another element worth mentioning is the restrictions that banks, especially branches of banks that have their head offices in the centre, put on the extension of credit towards the periphery, since the bases of information are more volatile in these regions. When these banks extend credit towards the periphery they prefer to do so to firms that are branches of firms of the centre, since they have greater confidence in these firms than in local firms. By doing so, they emphasise tendencies towards financial and regional leakages from the periphery towards the centre, since these firms are more integrated with the centre's economy than with the periphery's. This accentuates the tendency towards the easier credit and deposit creation in the centre and financial constraints in the periphery.

We emphasised the notion of the possibilities of creation of intra-regional linkages, real and financial, according to sectors and to the ownership of the firms operating in each sector. This is so because extra-regional firms tend to present low linkages, real and financial, within the host economy since the strategy of the firm is determined in the head-offices at the general level. At the same time, they tend to present low financial linkages with the host economy because the bases for the formation of expectations in the host economy are much more remote than in their original region. Therefore, the impacts of credit extended towards these firms are reduced in relation to the potential impacts of credit extended to firms that present a high intra-regional integration, as was earlier observed. Centre's banks tend to extend credit towards the periphery to projects of branches of centre's firms. So the impact of the extension of credit by these banks is also reduced.

The joint action of these elements tends to generate or accentuate a process of banking concentration in the centre. This intensifies still more the previous tendencies of financial constraints in the periphery and financial growth in the centre. Therefore, the joint action of real and financial elements in monetary production economies creates vicious circles which enforce the disparate regional growth.

Once the theoretical background was established, we embarked upon an analysis of the Brazilian case. Part II aimed to give an overview of the economic history of the regions of Brazil. We began our analysis with the settlement and observed how the economic dynamic of the regions changed over time under the agrarian export model. During this period, the main determinant of the dynamism of the regions was the joint action of natural resources and external markets. The financial sphere was important in terms of the development of the regions which were linked to the external sectors, since it allowed the development of crops demanded by international markets. At this stage, finance was mainly supplied by foreign banks and was a fundamental element in the extraction of surplus from the periphery by the international centres. It was mainly by the control of the financial and commercial spheres that first the Netherlands and later England extracted surplus from Brazil. The role that the financial system played during this phase of the economic development of the country is explained well by dependency theory. In this phase, there were serious monetary constraints in peripheral economies since the lack of contact with the dynamic activity marginalised them in the monetary economy. The transition from the agrarian export model to the import substitution model took place when the dynamic region was the Southeast and this was fundamental to the retention of economic dynamism by this region.

The structural characterisation of the regional economies during the period when dynamic activity was located in each one is important in order to observe their further development, mainly because the majority of the regions retained these structural elements. We can mention the case of the Northeast, which maintains the basic bequests of slavery and latifundia until nowadays, presenting a terrible land structure, very concentrated agriculture in few products for export and very tenuous labour relation. This avoids access by the great part of the population to the formal labour markets and reinforces the restrictions on this population to the financial sector. On the other hand, we have the Southeast which retained the more capitalist labour relations observed during the period of the coffee activity, a more diversified agriculture and a more diversified economic structure. This made for more widespread formal relations with labour and formal organisation of markets which made access easier to the financial system for the population.

In Part III, we analysed the regional question when the country entered the import substitution model. During this period, the regional economic dynamic was transferred from the external market to the internal market. To proceed with our analysis, we divided this part into two chapters. In Chapter 4, we analysed the real side of the regional economies, observed the internal financial mechanisms that it developed and analysed the impacts that general economic policies have had on the regional economies. We concluded that, at this stage, the regional economies followed the theoretical model presented in Chapter 2. That is, the peripheral economies showed an agricultural profile, the industries were traditional industries and there was higher instability in these economies. On the other hand, the central economy was mainly an industrial economy, concentrating dynamic sectors of the industry, presenting lower instability and a more developed institutional background to wage relations, contracts, financial system and so on. At the same time, we saw that the general economic policies led by the State had had an intense regional concentrating character.

During this period, the Brazilian economy and the regional economies were facing two types of new financial pressures which had to be met in order to allow continuation of growth: a) structural changes which demanded more sophisticated financial mechanisms and b) growth which by itself put the economy in a more illiquid position. The lack of proper financial mechanism did not find any solution in private financial schemes. The way of overcoming the financial limit to growth was found in some mechanisms which allowed internal finance by the firms and in funding schemes of the State. Both elements had impacts in the regional question.

In Chapter 5 we observed mainly the financial sector of these regional economies. Contrary to the real analysis, the regional financial dynamic has not received much attention in Brazil. Therefore, our analysis pioneered in this area, especially in the attempt to observe the financial dynamic under a Post Keynesian perspective. We centred our analysis in the banking system as a consequence of the great role that banks played in the financial dynamic of the country during this period. The lack of other financial mechanisms resulted in creating elements which allowed the continuation of the process of growth with internal finance or with funding provided by the state. However, as we observed, these mechanisms were extremely biased towards the centre and caused substantial damage to the periphery. We concluded that the theoretical model fitted well the Brazilian regional financial dynamic. We analysed the financial system in various aspects and concluded that a precise analysis of the regional dynamic asks for the integration of real and financial aspects. Therefore, we attempted to observe the meaning of certain relations, as in the case of the regional ratio of loans to deposits, in a broad sense in order to reach the deep meanings that they could present. We observed that the way that regions were integrated and the structural characteristics of each region explained the pattern followed by the financial system in regional terms. That is, the strong leakages, financial and real, observed in the peripheral economies were mainly responsible for the reduced role that banks played in these regions. On the other hand, the lower level of financial development in these regions reinforced the leakages of finance from the periphery to the centre, since it made agents prefer to manifest their liquidity preference in central assets. In this way, we have a real and financial vicious circle which was self-perpetuating and ended up by intensifying regional disparities. This also created a very concentrated banking system in the central regions, and what is worse, with a concentrating dynamic. This put limits to the credit creation in the periphery which accentuated the uneven pattern of regional development followed by the country.

In Part IV, we analysed the period 1960-90. The beginning of this period was marked by the change in the policy of the State to the peripheral regions, especially to the Northeast and later to the North. In this phase, we moved from an ad hoc policy of assistance for damages caused by droughts in the Northeast towards a policy of direct intervention in the economic structure of this region. Our main aim in this part was to analyse the results achieved by such a policy and to see if it caused any significant change in the pattern followed by the monetary and financial spheres in the regions. In Chapter 6, we analysed the policies adopted by the Federal Government to the regions and saw the impact they had on the real side of the periphery. We concluded that, although these policies did have significant effects in terms of changing the economic structures of the regions, industrialising the peripheral regions mainly through the transference of branches of firms from the centre to those regions, they had a reduced impact on the real economic problems of the regions and this was due to the way in which these policies were conducted, much more attuned to the needs of the central economies than to the necessities of the periphery, and this ended up aggravating some problems of the periphery.

As observed, industrialisation in the periphery had some characteristics, among them, the intense dependence on the centre, which resulted in intensifying leakages from the peripheral regions which did not allow retention of the benefits of these policies in the target region. Therefore, we can see in this phase a transformation in the relations of dependence but their nature was still maintained and was even more accentuated.

In Chapter 7, we analysed specifically the impacts of these policies on the financial sector. First, we observed a huge process of banking concentration at the national level which was stimulated by the government. This, however, did not reach the peripheral regions with the same intensity of the centre, since the policies that were responsible to a great extent for it also stimulated the extension of the banking network towards the periphery. However, when we analysed the variables associated with the action of the banks at the regional level, we did not notice important changes compared to the period observed in Part III. That is, the financial dynamic was still concentrated in the centre and the periphery continued to present constraints on the capacity to retain deposits. Therefore, the dynamic of credit creation, which led to increased investment, which increases income and generates deposits was broken, since there were tremendous leakages from the periphery, which had effects on both the income multiplier and the money multiplier. Furthermore, the type of industrialisation stimulated was one of the main causes of the increases in leakages. Therefore, the mechanisms created to promote growth in the periphery had features which undermined their effectiveness.

The kind of industrialisation promoted in the periphery intensified not only the real leakages. As industrialisation proceeded based on extra-regional firms these firms also speculated and held more centre assets than local assets. This caused strong financial leakages which reduced the impacts of credit extension or monetary expansion in the periphery.

During this period government-owned banks pursued policies of easy credit towards the periphery, contrary to private banks. However, the enormous leakages of finance from the periphery ended up by reducing the effects of those policies to the first round of the economic process. As finance leaked very soon to the centre, the main benefit of the credit extension in the periphery was captured by the centre, where the newly created finance played its role fully.

Therefore, the structural changes led by the state in the periphery after the 1960s, although having important impacts on the structure of the periphery had not broken the elements that create and perpetuate the vicious circles described in our theoretical model. On the contrary, the sort of industrialisation promoted in these regions resulted in reinforcing the dependence of these regions on the centre, which resulted in accentuating the vicious circles that stress disparate regional growth. Thus, the policies undertaken by the state did not have the effects that they were supposed to have and had little impact on overcoming the main problems of the peripheral regions in Brazil.

The Brazilian experience is extremely rich for demonstrating how a regional State intervention scheme that seemed to be adequate could have its impacts so reduced. This demonstrates that in spite of the State being the unique element able to break vicious circles generated in the private economic dynamic, its action is extremely complex. It is very easy for mechanisms that seem appropriate to tackle a specific problem to be captured by private mechanisms that end up destroying the original aim. This seems to be the case of the policies developed for the Northeast of Brazil in the period after 1960. Although these policies were aware about the creation of intra-regional linkages, absorption of labour etc.. Firms that were stimulated with these mechanisms were intrinsically against the principles postulated to overcome the backward position of the region. Therefore, the lack of appropriate mechanisms that counterbalanced the characteristics of these firms thwarted the expected effects of the scheme on the peripheral economies.

For such a scheme to realise its full potential it will be necessary to have a very well defined policy to stimulate projects that have a higher level of intra-regional linkages. And more, this stimulus must not be given only on an incentive basis. They must have a veto character: projects without certain potentialities in terms of creation of intra-regional linkages could not receive the benefits of such an incentive. In this way, the regional policy can attempt to assure the retention of a great part of the benefits of such a scheme in the target region. Putting the emphasis of the scheme in the linkages of projects is the best way to amplify the money, income and employment multipliers and in this way to change the expectations on the state of the peripheral economies.

Bibliography

Albuquerque, R.C. and Cavalcanti, C.V. (1976), *Desenvolvimento Regional no Brasil*, IPEA/IPLAN, Brasília.

Allen, K. and MacLennan, M.C. (1970), *Regional Problems and Policies in Italy and France*, George Allen and Unwin Ltd, London.

Almeida, J.G. de (1988), *Sistema Bancário Público e Privado: Mudança na Estrutura de Recursos e Tendências de Custo e Lucro (1985/1987)*, Texto para Discussão N. 13, FUNDAP, São Paulo.

Amadeo, E. and Dutt, A.K. (1987), "Os Keyensianos Neo-Ricardianos e os Pós-Keynesianos", *Pesquisa e Planejamento Econômico*, Vol. 17, N. 3.

Andrade, T.A. (1977), "Desigualdades Regionais no Brasil: Uma Seleção de Estudos Empíricos", *Pesquisa e Planejamento Econômico*, Vol. 7, N. 1.

Andrade, T.A. and Haddad, P. (1974), "Política Fiscal e Desequilíbrios Regionais", *Estudos Econômicos*, Vol. 4, N. 1.

Araújo, T.B. (1979), *La Division Interregional du Travail au Bresil et Le Exemple du Nord-est*, Unpublished Doctorat de 3 eme Cycle en Economie Publique Thesis, Universite de Paris I, Pantheon-Sorbonne, Paris.

Araújo, T.B. (1981), "Crescimento Industrial do Nordeste: Para Quem e Para Que?", *Revista Pernambucana de Desenvolvimento*, Vol. 8, N. 1.

Araújo, T.B. (1994), "Nordeste: Evolução Recente da Economia Regional" in *Balanço e Perspectiva do Federalismo Fiscal no Brasil*, FUNDAP/IESP, mimeo, Recife.

Aureliano, L.M. (1981), *No Limiar da Industrialização*, Brasiliense, São Paulo.

Banco Central do Brasil (1985), *Boletim Mensal do Banco Central do Brasil*, June.

Baer, W. (1965), *Industrialization and Economic Development in Brazil*, Richard D. Irwin, Illinois.

Baer, W. and Geiger, P.P. (1976), "Industrialização, Urbanização e a Persistência das Desigualdades Regionais do Brasil", *Revista Brasileira de Geografia*, Vol. 38, N. 2, abril/junho.

Baer, W.; Kerstenetzky, I. and Villela, A. (1973), " As Modificações no Papel do Estado na Economia Brasileira", *Pesquisa e Planejamento Econômico*, Vol. 3, N. 4, dezembro.

Baran, P.A. (1957), *The Political Economy of Growth*, John Calder, London.

Bear, J.B. (1976), "A Monetarist Model of Regional Business Cycle", *Journal of Regional Science*, Vol. 16, N. 1.

Bethell, L. (1970), *The Abolition of the Brazilian Slave Trade*, Cambridge University Press, Cambridge.

Bielschowsky, R.A. (1975), *Bancos e Acumulação de Capital na Industrialização Brasileira: Uma Análise Introdutória*, Unpublished Master Thesis, Universidade de Brasília, Brasília.

BNB (1992), *Matriz de Insumo-Produto do Nordeste. 1980 e 1985: Metodologia e Resultados*, BNB, Fortaleza.

Bodenheimer, S. (1971), "Dependency and Imperialism: The Roots of Latin American Underdevelopment". in Fann, K.T. and Hodges, D.C. (eds), *Readings in U.S. Imperialism*, Porter Sargent.

Boisier, S. (1975), "Localización, Tamaño Urbano y Productividad Industrial: Un Caso de Estudio del Brasil", *El Trimestre Economico*, N. 165, enero/marzo.

Bouzan, A. (1973), "Concentração e Economias de Escala nos Bancos Comerciais Brasileiros", *Revista de Administração de Empresas*, Vol. 13, N. 3, setembro.

Brandão, M.A.(1985), "A Regionalização da grande Indústria de Brasil: Recife e Salvador na Década de 70", *Revista de Economia Política*, Vol. 5, N. 4, outubro/dezembro.

Cameron, R. (1972), *Banking and Economic Development: Some Lessons of History*, New York, Oxford University Press.

Cano, W. (1977), *Raízes da Concentração Industrial em São Paulo*, DIFEL, São Paulo.

Cano, W. (1985), *Desequilíbrios Regionais e Concentração Industrial no Brasil, 1930-1970*, Global Editora & Editora da UNICAMP, São Paulo.

Cano, W. & Guimarães Neto, L. (1986), "A Questão Regional no Brasil: Traços Gerais de sua Evolução Histórica", *Revista de Económia Política*, N. 10, Julio-Diciembre.

Cardoso, F.H. (1960), "A Estrutura da Indústria em São Paulo", *Educação e Ciências Sociais*, Fevereiro.

Cardoso, F.H. (1972), "Dependency and Development in Latin America", *New Left Review,* July-August.
Cardoso, F.H. (1973), "Notas sobre o Estado dos Estudos sobre Dependência", *Cadernos CEBRAP*, N. 11, São Paulo.
Cardoso, F.H. (1978), "Capitalist Development and the State: Bases and Alternatives", *Ibero-Americana*, Vol. VII, N. 2.
Cardoso, F.H. (1982),"Development Under Fire" in Makler, H.; Martinelli, A. and Smelser, N., *The New International Economy*, Sage Publications, California.
Cardoso, F.H. and Faletto, E. (1979), *Dependence and Development in Latin America,* University of California Press, Berkeley.
Cardoso, F.H. and Muller, G. (1977), *Amazônia: Expansão do Capitalismo,* Brasiliense, São Paulo.
Carvalheiro, N. (1982), *Bancos Comerciais no Brasil- 1964/1976: Crescimento e Concentração*, Unpublished Master Thesis, Department of Economics, Universidade de São Paulo, São Paulo.
Carvalho, F.C.J. (1983-84), "On the Concept of Time in Shacklean and Sraffian Economics", *Journal of Post keynesian Economics,* Vol. VI, N. 2, winter.
Carvalho, F.C.J. (1988), *Fundamentos da Escola Pós-Keynesiana: A Teoria de uma Economia Monetária*, Texto Para Discussão, IEI/UFRJ, N. 176.
Carvalho, O. (1979), *Desenvolvimento Regional: Um Problema Político,* Campus, Rio de Janeiro.
Castro, A.B. (1980), *7 Ensaios sobre a Economia Brasileira*, Forense Universitária, Rio de Janeiro.
Castro, J. (1977), *The Geopolitics of Hunger*, Monthly Review Press, London.
CEPAL (1975), "O Desenvolvimento Recente do Sistema Financeiro na América Latina" in Serra, J. (org.), *América Latina-Ensaios de Interpretação Econômica,* Paz e Terra, Rio de Janeiro.
Chaloult, Y. (1978), *Estado, Acumulação e Colonialismo Interno: Contradições Nordeste/Sudeste, 1960 - 1977*, Editora Vozes, Petrópolis.
Chick, V. (1983), *Macroeconomics After Keynes*, MIT Press, Cambridge.
Chick, V. (1986), "The Evolution of the Banking System and The Theory of Saving, Investment and Interest", *Econommies et Societes*, vol.20, Serie Monnaie et Production.
Chick, V. and Dow, S.C. (1988), "A Post-Keynesian Perspective on the Relation Between Banking and Regional Development", in Arestis, P. (ed), *Post Keynesian Monetary Economics*, Elgar, Aldershot.
CIEF, Ministério da Fazenda, *Movimento Bancário do Brasil*, Several Issues.
Cohn, A. (1976), *Crise Regional e Planejamento,* Editora Perspectiva, São Paulo.

Davidson, P. (1980), "The Dual-Faceted nature of the Keynesian Revolution: Money and Money Wages in Unemployment and Production Flow Prices", *Journal of Post Keynesian Economics,* Vol. II, N.3, spring.

Davidson, P. (1982-83), "Rational Expectations: A Fallacious Foundation for Studying Crucial Decision-Making Processes", *Journal of Post Keynesian Economics,* Vol. V, N. 2, winter.

Davidson, P. (1986), "Finance, Funding, Saving, and Investment", *Journal of Post Keynesian Economics*, Vol. IX, N. 1, Fall.

Davidson, P. (1988), "A Technical Definition of Uncertainty and the Long-Run Non-Neutrality of Money", *Cambridge Journal of Economics*, Vol. 12, N. 3.

Davidson, P. (1990), "A Lei de Thirlwall", *Revista de Economia Política*, Vol. 10, N. 4, outubro-dezembro.

Davidson, P. and Kregel, J.A. (1980), "Keynes's Paradigme: A Theoretical Framework for Monetary Analysis" in Nell, E.J. (ed.), *Growth, Profits and Property. Essays in the Revival of Political Economy*, Cambridge University press, Cambridge.

Dean, W. (1969), *The Industrialization of São Paulo. 1880-1945*, University of Texas Press, Austin.

Delfim Netto, A. (1979), *O Problema do Café no Brasil*, Editora da Fundação Getúlio Vargas, Rio de Janeiro.

Denslow Jr., D. (1977), "As Origens da Desigualdade Regional no Brasil" in Versiani, F.R. & Barros, J.R.M., *Formação Econômica do Brasil: A Experiência da Industrialização,* Saraiva, São Paulo.

Dixon, R. and Thirlwall, A.P. (1975), "A Model of Regional Growth-Rate Differences on Kaldorian Lines", *Oxford Economic Papers*, Vol. 27.

Dos Santos, T. (1970), "The Structure of Dependence", *American Economic Review,* Vol. 60, N. 2.

Dos Santos, T. (1973),"The Crisis of Development Theory and the Problem of Dependence in Latin America" in Bernstein, H., *Underdevelopment and Development,* Penguin Books, Great Britain.

Dow, S.C. (1982), "The Regional Composition of the Money Multiplier Process", *Scottish Journal of Political Economy*, Vol. 29, N. 1.

Dow, S.C. (1985), *Macroeconomic Thought: A Methodological Approach, Blackwell,* Oxford.

Dow, S.C. (1987), "The Treatment of Money in Regional Economics", *Journal of Regional Science,* Vol. 27, N. 1.

Dow, S.C. (1988), "Incorporating Money in Regional Economic Models" in Harrigan, F. and McGregor, P.G., *Recent Advances in Regional Economic Modelling,* Pion Limited, London.

Dow, S.C. (1990), *Financial Markets and Regional Economic Development: The Canadian Experience*, Aldershot, Avebury.

Dow, S.C. (1992), "The Regional Financial Sector: A Scottish Case Study" in *Regional Studies*, Vol. 26, N. 7.

Dreese, G.R. (1973-74), "Banks and Regional Economic Development", *Southern Economic Journal*, Vol. 40.

Ferreira, A. (1983a), "A Dinâmica da Expansão Industrial Recente no Nordeste", *Revista Econômica do Nordeste*, Vol. 14, N. 2, abril/junho.

Ferreira, A. (1983b),"O Nordeste Brasileiro, Contraponto Inacabado de Acumulação?", *Revista de Economia Política*, Vol. 3, N. 3, julho/setembro.

FGV, *Conjuntura Econômica*, Several Issues.

Fishkind, H.H. (1977), "The Regional Impact of Monetary Policy: An Economic Simulation Study of Indiana 1958-1973", *Journal of Regional Science*, Vol. 17, N. 1.

Fishkind, H. and Roberts, R.B. (1979), "The Role of Monetary Forces in Regional Economic Activity: An Econometric Simulation Analysis", *Journal of Regional Science*, Vol. 19, N. 1.

Fishlow, A. (1977), "Origens e Consequências da Substituição de Importações no Brasil" in Versiani, F.R. & Barros, J.R.M., *Formação Econômica do Brasil: A Experiência da Industrialização*, Saraiva, São Paulo.

Frank, A.G. (1966), "The Development of Underdevelopment", *Monthly Review*, Vol. 18, N. 4, September.

Frank, A.G. (1967), *Capitalism and Underdevelopment in Latin America*, Monthly Review Press, New York.

Frick, O.O. (1991), *Reflexões sobre a Desconcentração Industrial em São Paulo*, Unpublished M.Sc. Thesis, Department of Economics, Universidade de São Paulo, São Paulo.

Friedman, J. (1972), "A General Theory of Polarized Development" in Hansen, N., *Growth Centers in Regional Economic Development*, The Free Press, New York.

Friedman, M. (1956), "The Quantity Theory of Money; A Restatment" in *Studies in the Quantity Theory of Money*, University of Chicago Press, Chicago.

Friedman, M. (1977), "A Theoretical Framework for Monetary Analysis" in Gordon, J. R. (ed.), *Milton Friedman Monetary Framework: A Debate with his Critics*, University of Chicago Press, Chicago.

Furtado, C. (1962), "O Problema do Nordeste" in *A Pré-Revolução Brasileira*, Fundo de Cultura, Rio de Janeiro.

Furtado, C. (1963), *Economic Growth of Brazil*, University of California Press, California.

Furtado, C. (1964), *Dialética do Desenvolvimento*, Fundo de Cultura, Rio de Janeiro.

Furtado, C. (1971), *Teoria e Política do Desenvolvimento Econômico*, Editora Nacional, São Paulo.

Furtado, C. (1971), *Formação Econômica do Brasil*, Companhia Editora Nacional, 11 ed.

Furtado, C. (1964), *Development and Underdevelopment*, University of California Press, Berkeley.

Furtado, C. (1982), *A Nova Dependência*, Paz e Terra, Rio de Janeiro.

Galvão, A.C.F. (1987), *O Capital Oligopólico em Marcha Sobre a Periferia Nordestina: Evolução da Organização Territorial, Divisão Territorial do Trabalho e Complementaridade Industrial*, Unpublished M.Sc. Thesis, Department of Economics, Universidade de São Paulo, São Paulo.

Galvão, O.J.A. (1979), "Políticas de Comércio Exterior no Pós-Guerra e a Exacerbação das Desigualdades Regionais no Brasil", *Revista Pernambucana de Desenvolvimento*, Vol. 6, N. 2, Jul./Dez..

Galvão, O.J.A. (1980), "A Integração Regional-Um Estudo dos Efeitos da Integração Econômica e do Comércio sobre as Desigualdades Regionais", *Revista Pernambucana de Desenvolvimento*, Vol. 7, N. 2, Jul./Dez..

Galvão, O.J.A. (1988), Regional Development in Brazil: A Study of Economic Integration in an Unevenly Developed Country, Unpublished Ph.D. Thesis, UCL, University of London.

Gazeta Mercantil, *Balanço Anual*, Several Issues.

Gentle, J.S.C.(1993), *The Financial Services Industry: The Impact of Corporate Reorganization on Regional Economic Development*, Avebury, Aldershot.

Gentle, J.S.C. and Marshall, N. (1992), "The Deregulation of The Financial Services Industry and The Polarization of Regional Economic Prosperity", *Regional Studies*, Vol. 26, N. 6.

Gerschenkron, A. (1962), *Economic Backwardness in Historical Perspective*, Harvard University Press, Cambridge.

Gomes, G.M. (1988), "Recessão e Crescimento nas Economias Brasileiras e Nordestina, 1980-1986". *Revista Pernambucana de Desenvolvimento*, Vol. 12, N. 2, julho/dezembro.

Goodhart, C.A.E. (1989), *Money, Information and Uncertainty*, MacMillan, London.

Goodman, D.E. and Albuquerque, R.C. (1974), *Incentivos à Industrialização e Desenvolvimento do Nordeste*, IPEA/INPES, Brasília.

GTDN (1978), *Uma Política de Desenvolvimento Econômico para o Nordeste*, Recife, SUDENE.

Guimarães Neto, L. (1978), "Urbanização e Emprego Urbano no Nordeste", *Revista Econômica do Nordeste*, Vol. 9, N. 2, abril/junho.

Guimarães Neto, L. (1982), "O Emprego no Nordeste: Sugestões de Políticas", *Revista Econômica do Nordeste*, Vol. 13, N. 3, julho/setembro.

Guimarães Neto, L. (1983), "Emprego em Pernambuco: Notas sobre a Experiência Recente (1960/82)", *Revista Pernambucana de Desenvolvimento*, Vol. 10, N. 1, janeiro/junho.
Guimarães Neto, L. (1989), *Introdução à Formação Econômica do Nordeste*, Editora Massangana, Recife.
Guimarães Neto, L. (1994), "Desigualdades Regionais e Federalismo (Exame do Conjunto das Regiões Brasileiras) in *Balanço e Perspectiva do Federalismo Fiscal no Brasil*, FUNDAP/IESP, mimeo, Recife.
Gurley, J.G. (1967), *American Economic Review*, Vol 57 (ii).
Haddad, P.R. (1989),"O Que fazer com o Planejamento Regional no Brasil da Póxima Década?", *Planejamento e Políticas Públicas*, N. 1.
Hahn, F.H. (1982), *Money and Inflation*, MIT Press, Cambridge Mass.
Hahn,F.H. (1984), "On some Problems of Producing the Existence of Equilibrium in a Monetary Economy" in Hahn, F.H., *Equilibrium and Macroenomics*, Basil Blackwell, Oxford.
Hansen, N.M. (1967), "Developments Poles and Economic Space", *KYKLOS*, Vol. 20, N. 3.
Harber Jr., R.P. (1982), "O Sistema de Incentivos Fiscais e o Nordeste: Uma Análise Econométrica", *Revista Econômica do Nordeste*, Vol. 13, N. 4, out/dez.
Hess, D.R. et al (1987), "A Evolução da Agricultura na Região Centro-Oeste na Década de 70", Rio de Janeiro, *Revista Brasileira de Geografia*, Vol. 49, N. 1, janeiro/ março.
Hicks, J.R. (1959), *Essays in World Economics*, Clarendon Press, Oxford.
Hill, J.M. and Moore, C.L. (1982), "Interregional Arbitrage and The Supply of Loanable Funds", *Journal of Regional Science*, Vol. 22.
Hirschman, A.O. (1958), *The Strategy of Economic Development*, Yale Uinversity Press, New Haven.
Hirschman, A.O. (1968/69),"Industrial Development in the Brazilian Northeast and the Tax Credit Scheme of Article 34/18", *Journal of Development Studies*, Vol. 5, N. 1.
Hirschman, A. (1971), *Journeys Toward Progress*, Greenwood, Westport.
Hirschman, A.O. (1981), *Essays in Trespassing: Economics to Politics and Beyond*, Cambridge University Press, Cambridge.
Hoare, A.G. (1978), "Industrial Linkages and the Dual Economy: The Case of Northern Ireland". *Regional Studies*, Vol. 12.
Hollanda, S.B. (1964), *História Geral da Civilização Brasileira*, II-II and II-III. Difusão Européia do Livro, São Paulo.
Hutchinson, R.W. and McKillop, D.G. (1990), "Regional Financial Sector Models: An Application to the Northern Ireland Financial Sector", *Regional Studies*, Vol. 24, N. 5.

Ianni, O. (1971), *Estado e Planejamento Econômico no Brasil: 1930/1970*, Civilização Brasileira, Rio de Janeiro.
IBGE, *Anuário Estatístico*, Several Issues.
IBGE, *Censo Demográfico*, Several Issues.
IBGE, *Censo Industrial*, Several Issues.
IBGE, *Censo Econômico*, Several Issues.
IBGE, *Pesquisa Nacional por Amostra de Domicílio*, Several Issues.
Kaldor, N. (1970), "The Case for Regional Policies", *Scottish Journal of Political Economy*, Vol. 17.
Kaldor, N. (1978), "The New Monetarism" in *Further Essays on Applied Economics*, Gerald Duckworth & Co. ltd, London.
Kaldor, N. (1985), *The Scourge of Monetarism*, Oxford University Press, Oxford.
Kaldor, N. and Trevithick, J. (1981), "A Keynesian Perspective on Money", *Lloyds Bank Review*, January.
Katzman, M.T. (1974), "Urbanização e Concentração Industrial: 1940/70", *Pesquisa e Planejamento Econômico*, Vol. 4, N. 3, dezembro.
Keynes, J.M. (1936), *The General Theory of Employment, Interest and Money*, The Collected Writtings of John Maynard Keynes, Vol. VII, Macmillan, Cambridge, 1991.
Keynes, J.M. (1937), "The General Theory of Employment", Quarterly Journal of Economics, N. 51, February.
Keynes, J.M. (1971), *A Treatise on Money: The Applied Theory of Money*, The Collected Writings of John Maynard Keynes, Vol VI, Macmillan, Cambridge.
Keynes, J.M. (1973a), *The General Theory. Part I: Preparation*, Collected Writings of John Maynard Keynes, Vol. XIII, Macmillan, Cambridge.
Keynes, J.M. (1973b), "Alternative Theories of the Rate of Interest", *The General Theory and After. Part II: Defence and Development*, Collected Writings of John Maynard Keynes, Vol.XIV, Macmillan, Cambridge.
Keynes, J.M. (1973c), "'Ex Ante' Theory of the Rate of Interest", *The General Theory and After. Part II: Defence and Development*, Collected Writings of John Maynard Keynes, Vol. XIV, Macmillan, Cambridge.
Keynes, J.M. (1979), *The General Theory and After: A Supplement*, The Collected Writings of John Maynard Keynes, Vol. XXIX, Macmillan, Cambridge.
Knight, F.H. (1933), *Risk, Uncertainty and Profit*, London School of Economics, London.
Kregel, J.A. (1986), "A Note on Finance, Liquidity, Saving, and Investment", *Journal of Post Keynesian Economics*, Vol. 9, N. 1, Fall.
Laclau, E. (1973), "Feudalismo y Capitalismo en America Latina" in Modos de Producción en América Latina, *Cuadernos de Passado y Presente*, N. 40, México.

Leff, N. (1972a), "Uma Perspectiva de Longo Prazo do Desenvolvimento e Subdesenvolvimento Brasileiro", *Revista Brasileira de Economia*, Vol. 26, N. 3, jul/set..

Leff,N. (1972b), "Economic Development and Regional Inequality: Origins of the Brazilian Case", *Quarterly Journal of Economics*, Vol. 86.

Lessa, C. (1981), *Quinze Anos de Política Econômica*, Brasiliense, São Paulo.

Lever, W. (1974), "Manufacturing Linkages and the Search for Suppliers and Markets" in Hamilton, F.E.I., *Spatial Perspective on Industrial Organization and Decision-Making*, John Willey & Sons, London.

Levy, M.B. (1979), *História Financeira do Brasil Colonial*, IBMEC, Rio de Janeiro.

Lima, H.F. (1976), *História Político-Econômica e Industrial do Brasil*, Companhia Editora Nacional, São Paulo.

Lipietz, A. (1988), *O Capital e seu Espaço*, Nobel, São Paulo.

Lodder, C.A. (1976), "Planejamento Regional: O Ponto de Vista Rural" in *Pesquisa e Planejamento Econômico*, Vol. 6, N. 3.

Lucas, R.E. (1973), "Some International Evidences on Output-Inflation Trade-Offs", *American Economic Review*, Vol. LXIII, N. 3.

Lyra, F.T. de (1981), "Raízes do Atraso Industrial do Nordeste", *Revista Pernambucana de Desenvolvimento*, Vol. 8, N. 2.

Macedo, R. (1982), "Salário Mínimo e Pobreza no Nordeste", *Revista Econômica do Nordeste*, Vol. 13, N. 2, abril/junho.

Magalhães, A. (1983), *Industrialização e Desenvolvimento Regional: A Nova Indústria do Nordeste*, IPEA/IPLAN, Brasília.

Magalhães, A. (1979), "Comércio e Desenvolvimento (Observações sobre as Relações Triangulares no Comércio da Região Nordeste)", *Revista Econômica do Nordeste*, Vol. 10, N. 4, out/dezembro.

Mahar, D.J. (1978), *Desenvolvimento Econômico da Amazônia*, IPEA/INPES, Rio de Janeiro.

Makler, H. (1982), "Financial Institutions, Credit Allocation and Marginalization in the Brazilian North-East: The Bahian Case" in Makler, H., Martinelli, A. and Smelser, N., *The New International Economy*, Sage Publications, California.

Marini, R.M. (1969), *Subdesarrollo Y Revolución*, Siglo XXI, México.

Marini, R.M. (1973), *Dialética de la Dependência*, Nueva Era, México.

Marques, N.F.S. (1982), *A Concentração Bancária Brasileira no Período Pós-1964*, Unpublished Master Thesis, Department of Economics, Universidade Federal de Pernambuco, Recife.

Marques, N.F.S. (1985), "A Concentração do Capital Bancário no Brasil (1964-1984)". *Revista Brasileira de Mercado de Capitais*, Vol. 11, N. 34 abril/junho.

Marshall, J.N. (1979), "Ownership, Organisation and Industrial Linkage: A Case Study in the Northern Region of England", *Regional Studies*, Vol. 13.

Martins, P.H.N. (1985), "Estado Burguês e Natureza do Planejamento no Nordeste" in *Revista de Economia Política*, Vol. 5, N. 3.

de Mattos, C.A. (1989), "Problemas y Politicas Regionales en el Ambito de Una Dinamica Concentradora", CEPAL, *Politicas Sociales en Uruguay: Planificacion, Educacion y Desarrollo Regional*, CEPAL, Montevideo.

McKillop, D.G. and Hutchinson, R.W. (1990), *Regional Financial Sectors in the British Isles, Aldershot*, Avebury.

McKillop, D.G. and Hutchinson, R.W. (1991), "Financial Intermediaries and Financial Markets: A United Kingdon Perspective" *Regional Studies*, Vol. 25, N. 6.

Mello, J.M.C. (1986), *O Capitalismo Tardio*, Brasiliense, São Paulo.

Mendes, A.G. (1978), "A Experiência de Planejamento Econômico no Brasil", in Cintra, A.O. and Haddad, P.R., *Dilemas de Planejamento Urbano e Regional no Brasil*, Zahar, Rio de Janeiro.

Mendes, A.L. (1988), *Concentração e Desintermediação Financeira no Brasil: (1964-1986)*, Unpublished Master Thesis, Department of Economics, Universidade de Brasília, Brasília.

Mendonça de Barros, J.R. and Galvão, A.C. (1984), "A Política de Industrialização do Nordeste em Face da Crise Econômica Brasileira", *Revsita Econômica do Nordeste*, Vol. 15, N. 3, julho/setembro.

Ministério da Fazenda, *Revista de Finanças Públicas*, Several Issues.

Minsky, H.P. (1986), *Stabilizing an Unstable Economy*, Yale University Press, Yale.

Moore, B.J. (1979-80), "The Endogenous Money Stock", *Journal of Post Keynesian Economics*, Vol. 2, N. 1.

Moore, B.J. (1983), "Unpacking the Post Keynesian Black Box: Bank Lending and the Money Supply", *Journal of Post Keynesian Economics*, Vol. 5, N. 4.

Moore, B.J. (1988), *Horizontalists and Verticalists: The Macroeconomics of Credit Money*, Cambridge University Press, Cambridge.

Moore, B.J. (1989), "A Simple Model of Bank Intermediation", *Journal of Post Keynesian Economics*, Vol. 12, N. 1.

Moore, C.L., Karaska, G.J. and Hill, J.A. (1985), "The impact of the Banking System on Regional Analyses",*Regional Studies*, Vol. 19, N. 1.

Moreira, R. (1979), *O Nordeste Brasileiro: Uma Política Regional de Industrialização*, Paz e Terra, Rio de Janeiro.

Moreira, R.M. (1984), "A Concentração Bancária e a Conglomeração Financeira", *Revista Brasileira de Mercado de Capitais*, Vol. 10, N. 32, abr/dez.

Morgan, E.V. (1973), "Regional Problems and Common Currencies", *Lloyds Bank Review*, October.

Myrdal, G. (1972), *Economic Theory and Under-Developed Regions*, Gerald Duckworth, London.

Neuhaus, P. (1975), *História Monetária do Brasil*, IBMEC, Rio de Janeiro.

Nicholls, W.H. (1970), "A Fronteira Agrícola na História Recente do Brasil: O Estado do Paraná, 1920-65", *Revista Brasileira de Economia*, Vol 24, N. 4, out./dez.

Nurkse, R. (1955), *Problemas de Formacion de Capital en los Países Insuficientemente Desarrollados*, Fondo de Cultura Económica, México.

O'Brien, F.S. and Salm, C.L. (1970), "Desemprego e Subemprego no Brasil" in *Revista Brasileira de Economia*, Vol. 24, N. 4.

O'Brien, P.J. (1975), "A Critique of Latin American Theories of Dependency" in Oxaal, I.(ed.), *Beyond the Sociology of Development*, Routledges & Kegan, London.

Oliveira, F. (1981), *Elegia para uma Re(li)gião*, Paz e Terra, Rio de Janeiro, 3rd edition.

Oliveira, F. (1984), *A Economia da Dependência Imperfeita*, Graal, 4th edition.

Palley, T.I. (1991-92), "Money, credit, and Prices in a Kaldorian Macro Model", *Journal of Post Keynesian Economics*, Vol. 14, N. 2.

Palma, G. (1981), "Dependency: A Formal Theory of Underdevelopment or a Methodology for the Analysis of Concrete Situations of Underdevelopment?" in Jolly, R. and Streeven, P. (eds), *Recent Issues in World Development*, Pergamon Press, Oxford.

Paz, P. and Sunkel, O. (1975), *El Subdesarrollo Latino Americano y La Teoria del Desarrollo*, Siglo Veintiuno, Mexico.

Pedrão, F. (1984), "A Posição do nordeste na Economica Nacional", *Revista Econômica do Nordeste*, Vol. 15, N. 1, janeiro/março.

Peláez, C.M. and Suzigan, W. (1976), *História Monetária do Brasil*, Editora Universidade de Brasília, Brasília.

Perdigão, L.A. (1983), *Conglomerados Financeiros: Análise de seu Desempenho no Brasil (1978/1981)*, IBMEC, Rio de Janeiro.

Perroux, F. (1967), *A Economia do Século XX*, Herder, Lisboa.

Petras, J. (1967), "The Roots of Underdevelopment", *Monthly Review*, Vol. 18, N. 9.

PIMES (1984), *Desigualdades Regionais no Desenvolvimento Brasileiro*, SUDENE, Recife.

Prado Jr., C. (1976), *História Econômica do Brasil*, Brasiliense, 19th ed., São Paulo.

Prado, E.F.S. (1981), *Estrutura Tecnológica de Desenvolvimento Regional*, Published for the Instituto de Pesquisa Econômica by Fundação Instituto de Pesquisa Econômica, Série Ensaios Econômicos, São Paulo.
Prebisch, R. (1949), "O Desenvolvimento Econômico da América Latina e seus Principais Problemas" in *Revista Brasileira de Economia*, Vol. 3, N. 3, Rio de Janeiro.
Prebisch, R. (1970), *Transformacion y Desarrollo: La gran Tarea de La América Latina*, Fondo de Cultura Económica, México.
Rattner, H. (1972), *Industrialização e Concentração Econômica em São Paulo*, FGV, Rio de Janeiro.
Rebouças, O. et al (1979), "Desenvolvimento do Nordeste: Diagnóstico e Sugestões de Políticas", *Revista Econômica do Nordeste*, Vol 10, N. 2, abril/junho.
Ricardo, D. (1970), "High Price of Bullion: A Proof of Depreciation of Bank Notes- 1810" in Sraffa, P.(ed.), *Works of David Ricardo*, Vol IIIa,Cambridge University Press, Cambridge.
Ricardo, D. (1973), *On the Principles of Political Economy and Taxation*, Dent, London.
Robock, S.H. (1963), *Brazil's Developing Northeast*, The Brookings Institution, Washington.
Rodriguez, O. (1981), *Teoria do Subdesenvolvimento da CEPAL*, Editora Forense-Universitária, Rio de Janeiro.
Rostow, W.W. (1971), *The Stages of Economic Growth*, 2nd ed., Cambridge University Press, Cambridge.
Rousseas, S.(1985), "A Mark-Up Theory of Bank Loan Rates", *Journal of Post Keynesian Economics*, Vol. 8, N. 1.
Santos, R.(1980), *História Econômica da Amazônia (1800-1920)*, T. A. Queiroz, São Paulo.
Sarmento, O.M. (1980), *Uncertainty and Inequality: The Case of Northeast Brazil*, Unpublished Ph.D. Thesis, University of Illinois at Urbana-Champaign.
Sayad, J. and Jatobá, S.J. (1980), "Efeitos Espaciais da Política Monetária e Financeira", *Separata of Revista Econômica do Nordeste*, Vol. 11, N. 1, jan/mar.
Schwartz, S.B.(1987), "Plantations and Peripheries". in Bethell, L. (ed.), *Colonial Brazil, The Cambridge History of Latin America*, Cambridge University Press, Cambridge.
Scott, Jr., I.O. (1955), "The Regional Impact of Monetary Policy", *Quarterly Journal of Monetary Policy*, Vol. 69.
Semple, R.K. and Gauthier, H.L. (1972) , "Tendências nas Desigualdades Regionais da Economia Brasileira: 1947/1966", *Dados*, N. 9.
Serra, J. and Cardoso, F.H. (1986), "As Desventuras da Dialética da

Dependência" in *Estudos CEBRAP*, N. 23, São Paulo.
Shackle, G.L.S.(1965), *A Scheme of Economic Theory*, Cambridge University Press, Cambridge.
Shackle, G.L.S.(1979), *Imagination and the Nature of Choice*, Edinburgh University Pess, Edinburgh.
Silva, S.(1976), *Expansão Cafeeira e Origens da Indústria no Brasil*, Alfa-Omega, São Paulo.
Simonsen, R.C.(1937), *História Econômica do Brasil*, Vol. I and II, Companhia Editora Nacional, São Paulo.
Simonsen, R.C.(1939), *Brazil's Industrial Evolution*, Escola de Sociologia e Política, São Paulo.
Singer, H.(1962), *Estudo sobre o Desenvolvimento Econômico do Nordeste*, Comissão de Desenvolvimento de Pernambuco, Recife.
Straszheim, M.R.(1971), "An Introduction and Overview of Regional Money Capital Markets" in Kain, J.F. and Meyer, J.R. (ed.), *Essays in Regional Economics*, Harvard University Press, Massachussets.
Studart, R.(1995), *Investment Finance in Economic Development*, Routledge, London.
SUDENE (1961), *I Plano Diretor do Desenvolvimento Econômico e Social do Nordeste (1961/63)*, Recife.
SUDENE (1963), *II Plano Diretor do Desenvolvimento Econômico e Social do Nordeste (1963/66)*, Recife.
SUDENE (1966), *III Plano Diretor do Desenvolvimento Econômico e Social do Nordeste (1966/68)*, Recife.
SUDENE (1968), *IV Plano Diretor do Desenvolvimento Econômico e Social do Nordeste (1969/73)*, Recife.
SUDENE (1979), *Legislação Básica*, Recife.
SUDENE (1990), *Produto e Formação Bruta de Capital: Nordeste do Brasil*, Recife.
SUDENE/BNB (1992), *Relatório da Pesquisa sobre o Desempenho da Indústria Incentivada do Nordeste 1988*, SUDENE, DPG/PLI, Recife.
Sunkel, O.(1973), *Past, Present and Future of Latin-American Underdevelopment*, Studies on Developing Countries, n.57, Center for Afro-Aasian Research of the Hungarian Academy of Science, Budapest.
Suzigan, W., Pereira, J.E.C., Almeida, R.A.G. (1972), *Financiamento de Projetos Industriais no Brasil*, IPEA/INPES, Rio de Janeiro.
Tavares, M.C. (1983), *Da Substituição de Importações ao Capitalismo Financeiro*, Zahar Editores, Rio de Janeiro.
Thirlwall, A.P.(1980), "Regional Problems Are Balance of Payments Problems", *Regional Studies*, Vol. 14.
Thurston, T.B. (1976), "Regional Interaction and the Reserve Adjustemnte Lag Within the Commercial Banking Sector", *Journal of Finance*, Vol. 31, December.

Tobin, J.(1982), "The Commercial Banking Firm: A Simple Model". *The Scandinavian Journal of Economics*, Vol. 84, N. 4.

Tsiang, S.C.(1978), "The Diffusion of Reserves and The Money Supply Multiplier". *Economic Journal*.

Versiani, F.R. & Versiani, M.T.R.O. (1977), "A Industrialização Brasileira Antes de 1930: Uma Contribuição" in Versiani, F.R. & Barros, J.R.M., *Formação Econômica do Brasil: A Experiência da Industrialização*, Saraiva, São Paulo.

Villela, A.V. & Suzigan, W. (1975), *Política do Governo e Crescimento da Economia Brasileira: 1889-1945*, IPEA/INPES, 2nd ed., Rio de Janeiro.

Weiskoff, R. and Wolff, E.(1977), "Linkages and Leakages: Industrial Tracking in an Enclave Economy", *Economic Development and Cultural Change*, Vol. 25, N. 4, July.

For Product Safety Concerns and Information please contact our EU representative GPSR@taylorandfrancis.com Taylor & Francis Verlag GmbH, Kaufingerstraße 24, 80331 München, Germany

Batch number: 10725921

Printed by Printforce, the Netherlands